Lecture Notes in Computer Science 15653

Founding Editors

Gerhard Goos
Juris Hartmanis

Editorial Board Members

Elisa Bertino, *Purdue University, West Lafayette, IN, USA*
Wen Gao, *Peking University, Beijing, China*
Bernhard Steffen◉, *TU Dortmund University, Dortmund, Germany*
Moti Yung◉, *Columbia University, New York, NY, USA*

The series Lecture Notes in Computer Science (LNCS), including its subseries Lecture Notes in Artificial Intelligence (LNAI) and Lecture Notes in Bioinformatics (LNBI), has established itself as a medium for the publication of new developments in computer science and information technology research, teaching, and education.

LNCS enjoys close cooperation with the computer science R & D community, the series counts many renowned academics among its volume editors and paper authors, and collaborates with prestigious societies. Its mission is to serve this international community by providing an invaluable service, mainly focused on the publication of conference and workshop proceedings and postproceedings. LNCS commenced publication in 1973.

Mark Manulis
Editor

Applied Cryptography and Network Security Workshops

ACNS 2025 Satellite Workshops:
AIHWS, AIoTS, QSHC, SCI, PrivCrypt, SPIQE,
SiMLA, and CIMSS 2025
Munich, Germany, June 23–26, 2025
Revised Selected Papers, Part I

Editor
Mark Manulis
Forschungsinstitut CODE
Universität der Bundeswehr München
Neubiberg, Germany

ISSN 0302-9743 ISSN 1611-3349 (electronic)
Lecture Notes in Computer Science
ISBN 978-3-032-01798-7 ISBN 978-3-032-01799-4 (eBook)
https://doi.org/10.1007/978-3-032-01799-4

© The Editor(s) (if applicable) and The Author(s), under exclusive license
to Springer Nature Switzerland AG 2026

This work is subject to copyright. All rights are solely and exclusively licensed by the Publisher, whether the whole or part of the material is concerned, specifically the rights of translation, reprinting, reuse of illustrations, recitation, broadcasting, reproduction on microfilms or in any other physical way, and transmission or information storage and retrieval, electronic adaptation, computer software, or by similar or dissimilar methodology now known or hereafter developed.
The use of general descriptive names, registered names, trademarks, service marks, etc. in this publication does not imply, even in the absence of a specific statement, that such names are exempt from the relevant protective laws and regulations and therefore free for general use.
The publisher, the authors and the editors are safe to assume that the advice and information in this book are believed to be true and accurate at the date of publication. Neither the publisher nor the authors or the editors give a warranty, expressed or implied, with respect to the material contained herein or for any errors or omissions that may have been made. The publisher remains neutral with regard to jurisdictional claims in published maps and institutional affiliations.

This Springer imprint is published by the registered company Springer Nature Switzerland AG
The registered company address is: Gewerbestrasse 11, 6330 Cham, Switzerland

If disposing of this product, please recycle the paper.

Preface

These proceedings contain papers that were selected for presentation at the satellite workshops and the poster session of the 23rd International Conference on Applied Cryptography and Network Security (ACNS 2025), which took place June 23–26, 2025 in Munich, Germany.

A total of nine satellite workshops, selected through a competitive call for workshops, were held in parallel to the ACNS conference. The following eight workshops organised independent calls for papers:

- 6th ACNS Workshop on Artificial Intelligence in Hardware Security (AIHWS 2025), chaired by Lejla Batina and Shivam Bhasin
- 7th ACNS Workshop on Artificial Intelligence and Industrial Internet-of-Things Security (AIoTS 2025), chaired by Dieter Gollmann and Mujeeb Ahmed
- 1st Workshop on Quantum-Safe Hybrid Cryptography (QSHC 2025), chaired by Ludovic Perret and Christoph Striecks
- 6th ACNS Workshop on Secure Cryptographic Implementation (SCI 2025), chaired by Jingqiang Lin and Bo Luo
- 1st International Workshop on Foundations and Applications of Privacy-Enhancing Cryptography (PrivCrypt 2025), chaired by Lucjan Hanzlik and Daniel Slamanig
- 1st Workshop on Secure Protocol Implementations in the Quantum Era (SPIQE 2025), chaired by Kenneth G. Paterson and Juraj Somorovsky
- 7th ACNS Workshop on Security in Machine Learning and its Applications (SiMLA 2025), chaired by Ye Dong and Yangguang Tian
- 5th ACNS Workshop on Critical Infrastructure and Manufacturing System Security (CIMSS), chaired by Zengpeng Li and Ahmed Amro

ACNS 2025 satellite workshops received a total of 87 paper submissions. Each workshop had its own program chairs and a Program Committee (PC) in charge of the review process. The submitted papers were evaluated by respective workshop PCs based on their significance, novelty, and technical quality. The review process was double-blind and submissions received 2-3 reviews each. Ultimately, 43 papers were selected for presentation, resulting in an acceptance rate of 49%.

The award for the Best Workshop Paper went to Tishya Sarma Sarkar, Kislay Arya, Siddhartha Chowdhury, Upasana Mandal, Shubhi Shukla, Sarani Bhattacharya and Debdeep Mukhopadhyay: "NETLAM: An Automated LLM Framework to Generate and Evaluate Stealthy Hardware Trojans" from the AIHWS workshop. The winning paper was selected by voting from papers nominated by different workshops.

ACNS 2025 satellite workshops also featured 15 invited talks:

- "Trustworthy AI: Hype or Hope? Challenges of Building Resilient and Secure Machine Learning Systems" by Alexandra Dmitrienko (University of Würzburg) and "OpenTitan: Landing the Open Source Root of Trust in Production" by Johann Heyszl (Google) at AIHWS

- "ChatIoT: LLM-based Security Assistant for Internet of Things with Retrieval-Augmented Generation" by Jianying Zhou (SUTD) at the AIoTS
- "EU actions for a quantum-safe future and efforts in bringing together communities" by Fabiana Da Pieve (European Commission) and "Hybridisation from an operator's perspective" by Felix Wissel (Deutsche Telekom) at QSHC
- "How the Microarchitecture undermines Confidentiality and Integrity" by Daniel Gruss (Graz University of Technology) at SCI
- "Malicious Cryptography and Privacy Illusion" by Mirosław Kutyłowski (NASK National Research Institute) and "Privacy-Enhancing Cryptography from Lattices" by Tjerand Silde (Norwegian University of Science and Technology) at PrivCrypt
- "Combiners for low entropy cryptography" by Julia Hesse (IBM Zurich), "Lattices give us KEMs and FHE, but where are the efficient lattice PETs?" by Martin Albrecht (Sandbox AQ), "The Post-Quantum Transition at Signal: Progress and Challenges" by Rolfe Schmidt (Signal), "Lessons learned from blackbox analyses of software and hardware cryptographic implementations" by Petr Svenda (Masaryk University) and "Google's PQC Journey: An Industry Perspective" by Christiane Peters (Google) at SPIQE
- "Taming Malicious Majorities in Federated Learning using Privacy-preserving Byzantine-robust Clustering" by Rui Wang (TU Delft) at SiMLA
- "Do not attribute to malice what you can attribute to incompetence" by Dieter Gollmann (TU Hamburg) at CIMSS

The International Workshop on Cryptography, Robustness, and Provably Secure Schemes for Female Young Researchers (CrossFyre), was held in parallel with the ACNS conference, without running a competitive call for papers.

The ACNS 2025 poster session was chaired by Daniel Slamanig. The session featured nine poster presentations and corresponding short poster papers were included in these proceedings. The award for the Best Poster went to Mirko Goldmann, Leonardo Del Bino and Michael Kissner: "A path towards all-optical DDoS detection on encrypted network traffic".

The organizing of the ACNS 2025 workshops was made possible by the joint efforts of many: We thank the authors of all submissions, program chairs of individual workshops, their PC members, and additional reviewers. We acknowledge Springer-Verlag for sponsoring the awards. We thank the ACNS 2025 General Chairs, Stefan Katzenbeisser and Johannes Kinder, along with all members of their organizing team. The ACNS 2025 workshop chair would like to acknowledge Jianying Zhou for his guidance and suggestions.

Last but not least, we thank all speakers, session chairs and attendees for their contribution to the success of the ACNS 2025 satellite workshops.

June 2025   Mark Manulis

AIHWS 2025

Sixth ACNS Workshop on Artificial Intelligence in Hardware Security

Program Chairs

Lejla Batina	Radboud University, Netherlands
Shivam Bhasin	Temasek Labs@NTU, Singapore

Program Committee

Stjepan Picek	Radboud University, Netherlands
Kota Yoshida	Ritsumeikan University, Japan
Dirmanto Jap	Nanyang Technological University, Singapore
Marc Stöttinger	RheinMain University of Applied Science, Germany
Kostas Papagiannopoulos	University of Amsterdam, Netherlands
Nikolaos Alachiotis	University of Twente, Netherlands
Vincent Verneuil	NXP Semiconductors, Germany
Durba Chatterjee	Radboud University, Netherlands
Maria Méndez Real	UBS, France
Łukasz Chmielewski	Masaryk University, Czech Republic
Lichao Wu	TU Darmstadt, Germany
Debapriya Basu Roy	IIT Kanpur, India
Sayandeep Saha	Indian Institute of Technology Bombay, India
Keerthi K	Nanyang Technological University, Singapore
Gorka Abad	Ikerlan Technology Research Centre, Netherlands

Additional Reviewers

Niklas Fassbender
Eunisse Nzetchuen
Trevor Yap

AIoTS 2025

Sixth ACNS Workshop on Artificial Intelligence and Industrial IoT Security

Program Chairs

Dieter Gollmann	TU Hamburg, Germany
Chuadhry Mujeeb Ahmed	Newcastle University, UK

Program Committee

Muhammad Muzammal	Northumbria University, UK
Yinhao Li	Newcastle University, UK
Arul Thileeban Sagayam	Bloomberg, UK
Rehmat Ullah	Newcastle University, UK
Magnus Almgren	Chalmers University of Technology, Sweden
Trinadh Reddy Pamulapati	Newcastle University, UK
Hasan Kivrak	Istanbul Technical University, Turkey
Luis Garcia	University of Utah, USA
James Ranjith Kumar Rajasekaran	Northumbria University, UK
Jide Edu	King's College London, UK
Devki Nandan Jha	Newcastle University, UK
Bo Wei	Newcastle University, UK
Sana Ullah Jan	Edinburgh Napier University, UK
Muhammad Azmi Umer	DHA Suffa University, Pakistan
Sibylle Fröschle	Hamburg University of Technology, Germany
Chris Poskitt	Singapore Management University, Singapore
Neetesh Saxena	Cardiff University, UK
Jairo Giraldo	University of Utah, USA
Daisuke Mashima	Singapore University of Technology and Design, Singapore
Saqib Hussain	Northumbria University, UK

QSHC 2025

First Workshop on Quantum-Safe Hybrid Cryptography

Program Chairs

Ludovic Perret	EPITA, Sorbonne University, France
Christoph Striecks	AIT Austrian Institute of Technology, Austria

Program Committee

Romain Alléaume	Télécom Paris, Institut Polytechnique de Paris, Inria, France
Christopher Battarbee	Sorbonne University, France
Carlos Cid	Simula UiB, Norway & Okinawa Institute of Science and Technology, Japan
Eleni Diamanti	CNRS, Sorbonne University, France
Benjamin Dowling	King's College London, UK
Alex Grilo	CNRS, Sorbonne University, France
Delaram Kahrobaei	CUNY QC, & University of York, UK & NYU, USA
Elham Kashefi	NQCC & University of Edinburgh, UK & CNRS, France
Vicente Martin	Universidad Politécnica de Madrid, Spain
Sebastian Ramacher	AIT Austrian Institute of Technology, Austria
Timothy Spiller	University of York, UK

Contents – Part I

AIHWS – Artificial Intelligence in Hardware Security

NETLAM: An Automated LLM Framework to Generate and Evaluate
Stealthy Hardware Trojans 3
   Tishya Sarma Sarkar, Kislay Arya, Siddhartha Chowdhury,
   Upasana Mandal, Shubhi Shukla, Sarani Bhattacharya,
   and Debdeep Mukhopadhyay

Attacking Single-Cycle Ciphers on Modern FPGAs: Featuring Explainable
Deep Learning 22
   Mustafa Khairallah and Trevor Yap

Can KANs Do It? Toward Interpretable Deep Learning-Based
Side-Channel Analysis 40
   Kota Yoshida, Sengim Karayalçin, and Stjepan Picek

Hamming Weight-Based Side Channel Analysis of HLS Kyber Hardware
Using Neural Networks 58
   Alexander Kharitonov, Tarick Welling, Maël Gay, and Ilia Polian

Jump, It Is Easy: JumpReLU Activation Function in Deep Learning-Based
Side-Channel Analysis 77
   Abraham Basurto-Becerra, Azade Rezaeezade, and Stjepan Picek

Arithmetic Masking Countermeasure to Mitigate Side-Channel-Based
Model Extraction Attack on DNN Accelerator 94
   Hirokatsu Yamasaki, Kota Yoshida, Yuta Fukuda, and Takeshi Fujino

Investigation of EM Fault Injection on Emerging Lightweight Neural
Network Hardware 113
   Bhanprakash Goswami, Reejit Chetry, J. Chithambara Moorthii,
   and Manan Suri

μ SCAN: Deep Learning Detection of Faulty Micro-architecture States
and Patterns from Scan-Chain Data 124
   Dillibabu Shanmugam, Zhenyuan Liu, Andrew Malnicof,
   and Patrick Schaumont

Let's Share a Secret: Share-Reduced Design of M&M for the AES S-Box 144
Haruka Hirata, Daiki Miyahara, Yuko Hara, Kazuo Sakiyama, and Yang Li

AIoTS – Artificial Intelligence and Industrial IoT Security

Protecting Privacy in IoT-Based Deep Learning: State-of-the-Art Methods
and Challenges 163
Martin Nocker, Florian Merkle, Pascal Schöttle, and Matthias Janetschek

Using Traditional Image Kernels and Image Processing Techniques
to Harden Convolutional Neural Networks Against Adversarial Attacks 185
Andrew Kiggins and Jide Edu

LAPIS: Layered Anomaly Detection System for IoT Security 204
Cheng Wang, Yan Lin Aung, Ye Dong, Trupil Limbasiya, and Jianying Zhou

IoTCat: A Multidimensional Approach to Categorize IoT Devices in Order
to Identify a Delegate for Cybersecurity Functions 222
Emiliia Geloczi, Nico Mexis, Benedikt Holler, Henrich C. Pöhls, and Stefan Katzenbeisser

QSHC – Quantum-Safe Hybrid Cryptography

Field-Tested Authentication for Quantum Key Distribution and DoS
Attacks 245
Antoine Gansel, Juliane Krämer, Tim Schumacher, Patrick Struck, Maximilian Tippmann, and Thomas Walther

Integration of PQC and QKD: Applications, Challenges
and Implementation Frameworks 266
Elina Kalnina, Rihards Balodis, Edgars Celms, Sergejs Kozlovics, Inara Opmane, Krisjanis Petrucena, Edgars Rencis, and Juris Viksna

Author Index 285

Contents – Part II

SCI – Secure Cryptographic Implementation

Improved PACD-Based Attacks on RSA-CRT: Breaking the Signature
Verification Countermeasure 3
    Guillaume Barbu, Laurent Grémy, and Roch Lescuyer

One Time is Enough: Chosen-Ciphertext Side-Channel Attack
on ML-KEM Cryptosystems 23
    *Yuhan Qian, Jing Gao, Yuchen Zhong, Yaoling Ding, Jingjie Wu,
Weiping Gong, Zihe Lin, and An Wang*

A Review of Lattice Cryptography Attack Cost Model 41
    Xi Hu, Yunfei Cao, and Hong Xiang

Exploring the HTTPS OCSP Ecosystem: A Comprehensive Study 61
    HengSheng Wang, ShuShang Wen, and Wei Wang

Differential Fault Analysis Against White-Box SM4 Implementations 81
    Liangju Zhao, Luoqi Chen, Yufeng Tang, and Zheng Gong

Leveled Software Implementation of Polka and Comparison
with Uniformly Masked Kyber 101
    *Thibaud Schoenauen, Clément Hoffmann, Charles Momin,
Thomas Peters, and François-Xavier Standaert*

Research on the Security Estimation Framework for Code-Based Public
Key Cryptography Algorithms 118
    Haoyue Fu, Yunfei Cao, Hong Xiang, and Congyi Zhang

Paper Document Anti-counterfeiting System Based on Digital Signatures
and Image Processing 132
    Yiyan Zhao, Jiwu Jing, Junlin He, Fangyu Zheng, and Chunjing Kou

PQMagic: Towards Secure and Efficient Post Quantum Cryptography
Implementations 152
    Yituo He, Xinpeng Hao, Juanru Li, and Yu Yu

Stateless Hash-Based Signatures for Post-Quantum Security Keys 173
    Ruben Gonzalez

ChatGPT as Preprocessing Agents: A Case Study on Cryptographic
Side-Channel Analysis 193
    Zhen Li, Anjiang Liu, An Wang, and WeiJia Wang

Improved Functional Bootstrapping of SM4 for Hybrid Homomorphic
Encryption 211
    Jin Peng, Dachao Wang, and Zheng Gong

RCE-HVE: Plausible Deniability Against Multi-snapshot Adversaries
with Amplified Storage 229
    Haoyang Xing, Chongyu Long, Anda Che, Fangyu Zheng, and Jiwu Jing

PrivCrypt – Foundations and Applications of Privacy-Enhancing Cryptography

Enhancing E-Voting with Multiparty Class Group Encryption 251
    Michele Battagliola, Giuseppe D'Alconzo, Andrea Gangemi, and Chiara Spadafora

Hierarchical Identity-Based Matchmaking Encryption 274
    Sohto Chiku, Keisuke Hara, and Junji Shikata

Silentium: Implementation of a Pseudorandom Correlation Generator
for Beaver Triples 296
    Vincent Rieder

Towards Privacy and Integrity: SNARK-Driven Verifiable FHE
for Outsourced Computation 318
    Rohitkumar R. Upadhyay, Sahadeo Padhye, Rajeev Anand Sahu, and Vishal Saraswat

SPIQE – Secure Protocol Implementations in the Quantum Era

Public Key Linting for ML-KEM and ML-DSA 337
    Evangelos Karatsiolis, Franziskus Kiefer, Juliane Krämer, Mirjam Loiero, Christian Tobias, and Maximiliane Weishäupl

Author Index 363

Contents – Part III

SiMLA – Security in Machine Learning and Its Applications

TIRE: Advancing Threat Intelligence Relation Extraction with a Novel Data-Centric Framework 3
    Inoussa Mouiche and Sherif Saad

JailFact-Bench: A Comprehensive Analysis of Jailbreak Attacks vs. Hallucinations in LLMs 23
    Sanjana Nambiar and Christina Pöpper

ReDASH: Fast and Efficient Scaling in Arithmetic Garbled Circuits for Secure Outsourced Inference 43
    Felix Maurer, Jonas Sander, and Thomas Eisenbarth

Winning at All Cost: A Small Environment for Eliciting Specification Gaming Behaviors in Large Language Models 52
    Lars Malmqvist

United We Log, Divided We Identify: A Decentralized Approach for Automated Log Analysis 70
    Elnaz Rabieinejad, Ali Dehghantanha, Fattane Zarrinkalam, and Jeff Schwartzentruber

A Study of Effectiveness of Brand Domain Identification Features for Phishing Detection in 2025 89
    Rina Mishra and Gaurav Varshney

Evaluating Membership Inference Attacks in Heterogeneous-Data Setups 109
    Bram van Dartel, Marc Damie, and Florian Hahn

CIMSS – Critical Infrastructure and Manufacturing System Security

Spying by SPi, I Got the Birds-Eye 121
    Awais Yousaf, Lee Ling Yi Kalvin, Meixuan Li, and Jianying Zhou

Fast and Robust Fragile Watermarking Enabling Real-Time Self-recovery for UAS 141
    Laurens Le Jeune, Anna Hristoskova, and Farhad Aghili

Standardized and Usage-Controlled Alert Analysis for Improved Cyber
Threat Intelligence 162
  Hendrik Meyer Zum Felde, Radhouene Azzabi, Cédric Gouy-Pailler,
  Gilles Lehmann, and Amaia Gil

Poster Papers

HatMob: An All-Encompassing Mobile Pentesting Suite 179
  Caleb Lee Jia Jing, He Haiqi, and Vivek Balachandran

An Information-Theoretically Secure QKD Protocol for One-Time Pad
Encryption 185
  Sergejs Kozlovičs, Krišjānis Petručeça, and Juris Vīksna

A Path Towards All-Optical DDoS Detection on Encrypted Network Traffic ... 191
  Mirko Goldmann, Leonardo Del Bino, and Michael Kissner

A Hybrid Encryption Framework Combining Classical, Post-Quantum,
and QKD Methods 197
  Amal Raj and Vivek Balachandran

POSTER: Tortoise: An Authenticated Encryption Scheme 202
  Kenneth Odoh

Optimized Noise Bound in BFV Homomorphic Encryption 207
  Akshit Aggarwal, Yang Li, and Srinibas Swain

Private LGBTQ Searches Without a Trace 213
  Akshit Aggarwal, Yang Li, and Srinibas Swain

Security Proof Techniques for QKD and Applications to Critical
Infrastructures 218
  Meret Kristen and Jürgen Mottok

Privacy and Latency-Aware Dynamic Split Computing 223
  Kenshiro Ise and Yuko Hara

Author Index 229

AIHWS – Artificial Intelligence in Hardware Security

NETLAM: An Automated LLM Framework to Generate and Evaluate Stealthy Hardware Trojans

Tishya Sarma Sarkar[1(✉)], Kislay Arya[2], Siddhartha Chowdhury[1], Upasana Mandal[1], Shubhi Shukla[3], Sarani Bhattacharya[1], and Debdeep Mukhopadhyay[1]

[1] Department of Computer Science and Engineering, Indian Institute of Technology, Kharagpur, India
{tishya,mandal.up98}@kgpian.iitkgp.ac.in,
{sarani,debdeep}@cse.iitkgp.ac.in

[2] Department of Electronics and Electrical Communication Engineering, Indian Institute of Technology, Kharagpur, India
kislayarya536@kgpian.iitkgp.ac.in

[3] Centre for Computational and Data Sciences, Indian Institute of Technology, Kharagpur, India
shubhishukla@kgpian.iitkgp.ac.in

Abstract. Securing externally sourced hardware designs is essential to prevent adversaries from embedding hardware Trojans. Trojans are stealthy modifications that leak data or create backdoors. Existing benchmarks like *Trust-Hub* provide only a limited set of Trojans (106), while the possibilities are virtually infinite. To address this, we propose **NETLAM**, a comprehensive framework utilizing multiple LLM-based tools to generate previously undiscovered Trojans not included in *Trust-Hub*. The first tool converts hardware netlists into Directed Acyclic Graphs (DAGs) to identify vulnerable nets and components in digital designs. Using these insights, the second tool generates stealthy Trojan-infected versions of the original design. To evaluate the stealthiness of these Trojans, we use an LLM-based equivalence checker, where stealthier Trojans pass equivalence checks while others are detected. We evaluate **NETLAM** using the AES dataset from *Trust-Hub* consisting of 28 Trojans. We identified 5 new Trojans, with high Common Vulnerability Scoring System (CVSS) scores, demonstrating their stealthiness. To prove the efficacy of the **NETLAM** generated Trojans, we further utilize an open-source formal equivalence checker to perform a functional equivalence check between the golden and the **NETLAM** generated Trojan-infected circuits. All of the suggested Trojans pass the formal equivalence check. However, the same Trojan-infested circuits fail in the **NETLAM** equivalence test, thus validating the effectiveness of our proposed framework. We show that LLMs and Generative AI models, such as GPT-4o and Gemini, can enhance Trojan detection by using semantic and probabilistic analysis rather than strict logical equivalence (GitHub Repository: https://github.com/shubhishukla10/NETLAM).

© The Author(s), under exclusive license to Springer Nature Switzerland AG 2026
M. Manulis (Ed.): ACNS 2025 Workshops, LNCS 15653, pp. 3–21, 2026.
https://doi.org/10.1007/978-3-032-01799-4_1

Keywords: Hardware Trojans · Large Language Models · Vulnerability Detector · Equivalence Checker · Directed Acyclic Graphs

1 Introduction

In today's technology-driven world, hardware devices are everywhere, supporting important applications in communication, healthcare, defense, transportation, and consumer electronics. These devices are the foundation of modern infrastructure, making their security and reliability very important. However, the fast growth of hardware components and their dependence on complex global supply chains have created new risks. One of the most serious threats is hardware Trojans, which are hidden and dangerous modifications that can harm the functionality and trustworthiness of these devices.

Hardware Trojans (HTs) are harmful changes intentionally added to digital designs to disrupt their normal behaviour, steal sensitive information, or disable important functions at the right moment. These changes can take different forms, such as adding extra logic gates, altering connections, or creating small timing changes [14]. Trojans are usually made to stay hidden during normal use and testing, only becoming active under specific conditions, which makes them very hard to detect. The effects of these attacks can be severe: in defense systems, they can threaten national security, while in consumer devices, they can cause serious privacy leaks and financial losses. Consequently, identifying, mitigating, and minimizing these risks has emerged as a crucial research focus.

Existing research in HTs largely focuses on either insertion or detection, often addressing them in isolation. For instance, [1] utilizes large language models (LLMs) to autonomously generate synthesizable HTs from high-level design specifications, enabling rapid exploration of the attack surface. Similarly, [4] applies machine learning techniques to dynamically insert Trojans by analyzing structural and functional features of existing designs. Expanding on these efforts, [9] demonstrates the application of LLMs in offensive hardware security, showcasing their ability to identify vulnerable modules, insert HTs, and craft sophisticated attacks on complex designs like RISC-V CPUs. The study addresses LLM context-length limitations by focusing on register transfer level (RTL) code, validating the inserted HTs through FPGA-based testing on CPU integrity and availability. On the detection front, [3] introduces SPICED, an LLM-based framework for detecting and localizing analog Trojans and syntactical bugs in circuit netlists. By leveraging chain-of-thought reasoning and few-shot learning, SPICED achieves 93.32% average Trojan coverage and 93.4% true positive rate on analog benchmarks without requiring hardware modifications or explicit training, providing an effective software-based solution for analog and mixed-signal circuits. Furthermore, [18] presents a golden reference-free HT detection method using Graph Neural Networks (GNNs). Representing hardware designs as Data Flow Graphs (DFGs), this approach achieves 97% recall for RTL in 21.1 ms and 84% recall for gate-level netlists in 13.42 s, demonstrating scalability and efficacy. Additionally, [17] proposes a golden-free multidimensional self-referencing technique, which detects hardware Trojans by analyzing side-channel signatures in time and frequency domains, expanding Trojan coverage and reducing process variations. The automated framework includes test generation, signal processing, and decision-making, achieving high detection sensitivity. Evaluated on 96 Trojan-inserted chips, it effectively detects even small, hard-to-detect Trojans. Although these advancements have improved detection techniques, pre-silicon verification continues to face challenges due to security gaps. Such security gaps encompass incomplete threat models, limited detection of hardware Trojans, insufficient formal verification procedures, inadequate test input sets during simulation for rare events, and most importantly, hidden vulnerabilities in the RTL designs. To address this, a formal verification approach [5] has been introduced, enabling exhaustive detection of sequential HTs at the RTL level, independent of golden models or payload behavior, effectively identifying complex HTs in *Trust-Hub* accelerators. Apart from these, Vul-FSM [11] introduces a database of 10,000 vulnerable finite state machine (FSM) designs, generated using the SecRT-LLM framework. Leveraging LLMs like GPT-3.5-turbo, the framework achieves high accuracy in vulnerability insertion and detection, showcasing its potential for efficiently creating and analyzing hardware security benchmarks. *Despite significant advancements, current research lacks a comprehensive tool capable of identifying all potential Trojans that could be inserted into a given design. While existing repositories like Trust-Hub [12], [13] provide only a handful of Trojan examples, and tools like Vul-FSM [11] focus on FSM vulnerabilities, they represent just a fraction of the infinite possibilities. This limitation highlights the need for an automated and versatile solution to systematically discover, analyze, and generate new, previously unknown Trojans across diverse hardware designs, motivating us to develop such a tool.*

In this work, we introduce **NETLAM**, a comprehensive framework leveraging multiple LLM-based tools, developed by us, with distinct functionalities to identify, generate, and evaluate Trojans within a given design. First, we develop an LLM-based equivalence checker and demonstrate its effectiveness using Trojan examples from *Trust-Hub*. Next, we create an LLM-based tool to convert digital netlists or Verilog code into directed acyclic graphs (DAGs), enabling the identification of potential Trojan insertion points. This step is crucial because it gives a direct insight into the vulnerable and candidate trigger points of the hardware design under test. Thus, it allows the designer to secure the design to avoid possible threats. Finally, we design an LLM-based Trojan injector capable of generating Verilog code with injected Trojans. Together, these tools form the **NETLAM** framework, which takes a design as input, identifies vulnerabilities by analyzing DAGs generated from the netlist, produces Trojan-injected Verilog code based on these vulnerabilities, and evaluates the stealthiness of the Trojans using the equivalence checker. We specifically evaluated our tool on the AES design from *Trust-Hub*, which includes 28 reported Trojans. Our tool successfully identified and generated 5 new Trojans that were not part of *Trust-Hub*, with high CVSS scores. For ranking the effectiveness of the **NETLAM** generated Trojans, we further test their equivalence with the golden designs using a formal equivalence checker, EQY, which is included in the Yosys synthesis suite

[8,16]. EQY is an open-source automated tool that performs a logical and functional equivalence between two given designs by exploiting miter circuits. As a result, a formal functional uniformity is examined. Nonetheless, there are innumerable instances of Trojans, which surreptitiously hide within the design and get activated by rare inputs or triggers. In such cases, a functional equivalence might not always provide an intended result and can render a Trojan-infected design equivalent to the golden design due to its sporadic nature. At this point, our LLM-based equivalence checker can come to the rescue by building a graph-based representation of the circuit and detecting redundant or suspicious logic paths. Our LLM-based equivalence checker also provides a semantic analysis of the two designs under test, thus detecting any additional circuitry or variable introduced in the victim modules. This step allows us to claim that our proposed tool, **NETLAM** succinctly generates and evaluates powerful Trojans.

1.1 Contributions

The contributions of this work are as follows:

- **LLM-Based Equivalence Checker:** We develop an LLM-based equivalence checker capable of verifying the functional equivalence between designs and identifying Trojan injections. Its effectiveness is demonstrated through evaluation on *Trust-Hub* Trojan examples.
- **LLM-Based DAG Generator and Vulnerability Identifier:** We propose a tool that converts hardware netlists or Verilog code into directed acyclic graphs (DAGs) and identifies the most stealthy Trojan-vulnerable points within the design, highlighting potential insertion locations.
- **LLM-Based Trojan Injector:** We introduce an LLM-based Trojan injector that generates Verilog code with stealthily inserted Trojans, creating novel Trojan-infected designs.
- **Comprehensive Framework - NETLAM:** We consolidate the above tools into **NETLAM**, a unified framework that takes a design as input, identifies vulnerabilities via DAG generation, generates Trojan-injected Verilog code from identified vulnerabilities, and evaluates the stealthiness of the generated Trojans using the equivalence checker.

The rest of the paper is organized as follows. Section 2 provides essential background on HTs, LLMs, and equivalence checking, while reviewing existing methods in HT detection and insertion. Section 3 describes the **NETLAM** framework, including its three key components: the LLM-based DAG generator for identifying vulnerabilities, the Trojan injector for creating stealthy HTs, and the equivalence checker for validating stealthiness. Section 4 details the experimental setup and evaluates **NETLAM** on AES designs from *Trust-Hub*, showcasing its ability to generate novel Trojans with high CVSS scores. Finally, Sect. 5 concludes the paper, summarizing its contributions and emphasizing the need for an integrated framework to advance HT research.

2 Background

2.1 Large Language Models (LLMs)

Large Language Models (LLMs) such as GPT, LLaMa, and Gemini are based on the transformer architecture, which leverages the attention mechanism to compute dynamic relevance scores for input tokens. This enables the model to focus on semantically significant parts of the input. The self-attention module, a core component, computes contextual dependencies across the entire input sequence in parallel, overcoming the sequential limitations of RNNs [10] and LSTMs [6]. Additionally, positional encodings are employed to encode token order, compensating for the model's inherent lack of sequential processing capability. In this work, we utilize multiple LLMs to develop our tool **NETLAM**, which can generate stealthy and robust trojans injected benchmarks.

2.2 Hardware Trojans

Hardware Trojans (HTs) [15] threaten the security of integrated circuits, especially in third-party design and manufacturing. These stealthy modifications can compromise system confidentiality, integrity, and availability, often lying dormant until triggered. Detection techniques like side-channel analysis, runtime monitoring, and formal verification, alongside advanced methods using machine learning and Hardware Performance Counters (HPCs), help identify anomalies. Prevention strategies include split manufacturing, logic locking, and post-silicon power and delay analysis. As hardware underpins critical systems like smart grids, IoT, and autonomous vehicles, robust defenses against HTs are vital for ensuring security and reliability

2.3 Register Transfer Level (RTL) and Gate-Level Netlists

In digital design, netlists serve as textual descriptions of circuits, detailing their components and interconnections. These representations exist at varying levels of abstraction, with the most common being the Register-Transfer Level (RTL) and gate-level. RTL netlists depict a design at a high level of abstraction, focusing on the flow of data and control signals between registers. Written in hardware description languages (HDLs) such as Verilog or VHDL, RTL netlists emphasize functionality over implementation specifics. They describe algorithmic behavior using constructs like conditional statements, loops, and procedural blocks, enabling designers to focus on the logic and operation of the circuit.

Gate-level netlists, on the other hand, offer a detailed view of the circuit after synthesis. These netlists consist of interconnected logic gates, flip-flops, and hardware primitives, representing the actual implementation of the design based on a specific technology library. Gate-level netlists are essential for detailed analysis tasks such as timing verification, power estimation, and functional equivalence checking. Bridging the abstraction gap between RTL and gate-level netlists is a critical aspect of hardware verification. Ensuring that the synthesized gate-level netlist faithfully implements the intended behavior of the RTL design is key to detecting functional errors and identifying potential hardware Trojans.

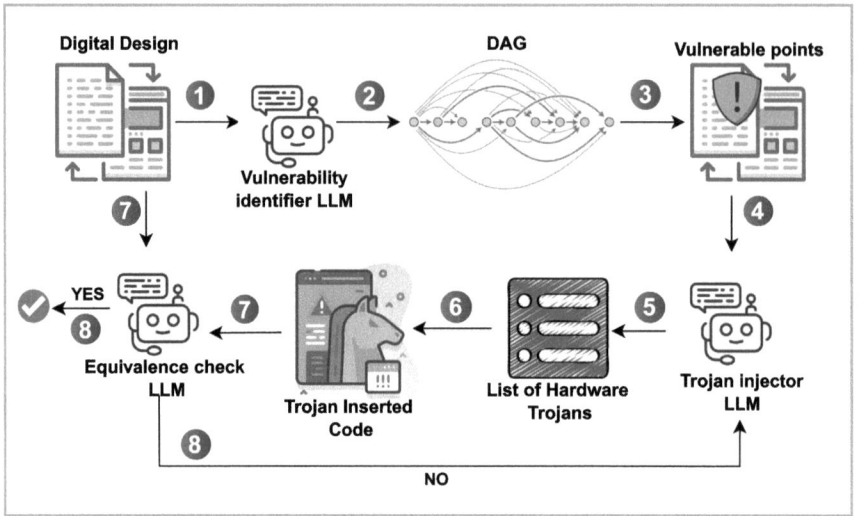

Fig. 1. Workflow of the Proposed **NETLAM** Framework. The three LLM modules, labeled as Vulnerability Identifier LLM, Trojan Injector LLM, and Equivalence Check LLM, are three separate LLM instantiations. The DAG generated by the Vulnerability Identifier is an adjacency list representation of the complex netlist. The vulnerable points include the probable trigger nets in the design. The Trojan inserted code is a maliciously modified version of the target Verilog module.

3 NETLAM Framework

We propose an automated framework, **NETLAM**, that integrates three powerful LLM-based tools: a DAG generator and vulnerability identifier, a Trojan injector, and an equivalence checker. Together, these tools systematically identify vulnerabilities, generate stealthy hardware Trojans, and evaluate their impact, providing a comprehensive solution for uncovering new Trojans and enhancing existing benchmarks like *Trust-Hub*, which is currently limited to 106 Trojan examples. **NETLAM** aims to create a significantly larger set of Trojans while ensuring their stealthiness through advanced equivalence evaluation. Simultaneously, our methodology aims to assist a designer to assess the susceptibility of the RTL design under test to probable threats by exploring the vulnerable nets and unknown hardware Trojans that can be implanted in those points. This methodology is compatible with two state-of-the-art LLM models, Gemini-1.5-flash00 and ChatGPT-4, to enable robust and automated hardware security analysis. The workflow for **NETLAM** is illustrated in Fig. 1, wherein the input is an RTL design or a gate-level netlist and the output is a set of undiscovered hardware Trojans that pass the equivalence check.

> **1. Instruction for Vulnerability Identification and DAG Creation**
>
> The following are two synthesized gate-level netlists. You are tasked with the following:
>
> 1. DAG Conversion and Analysis: Give a small description of the circuit, what it does and what are the components involved. Convert the Verilog code to a Directed Acyclic Graph (DAG) to map all signals, registers, and logic blocks. Provide the DAG in a clear adjacency list format for readability and the nodes in the DAG must be -
>   a. input and output ports and registers
>   b. wires
>   c. input and output ports of the components.
>
> 2. Identify Vulnerable Points: Detect vulnerable locations (e.g., specific registers, data paths, logic gates) in the first netlist that could be exploited for hardware Trojans utilizing the DAG. Evaluate vulnerabilities based on placement, signal flow, and sensitivity to conditions. For each vulnerable point, recommend the most stealthy Trojan types that should pass any functional equivalence check with the original design, including: Trigger mechanisms (e.g., specific input sequences, clock cycles) Payload actions (e.g., bit-flipping, signal tampering) Stealth features (e.g., random activation, intermittent triggering) Rank the top 5 Trojans with descriptions that align with the vulnerabilities identified. Print the DAG as an adjacency list. List the top 5 Trojans with targeted vulnerable points in the design. Rank the Trojans using the CVSS framework, evaluating its stealth, impact, and exploitability.

3.1 Vulnerability Identifier and DAG Generator

The first tool in **NETLAM** systematically identifies vulnerabilities in Verilog codes, RTL, and gate-level netlists. It converts the design into a DAG representation, revealing the logical flow of operations and structural dependencies. We provide specific preliminary instructions to the LLM which broadly include (i) Understanding the functionality of each module of the provided design, (ii) Constructing a DAG specific to each module in the form of an adjacency matrix, (iii) Identifying all the vulnerable points or modules from the DAG where critical Trojans can be inserted. A snippet of the predefined instruction is provided in the listing **1. Instruction for Vulnerability Identification and DAG Creation**. We provide complete instructions in the GitHub repository. The DAG serves as a blueprint for identifying exploitable points in the design. The LLM evaluates the DAG using a context-aware analysis, considering critical factors such as timing, data dependencies, and logic sensitivity. This analysis identifies the top five most stealthy Trojan-vulnerable points, which may include specific registers, signals, or logic blocks. These points represent locations where Trojans can be inserted with minimal functional disturbance, providing a detailed vulnerability map to guide the Trojan injection phase.

> **2. Instruction for Trojan Generation**
>
> The following are the Verilog codes of an AES block cipher design. You are tasked with the following:
>
>   1. Identify the 'S' module in the provided Verilog files.
>
>   2. Implement a Gate-Level Trojan only in the 'S' module which gets triggered by specific input combinations.
>
>   – Do not modify any other modules.
>   – Ensure there are no apparent hints of the Trojan inclusion.
>   – Make the Trojan as stealthy as possible.
>
>   3. Modify the original Verilog code by inserting the newly suggested Trojan into the identified vulnerable points. Ensure that the modified code integrates seamlessly into the design without introducing apparent anomalies. Test the new Trojan-injected design for operational correctness while ensuring the Trojan remains functional. After creating the new Trojan, rank it using the CVSS framework, evaluating its stealth, impact, and exploitability. Provide a justified CVSS score and a comparison with the original Trojan to highlight improvements in stealth and effectiveness.
>
>   4. Provide the entire modified Verilog code with well-labeled comments where the Trojan is included.

3.2 Trojan Injector and Trojan Generation

The second tool focuses on generating Trojan-injected versions of the original design based on the vulnerabilities identified in the DAG analysis. We provide specific preliminary instructions to the LLM to build this tool which broadly include (i) Identifying the top 5 stealthy Trojans that can be inserted in the specific vulnerable modules, (ii) Ranking the suggested Trojans based on their CVSS scores, and (iii) Modifying the existing module and generating the Trojan-infected module. A snippet of the detailed instruction is provided in the listing **2. Instruction for Trojan Generation**. We provide complete instructions in the GitHub repository. This Trojan injector creates modified Verilog code, embedding stealthy hardware Trojans that exploit the identified vulnerabilities while ensuring operational correctness. The tool classifies the generated Trojans into categories, such as key-dependent, payload-triggered, or side-channel-based, and evaluates their potential impact on the design's behavior and security. To enhance stealth, techniques such as delayed activation or seamless integration into legitimate components are employed. The Trojan injector generates a range of Trojans, from simple to highly stealthy, broadening the scope of Trojan possibilities for hardware designs.

> **3. Instruction for Equivalence Check**
>
> The following are two synthesized gate-level representations of two Verilog designs. You are tasked with the following:
>
> 1. Construct a miter circuit to check the functional equivalence of the two provided gate-level netlists. Provide a detailed analysis of their functional behavior and determine if they are equivalent at the RTL-level, despite having varying top modules or additional sub-modules. Focus on input-output behavior and logical equivalence, ignoring optimizations or naming differences or gate implementations or additional Verilog modules. Is there any additional circuitry or malicious alteration in any of the two files?
>
> 2. If a Trojan is detected in either netlist, analyze its characteristics and impact on the design. Start by identifying the Trojan type, such as key-dependent, payload-triggered, or side-channel-based, through structural and behavioral analysis of the netlist. Next, assess how the Trojan affects the overall design, focusing on vulnerabilities introduced, disruptions caused to timing or functionality, and potential security implications. Provide a thorough explanation of the Trojan's behavior and its operational consequences.
>
> 3. Based on the equivalence check outcome, determine whether the Trojan passes or fails the check. If the Trojan remains undetected during functional equivalence testing, evaluate its stealth and impact using the Common Vulnerability Scoring System (CVSS). Rank the Trojan and justify its score with detailed observations. If the Trojan is easily detected during equivalence testing, proceed to create a more stealthy alternative. Identify vulnerable points or modules in the design, such as unused registers, infrequent logic, or weak constraints, and propose a new Trojan designed to blend into the original structure using techniques like delayed activation, payload encryption, or integration into legitimate components.

3.3 Equivalence Checker and Stealth Assessment

The procedure of building the third tool, an equivalence checker, involves converting a complex digital design into gate-level netlists using *Yosys* [16], an open-source Verilog RTL synthesis tool, to synthesize Verilog files for functional equivalence analysis. The golden reference and Trojan-infected Verilog source codes are sourced from the AES-based Trojan attack variants provided in *TrustHub* [12,13]. Each Verilog file undergoes a sequence of transformations in Yosys, including reading the design, mapping it to standard cells using a provided liberty file, optimizing the design, and generating mapped netlists.

We use the *freePDK45* 45 *nm* [7] variant open-source Process Design Kit (PDK) to map the synthesized Verilog designs into the gate-level netlists. These netlists are then fed into a Generative AI model as part of a carefully constructed and pre-defined prompt, requesting an analysis to determine their functional equivalence based on logical behavior and structural characteristics. This approach avoids the need to upload files to external services by directly embedding the netlist content into the prompt, thereby streamlining the process. The AI's response provides a comprehensive comparison and insight into the equivalence or differences between the two Verilog designs.

In scenarios where a Verilog designer needs to verify whether an outsourced design has been tampered with or contains malicious alterations, the equivalence checker proves invaluable. The designer inputs the golden reference design alongside the manufactured IC design into the checker, which analyzes the two netlists for additional logic blocks, structural modifications, or any alterations that could pose security threats. The equivalence checker operates based on pre-defined instructions to detect such malicious changes, without any prior knowledge of the presence, absence, or potential types of Trojans, or which netlist is Trojan-infected in the provided designs. We provide detailed preliminary instructions to the LLM to build our tool, which broadly includes (i) Performing a rigorous functional equivalence checking of the two gate-level netlists, ignoring any additional modules or input/output variables. (ii) Justifying whether the modified module passes or fails the checking procedure, (iii) If any Trojan is detected, then rank the same using CVSS score and provide a more stealthy Trojan, which should have a higher CVSS score than the provided one. A snippet of the detailed instruction is provided in the listing **3. Instruction for Equivalence Check**. We provide complete instruction in the GitHub repository. Importantly, the checker requires gate-level netlists for accurate analysis, as Verilog source codes often include procedural blocks that are challenging to model effectively.

If the equivalence checker identifies any such malicious alterations in either of the netlists in comparison to the other, it proceeds to determine the type of Trojan that has been inserted in the victim netlist. The stealth of the Trojan is decided based on a hypothetical Common Vulnerability Scoring System (CVSS) score. The CVSS score quantifies the severity of security vulnerabilities. It considers factors like exploitability and impact to assign a numerical rating between 0 and 10, where 0 indicates no severity and 10 indicates critical severity. This process also enables the designer to assess the impact of the inserted Trojan and identify vulnerable points within the design. The equivalence checker's output is further leveraged by the **NETLAM** tool to pinpoint vulnerabilities and explore the possibility of inserting alternative Trojans with higher CVSS scores into the same design. To further validate the credibility of our tool and the stealth of the generated Trojans, we evaluate the equivalence between the golden design and the Trojan-infected design using the formal equivalence checker (EQY) included within the Yosys suite [8]. This is a miter circuit-based equivalence checker, which strategically checks the functional equivalence between two designs by comparing the outputs of the two designs. If the outputs vary then there is a potential modification in either of the designs.

We now evaluate this comprehensive framework in the next section by uncovering new stealthy Trojans that were previously unknown.

4 Experimental Results

In this section, we discuss the comprehensive results of our proposed tools. We specifically target the AES-based Trojan attacks included in *Trust-Hub* for analyzing the security-critical aspect of our proposed tool. The authors propose

Table 1. Comparison of NETLAM with state-of-the-art tools for hardware Trojan generation.

Feature	NETLAM	[1]	[11]	[2]	[4]	[3]
Approach	Uses LLMs for vulnerability identification, Trojan insertion, and equivalence checking	Uses LLMs to analyze and generate Trojans based on Trust-Hub benchmarks	Uses LLMs for vulnerability insertion, detection, and validation using fidelity checks	Automated framework for generating and benchmarking Trojans on PCB designs	ML-based Trojan detection using trigger-net classification	Uses LLMs to detect and localize stealthy Trojans in circuit netlists using chain-of-thought reasoning
Equivalence Checking	LLM-based equivalence checker with functional analysis	Not mentioned	Hybrid verification approach combining static analysis, formal verification, and manual review	Not a primary focus	Not mentioned	Not applicable (focused on analog circuit analysis)
Vulnerability Analysis	Identifies and ranks vulnerable points in RTL/netlists using DAG representation	Cannot identify vulnerable points in the design	Uses LLMs for vulnerability detection, categorization, and validation	Analyzes trigger and payload selection for board-level Trojans	Uses ML models to classify trigger nets based on probability estimates	Cannot identify vulnerable points in the design
Trigger Net Selection	Identifies stealthy nets using DAG-based vulnerability mapping	User prompt-based trigger net selection	Uses guided prompting for vulnerability selection	Uses signal probability analysis for rare node detection	Uses ML-based classification to predict high-probability trigger nets	Extracts trigger locations based on LLM prompts
Learning Time	Uses pre-trained LLMs, reducing training overhead	Uses pre-trained LLMs, reducing training overhead	Uses GPT models with iterative refinement to improve accuracy	No explicit learning; relies on automation heuristics	Requires training time for ML models	Uses pre-trained LLMs, reducing training overhead
Scalability	Can be extended to any RTL designs	Platform-independent but focused on FPGA/ASIC designs	Evaluates 10,000 FSM-based designs for security weaknesses	Benchmarks multiple PCB designs with different Trojan instances	Scales well with ML training but requires dataset availability	Analog/mixed signal circuits only
Automation Level	Fully automated	Fully automated	Semi-automated, requiring manual validation in some cases	Fully automated	Semi-automated	Fully automated
Integration with EDA Tools	Uses Yosys for netlist processing and formal verification	Works with FPGA tools (Xilinx Vivado)	Integrates JasperGold Superlint and ARC-FSM Trojan insertion tool for verification	Primarily uses a custom Trojan insertion tool	Integrates with Synopsys and Cadence ATPG tools for Trojan validation	No integration with traditional EDA tools

an LLM-based framework capable of generating stealthy Trojans in [1]. However, they do not assess the vulnerabilities of the victim RTL designs. On the other hand, [3] proposes a tool that identifies stealthy analog Trojans, but does not insert them. Moreover, this work does not explore the vulnerabilities in a digital design. The authors of [11] propose a comprehensive benchmark dataset based on finite state machines (FSMs) and proposes a semi-automated tool to evaluate 10,000 FSM-based designs. However, this work uses guided prompting for vulnerability selection. As our tool comprehensively discovers the probable trigger nets/payloads in the design from the generated DAGs, it provides a better understanding of the design. Specifically, a designer can also use the vulnerability detector before manufacturing to discover any design shortcomings. A detailed state-of-the-art survey is provided in Table 1. During equivalence checking, our tool has effectively detected several highly stealthy Trojans from the benchmark dataset provided by *Trust-Hub*, which are otherwise challenging to identify during the standard operation of an AES encryption process. The Trojan-infected designs comprise additional modules that make the detection of Trojans easier. Moreover, the synthesized netlists of the same comprise additional circuitry as compared to the original design, further altering the structural uniformity. Few of the state-of-the-art Trojans such as the side-channel-based or payload-triggered Trojans do not alter the normal functionality, thus making detection difficult.

Table 2. Comprehensive Results of Equivalence Checking

Sl. No.	AES Variant	Equivalence Check (EQY)	Equivalence Check (NETLAM)	Trojan Provided	CVSS Score
1	T100	Fail	Fail	Side-channel, key-dependent	7.5
2	T1000	Fail	Fail	Payload-triggered	7.8
3	T1100	Fail	**Pass**	Side-channel-based	8
4	T1200	Fail	Fail	Side-channel-based	7.5
5	T1300	**Pass**	Fail	Data-dependent	9
6	T200	Fail	Fail	Data-dependent	8.5
7	T300	**Pass**	**Pass**	Side-channel-based	9.6
8	T900	Fail	**Pass**	Payload-triggered, key-dependent, side-channel Trojan	9.8
9	T1500	**Pass**	**Pass**	Side-channel-based	9.8
10	T700	Fail	Fail	Payload-triggered	7.8

Among the 28 instances of AES-based Trojan attacks, Table 2 showcases 10 of the most powerful Trojan-infected AES designs. We carry out the equivalence in two methods: preliminarily, we utilize the formal equivalence checker of Yosys, EQY, to find the functional equivalence between the golden design and the Trojan-infested designs. This gives us a comprehensive idea of the functional and logical similarities/dissimilarities. Finally, we check the equivalence by exploiting our LLM-based equivalence checker. This allows us to further extend the investigation if the Trojan is not visible by EQY. Out of the 10 variants, 7 fails the functional equivalence check using EQY, while the remaining 3 passes due to their high level of stealth. Although most of the Trojans are very difficult to trace, a considerable number of the Trojans are identifiable by our LLM-based equivalence checker. **NETLAM** equivalence checker can successfully detect 6 Trojans. The Trojans of the attack variants that pass the equivalence test are mainly side-channel-based, data or key-dependent and payload-triggered Trojans.

---

4. Functional Equivalence Check

A direct comparison of File 1 and File 2 reveals significant differences. While both files implement an AES-128 encryption algorithm with similar sub-modules (S, S4, T, expand_key_128, final_round, one_round, table_lookup), File 2 contains an additional module: 'TSC' and 'Trojan_Trigger'. File 1's 'top' module only includes an AES-128 instance, while File 2's 'top' module includes the AES-128 instance, a 'Trojan_Trigger' module, and a 'TSC' module. The 'TSC' module acts as a Trojan. It takes the key and data as input and, when triggered by 'Tj_Trig', produces an output ('Capacitance') that is derived from the input data and XORed with portions of the key. This output is not part of the legitimate AES-128 functionality. The Trojan_Trigger module generates the trigger signal 'Tj_Trig' based on a large counter, making its activation seemingly random and hard to predict during normal operation. The counter's logic seems convoluted and designed to make it difficult to analyze at a glance. Therefore, the two netlists are **not functionally equivalent**. File 2 includes additional circuitry in the form of a Trojan that leaks information.

Side-channel-based Trojans are difficult to detect through functional equivalence since they do not alter the primary operation of the circuit. Data or Key-dependent Trojans, on the other hand, remain dormant for extended periods, becoming active only when the target key or data pattern appears, making them extremely hard to detect during standard testing. Payload-triggered Trojans are triggered only when the rare signal pattern occurs. The corresponding CVSS scores of the undetected Trojans are considerably high, with the side-channel-based Trojans being the most critical ones. The outputs of the equivalence checker, provided in the listings **4. Functional Equivalence Check** and **5. Trojan Detection and Stealth Evaluation** portray the structural as well as functional discrepancies among the Trojan-free and Trojan-infected designs of the **AES-T1200** variant. Additionally, the listing **5. Trojan Detection and Stealth Evaluation** presents the strength of the particular Trojan. Furthermore, our proposed **NETLAM** tool performs an overview of the different sub-modules present in the design, describing the functionality of each of them to better understand the vulnerable sites where Trojans can be inserted. Such an output is provided in the listing **6. NETLAM output for Circuit Description**.

5. Trojan Detection and Stealth Evaluation

The Trojan fails the simple functional equivalence check because of the added modules and outputs. However, detecting it requires a more sophisticated side-channel analysis method rather than a simple input-output comparison.

To evaluate the stealth of the original Trojan, we can use the CVSS framework. A possible CVSSv3 score for the original Trojan could be:

Attack Vector (AV): Local (L) – Assuming the attacker has physical access to the device. Attack Complexity (AC): High (H) - Requires specific side-channel analysis techniques.
Privileges Required (PR): None (N) - No specific privileges are needed beyond physical access.
User Interaction (UI): None (N) - The Trojan activates autonomously.
Scope (S): Unchanged (U) - The Trojan doesn't affect other system parts.
Confidentiality Impact (C): High (H) – Potential data and key leakage.
Integrity Impact (I): None (N) - No data modification.
Availability Impact (A): None (N) - No denial of service.
This yields a CVSSv3 base score of approximately **7.5 (High)**. This reflects the high confidentiality impact, but the high attack complexity slightly reduces the score.

6. NETLAM output for Circuit Description:

The top-level module top instantiates three main modules:

aes_128: This module performs the core AES-128 encryption process. It takes a 128-bit state (plaintext) and a 128-bit key as input and produces a 128-bit ciphertext as output. The encryption involves multiple rounds, each consisting of several sub-operations (SubBytes, ShiftRows, MixColumns, AddRoundKey).

Trojan_Trigger: This module acts as a trigger for a hardware Trojan. It's a counter that generates a trigger signal ('Tj_Trig') based on a specific internal counter value. The trigger condition is not explicitly defined in the provided code but is implicitly controlled by the internal state of the counter.

TSC(Trojan State Controller): This module is the Trojan itself.It takes the trigger signal ('Tj_Trig'), the AES key, and the AES state (plaintext) as input. When the 'Tj_Trig' signal is asserted, it loads a potentially modified version of the state into the 'Capacitance' output, which is not part of the original AES functionality and could be used to leak information or manipulate the output.

After a comprehensive understanding of the functionalities of the different modules in the design, the LLM tool creates a DAG in the form of an adjacency list, which aids in determining the interconnections and intermediate registers and signals of the design. A snippet of the query output by the LLM is provided in the listing **7. NETLAM output for DAG Creation**. Then the LLM identifies the most vulnerable nets or modules in the design using the DAG. An instance of the query output is illustrated in the listing **8. Identifying Vulnerable Points**.

7. NETLAM output for DAG Creation

Creating a complete DAG for such a large circuit would be extremely cumbersome to represent as a simple adjacency list. However, I can illustrate the DAG concept with a simplified example focusing on a small section and showing the general approach.

Let's consider a part of the 'S' module:
```
module S(...);
input [7:0] in;
wire _081_ = ~ in[7];
wire _092_ = ~ in[6];
INV_X1 _492_ (.A(in[7]), .ZN(_081_));
INV_X1 _493_ (.A(in[6]), .ZN(_092_));
endmodule
```
The DAG for this snippet would be like this (adjacency list representation):
in[7]: _081_
in[6]: _092_
_081_:
_092_:

8. Identifying Vulnerable Points

Given the structure, vulnerable points in the TjFree netlist are likely within the aes_128 module's internal registers and the data paths leading to the out ports. The Trojan could be stealthy if it manipulates signals only when specific conditions are met by the trigger.

Vulnerable Point 1: Registers within the aes_128 module (Specifically the DFFs storing intermediate results of the AES rounds). A Trojan could subtly alter data stored in these registers under specific conditions, without affecting the overall functionality during normal operation.

Vulnerable Point 2: The data paths between combinational logic blocks in aes_128 (between SubBytes, ShiftRows, MixColumns, AddRoundKey operations). Trojans could insert small, conditional changes within these data paths, especially around the AddRoundKey operation that combines round keys and state.

Vulnerable Point 3: The output registers of the aes_128 module (DFFs feeding the out port). A Trojan could flip bits conditionally before the final output is latched.

After pinpointing the vulnerable points in the design, the LLM is asked to propose the top 5 Trojans specific to those vulnerable sites. The top 10 Trojans suggested by the LLM across various AES-based Trojan attack variants are listed in Table 3. These Trojans have significantly high CVSS scores, and notably, 5 of them have not been identified earlier and are not part of the *Trust-Hub* benchmark dataset. We perform the two-stage equivalence checking of these 5 newly suggested Trojans, which are not included in *Trust-Hub*, to justify the credibility of our proposed tool. Surprisingly, all of the suggested Trojans pass the EQY functional equivalence check. However, 4 of them fail the **NETLAM** equivalence checker, thus strengthening our claim of evaluating such surreptitious Trojans. The Trojans fail in the equivalence test mainly because it incurs

Table 3. Stealthy Trojans suggested by **NETLAM** and their corresponding target modules, trigger mechanism, payload action, stealth features and CVSS Scores. The proposed Trojans are applicable across various AES-based Trojan attack variants.

Rank	Trojan Description	Vulnerable Point	Trigger Mechanism	Payload Action	Stealth Features	Included in Trust-Hub
1	Data-Dependent Bit-Flip	'aes_128' registers	Specific input patterns, clock cycle	Flip a bit in a selected register	Random activation, low probability	Yes
2	Conditional Key Modification	expand_key_128 XOR gates	Specific input patterns	Modify a few bits in a round key	Intermittent triggering	Yes
3	Intermittent Signal Tampering	Data path in 'aes_128'	Trigger count, specific data	Add small bias to an intermediate value	Rare activation	No
4	Clock Gating Trojan	Clock signal in 'aes_128'	Counter value, external signal	Temporarily halt clock signal to block	Random activation	No
5	Data Tampering Trojan	'xS' module	Complex trigger	Modifies specific bits of the intermediate state in each encryption round	Data-dependent, complex trigger	No
6	Data Dependent Trojan	Module final_round	Conditional trigger	Affects the final output directly	Data-dependent, complex trigger	Yes
7	Logic-level Trojan	'table_lookup' module	Always active	Modifies lookup table values	Small, localized modification	No
8	Gate-level Trojan	'S' module gates	Specific input combinations	Bit-flipping	Random activation, low frequency	No
9	Clock Glitch Trojan	Clock input to 'S'	Random clock glitches	Data corruption	Very low frequency	Yes
10	Delay-based Trojan	'aes_128' module critical path	Always active	Introduces intentional delay	Change in delay not visible during functional tests	Yes

additional circuitry in the victim modules. A brief analysis is provided in Table 4. As the LLM-based equivalence checker performs a one-to-one matching between the circuitry as well as the hierarchy of the designs, it is easier to detect stealthy Trojans using such tools.

Nevertheless, seldom in formal equivalence and verification tools, the user does not have access to the golden reference design [5]. In such cases, it is hard for the verification tool to detect the discrepancies in the Trojan-infected designs. Thus, a more reliable metric in such cases is the CVSS score. Moreover, this

Table 4. Comprehensive Results of Equivalence Checking for **NETLAM** suggested Trojans

Rank	Trojan Description	CVSS Score	Equivalence Check (EQY)	Equivalence Check (NETLAM)
1	Intermittent Signal Tampering	9	Passed	Failed due to presence of additional circuitry
2	Clock Gating Trojan	8.8	Passed	Failed due to presence of the additional clock-gating circuitry
3	Data Tampering Trojan	8.5	Passed	Failed due to difference in the 'xS' module's logic
4	Logic-level Trojan	8	Passed	Passed
5	Gate-level Trojan	7.8	Passed	Failed due to additional circuitry in 'xS' module

work is a preliminary exploration of the capabilities of LLM tools in detecting hardware Trojans in digital designs. We aspire to enhance the capacity of our tool further and uncover more stealthy Trojans capable of even passing the golden-input inclusive equivalence check to broaden the scope of benchmarks like *Trust-Hub* further. The ultimate instruction given to the LLM is to devise a Trojan specific to the vulnerable sites that is more stealthy than the one initially provided. This is illustrated in the listing **9. Trojan Inserted Benchmark**.

---

9. Trojan Inserted Benchmark

A more stealthy Trojan could be integrated within the existing AES-128 module, specifically within the 'expand_key_128' module. This module has many unused intermediate wires and registers, which present perfect camouflage.
This example adds a simple XOR operation to modify a single bit in the key expansion. Note: Actual implementation would involve a more sophisticated method.

```
 module expand_key_128(clk, in, out_1, out_2, rcon);
// ... existing code ...
// Trojan: XOR with a bit of the input data, conditionally
always @(posedge clk) begin
if (Counter[0] & Counter[1]) begin // Conditional activation, even more subtle
k0a[0] <= k0a[0] ^ in[0]; //Modifying the first bit of k0a
end
// ... existing code ...
endmodule
 module Trojan_Trigger(clk, rst, out, Tj_Trig);
//The counter can now use outputs of the key expansion instead of the state
// ... modified counter logic ...
always @(posedge clk) begin
if (rst) begin
Counter <= 0;
end else begin
Counter <= Counter + 1;
end
end
assign Tj_Trig = Counter[0] & Counter[1]; // A simple, but subtle trigger
endmodule
```

---

5 Conclusion

In this work, we present **NETLAM**, a comprehensive framework leveraging multiple LLM-based tools to tackle the challenge of identifying and generating hardware Trojans in digital designs. By combining an LLM-based equivalence checker, a DAG generator with vulnerability identification capabilities, and a Trojan injector, **NETLAM** provides a systematic approach to uncovering new, previously undiscovered Trojans. Our evaluation of *Trust-Hub's* AES dataset demonstrates the framework's ability to generate novel Trojans with high CVSS scores. We demonstrate that LLM models, such as GPT-4o and Gemini, can improve Trojan detection by leveraging semantic and probabilistic analysis instead of relying solely on strict logical equivalence. The functional, logical, and structural equivalence test is critical in the domain of hardware Trojan detection, thus necessitating the need for more open-source and accessible tools for performing such routine tests. Our proposed tool **NETLAM** paves the way for such design-critical validation by using a hybrid model for inspecting digital designs that include a formal verification tool for deterministic logic checks and a Generative AI for anomaly detection, trigger analysis, and structural mapping. Importantly, **NETLAM** not only identifies vulnerabilities but also contributes to enhancing Trojan research by uncovering more potential Trojans, thus paving the way for expanding benchmarks like *Trust-Hub*.

Acknowledgements. This work is supported by the Information Security Education and Awareness (ISEA) project under the Ministry of Electronics and Information Technology (MeitY).

References

1. Bhandari, J., Sadhukhan, R., Krishnamurthy, P., Farshad Khorrami, and Ramesh Karri. SENTAUR: security enhanced trojan assessment using llms against undesirable revisions. CoRR, abs/2407.12352 (2024)
2. Bhattacharyay, A., Yang, S., Cruz, J., Chakraborty, P., Bhunia, S., Hoque, T.: An automated framework for board-level trojan benchmarking. IEEE Trans. Comput. Aided Des. Integr. Circuits Syst. **42**(2), 397–410 (2023)
3. Chaudhuri, J., Thapar, D., Chaudhuri, A., Firouzi, F., Chakrabarty, K.: SPICED: syntactical bug and trojan pattern identification in A/MS circuits using llm-enhanced detection. CoRR, abs/2408.16018 (2024)
4. Cruz, J., Gaikwad, P., Nair, A., Chakraborty, P., Bhunia, S.: Automatic hardware trojan insertion using machine learning. CoRR, abs/2204.08580 (2022)
5. Duque Antón, A.L., et al.: A golden-free formal method for trojan detection in non-interfering accelerators. In: 2024 Design, Automation & Test in Europe Conference & Exhibition (DATE), pp. 1–6 (2024)
6. Hochreiter, S., Schmidhuber, J.: Long short-term memory (lstm). Neural Comput. **9**(8), 1735–1780 (1997)
7. The freePDK45 process design kit (PDK)
8. Klemmer, L., Bonora, D., Grosse, D.: Large-scale gatelevel optimization leveraging property checking. In: DVCon Europe 2023; Design and Verification Conference and Exhibition Europe, pp. 86–93 (2023)
9. Kokolakis, G., Moschos, A., Keromytis, A.D.: Harnessing the power of general-purpose llms in hardware trojan design. In: Andreoni, M. (ed.) Applied Cryptography and Network Security Workshops, pp. 176–194. Springer, Cham (2024)
10. Rumelhart, D.E., Hinton, G.E., Williams, R.J.: Recurrent neural network (rnn). Nature **323**, 533–536 (1986)

11. Saha, D., Yahyaei, K., Saha, S.K., Tehranipoor, M., Farahmandi, F.: Empowering hardware security with llm: the development of a vulnerable hardware database. In: 2024 IEEE International Symposium on Hardware Oriented Security and Trust (HOST), pp. 233–243 (2024)
12. Salmani, H., Tehranipoor, M., Karri, R.: On design vulnerability analysis and trust benchmarks development. In: 2013 IEEE 31st International Conference on Computer Design (ICCD), pp. 471–474 (2013)
13. Shakya, B., He, M.T., Salmani, H., Forte, D., Bhunia, S., Tehranipoor, M.M.: Benchmarking of hardware trojans and maliciously affected circuits. J. Hardware Syst. Secur. **1**, 85–102 (2017)
14. Skorobogatov, S., Woods, C.: Breakthrough Silicon Scanning Discovers Backdoor in Military Chip. In: Prouff, E., Schaumont, P. (eds.) CHES 2012. LNCS, vol. 7428, pp. 23–40. Springer, Heidelberg (2012). https://doi.org/10.1007/978-3-642-33027-8_2
15. Tehranipoor, M., Koushanfar, F.: A survey of hardware trojan taxonomy and detection. IEEE Design & Test of Computers **27**(1), 10–25 (2010)
16. Wolf, C., Glaser, J., Kepler, J.: Yosys-a free verilog synthesis suite (2013)
17. Yang, S., Hoque, T., Chakraborty, P., Bhunia, S.: Golden-free hardware trojan detection using self-referencing. IEEE Trans. Very Large Scale Integr. (VLSI) Syst. **30**(3), 325–338 (2022)
18. Yasaei, R., Chen, L., Yu, S.-Y., Abdullah Al Faruque, M.: Hardware trojan detection using graph neural networks. IEEE Trans. Comput.-Aided Des. Integrated Circuits Syst. **1** (2022)

Attacking Single-Cycle Ciphers on Modern FPGAs
Featuring Explainable Deep Learning

Mustafa Khairallah[1,2](✉) and Trevor Yap[1]

[1] Nanyang Technological University, Singapore, Singapore
trevor.yap@ntu.edu.sg
[2] Department of Electrical and Information Technology, Lund University, Lund, Sweden
m.khairallah@ntu.edu.sg

Abstract. In this paper, we revisit the question of key recovery using side-channel analysis for unrolled, single-cycle block ciphers. In particular, we study the Princev2 cipher. While it has been shown vulnerable in multiple previous studies, those studies were performed on side-channel friendly ASICs or older FPGAs (*e.g.,* Xilinx Virtex II on the SASEBO-G board), and using mostly expensive equipment. We start with the goal of exploiting a cheap modern FPGA and board using power traces from a cheap oscilloscope. Particularly, we use Xilinx Artix 7 on the Chipwhisperer CW305 board and PicoScope 5000A, respectively.

We split our study into three parts. First, we show that the new set-up still exhibits easily detectable leakage, using a non-specific t-test. Second, we replicate attacks from older FPGAs. Namely, we start with the attack by Yli-Mäyry *et al.*, which is a simple chosen plaintext correlation power analysis attack using divide and conquer. However, we demonstrate that even this simple, powerful attack does not work, demonstrating a peculiar behavior. We study this behavior using a stochastic attack that attempts to extract the leakage model, and we show that models over a small part of the state are inconsistent and depend on more key bits than what is expected. We also attempt classical template attacks and get similar results.

To further exploit the leakage, we employ deep learning techniques and succeed in key recovery, albeit using a large number of traces. We perform the explainability technique called Key Guessing Occlusion (KGO) to detect which points the neural networks exploit. When we use these points as features for the classical template attack, although it did not recover the secret key, its performance improves compared to other feature selection techniques.

Keywords: Deep Learning · Side-Channel Analysis · Princev2 · Low Latency · FPGA

© The Author(s), under exclusive license to Springer Nature Switzerland AG 2026
M. Manulis (Ed.): ACNS 2025 Workshops, LNCS 15753, pp. 22–39, 2026.
https://doi.org/10.1007/978-3-032-01799-4_2

1 Introduction

Block ciphers with unrolled implementations have gained popularity over the recent years with the emergence of ciphers such as Prince [7,8] (with both its versions), Bipbip [4], SCARF [10], Speedy [14], Orthros [3], Gleeok [2], and several others. These ciphers are typically designed with smaller security margins and are popular in applications such as memory and/or cache encryption. In these applications, the top priority is to perform the encryption and decryption as fast as possible. Unlike older and more classical designs, these block ciphers are typically implemented such that they take only one clock cycle using dedicated hardware.

This strategy presents a challenge for side-channel adversaries. In fact, unrolling the implementation of a cipher (performing several rounds of the block cipher in one clock cycle using dedicated hardware) provides some basic resistance against side-channel attacks [6]. However, advanced attacks are still feasible [16,19–21].[1] Nonetheless, the demonstrated attacks have been significantly more complicated than attacks on classical unprotected ciphers.

While investigating these attacks, we have noticed that the majority of them were performed on FPGAs that are two decades old, with the exception of [16], where the attack was performed using a dedicated side-channel friendly ASIC. More importantly, the traces were acquired using expensive equipment that is typically found in well-established labs. More and more attacks on other ciphers are being performed using cheaper equipment that can even potentially be operated in the field. Thus, we set out to investigate the vulnerability of the Princev2 cipher to side-channel analysis using cheaper setups. We use the Chipwhisperer CW305 board with Xilinx Artix 7 FPGA and the PicoScope portable oscilloscope for acquiring power traces. Compared to the oscilloscopes used in previous experiments, the PicoScope has a significantly lower sampling frequency and cost. It is hard to tell apriori whether the sampling frequency is even sufficient for the task at hand. Typically, we would use the Nyquist criterion to determine if the sampling frequency is sufficient relative to the measured signal. However, in the case of unrolled implementations, the measured signal is not related to the clock frequency but rather to the delay of the individual gates, as we hope to be able to isolate different parts of the execution.

At the end of our study, we answer our research question in the affirmative: even with this cheap setup, the implementation is still vulnerable to side-channel attacks with reasonable resources. However, the road to this answer is more interesting than the destination. Quickly, we found out that the traces still exhibit observable leakage using Test Vector Leakage Assessment (TVLA), with very few traces. However, when applying known attacks, particularly the correlation power analysis in [19], we observe a peculiar behavior. While the attack converged, indicating a uniquely recovered key, it turned out the recovered key was wrong. This behavior was consistent with different parameters and with different leakage models: Hamming distance, Hamming weight, and Identity leakage

---

[1] This is a comprehensive but non-exhaustive list.

models. To understand what is happening, we diverged our attention to a model extraction profiling attack, namely the stochastic attack [17]. The stochastic attack requires training on known keys and assumes only a polynomial leakage model. For instance, a Hamming weight leakage model is a polynomial leakage model where all the bits of the targeted value contribute linearly and equally to the leakage. However, we again observed that this polynomial model does not hold. When we train with a fixed known key, we see that the model changes depending on the value of the key, and when we train with many random keys, we get inconsistent models.

Subsequently, we opted to use more modern and advanced tools: Deep-Learning-based Side-Channel Analysis (DLSCA). It has been shown that DLSCA has obtained significant performance over classical side-channel attacks [5,15]. Specifically, in the presence of jitter/desynchronized and masking countermeasures, it has been demonstrated that DLSCA can recover the secret key without much preprocessing needed [9]. In fact, using a single-cycle cipher introduces natural desynchronization [6]. Therefore, DLSCA is the most suitable tool for exploiting the leakage within the traces. To the best of our knowledge, this is the first time DLSCA has been applied to traces of an unrolled, single-cycle block cipher. Furthermore, we utilize an explainability technique called Key Guessing Occlusion (KGO) [18] on the well-performing Deep Neural Network (DNN). This allows us to understand which timestamp/sample points the DNN is exploiting. We further use these relevant sample points for template attacks. The performance of the classical template attack improves compared to other feature selection tools or without any feature selection tools.

Part of the outcome of our study is the dataset that can be used to study advanced template attacks. To help further investigation, the dataset can be found at

$$\text{https://shorturl.at/yLIMR}$$

Outline. The paper is organized as follows: In Sect. 2, we give a brief description of the Princev2 cipher and the targeted operation. In Sect. 3, we show the vulnerability of the implementation to TVLA. In Sect. 4, we apply correlation power analysis and show the odd behavior that the traces exhibit. While in Sect. 5, we study this behavior in more detail using the stochastic attack. Next, the use of DLSCA is explored in Sect. 6. Finally, we conclude the paper in Sect. 7.

2 The Princev2 Block Cipher

Princev2 [8] is an update to the design of Prince [7]. The only difference between the two ciphers is in the key schedule. Thus, side-channel attacks, at least on the first round, are still applicable. Princev2 has a 64-bit block size and 128-bit key size. It is designed to have very small encryption critical path. The key is split into two 64-bit halves, and the round keys alternate between these two halves.

It consists of 10 iterative rounds and one middle round. The first five rounds are of the form
$$\text{AddRoundKey} \to \text{Sbox} \to \text{LinearLayer}$$
while the last 5 rounds are of the form
$$\text{LinearLayer} \to \text{Sbox}^{-1} \to \text{AddRoundKey}.$$

The linear layer is an involution, so its inverse is the same as itself. Thus, the last 5 rounds are essentially the inverse of the first 5 rounds if the round keys were the same. The middle round is of the form
$$\text{Sbox} \to \text{LinearLayer} \to \text{Sbox}^{-1}.$$

The block cipher is designed with this structure so that the same circuit can be used for both encryption and decryption. In order to recover the full secret key, we need to recover two different round keys. In our attacks, we target the first two round keys. In particular, our attacks target the output of the operation:
$$Sbox(K \oplus P),$$
where K and P are 4-bit variables. In the classical attacks (Sects. 4 and 5), we target one nibble at a time. In other words, we need one set of traces for each targetted nibble. In the DLSCA (Sect. 6), we collect one set of traces which can be used to attack different nibbles.

3 Experimental Set-up and Detecting Non-specific Leakage

For our experiments, we use the Artix 7 xc7a35t FPGA, on the ChipWhisperer CW305 development board. We use PicoScope PS5000a as our oscilloscope. We use two oscilloscope channels, one for triggering, set at a range of 20V, and one for measurement, set at a range of 200mV. The FPGA runs at 10 MHz and the oscilloscope is set to time-base 2 (4ns sampling interval). This implies that each clock cycle is represented in the trace approximately 25 samples. In order to verify that the setup gives meaningful traces and that we can detect leakage at all, we perform Welsh's t-test using the TVLA framework. We used 1000 traces that randomly switch between random and fixed plaintexts, with 483 traces with a fixed plaintext and 517 random plaintexts. As expected, we can easily detect non-specific leakage with $t > 20$. The result is shown in Fig. 1. Despite this positive and expected result, it is well known that TVLA does not give an indication of how the observable leakage can be exploited in a meaningful attack. In the remainder of the paper, we will attempt to exploit the leakage, first using known attacks and then using DLSCA.

Several side-channel attacks on single-cycle ciphers have been proposed over the years. [16,19–21] is a comprehensive (but non-exhaustive) list of examples.

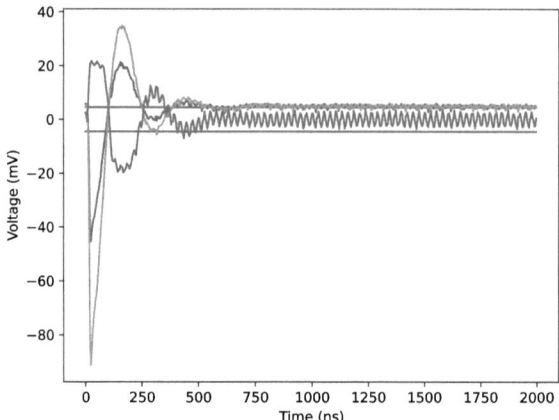

Fig. 1. TVLA result against Princev2. Green is the t value, blue is the mean of all the fixed plaintext traces and orange is the mean of all the random plaintext traces. The red lines are set at ±4.5, the widely accepted standard for significant leakage. (Color figure online)

The main challenge in attacking single-cycle ciphers is their unrolled combinational circuit. This means that the measured power includes the switching activity from all the gates of the combinational circuit. On the other hand, side-channel attacks achieve the best results when we are able to perform attacks in a divide-and-conquer manner: the attacker targets a small part of the computation at a time, *e.g.* one substitution box (sbox) or a handful of sboxes. In this framework, everything that is simultaneous to the targeted operation is seen as algorithmic noise. Thus, if we target one sbox in a single-cycle implementation, almost the whole cipher contributes to the noise. With a high-resolution, powerful oscilloscope, we can somehow reduce this effect by having more samples per cycle and somewhat having a better resolution in identifying the logic propagation patterns in the trace. Our setup is, however, geared towards studying the other end of this spectrum: a cheap low-resolution oscilloscope, a cheap board, and relatively high-frequency implementation. While the TVLA result shows significant observable leakage, it also shows that during the first clock cycle after the trigger, the power consumption is quite high with significant peaks.

4 Correlation Power Analysis

Yli-Mäyry *et al.* [19] proposed a CPA attack on prince using the Tektronix DPO7254 oscilloscope with 0.2 ns sampling interval and Xilinx Virtex II FPGA. Information on the clock frequency does not seem to be reported. They were successful in recovering one round key with around 50,000 traces. Yli-Mäyry *et al.* [20] proposed a new technique for reducing the algorithmic noise. Instead of collecting one set of traces with random plaintexts, they collected a separate set of traces for each targeted sbox, where the plaintext nibble corresponding to that sbox varies randomly, and the rest are set to zeros. This reduces the switching activity and algorithmic noise in the first sbox layer. They used the same oscilloscope as [19], but set to an even higher sampling frequency: 0.025 ns sampling interval. They were able to find the first round key with 16 × 500 traces. This is significantly better than [19]. They also attack the second round key but the number of traces increases by 10−40×. The authors seem to attribute the improved performance of [20] compared to [19] solely to the new strategy. While the strategy plays a major role, it should not be missed that the sampling frequency is increased by 8 folds. We also note that both papers use the Sasebo-G board, with Xilinx Virtex II FPGA[2]. The Sasebo-G board is heavily engineered to ease side-channel analysis. The Virtex II board is quite outdated in 2024.

Moos [16] studied the problem of attacking Princev2 on a custom 40 nm side-channel-friendly ASIC. He performed two studies. The first is based on dynamic power analysis, using Teledyne LeCroy WaveRunner 8254M and 0.025 ns sampling interval. He also used a high-frequency electromagnetic probe to get high-resolution power traces. In this case, he was able to recover the key with about 500,000 traces. In the second study, he targeted static power. He used Teledyne LeCroy HRO 66Zi and 0.5 ns sampling interval. He was able to recover most of the first round key using an estimate of 16 × 50,000 traces.

While these attacks are powerful, they are also quite costly. Each of the three oscilloscopes used in these experiments costs upwards of 10k Euros. Besides, these oscilloscopes are only useful for attacks that can be performed in a lab, as they lack portability. The oscilloscope we use (PicoScope 5000a) is portable, can be powered by a laptop and costs < 2.5k Euros. We also needed an SMA-BNC cable to interface between the oscilloscope and the CW305 board, which cost about 30 Euros. We set to find out if the previous attacks are effective in this cheap setting. We performed the CPA of [20]. A random fixed key is generated at the beginning of the experiment and loaded to the FPGA. Next, we select which nibble we want to target and set all other plaintext nibbles to 0. When targeting the nibble at index i, the plaintext for trace j is on the form:

$$0x000000000000000r_j << (4i)$$

where r_j is a random nibble.

We collected 100,000 traces per nibble and observed that the CPA attack converges towards one key guess. It seemed to converge with the maximum correlation coefficient ≈ 0.08. However, upon further inspection, it seemed that the attack was always converging but not the correct value. For instance, the results for one nibble for each key guess are displayed in Fig. 2, with 8 as the key guess with the highest correlation coefficient. The figure depicts the first two clock cycles and corresponds to the first two peaks in the power traces in Fig. 1. There is also a clear ordering of the guess throughout the computation. Figure 3 shows the maximum correlation coefficient for each key nibble guess. Showing the correct guess should have been 0, but the attack guessed 8.

---

[2] [20] lists the board as Sasebo-G II, but Sasebo-G II came with Virtex 5, not Virtex II.

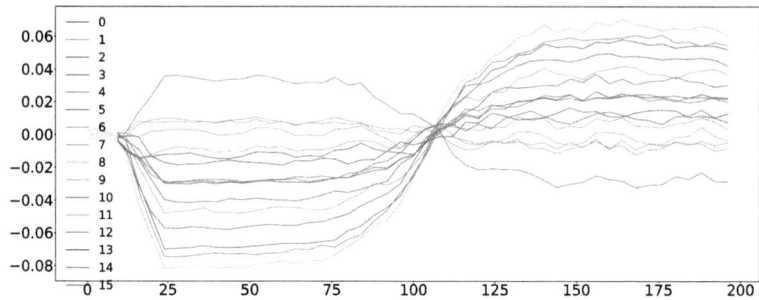

Fig. 2. Correlation coefficient for a key nibble in the first two clock cycles.

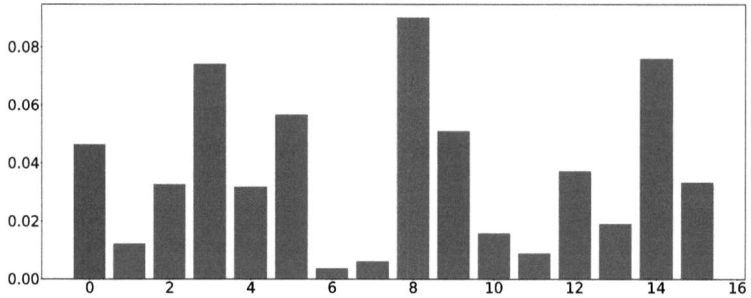

Fig. 3. Maximum correlation coefficient for a key nibble in the first two clock cycles. Red is the guessed key nibble, while green is the correct key nibble. (Color figure online)

We tried this experiment numerous times and could not identify any pattern for why this behavior was happening. It seems that the wrongly guessed key value for the same nibble location and the same correct key nibble value also change by changing the full key, while it remains the same for the same key. In other words, consider the two round keys

$$0x0ae6568fd3cfa120$$

$$0xf27667ef4441a520$$

with plaintexts

$$0x000000000000000r_j.$$

Both keys have a targeted key nibble of value 0, but during the attack, each key will lead to a different wrong guess. Figures 2 and 3 have been generated using the Hamming distance model at the output of the first sbox layer. However, the same behavior was observed using the Hamming weight model.

5 Stochastic Attacks

To get one step closer to understanding the root cause of the behavior observed in the CPA attack, we perform a stochastic attack. During CPA, we assume a specific leakage model, such as Hamming weight or Hamming distance. During the stochastic attack, we assume a polynomial leakage model, typically linear. In particular, if the target variable is

$$X = S(K \oplus P)$$

and X consists of 4 bits x_3, x_2, x_1 and x_0, then we assume the model

$$L(X) = \sum_{i=0}^{15} a_i x_0^{i_0} x_1^{i_1} x_2^{i_2} x_3^{i_3}$$

where $a_i \in \mathbb{R}$ and $i_3 i_2 i_1 i_0$ is the bit representation of the integer i for all $0 \leq i \leq 15$. Note that if $i = 0$, this is the DC offset in the model. If $a_i = 0$ for every $i \notin \{0, 1, 2, 4, 8\}$, then the model is linear. The stochastic attack is a model extraction attack. In other words, its goal is not to recover a secret key but to recover the hardware leakage model, assuming it is a polynomial model. We collect many traces with known values of X. For the target nibble, the stochastic attack performs a form of regression to recover the coefficients a_i for the values of X (which are known) and the measured traces. We refer to [17] for full details on the computational part of the attack. If the Hamming weight model is correct, then we would expect $a_0 \neq 0, a_1 \approx a_2 \approx a_4 \approx a_8 \neq 0$ and $a_i \approx 0$ for the other values of i. Our stochastic analysis was performed with 10,000 traces per experiment. It shows two peculiar observations:

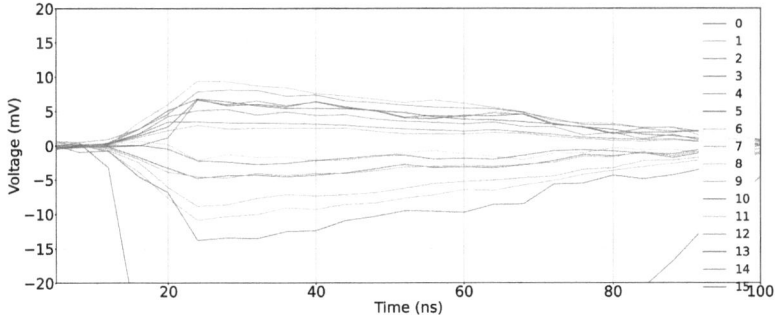

Fig. 4. Example of the model extracted by the stochastic attack

1. The model returned by the stochastic analysis is non-linear. For instance, when we use the key

$$0x398c46c68f4664cd6afc2ccca4b2eb9f$$

and vary the target plaintext nibble randomly, we get a uniform distribution for X. The model we get is shown in Fig. 4. The blue cropped curve corresponds to a_0, which is the constant part of the polynomial. We expect 4 more curves to have significant non-zero values, but we can see that this is not the case.

2. By changing the key values during the training phase, we get different leakage models. This is demonstrated in Figs. 5 and 6, by showing the linear part of the model for different keys used in the training, with both random and chosen examples. Note that while in these experiments, we use one key for each iteration, the plaintext varies uniformly at random for each trace. Thus, the distribution of X is the same for all experiments.

Moreover, changing the key for each trace does not help achieve a reliable model either. In Fig. 7, we give three identical experiments targeting the same nibble and varying the full key randomly for each trace, each with $10,000$ traces. We observe that the three experiments give different weights for different bits. The observations from the TVLA test, CPA attack and stochastic attack lead us to conclude that while the traces from our setup include enough information for observable non-specific leakage, they do not include enough information to be exploited by conventional attacks, both profiled and non-profiled. This begs the question: is the implementation secure against our attack setup? We answer this question negatively in the next section, using DLSCA.

6 Deep Learning-Based Side-Channel Attack

In recent years, DLSCA has garnered significant interest due to its impressive performance despite the presence of hiding and masking countermeasures. Therefore, in this section, we explore the capability of DLSCA on unrolled, single-cycle block ciphers. We will first recall the profiling attack.

6.1 Profiling Attack

Suppose Z and $\boldsymbol{T}$ to be random variables of the sensitive variable and traces, respectively. There are two phases in a profiling attack: the profiling phase and the attack phase. In the profiling phase, a clone device is used to build a distinguisher $\mathcal{F}$. The adversary either has the knowledge of the key or can manipulate the key of the clone device. Profiling traces of a known set of random public variables (plaintexts or ciphertexts) are then collected from the clone device to build $\mathcal{F}$. Next, in the attack phase, several attack traces (using another set of known public variables) are collected using the target device. Then, the attack traces are given to $\mathcal{F}$ to output a probability score for each hypothetical sensitive value i.e., $\boldsymbol{y}_i = \mathcal{F}(\boldsymbol{t}_i)$ for each attack traces $\boldsymbol{t}_i$ acquired from the target device. For key recovery, the log-likelihood score for each key $k \in \mathcal{K}$ is calculated:

$$score(k) = \sum_{i=1}^{N_a} \log(\boldsymbol{y}_i[z_{i,k}])$$

with N_a as the number of attack traces used and $z_{i,k} = Crypt(pt_i, k)$ are the hypothetical sensitive values based on the key k with pt_i being the corresponding public variable to the trace $\boldsymbol{t}_i$. In this work, we set $Crypt$ to be the sbox of

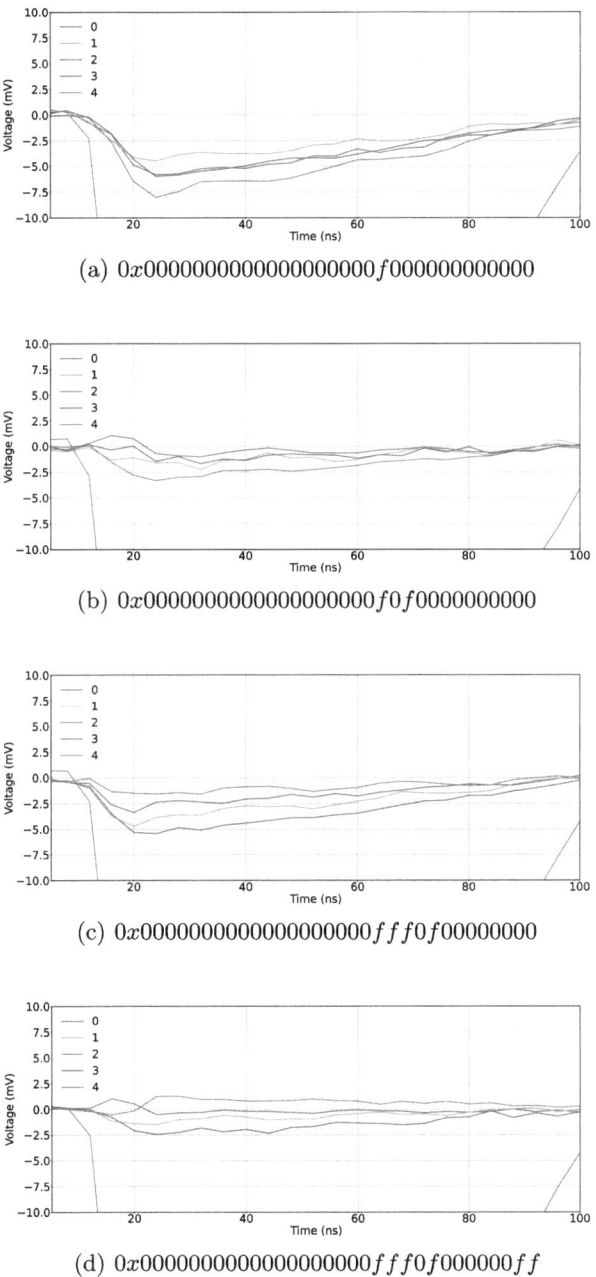

Fig. 5. Different linear leakage models obtained for different chosen training keys.

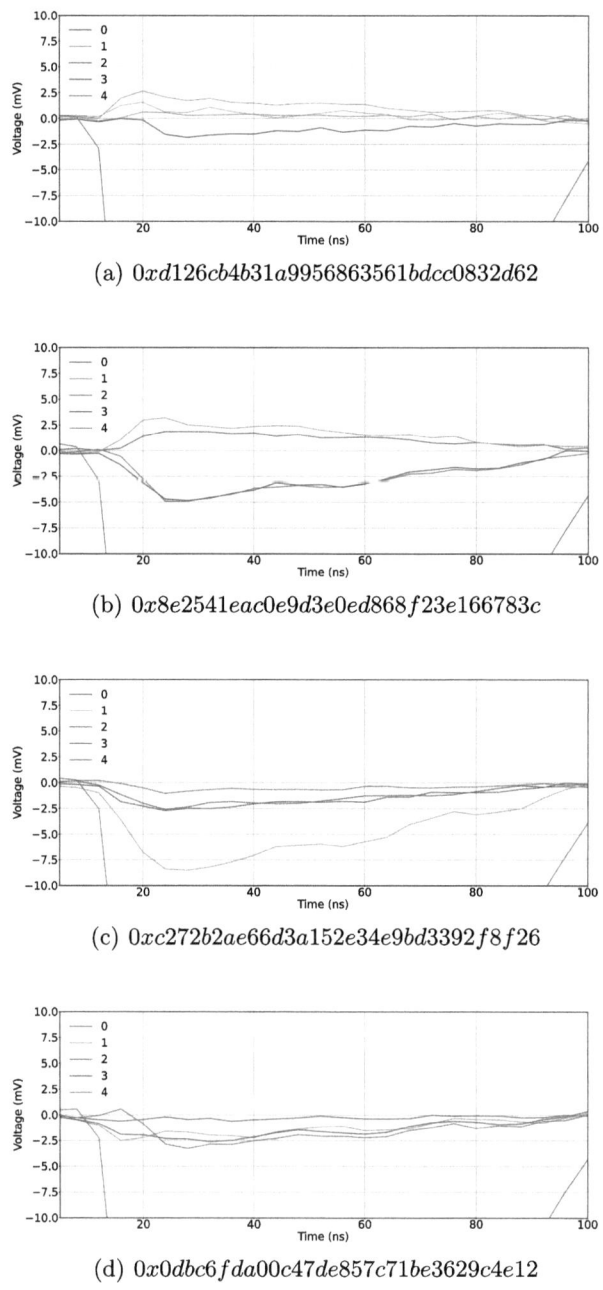

Fig. 6. Different linear leakage models obtained for different random training keys.

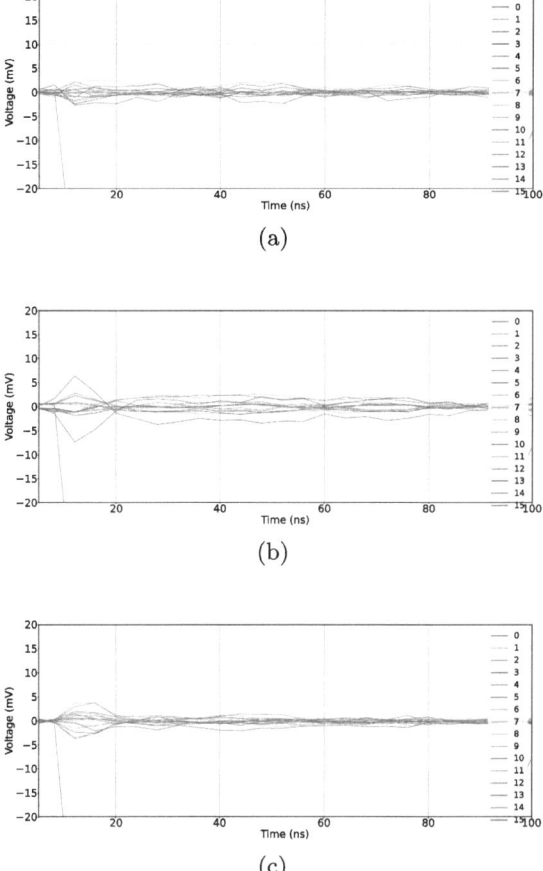

Fig. 7. Different linear leakage models obtained from three experiments where the key varies for each trace.

Princev2. The scores are then sorted in a guess vector, $\boldsymbol{G} = [G_0, G_1, \ldots, G_{|\mathcal{K}|-1}]$ where G_0 is the most likely key candidate while $G_{|\mathcal{K}|-1}$ is the least likely key candidate. The rank of the key is defined as the index of $\boldsymbol{G}$. We define GE as the average rank correct secret key. Therefore, we recover the key successfully when $GE = 0$. Furthermore, we denote $NTGE$ as the least number of attack traces required to attain $GE = 0$.

For the classical template attack, the conditional probability $Pr(\boldsymbol{T}|Z = z)$ is assumed to be a multivariate Gaussian distribution and uses Bayes' Theorem to build the distinguisher. On the other hand, for a typical profiled DLSCA, a DNN is trained as a distinguisher with traces as the input and sensitive values as the labels [11,22].

Table 1. Hyperparameter search space.

Hyperparameter	Options
MLP	
Number of Dense Layers	1 to 8 (step 1)
Neurons per layer	$10, 20, 50, 100, 200$
CNN	
Convolution layers	1 to 4 (step 1)
Convolution filters	4 to 16 (step 4)
Kernel size	26 to 52 (step 2)
Padding	0 to 16 (step 2)
Pooling type	Average or Max
Pooling size	2 to 10 (step 2)
Number of Dense Layers	1 to 8 (step 1)
Neurons per layer	$10, 20, 50, 100, 200$
Others	
Batch size	100 to $1,000$ in a step of 100
Activation function	$ReLU, SeLU, ELU$ or $tanh$
Optimizer	Adam or RMSprop
Learning Rate	$1e^{-3}, 1e^{-4}, 5e^{-4}, 1e^{-5}, 5e^{-5}$
Weight Initializer	Random Uniform or Glorot Uniform or He Uniform

6.2 Experimental Setting

Hyperparameter Search Space: Among the many different DNN architectures, the Multilayer Perceptron (MLP) and Convolutional Neural Network (CNN) are the most commonly used architecture within the side-channel domain [1,11,22]. We utilize random search, a popular hyperparameter tuning strategy, sampling 100 DNN configurations from the defined hyperparameter search space stated in Table 1. As with many works, we use the softmax activation function [13] in the last layer for every DNN used and train each DNN with 100 epochs using the categorical-cross entropy loss function.

Dataset: The dataset consists of $50,000$ profiling traces collected under random key settings and $50,000$ attack traces obtained using a fixed key setting. We truncate the traces such that it only includes the encryption portion ranging from sample point 5 to 31.[3] Each of the traces consists of 26 sample points. We use the output sbox of the first round of Princev2 as the label for our attack.[4]

---

[3] We also manage to recover the secret key with full traces using DLSCA successfully.
[4] We have also applied its Hamming weight as the label. However, we see superior results with just the output of the sbox and will only present these results here.

6.3 Experimental Results

We target all 16 nibbles of the first round key and present our results in Table 2. Using DLSCA, we successfully recovered the first round keys for all nibbles using fewer than 20,000 attack traces. Nibbles 3 and 8 were the easiest to attack, with a NTGE of less than 17,000. In contrast, nibble 14 proved the most challenging to recover, as the MLP failed to retrieve the key, while the CNN required an NTGE of 19,997.

Next, we apply DLSCA to all 16 nibbles of the second-round key and display the results in Table 3. Similar to the first-round keys, we successfully recover all nibbles using fewer than 20,000 attack traces. Notably, we can easily recover nibbles 2 and 7 with less than 18,000 attack traces. Using both MLP and CNN, we are able to recover the entire second-round key. Overall, we successfully recover the full Princev2 key using DLSCA.

6.4 Explanability of Deep Neural Network

In order to understand which sample points the DNNs are using for key recovery, we employ the explainability techniques called KGO proposed by [18]. KGO utilizes a technique called occlusion, which replaces each sample point with a default baseline value. The KGO algorithm iteratively occludes each sample point to obtain the minimum set of sample points that is necessary for a trained DNN to recover the secret key. These minimum set of relevant sample points are called OccPoIs. [18] also proposed an algorithm called 1-KGO to state how much contribution an OccPoI is to the DNN. This is done by occluding each OccPoI one by one and obtaining the GE values for each OccPoI occluded. If the GE is high, this means that this OccPoI has a high contribution to the key recovery, while if the GE is low, it means that it contributes less for the DNN to recover the key. We focus only on the best-performing MLP for nibble 0 as the technique can extend to other well-performing networks. Using KGO, we acquire the sample points 7 and 15 as OccPoIs. Then we apply the 1-KGO algorithm and obtain the GE values 11 and 2 for sample points 7 and 15, respectively. This means that the sample point 7 has the most contribution compared to 15. This aligns with the TVLA result that sample point 7 leaks the most. We plot the OccPoIs and their contribution in Fig. 8 (blue plot).

To evaluate OccPoIs' relevance in classical SCA, we conducted a template attack utilizing OccPoIs. Notably, the GE converged to 2, outperforming the $GE = 11$ achieved without feature selection on truncated traces. We also compare its performance with two other feature selection tools, namely SOSD and SOST [12], by selecting the same number of sample points as OccPoIs. SOSD selected the sample points at 6 and 12 while SOST selected the sample points at 2 and 13 (illustrated in Fig. 8). We apply template attack with these sample points only and observe that both SOSD an SOST have high GE, suggesting that SOSD and SOST fail to recover the secret key. This demonstrates that OccPoIs, selected via DNNs with KGO, effectively exploit leakages and enhance classical attack effectiveness (Table 4).

Table 2. Performance using DLSCA. Random key setting with truncated traces for first round.

Nibble	0	1	2	3	4	5	6	7
MLP	19847	19599	19971	15065	19353	18850	19959	18523
Nibble	8	9	10	11	12	13	14	15
MLP	16771	19677	19997	19345	19881	17300	$(GE=3)$	18372
Nibble	0	1	2	3	4	5	6	7
CNN	19771	18048	19745	16416	19118	18843	19453	18025
Nibble	8	9	10	11	12	13	14	15
CNN	15246	19386	19866	19445	18924	17811	19997	18348

Table 3. Performance using DLSCA. Random key setting with truncated traces for second round.

Nibble	0	1	2	3	4	5	6	7
MLP	18778	19846	17144	19901	19144	17510	19996	15436
Nibble	8	9	10	11	12	13	14	15
MLP	19995	19985	19188	19519	18381	$(GE=2)$	19273	19829
Nibble	0	1	2	3	4	5	6	7
CNN	19199	19863	17036	18036	17110	19047	18620	15883
Nibble	8	9	10	11	12	13	14	15
CNN	$(GE=1)$	19932	17299	19503	$(GE=1)$	19994	19972	19260

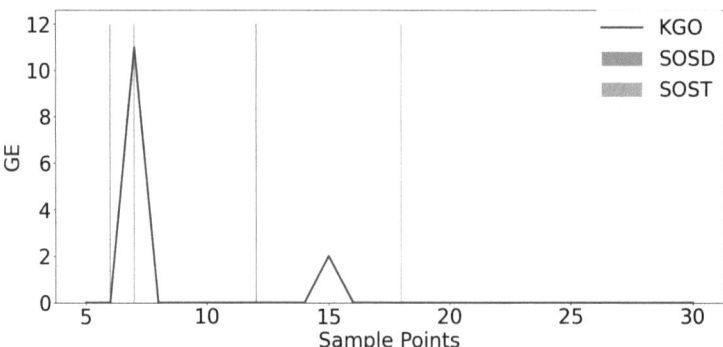

Fig. 8. Sample Points Selected by Various Feature Selection Tools. (Color figure online)

Table 4. Performance using Template Attack with Feature Selection Used.

Technique Used	Template Attack Performance
No Feature Selection	$GE = 11$
KGO	$GE = 2$
SOSD	$GE = 13$
SOST	$GE = 11$

7 Conclusion

In this paper, we investigated the vulnerability of the hardware implementation of Princev2 on Artix 7 to power analysis using cheaper and portable oscilloscopes. We demonstrated that the setup can still easily observe leakage and can perform key recovery using DLSCA. We also presented the challenges of extending these attacks to classical attacks that are not based on deep learning. Furthermore, we investigated which sample points are useful (i.e., OccPoIs) to the neural network for key recovery through the KGO explainability technique. We improve the classical template attack by using these relevant sample points. As part of future work, we plan to investigate the leakage model and the reasons behind the observed inconsistencies in classical attacks in more detail.

Acknowledgment. Mustafa Khairallah is supported by the Wallenberg-NTU Presidential Postdoctoral Fellowship and worked on the experiments in the paper while at Lund University Sweden. We would like to thank Shivam Bhasin for suggestions and support during these experiments.

References

1. Acharya, R.Y., Ganji, F., Forte, D.: Information theory-based evolution of neural networks for side-channel analysis. IACR Trans. Cryptogr. Hardw. Embed. Syst. **2023**(1), 401–437 (2023). https://doi.org/10.46586/TCHES.V2023.I1.401-437
2. Anand, R., et al.: Gleeok: a family of low-latency prfs and its applications to authenticated encryption. IACR Trans. Cryptogr. Hardw. Embed. Syst. **2024**(2), 545–587 (2024). https://doi.org/10.46586/TCHES.V2024.I2.545-587
3. Banik, S., Isobe, T., Liu, F., Minematsu, K., Sakamoto, K.: Orthros: A low-latency PRF. IACR Trans. Symmetric Cryptol. **2021**(1), 37–77 (2021). https://doi.org/10.46586/TOSC.V2021.I1.37-77
4. Belkheyar, Y., Daemen, J., Dobraunig, C., Ghosh, S., Rasoolzadeh, S.: Bipbip: A low-latency tweakable block cipher with small dimensions. IACR Trans. Cryptogr. Hardw. Embed. Syst. **2023**(1), 326–368 (2023). https://doi.org/10.46586/TCHES.V2023.I1.326-368
5. Benadjila, R., Prouff, E., Strullu, R., Cagli, E., Dumas, C.: Deep learning for sidechannel analysis and introduction to ASCAD database. J. Cryptogr. Eng. **10**(2), 163–188 (2020). https://doi.org/10.1007/S13389-019-00220-8

6. Bhasin, S., Guilley, S., Sauvage, L., Danger, J.-L.: Unrolling cryptographic circuits: a simple countermeasure against side-channel attacks. In: Pieprzyk, J. (ed.) CT-RSA 2010. LNCS, vol. 5985, pp. 195–207. Springer, Heidelberg (2010). https://doi.org/10.1007/978-3-642-11925-5_14
7. Borghoff, J., et al.: PRINCE - a low-latency block cipher for pervasive computing applications - extended abstract. In: Wang, X., Sako, K. (eds.) ASIACRYPT 2012. LNCS, vol. 7658, pp. 208–225. Springer, Cham (2012). https://doi.org/10.1007/978-3-642-34961-4_14
8. Bozilov, D., et al.: Princev2 - more security for (almost) no overhead. In: Dunkelman, O., Jr., M.J.J., O'Flynn, C. (eds.) SAC 2020. LNCS, vol. 12804, pp. 483–511. Springer (2020https://doi.org/10.1007/978-3-030-81652-0_19
9. Cagli, E., Dumas, C., Prouff, E.: Convolutional neural networks with data augmentation against jitter-based countermeasures. In: Fischer, W., Homma, N. (eds.) CHES 2017. LNCS, vol. 10529, pp. 45–68. Springer, Cham (2017). https://doi.org/10.1007/978-3-319-66787-4_3
10. Canale, F., Güneysu, T., Leander, G., Thoma, J.P., Todo, Y., Ueno, R.: SCARF - a low-latency block cipher for secure cache-randomization. In: Calandrino, J.A., Troncoso, C. (eds.) 32nd USENIX Security Symposium, USENIX Security 2023, Anaheim, CA, USA, August 9-11, 2023, pp. 1937–1954. USENIX Association (2023). https://www.usenix.org/conference/usenixsecurity23/presentation/canale
11. Eng, T.Y.H., Bhasin, S., Weissbart, L.: Train Wisely: Multifidelity Bayesian Optimization Hyperparameter Tuning in Side-Channel Analysis. IACR Cryptol. ePrint Arch., p. 170 (2024). https://eprint.iacr.org/2024/170
12. Gierlichs, B., Lemke-Rust, K., Paar, C.: Templates vs. stochastic methods. In: Goubin, L., Matsui, M. (eds.) CHES 2006. LNCS, vol. 4249, pp. 15–29. Springer, Heidelberg (2006). https://doi.org/10.1007/11894063_2
13. Goodfellow, I.J., Bengio, Y., Courville, A.C.: Deep Learning. Adaptive computation and machine learning, MIT Press (2016). http://www.deeplearningbook.org/
14. Leander, G., Moos, T., Moradi, A., Rasoolzadeh, S.: The SPEEDY family of block ciphers engineering an ultra low-latency cipher from gate level for secure processor architectures. IACR Trans. Cryptogr. Hardw. Embed. Syst. **2021**(4), 510–545 (2021). https://doi.org/10.46586/TCHES.V2021.I4.510-545
15. Maghrebi, H., Portigliatti, T., Prouff, E.: Breaking cryptographic implementations using deep learning techniques. In: Carlet, C., Hasan, M.A., Saraswat, V. (eds.) SPACE 2016. LNCS, vol. 10076, pp. 3–26. Springer, Cham (2016). https://doi.org/10.1007/978-3-319-49445-6_1
16. Moos, T.: Unrolled cryptography on silicon A physical security analysis. IACR Trans. Cryptogr. Hardw. Embed. Syst. **2020**(4), 416–442 (2020). https://doi.org/10.13154/TCHES.V2020.I4.416-442
17. Schindler, W., Lemke, K., Paar, C.: A stochastic model for differential side channel cryptanalysis. In: Rao, J.R., Sunar, B. (eds.) CHES 2005. LNCS, vol. 3659, pp. 30–46. Springer, Heidelberg (2005). https://doi.org/10.1007/11545262_3
18. Yap, T., Bhasin, S., Picek, S.: OccPoIs: Points of Interest based on Neural Network's Key Recovery in Side-Channel Analysis through Occlusion. IACR Cryptol. ePrint Arch., p. 1055 (2023). https://eprint.iacr.org/2023/1055
19. Yli-Mäyry, V., Homma, N., Aoki, T.: Improved power analysis on unrolled architecture and its application to PRINCE block cipher. In: Güneysu, T., Leander, G., Moradi, A. (eds.) LightSec 2015. LNCS, vol. 9542, pp. 148–163. Springer, Cham (2015). https://doi.org/10.1007/978-3-319-29078-2_9

20. Yli-Mäyry, V., Homma, N., Aoki, T.: Chosen-input side-channel analysis on unrolled light-weight cryptographic hardware. In: 18th International Symposium on Quality Electronic Design, ISQED 2017, Santa Clara, CA, USA, March 14-15, 2017, pp. 301–306. IEEE (2017). https://doi.org/10.1109/ISQED.2017.7918332
21. Yli-Mäyry, V., Ueno, R., Miura, N., Nagata, M., Bhasin, S., Mathieu, Y., Graba, T., Danger, J., Homma, N.: Diffusional side-channel leakage from unrolled lightweight block ciphers: A case study of power analysis on PRINCE. IEEE Trans. Inf. Forensics Secur. 16, 1351–1364 (2021). https://doi.org/10.1109/TIFS.2020.3033441
22. Zaid, G., Bossuet, L., Habrard, A., Venelli, A.: Methodology for efficient CNN architectures in profiling attacks. IACR Trans. Cryptogr. Hardw. Embed. Syst. **2020**(1), 1–36 (2020). https://doi.org/10.13154/TCHES.V2020.I1.1-36

Can KANs Do It? Toward Interpretable Deep Learning-Based Side-Channel Analysis

Kota Yoshida[1(✉)], Sengim Karayalçin[2], and Stjepan Picek[3]

[1] Ritsumeikan University, Kyoto, Japan
y0sh1d4@fc.ritsumei.ac.jp
[2] Leiden University, Leiden, The Netherlands
s.karayalcin@liacs.leidenuniv.nl
[3] Radboud University, Nijmegen, The Netherlands
stjepan.picek@ru.nl

Abstract. Recently, deep learning-based side-channel analysis (DLSCA) has emerged as a serious threat against cryptographic implementations. These methods can efficiently break implementations protected with various countermeasures while needing limited manual intervention. To effectively protect implementation, it is therefore crucial to be able to interpret **how** these models are defeating countermeasures. Several works have attempted to gain a better understanding of the mechanics of these models. However, a fine-grained description remains elusive. To help tackle this challenge, we propose using Kolmogorov-Arnold Networks (KANs). These neural networks were recently introduced and showed competitive performance to multilayer perceptrons (MLPs) on small-scale tasks while being easier to interpret. In this work, we show that KANs are well suited to SCA, performing similarly to MLPs across both simulated and real-world traces. Furthermore, we find specific strategies that the trained models learn for combining mask shares and are able to measure what points in the trace are relevant.

1 Introduction

Since the seminal work of Kocher [13], side-channel analysis (SCA) has received significant attention from the research community. Chari et al. [6] proposed template attacks to assess the security of cryptographic implementations under worst-case assumptions. For these attacks, the adversary uses a copy of the device they are attacking with known key(s), i.e., a profiling device, to create a model for the computation of the target device. This model can then be used to attack the target device more efficiently. However, classical profiling attacks still require significant manual intervention in the feature engineering phase [1,15,27].

To address this limitation, deep learning-based profiling attacks have recently emerged with the promise to automate much of the labor-intensive aspects of

---

K. Yoshida and S. Karayalçin—Equal contribution.

SCA evaluations [5,11,17]. In these works, neural networks are trained to directly predict sensitive intermediate values from traces of protected implementations, leading to state-of-the-art attacking results. While these models result in (more) automated and efficient attacks than classical profiling methods, several open challenges still limit the reliability of deep learning-based SCA in practice [26].

One of the key limitations of using neural networks is that the (trained) networks are a black-box. In the context of SCA, a network resulting in key retrieval clearly indicates that exploitable leakage is present in the traces. However, actionable feedback about what information is leaking and where is difficult to extract. To address this challenge, several works have explored input attribution methods to visualize what parts of the trace are contributing to the neural network predictions [10,20,22,38], implicitly working on the second condition. Further works attempted to gain a better understanding of the internal operations of the neural network [23,34]. Finally, in [35], a specific type of network architecture is used that is more interpretable. While these works make significant progress towards understanding aspects of the trained networks, only [35] provides explanations on the internals that reflect on how networks are combining secret shares to avoid masking countermeasures. However, this requires specialized architectures and results in significantly degraded attack performance.

Indeed, in the context of leakage-assessments, Gao and Oswald [8] define explainable key leakage detection to comprise three main elements: 1) a list of intermediate values that leak; 2) the trace points where these intermediate values leak; 3) the creation of a concrete attack path to extract the key. A trained neural net that results in key extraction directly fulfills the third condition. Furthermore, some of the above works fill in parts of the first two conditions. The input attribution methods can indicate the leakage points the network is exploiting. Furthermore, with access to masking randomness the work in [23] can determine which intermediate values are (not) used by the network. Combining these, we can then fulfill all three conditions. However, when masking randomness is not available to the evaluator (see [18] for a discussion on the relevance of this setting in practice), only the specialized architecture from [35] can fulfill all the conditions, but this results in significantly degraded attack performance in practical settings which is problematic if we aim to provide feedback on what the optimal attack path is.

To address this gap, we propose using the recently introduced Kolmogorov-Arnold Networks (KAN) [16]. KANs are a novel alternative to the widely used multilayer perceptron (MLP) with several key benefits for our application. KANs can achieve similar performance to MLPs with much fewer trainable parameters on several tasks and result in (qualitatively) far more interpretable networks. Considering the challenges related to explaining how neural networks effectively break implementations discussed above and the fact that (relatively) small models often work quite well in SCA [23,38], exploring whether KANs can provide competitive performance while improving interpretability is relevant. With simulation and real traces, we demonstrate that KANs can achieve comparable performance to MLPs and can interpret what profiling models learned in DLSCA.

The main contributions of this paper are as follows:

1. This is the first report on applying KANs in SCA. We demonstrate that KAN performs similarly to MLP in DLSCA. KANs can effectively retrieve the sub-key from (the truncated) ASCAD traces in ≈ 300 traces, which is comparable to early, less-optimized[1] MLPs [2].
2. We simulate side-channel leakage and show the function learned by KANs. More precisely, we simulated Hamming weight (HW) leakage from a software-implemented cryptographic algorithm with a masking countermeasure. Focusing on LSB labeling, we showed that KANs learned an expectation maximization function for each leakage pattern. This function can achieve 53.74% accuracy on the 2-share masking countermeasure, which indicates that more shares are needed to mitigate SCA risks.
3. We evaluated the interpretability of KANs with the ASCAD dataset, which contains power traces acquired from software-implemented AES with a 2-share masking countermeasure. We showed that the same result as the simulation can be obtained with real traces.

A repository containing the code for this paper is provided at https://github.com/Sengim/kansca.

2 Side-Channel Analysis

Profiling SCA with Deep Learning. In the profiled SCA scenario, the adversary has access to a clone device on which they have access to the secret key(s) [6]. The adversary's first step is to create a model (with uncertainty) to predict a secret-dependent intermediate value of cryptographic operations from side-channel leakage. Since the intermediate value depends on a key, the adversary can reveal the key from the intermediate value. Here, we consider that the cryptographic algorithm is AES, and the side-channel leakage is the target device's power consumption. The intermediate value is generally set to the output of the AES Sbox, i.e., $SBox[p_i \oplus k_i]$ where p_i and k_i are the i'th bytes of the plaintext and key, respectively.

The adversary prepares a dataset that consists of measured power traces (input) $\mathcal{X}_p$ and corresponding intermediate values (label) $\mathcal{Y}_p$. These intermediate values can be transformed to effectively train the model using a leakage model representing how the value influences the physical measurements. The adversary trains a neural network-based classification model parameterized with trainable θ, $\mathcal{M}_\theta : \mathbf{X} \mapsto \mathbf{Y}$ with the dataset with gradient descent to minimize a loss function. This then results in the model predicting a probability distribution over the possible label values for a trace. This step is commonly denoted by the training or profiling step.

---

[1] We note that better performance has been achieved for this target with more optimized architectures [33,38], but similar performance improvements should be possible for KANs with more research.

The second step is to reveal the most likely secret key using the trained model $\mathcal{M}_\theta$ and newly acquired traces $\mathcal{X}_a$ from the target device. The adversary can leverage to score key candidates $k \in \mathcal{K}$ according to the log-likelihood of the intermediate values y_k the model predicts $score(k) = \sum_{\mathbf{x}_i \in \mathcal{X}_a} log(\mathcal{M}(\mathbf{x}_i)_\theta(\mathbf{x}[y_{k,i}]))$.

These scores can then be ordered, which allows us to rank the key candidates accordingly. As only the actual key $k*$ should generate intermediate values processed in the traces, the highest rank key should be the correct one if the model is well-trained. By simulating different attacks with varying random subsets of attack traces, we can effectively simulate different attacks and estimate the guessing entropy of the correct key by taking the average rank of the correct key over these simulated attacks [30].

Leakage Models and Labeling Techniques. The Hamming weight (HW) leakage model is generally assumed when attacking software-implemented AES [26]. In this model, we can observe power consumption correlated to the HW of the transferred value on the data bus. A template attack, a typical profiled SCA technique, sets the HW of the intermediate value (i.e., Sbox output) as the prediction target. On the other hand, the HW labeling can be problematic for SCA using machine (deep) learning because of label imbalance problems [25]. As such, Identity [2] and bitwise [31] labelings are frequently used. The Identity labeling sets the target intermediate value directly as a classification target. The bitwise labeling sets a specific bit of the target intermediate value as a classification target. Specific leakage models that assume bitwise leakage are the least significant bit(LSB) and most significant bit(MSB) leakage models. This label can be regarded as focusing on a specific wire on the data bus, which can occur if there is some physical bias towards that wire in the power/EM measurements.

3 Kolmogorov–Arnold Networks

Kolmogorov–Arnold Networks (KANs) are a novel type of neural network architecture introduced by Liu et al. [16] based on the Kolmogorov-Arnold representation theorem [14]. In this section, we aim to give a (relatively) brief overview of the main concepts behind KANs and discuss the benefits concerning interpretability. For more details, we refer the reader to [16].

3.1 Kolmogorov-Arnold Representation Theorem

The Kolmogorov-Arnold representation theorem [14] states that any multivariate continuous function $f(X) : [0,1]^n \mapsto \mathbf{R}$ can be represented by a finite superposition of univariate functions:

$$f(x_1, \cdots, x_n) = \sum_{q=1}^{2n+1} \Phi_q(\sum_{p=1}^{n} \phi_{q,p}(x_p)). \tag{1}$$

Here, $\phi_{q,p}$ are univariate functions s.t. $\phi_{q,p} : [0,1] \mapsto \mathbf{R}$ and $\Phi_q : \mathbf{R} \mapsto \mathbf{R}$. As these are all univariate functions, we can parameterize each as a basis spline curve [7] composed of local learnable basis spline functions.

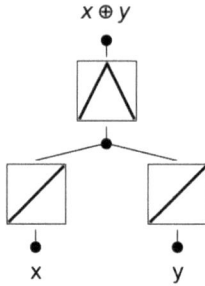

Fig. 1. Simple KAN implementing $x \oplus y$.

3.2 KAN Architecture

The key insight in [16] is then that these functions Φ_q can be used as a network layer, analogous to fully connected layers in multilayer perceptrons and that these layers can be stacked to create deeper networks. A KAN layer with n_{in} input and n_{out} output variables is expressed as:

$$\Phi = \{\phi_{q,p} | p \in \{1, \cdots, n_{in}\}, q \in \{1, \cdots, n_{out}\}\}. \tag{2}$$

The function in Eq. (1) is then a composition of two of these layers, where the first has n inputs and $2n + 1$ outputs and the second has $2n + 1$ inputs and one output. Deeper networks are a further concatenation of an arbitrary number of these layers. Hereafter, we define a representation of KAN's network architecture by an integer array $\text{KAN}[n_0, n_1, ..., n_L]$ where n_i is the number of nodes in the i-th layer of the KAN's graph by following the paper [16].

3.3 Interpretability of KANs

In this section, we discuss why KANs are more interpretable than other types of networks. The key attributes that result in easier interpretation are that the number of parameters to achieve similar accuracy is lower and that each of the learned activation functions $\phi_{q,p}$ can be easily visualized. This allows for a more intuitive understanding of the information flow in a network when compared to the more opaque nature of (large) weight matrices in MLPs.

To illustrate, Fig. 1 contains a KAN[2,1,1] with two inputs x, y, which can be either 0 or 1. In the figure, we can see a plot of the learned activation function on each edge. We can see that the initial two activation functions are linear, i.e., 0 if the input is 0 and 1 if the input is 1, and these are summed together in the first node. Then, the final activation with inputs ranging from (rescaled) 0–2 is 1 if its input is around 1 and 0 otherwise. This results in a function that is 1 if $x \neq y$ and thus implements an XOR operation on these two inputs. For more examples, we again refer to [16].

3.4 Additional Hyperparameters and Trainable Parameter Counts

When compared with MLPs, which have a number of layers **L** and a number of nodes in each layer **N**, KANs introduce two additional architectural parameters: the order of the basis-spline functions that are used to **k** and the number of grid intervals **G** on which the basis-spline curves are defined.

For a network with **L** layers each with equal number of nodes **N** this then results in $O(LN^2)$ parameters for an MLP vs. $O(LN^2(G+k))$ for a KAN. While the number of parameters for a KAN with the same number of layers and nodes is higher, generally the number of nodes per layer should be significantly lower for a KAN that achieves similar accuracy. The order **k** should also not be too high to avoid optimization issues for the basis-spline curves and is generally fixed to a low constant (3 in [16]).

One of the main benefits of this formulation of KANs is that the number of grid intervals can be increased during training to increase the capacity of the networks without re-training the entire network. This allows for more conservative starting settings of **G** which can then be (algorithmically) increased during training to achieve desired levels of accuracy.

4 Related Work

As deep learning-based side-channel analysis (DLSCA) has grown in popularity over recent years [26], several works have investigated the interpretability/explainability perspectives.

Earlier works introduced input attribution methods that identify which parts of the input traces influence the network's predictions [10]. Works in this area include using gradient visualization methods [19], heatmaps [38], Layerwise Relevance Propagation [10,22], and saliency maps [10]. Schamberger et al. introduced the concept of n-occlusion to examine how the window of occlusion impacts key recovery [29]. Later, Yap et al. developed a novel approach based on occlusion to find minimal sample points for a neural network key recovery [36]. Besides works that investigate the importance of features for a neural network, there are also works that concentrate on feature engineering techniques (selection or construction of points of interest). Rioja et al. considered using metaheuristics known as Estimation of Distribution Algorithms to help automate the selection of the PoIs in both unprotected and masking settings [28].

While these works effectively highlight/select which parts of the traces are utilized by the networks, the internal processes of the network largely remain a black-box. Van der Valk et al. first explored using Vector Canonical Correlation Analysis to compare neural network internal representations. Subsequently, Wu et al. [34] explored ablating layers of trained networks to investigate what specific layers are doing in the network, focusing on challenges related to the portability of the networks. Perin et al. provided a metric based on the Information Bottleneck theory to visualize the information the deep neural network is learning for each epoch [21]. Perin et al. [24] employed probes on networks trained to circumvent the masking countermeasure and visualize where in the network secret shares are recombined to the target values. Zaid et al. designed a generative model by combining it with a stochastic attack using an autoencoder called Conditional Variational Autoencoder, providing equations of the leakage in the trace through the autoencoder's weights [37]. Masure et al. [18] then provide a method for a priori embedding the secret share combination in the network as a novel layer. Yap et al. [35] proposed using an adapted network structure to be able to extract SAT equations from trained networks and precisely show the internal workings of networks.

The above papers show several methods that can provide a broad understanding of the 'behavior' of the network by 1) showing important input features [10,20,22,38], 2) in which layers certain information is processed [18,23,34], or 3) estimate the physical leakage model explicitly using masks [37]. However, these works either are restricted to characterizing inputs [10,20,22,37,38], and/or require a priori assumptions about what leakage is exploitable (e.g., characterizing the network behavior in terms of known secret shares [24] or masking scheme [18]). Concretely, only the work in [35] attempts to gain a more precise understanding of the internals of the networks without requiring strong assumptions, but this requires a specialized architecture, resulting in reduced attack performance and computationally costly training procedures. This makes applying these models in practice much more difficult, especially when considering practical targets with long traces.

5 Simulations

In this section, we always use batch size 256 and train for 3000 steps. The optimizer is Adam [12] with a learning rate of `1e-3`. The grid and k parameters are both set to 3. The outputs of the KAN are transformed using a softmax function to rescale to a probability function, and the loss function is categorical cross-entropy. Based on the recommendations by Liu et al. that KAN's training starts from a simple setup, especially a small KAN shape and small grid size,[2] we run some basic experiments with minimal KANs (i.e., from KAN[2, 1, 2] to KAN[2, 3, 2]) and determine that the additional nodes do not improve accuracy. As such, we use KAN[#inputs, 1, 2] unless mentioned otherwise.

5.1 Bitwise Leakage

We first examine how KANs fit a Boolean masking scheme where a single bit for each share is leaked. In this case, we simulate n points corresponding to n shares and include the leakage for 1 bit in each of these. We add noise with zero mean and varying standard deviations to each of these points to simulate more or less noisy side-channel traces. The label for each of these simulated traces is then the recombination (or bitwise XOR) of these shares. The number of KAN's output is set to 2 and activated by the softmax function. The output represents the confidence value corresponding to the prediction output of 0 or 1.

---

[2] https://github.com/KindXiaoming/pykan.

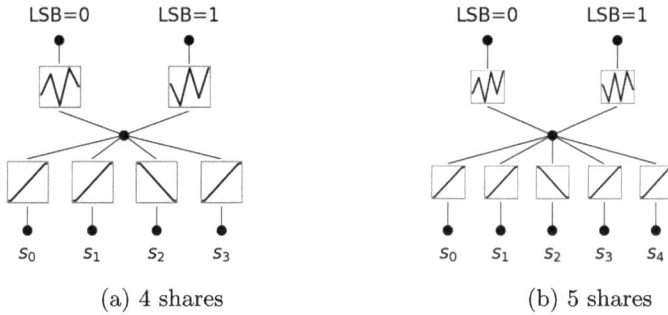

Fig. 2. Low-noise (mean 0, std 0.1) KAN models for bitwise leakage.

The results with low noise in Fig. 2 show a pattern for increasing security orders (which we verify also holds for higher/lower orders). The basic algorithm that we can visually identify in the graph and activations in Fig. 2 is to first linearly add the leakage for several shares together in a single node, and subsequently apply a periodic activation with a number of highs/lows that correspond to the masking order. To illustrate, imagine recombining 3 shares with perfect information. We first sum the 3 shares together, i.e., $1 + 1 + 0$. Clearly, if the result is even, the 1-bits cancel each other out, and the result should be 0. Conversely, if the result is odd, i.e., $1 + 0 + 0$, the result should be 1. More generally, we can compute xor for n-shares, $s_1, \cdots s_n \in \{0,1\}$ by taking $(\sum_{i=1}^{n} s_i) \bmod 2$. To achieve these results, KAN can fit sinusoid-like activations (top activations in Fig. 2 and Fig. 3) that are on/off (1/0) when inputs are even or odd. Note that intermediate values can be rescaled while keeping the algorithm identical; if inputs are scaled by 0.5, then as opposed to even/odd, the functions can fit on these ranges (whole vs. not whole numbers) similarly.

With higher noise values added to the inputs, the pattern of additional peaks/valleys for higher masking orders remains. In Fig. 3, the learned activations in the output layer closely resemble those in Fig. 2. The main difference between these scenarios is in the input layer, where we see that the activation remains 1/0 for inputs corresponding to the 1/0 distributions of the leakage.

Finally, when we consider scenarios with additional uninformative samples in Fig. 4, which is common in practical SCA, KANs still learn similar structures and effectively ignore additional samples.

5.2 HW Leakage

We next look at how KANs learn from 8-bit HW leakage on the 2-share Boolean masking scheme. We trained KAN with simulation traces without noise. The label for these simulated traces is then the LSB of XOR of these shares. The left of Fig. 5 shows the trained KAN's graph. To obtain a more interpretable KAN graph, we set linear functions to activations belonging to input nodes, and the trained graph is shown in the center of Fig. 5. Here, we considered sine,

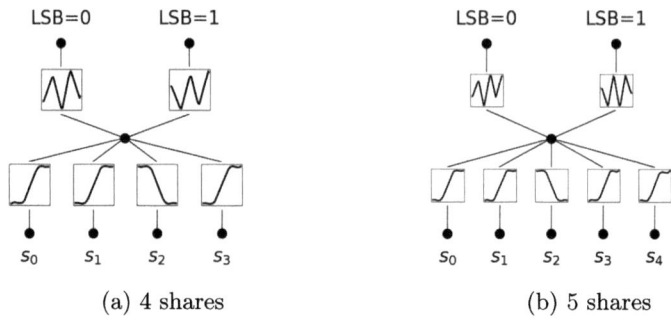

Fig. 3. Higher-noise (mean 0, std 0.1) KAN models for bitwise leakage.

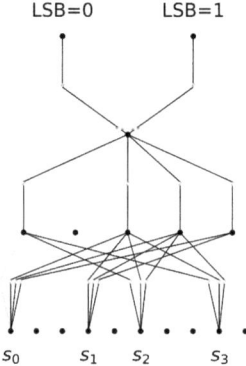

Fig. 4. 4 share KAN [10, 5, 1, 2] with uninformative samples.

quartic, and other functions in addition to linear functions to make the input activation symbolic. As the error of the input activation can be corrected in the subsequent ones, we first adopted the simplest one: a linear function. Since it decreases the classification accuracy to 53.10%, we set a larger grid size to enhance the representation and re-train the KAN. We chose the grid size of 17 because the intermediate node's output $(HW(s_1) + HW(s_2))$ has 17 patterns. The last graph is shown on the right of Fig. 5, and it achieves 53.26% accuracy. According to the graph, the intermediate node calculates $HW(s_1) + HW(s_2)$, and the activations belonging to output nodes determine the confidence of each class (LSB = 0 or LSB = 1).

Let us consider the occurrence distribution of 0 and 1 of LSB. The HW leakage model supposes all the lines on the data bus to contribute equally to power consumption. We cannot distinguish combinations with the same HW: e.g., both HW of "01" and "10" are 1. On the other hand, some combinations have a biased frequency of occurrence; we consider the aggregation based on $HW(s_1) + HW(s_2)$, which is the output of the intermediate node of the finally obtained KAN (right one) in Fig. 5. Table 1 provides the number of occurrences

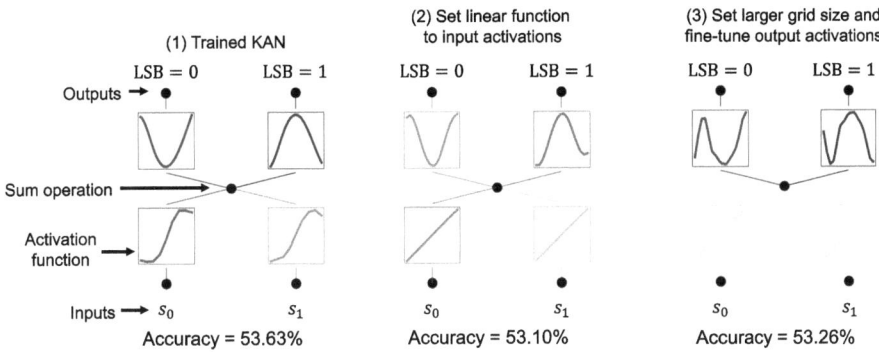

Fig. 5. Interpretation procedure for profiling model on 2-share Boolean masking using KAN.

Table 1. Number of occurrences of each LSB in $\text{HW}(s_1) + \text{HW}(s_2)$

$\text{HW}(s_1) + \text{HW}(s_2)$	$\text{LSB}(s_1 \oplus s_2) = 0$	$\text{LSB}(s_1 \oplus s_2) = 1$
0	1	0
1	14	2
2	92	28
3	378	182
4	1092	728
5	2366	2002
6	4004	4004
7	5434	6006
8	6006	6864
9	5434	6006
10	4004	4004
11	2366	2002
12	1092	728
13	378	182
14	92	28
15	14	2
16	1	0

of each LSB in all patterns of $\text{HW}(s_1) + \text{HW}(s_2)$. A reasonable way to predict LSB by using $\text{HW}(s_1) + \text{HW}(s_2)$ is by choosing ones with a higher expected value on each combination, such as the greyed cells in Table 1. Hereafter, we denote this approach by "expected value maximization (EVM) strategy". This strategy achieves 53.74% accuracy on 2-share masking; it is close to the KAN's accuracy. Figure 6 plots the results in Table 1 and their differences. Looking at the difference graph, we can see that it matches the graph learned by the

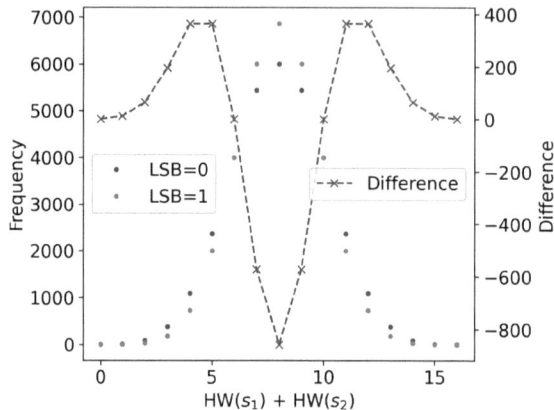

Fig. 6. Expectation value graph for the EVM strategy.

Table 2. List of known leakages about the third byte in the first round.

Name	Type	Definition of the target variable	PoI Fixed	Random
$snr1$	unmasked SBox output	$\text{SBox}(p[3] \oplus k[3])$	559	147
$snr2$	masked SBox output	$\text{SBox}(p[3] \oplus k[3]) \oplus r_{out}$	492	1000
$snr3$	common SBox output mask	r_{out}	149	188
$snr4$	masked SBox output in linear part	$\text{SBox}(p[3] \oplus k[3]) \oplus r[3]$	517	1071
$snr5$	SBox output mask in linear part	$r[3]$	156	188

KAN. From these results, we can consider that KANs have learned the EVM strategy because the activation in the KAN closely matches the graph of the EVM strategy, and their accuracy is comparable.

6 Real-World Targets

6.1 ASCAD Datasets

ASCADv1 dataset [2] is a public dataset for evaluating side-channel attacks. The dataset contains power traces acquired from software-implemented AES-128 running on ATMega8515, which has a masking countermeasure. The dataset provides plaintexts, ciphertexts, keys, masks, and traces. It is divided into profiling and attack subsets to evaluate profiling attack scenarios. It has two variants depending on how the key is provided during the trace acquisition. The fixed key dataset was acquired with a single key in both the profiling and attack subsets. There are 50 000 traces in the profiling and 10 000 traces in the attack subset. The variable key dataset was acquired with a random key in the profiling and a single key in the attack subset. There are 200 000 traces in the profiling and 100 000 traces in the attack subset. To evaluate elementary attacks, the first two bytes of the AES state during the first round are not masked. Our attack experiments reported in the rest of the paper only target the third SBox processing during the first round, as it is the first masked byte. Each trace has 700 (fixed key) and 1400 (variable key) sample points, covering the calculation of the first round, as recommended by the authors of the datasets.

The countermeasure implementation has two masked states; the linear part is secured by 16 different masks with a table re-computation method, and the SubBytes processing is secured by the same input and output mask pair used for each state element. This means the leakage about an unprotected intermediate value (unmasked SBox output), which is strongly related to the key, is expected to be hidden. On the other hand, the leakage of shares made by the masking procedure can be observed from traces. Hereafter, we call these known leakages snr1-5 following Benadjila et al. [2], as shown in Table 2. Each snr2-3 and snr4-5 pair is supposed to correspond to the pair of $share_1$ and $share_2$ in the simulation in the previous section. The PoI column in the table lists the sample point that achieved the highest value based on the F-test for each snr, which are the sample points where the snrs are expected to be leaked at most. The F-test was conducted with a scenario where the tester knows the key/mask values.

6.2 Revealing What Models Learned

In this section, we evaluate the attack performance and explainability of KANs in real-world settings. We chose MLP as a comparison target in this paper because KAN was proposed as a promising alternative to MLP [16]. We trained MLP and KAN using the ASCAD dataset. Models receive all sample points: 700 on fixed key and 1400 points on variable key dataset. To select the MLP architecture, we considered model architecture MLP_{exp} from [31] and MLP_{best} from [2]. The former is designed for the LSB labeling, and the latter is for the Identity labeling. These achieved almost the same classification accuracy with LSB labeling, but the MLP_{exp} is a significantly smaller architecture than the MLP_{best}; thus, we picked MLP_{exp} in this paper. The architecture of MLP_{exp} is [#inputs, 20, 10, 2] and has ReLU activation for each intermediate layer. KAN is set to [#input_samples, 5, 1, 2]. To design this architecture, we considered that the number of inputs significantly increased from the simulation settings in Sect. 5. We added a new layer after the input layer, intended to aggregate and organize features from traces. The number of nodes in the layer was set to 5 as the minimum number that each node can represent snr1-5, respectively. Note that this does not guarantee each node represents one share in the trained KAN.

Table 3 lists the classification accuracy of models on the test set. The MLPs achieved 60.46% on the fixed key and 58.00% on the variable key datasets. The KANs achieved 61.18% on the fixed key and 59.17% on the variable key datasets. These results indicate that MLP and KAN achieved similar classification accuracy on each dataset. In addition, we calculated guessing entropy with these trained models (Fig. 7). The number of traces for GE = 0 is listed in Table 3. The classification accuracy of MLPs was slightly lower than that of KANs. However, the number of traces to achieve GE = 0 was lower for MLP than for

KANs. We assume this happened because the GE calculation is affected by both classification accuracy and confidence in each prediction.

Table 3. Attack results on ASCADv1 dataset with MLP and KAN

Model	Classification accuracy		#traces to achieve GE = 0	
	fixed key	variable key	fixed key	variable key
MLP	60.46%	58.00%	222	388
KAN	61.18%	59.17%	315	476

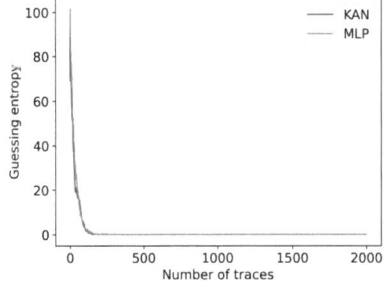
(a) ASCADv1 fixed key dataset.

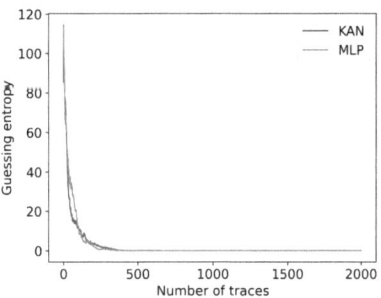
(b) ASCADv1 variable key dataset.

Fig. 7. Guessing entropy with MLP and KAN.

Figure 8 shows the SNR (F-test) value of each snr and the models' input-based sensitivity. The sensitivity of the MLP model is the partial derivative of the model output with regard to the given input, the same approach as [31]. The sensitivity of the KAN model is calculated by summing $output\_range/input\_range$ of activations belonging to each input sample, which is the score for the importance of each node (inputs) used for pruning KAN nodes [16]. Since KAN and MLP achieved similar classification accuracy and showed similar sensitivity distributions, this suggests that they learned a similar function. We can see sample points with high sensitivity that coincide with the points corresponding to the peaks of snr3, 4, and 5. Since the peak positions of snr3 and 5 are almost the same, and the model did not focus on snr2, it is reasonable to assume that the principal part of the learned function focuses on the pair of snr4 and snr5.

Next, we trained KANs with the peak point of the $snr4$ and 5. The chosen sample point pairs are 517 ($snr4$) and 156 ($snr5$) on the fixed key dataset and 1071 ($snr4$) and 188 ($snr5$) on the variable key dataset. Since the number of input nodes is reduced to 2, the KAN's architecture is the same as the simulation: KAN[2, 1, 2]. The trained KANs' graphs are shown in Fig. 9, which was trained

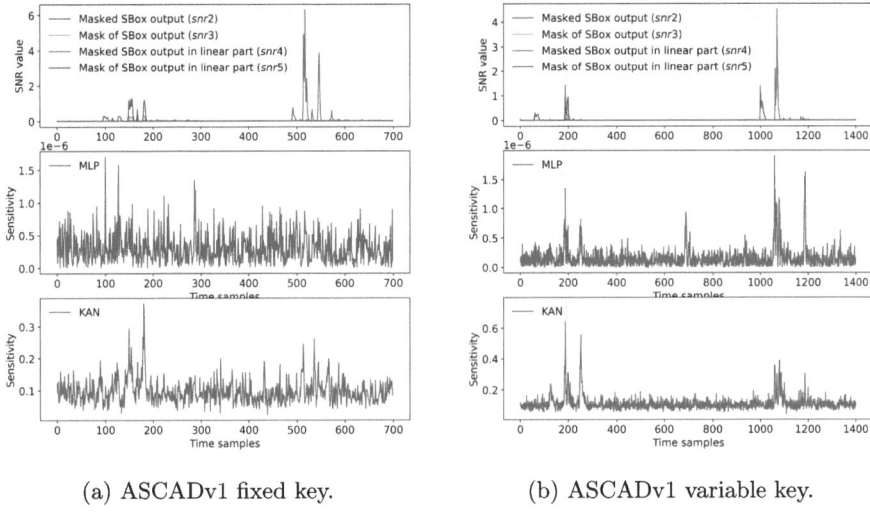

(a) ASCADv1 fixed key. (b) ASCADv1 variable key.

Fig. 8. Sensitivity results.

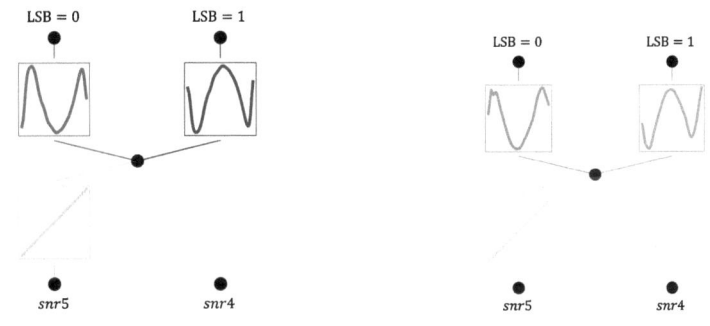

(a) ASCADv1 fixed key dataset. (b) ASCADv1 variable key dataset.

Fig. 9. Trained KAN's graph after setting linear function and fine-tuning. The output activations exhibited a shape similar to the graph from the EVM strategy.

using the same settings as the simulation, and the grid size is set to 17, where the input activations are set to the linear function for the same reasons as in the simulation. These KANs achieved 56.79% classification accuracy for the fixed key and 55.33% for the variable key dataset. Comparing KAN's graph on the right of Fig. 5 and Fig. 9, they have the same input activations and similar output activations. This indicates that KANs learned the same graph as the simulation, which is the EVM strategy, from real traces (ASCADv1 dataset).

7 Discussion

As showcased by our results in Sect. 5, KANs can effectively learn understandable mechanisms to combine mask shares in both bitwise and Hamming weight leakage models. In these smaller settings, the model plots clearly show activation patterns that match either an EVM strategy for HW simulations or a switching strategy for bit-leakage simulations. These explanations are significantly more fine-grained than those accomplished in the simulation experiments from [35]. Yap et al. can decompose the operations into a SAT equation where they can deduce what samples are being recombined, while our results show the precise strategy by which the models recombine shares. Further experiments with irrelevant input features also showcase that KANs learn to ignore those features quickly and that the standard model visualization functionality clearly shows what features are (ir)relevant. Altogether, these results indicate that KANs can generate explanations at the input level by attributing predictions to specific input features, matching the input visualization tools from related works [9], while also providing solid explanations of how models are actually recombining shares, improving over [35].

When we subsequently consider targeting real-world traces, we show with input visualization tools that the network learns from the correct leakage points. Moreover, when we select the most important points and retrain the KAN on those, we can match the learned combination scheme to the strategies found in simulations. While it is plausible that the same can be done directly for the models trained on full traces, selecting features makes it significantly easier as the models are much smaller, allowing for a much simpler visual inspection of the resulting network graphs. The attack performance of the model is also reasonable, being competitive with MLP models and significantly outperforming architectures specialized for interpretability.[3] While the performance here is behind state-of-the-art models [33,38], further work in optimizing KAN training setups could help close this gap.

In general, KANs seem like a viable alternative to MLPs in terms of attack performance. On the side of interpretability, KANs clearly improve over MLPs. For now, the only real downside to using KANs seems to be the computational overhead of training them with larger input dimensions. In our computing environment[4], training KAN[700,5,1,2] in $\#steps = 5000$ and $batch\_size = 256$ takes 6 h, and KAN[1400,5,1,2] in $\#steps = 7000$ and $batch\_size = 256$ takes 13 h. In contrast, the training of MLPs is finished within 15 min. However, as mentioned in [16], no significant effort has been put into optimizing implementations and considering the interest of the ML community in utilizing KANs (see, e.g., [3,4,32]) it seems reasonable to expect the computational performance to be improved.

---

[3] In [35], retrieving a key-byte from the ASCADv1 fixed key dataset requires 7222 traces.
[4] Intel Core i7-13800H CPU, Nvidia GeForce RTX 4060 Laptop GPU, 64GB RAM.

One of the main limitations of this interpretability in KANs is that for full-length traces, it is still difficult to do detailed analyses of the learned activations. In the controlled scenario where we select features, we can directly find the EVM strategies the network uses for classification. Additionally, in both bitwise and HW simulations, we can find the learned structure straightforwardly. However, for longer real-world traces, the interpretability results are still similar to those of standard input visualization methods that indicate where the leakage occurs. We chose this experimental setup with both simulations and selected features to mimic the setups in [35]. Here, the attacks against longer traces exhibit similar limitations, while the explanations for network internals in more toy settings are restricted to boolean formulas of the inputs.

8 Conclusions and Future Work

In this paper, we propose using KANs as an alternative to MLPs for side-channel analysis. Our results across both simulated and real-world traces indicate that KANs can be competitive regarding attack performance. Furthermore, we can reverse-engineer the method the networks use to recombine mask shares on simulations. Subsequently, we train KANs on the ASCAD dataset, resulting in a key recovery in ≈ 300 traces, performing competitively with a basic MLP from [2]. Moreover, we can find the share combination methods from simulations in the trained networks. In future work, we plan to interpret profiling models using other labeling techniques, especially Identity labeling. We also plan to explore whether embedding KAN layers as part of larger networks, e.g., to replace the fully connected parts of CNNs from [38], can be an effective strategy to mitigate the computational overhead of training KANs on full traces.

References

1. Archambeau, C., Peeters, E., Standaert, F.-X., Quisquater, J.-J.: Template attacks in principal subspaces. In: Goubin, L., Matsui, M. (eds.) CHES 2006. LNCS, vol. 4249, pp. 1–14. Springer, Heidelberg (2006). https://doi.org/10.1007/11894063_1
2. Benadjila, R., Prouff, E., Strullu, R., Cagli, E., Dumas, C.: Deep learning for side-channel analysis and introduction to ASCAD database. J. Cryptographic Eng. **10**(2), 163–188 (2020)
3. Bozorgasl, Z., Chen, H.: Wav-kan: Wavelet kolmogorov-arnold networks. CoRR abs/2405.12832 (2024)
4. Bresson, R., Nikolentzos, G., Panagopoulos, G., Chatzianastasis, M., Pang, J., Vazirgiannis, M.: Kagnns: Kolmogorov-arnold networks meet graph learning. CoRR, abs/2406.18380 (2024)
5. Cagli, E., Dumas, C., Prouff, E.: Convolutional neural networks with data augmentation against jitter-based countermeasures. In: Fischer, W., Homma, N. (eds.) CHES 2017. LNCS, vol. 10529, pp. 45–68. Springer, Cham (2017). https://doi.org/10.1007/978-3-319-66787-4_3
6. Chari, S., Rao, J.R., Rohatgi, P.: Template attacks. In: Kaliski, B.S., Koç, K., Paar, C. (eds.) CHES 2002. LNCS, vol. 2523, pp. 13–28. Springer, Heidelberg (2003). https://doi.org/10.1007/3-540-36400-5_3

7. De Boor, C., De Boor, C.: A practical guide to splines, vol. 27. Springer, New York (1978)
8. Gao, S., Oswald, E.: A novel framework for explainable leakage assessment. In: Joye, M., Leander, G. (eds.) Advances in Cryptology - EUROCRYPT 2024 - 43rd Annual International Conference on the Theory and Applications of Cryptographic Techniques, Zurich, Switzerland, May 26-30, 2024, Proceedings, Part III, vol. 14653, pp. 221–250. Springer (2024)
9. Golder, A., Bhat, A., Raychowdhury, A.: Exploration into the explainability of neural network models for power side-channel analysis. In: Savidis, I., Sasan, A., Thapliyal, H., DeMara, R.F. (eds.) GLSVLSI '22: Great Lakes Symposium on VLSI 2022, Irvine CA USA, June 6 - 8, 2022, pp. 59–64. ACM (2022)
10. Hettwer, B., Gehrer, S., Güneysu, T.: Deep neural network attribution methods for leakage analysis and symmetric key recovery. In: Paterson, K.G., Stebila, D. (eds.) Selected Areas in Cryptography - SAC 2019 - 26th International Conference, Waterloo, ON, Canada, August 12-16, 2019, Revised Selected Papers, vol. 11959. LNCS, pp. 645–666. Springer (2019)
11. Kim, J., Picek, S., Heuser, A., Bhasin, S., Hanjalic, A.: Make some noise. unleashing the power of convolutional neural networks for profiled side-channel analysis. IACR Transactions on Cryptographic Hardware and Embedded Systems, pp. 148–179 (2019)
12. Kingma, D.P., Ba, J.: Adam: a method for stochastic optimization. In: Bengio, Y., LeCun, Y. (eds.) 3rd International Conference on Learning Representations, ICLR 2015, San Diego, CA, USA, May 7-9, 2015, Conference Track Proceedings (2015)
13. Kocher, P.C., Jaffe, J., Jun, B.: Differential power analysis. In: Proceedings of the 19th Annual International Cryptology Conference on Advances in Cryptology, CRYPTO '99, pp. 388–397. Springer, London (1999)
14. Kolmogorov, A.N.: On the representation of continuous functions of many variables by superposition of continuous functions of one variable and addition. In Doklady Akademii Nauk, vol. 114, pp. 953–956. Russian Academy of Sciences (1957)
15. Lerman, L., Poussier, R., Markowitch, O., Standaert, F.: Template attacks versus machine learning revisited and the curse of dimensionality in side-channel analysis: extended version. J. Cryptogr. Eng. **8**(4), 301–313 (2018)
16. Liu, Z., et al.: KAN: kolmogorov-arnold networks. CoRR, abs/2404.19756 (2024)
17. Maghrebi, H., Portigliatti, T., Prouff, E.: Breaking cryptographic implementations using deep learning techniques. In: International Conference on Security, Privacy, and Applied Cryptography Engineering, pp. 3–26. Springer (2016)
18. Masure, L., Cristiani, V., Lecomte, M., Standaert, F.: Don't learn what you already know scheme-aware modeling for profiling side-channel analysis against masking. IACR Trans. Cryptogr. Hardw. Embed. Syst. **2023**(1), 32–59 (2023)
19. Masure, L., Dumas, C., Prouff, E.: Gradient visualization for general characterization in profiling attacks. In: Polian, I., Stöttinger, M. (eds.) COSADE 2019. LNCS, vol. 11421, pp. 145–167. Springer, Cham (2019). https://doi.org/10.1007/978-3-030-16350-1_9
20. Masure, L., Dumas, C., Prouff, E.: A comprehensive study of deep learning for side-channel analysis. IACR Trans. Cryptogr. Hardw. Embed. Syst. **2020**(1), 348–375 (2020)
21. Perin, G., Buhan, I., Picek, S.: Learning when to stop: a mutual information approach to prevent overfitting in profiled side-channel analysis. In: Bhasin, S., De Santis, F. (eds.) Constructive Side-Channel Analysis and Secure Design, pp. 53–81. Springer, Cham (2021)

22. Perin, G., Ege, B., Chmielewski, L.: Neural network model assessment for side-channel analysis. Cryptology ePrint Archive, Paper 2019/722 (2019)
23. Perin, G., Wu, L., Picek, S.: Exploring feature selection scenarios for deep learning-based side-channel analysis. IACR Trans. Cryptographic Hardware Embedded Syst. **2022**(4), 828–861 (2022)
24. Perin, G., Wu, L., Picek, S.: I know what your layers did: Layer-wise explainability of deep learning side-channel analysis. IACR Cryptol. ePrint Arch., p. 1087 (2022)
25. Picek, S., Heuser, A., Jovic, A., Bhasin, S., Regazzoni, F.: The curse of class imbalance and conflicting metrics with machine learning for side-channel evaluations. IACR Trans. Cryptogr. Hardw. Embed. Syst. **2019**(1), 209–237 (2019)
26. Picek, S., Perin, G., Mariot, L., Wu, L., Batina, L.: SoK: deep learning-based physical side-channel analysis. ACM Comput. Surv. **55**(11), 227:1–227:35 (2023)
27. Rechberger, C., Oswald, E.: Practical template attacks. In: Lim, C.H., Yung, M., (eds.) Information Security Applications, 5th International Workshop, WISA 2004, Jeju Island, Korea, August 23-25, 2004, Revised Selected Papers. LNCS, vol. 3325, pp. 440–456. Springer (2004)
28. Rioja, U., Batina, L., Flores, J.L., Armendariz, I.: Auto-tune pois: estimation of distribution algorithms for efficient side-channel analysis. Comput. Netw. **198**, 108405 (2021)
29. Schamberger, T., Egger, M., Tebelmann, L.: Hide and seek: Using occlusion techniques for side-channel leakage attribution in cnns. In: Zhou, J., et al. (eds.) Applied Cryptography and Network Security Workshops, pp. 139–158. Springer, Cham (2023)
30. Standaert, F.-X., Malkin, T.G., Yung, M.: A unified framework for the analysis of side-channel key recovery attacks. In: Joux, A. (ed.) EUROCRYPT 2009. LNCS, vol. 5479, pp. 443–461. Springer, Heidelberg (2009). https://doi.org/10.1007/978-3-642-01001-9_26
31. Timon, B.: Non-profiled deep learning-based side-channel attacks with sensitivity analysis. IACR Trans. Cryptogr. Hardw. Embed. Syst. **2019**(2), 107–131 (2019)
32. Vaca-Rubio, C.J., Blanco, L., Pereira, R., Caus, M.: Kolmogorov-arnold networks (kans) for time series analysis. CoRR abs/2405.08790 (2024)
33. Wouters, L., Arribas, V., Gierlichs, B., Preneel, B.: Revisiting a methodology for efficient cnn architectures in profiling attacks. IACR Trans. Cryptographic Hardware Embedded Syst. **2020**(3), 147–168 (2020)
34. Wu, L., Won, Y.-S., Jap, D., Perin, G., Bhasin, S., Picek, S.: Ablation analysis for multi-device deep learning-based physical side-channel analysis. IEEE Trans. Dependable Secure Comput. **21**(3), 1331–1341 (2024)
35. Yap, T., Benamira, A., Bhasin, S., Peyrin, T.: Peek into the black-box: Interpretable neural network using SAT equations in side-channel analysis. IACR Trans. Cryptogr. Hardw. Embed. Syst. **2023**(2), 24–53 (2023)
36. Yap, T., Bhasin, S., Picek, S.: OccPoIs: Points of interest based on neural network's key recovery in side-channel analysis through occlusion. Cryptology ePrint Archive, Paper 2023/1055 (2023)
37. Zaid, G., Bossuet, L., Carbone, M., Habrard, A., Venelli, A.: Conditional variational autoencoder based on stochastic attacks. IACR Trans. Cryptogr. Hardw. Embed. Syst. **2023**(2), 310–357 (2023)
38. Zaid, G., Bossuet, L., Habrard, A., Venelli, A.: Methodology for efficient cnn architectures in profiling attacks. IACR Trans. Cryptographic Hardware Embedded Syst. **2020**(1), 1–36 (2019)

Hamming Weight-Based Side Channel Analysis of HLS Kyber Hardware Using Neural Networks

Alexander Kharitonov[✉], Tarick Welling, Maël Gay, and Ilia Polian

University of Stuttgart, 70174 Stuttgart, Germany
sci@blockworker.de

Abstract. With continued improvements in the quantum computing area, the future security of current encryption schemes is uncertain. The National Institute of Standards and Technology (NIST) has standardized post-quantum lattice-based ciphers, such as CRYSTALS-Kyber (as ML-KEM), for this purpose. While a significant amount of research on potential weaknesses of such new encryption schemes has been performed, their implementations may still remain vulnerable to Side Channel Analysis (SCA). In this paper, we investigate the possibility of leveraging the power side channel on a hardware implementation of ML-KEM. The circuit under attack has been obtained by High-level Synthesis (HLS). This complicates the attack, as no details about the internal implementation are known to the attacker, though points of interest in the captured power traces can be identified using known methods. While several methods exist to perform SCA, we make use of Neural Networks (NNs) to extract information about intermediate decryption values from the implementation's power consumption. With our attack method, we find that it is feasible to recover the secret decryption key from power consumption information, assuming the attacker is able to provide arbitrary ciphertexts for decryption.

Keywords: PQC · Side Channel · Neural Network

1 Introduction

Secure encryption is critically important for many aspects of the modern world, forming the basis for online privacy and security, and for embedded devices. However, quantum computers pose a severe theoretical threat to many modern encryption schemes. For instance, the RSA cryptosystem can be attacked using Shor's algorithm [23]. As quantum computers become more advanced and powerful, this threat may become a reality in the foreseeable future.

Because of this, there has been an increased effort in recent years to develop new *post-quantum* encryption schemes, designed to be secure against quantum attacks. One such scheme is CRYSTALS-Kyber (or simply Kyber), which has been standardized as ML-KEM for global use, meaning it is likely to be used widely for post-quantum secure encryption in the near future. In this work, we use ML-KEM and Kyber interchangeably.

As with other important encryption primitives, there is a need for Kyber to be scrutinized and potential weaknesses identified. One family of threats are Side Channel Analysis (SCA) attacks [25], which focus on the implementations of encryption schemes. Such implementations will leak information about the secret key through "side channels", e. g., the implementation's power consumption [19]. Recent SCAs incorporate machine learning techniques as well, e. g., Neural Networks (NNs) [18], as they are often more efficient (requiring a lower number of measurements) as opposed to other approaches.

In this work, we investigate the viability of such an SCA on a hardware implementation of Kyber. In particular, we perform our attack on a Highlevel Synthesis (HLS) implementation of Kyber, meaning we do not have any knowledge or control over the actual hardware implementation (e.g. we take the HLS output, which is not easily modifiable). This implementation is then ran on the CW305 ChipWhisperer platform. We record power traces and analyze the power consumption of the implementation to determine whether it reveals any useful information. Next, we train NNs for this side channel information analysis, to extract the secret key from the implementation's power consumption. Our methodology does not characterize the secret key values from the NNs directly. Instead, we make use of extracted information on the Hamming weights of intermediate values to predict parts of the secret key, with the possibility of eventually extracting the entire key.

Our contributions are as follows:

- We propose a new NN-based key recovery SCA against Kyber using the Hamming weight of the intermediate multiplication coefficients.
- We perform our attack on an unprotected FPGA-based hardware implementation of Kyber and successfully recover the first key coefficients, extrapolating the overall feasibility of our attack if all coefficients are considered.
- To our knowledge, this is the first NN-based key-recovery attack on a hardware implementation of Kyber.

The remainder of this paper is organized as follows. Section 2 provides the background on Kyber, SCA and NNs. Section 3 describes the details about how we approach the analysis and design of an SCA on Kyber, as well the methods we use to implement this approach in practice. Section 4 presents our results with regard to the key extraction. Section 5 summarizes this work and its results, as well as giving an outlook to potential future work.

2 Background

In this section, we introduce the necessary background information. First, we will outline the required context for Kyber. We then will explain SCA and NNs.

2.1 CRYSTALS-Kyber

CRYSTALS-Kyber [2,4], standardized as ML-KEM by the National Institute of Standards and Technology (NIST), is a lattice based Key Encapsulation Method (KEM). It uses the Module-Learning With Errors (LWE) [15] construction to create an asymmetric encryption scheme, which is an extension of the LWE [20] construction. Both are specializations of the original lattice scheme introduced by Regev [21].

The Kyber encryption scheme, which is chosen-plaintext-attack (CPA) secure, is used to create a chosen-ciphertext-attack (CCA) secure KEM through the Fujisaki-Okamoto transform. Although only the KEM is adopted for use, our approach is not affected by the outer layer of the KEM. As such, we consider the Public Key Encryption (PKE) in isolation of the broader usage context. For our attack, we consider specification version 3.02 [2] of Kyber, with the following parameters: $q = 3329, n = 256$ and the security parameter $k \in \{2, 3, 4\}$.

Mathematical Principle. In this work, $\mathbb{Z}_q$ is the ring of integers modulo a prime q. The ring of integer polynomials modulo q is denoted as $\mathbb{Z}_q[x]$. The ring $R_q = \mathbb{Z}_q[x]/(x^n + 1)$ denotes polynomials which are both modulo q and $x^n + 1$. In the remainder of the paper, vectors are represented as bold lowercase letters, $\mathbf{u} \in R_q^k$ and matrices as bold uppercase ones, $\mathbf{A} \in R_q^{k*k}$.

In Kyber, computations are performed both in the canonical domain and the Number-Theoretic Transform (NTT) domain. The advantage of the latter is efficient polynomial multiplication – given $n = 256$, what would be a degree-255 polynomial multiplication in the canonical domain becomes 128 simple degree-1 polynomial multiplications in the NTT domain. Given NTT-domain input polynomials a and b, the result polynomial c is calculated as follows in the Kyber NTT implementation, for $i \in [0, 127]$:

$$c_{2i} = (a_{2i} \cdot b_{2i} \mod {}^{\pm} q) + (a_{2i+1} \cdot b_{2i+1} \cdot \zeta_i' \mod {}^{\pm} q) \quad (1)$$
$$c_{2i+1} = (a_{2i} \cdot b_{2i+1} \mod {}^{\pm} q) + (a_{2i+1} \cdot b_{2i} \mod {}^{\pm} q) \quad (2)$$

where ζ_i' are constants.

The secret key of a Kyber key pair is the secret vector $\mathbf{s} \in R_q^k$, whereas the public key is $(\mathbf{A}, \mathbf{As} + \mathbf{e})$ with $\mathbf{A} \in R_q^{k \times k}$ and $\mathbf{e} \in R_q^k$ randomly generated. This public key corresponds to a set of k samples for the Module-LWE problem.

Encryption of a message m is done as $(\mathbf{u} = \mathbf{A}^\top \mathbf{r} + \mathbf{e}_2, v = \mathbf{t}^\top \mathbf{r} + e_3 + \frac{q}{2}m)$, creating a ciphertext tuple in $R_q^k \times R_q$. With a high likelihood, the decryption will result in the original message: $\mu = \lceil v - \mathbf{s}^\top \mathbf{u} \rfloor$. This likelihood is guaranteed by the error distributions used in generating the errors in Kyber.

Decryption Algorithm. With an asymmetric encryption scheme, the main target of potential attacks is the private (decryption) key. Therefore, for the purposes of an attack, such as the one considered in this work, the decryption algorithm/implementation is the target.

In practice, the algorithm implementation used in this work is shown in Listing 1.1, which is in C and is used as HLS input. The parameter and variable assignments are as follows:

Listing 1.1 Kyber decryption implementation used in this work

```
void indcpa_dec(uint8_t m[KYBER_INDCPA_MSGBYTES],
                const uint8_t c[KYBER_INDCPA_BYTES],
                const uint8_t sk[KYBER_INDCPA_SECRETKEYBYTES]) {
    polyvec b, skpv; poly v, mp;
    unpack_ciphertext(&b, &v, c);
    unpack_sk(&skpv, sk);
    polyvec_ntt(&b);
    polyvec_basemul_acc_montgomery(&mp, &skpv, &b);
    poly_invntt_tomont(&mp);
    poly_sub(&mp, &v, &mp);
    poly_reduce(&mp);
    poly_tomsg(m, &mp);
}
```

- m: Resulting plaintext message (output).
- c: Ciphertext in compressed form and canonical polynomial domain.
- sk: Secret key encoded in binary, in NTT domain.
- b: Decoded polynomial vector **u** of the ciphertext $(\mathbf{u}, v)$.
- skpv: Decoded polynomial vector **s** of the secret key (in NTT domain).
- v: Decoded polynomial v of the ciphertext $(\mathbf{u}, v)$.
- mp: Polynomial buffer for intermediate calculation results.

In short, the algorithm starts by decompressing the ciphertext and decoding the secret key (lines 5–6). Since the multiplication $\mathbf{s}^\top \mathbf{u}$ should be done in the NTT domain for efficiency, the NTT is then applied to the vector **u** (line 7). Afterwards, the product $\mathbf{s}^\top \mathbf{u}$ is calculated in the NTT domain (line 8) and the inverse NTT is applied to the result, converting it back to the canonical polynomial domain (line 9). With this, we can subtract this result from the ciphertext polynomial v (lines 10–11), and finally extract the plaintext message bits (line 12).

2.2 Neural Networks

Like many machine learning algorithms, the goal of NNs is to use an automated learning algorithm to learn a function using an existing *training dataset*, consisting of input values paired with corresponding expected output values. Once trained, the NN can then be used to predict/approximate the value of the learned function, even for input values that do not appear in the training dataset. These functions may be (and typically are) quite complicated, making them very difficult and often infeasible to approximate using traditional mathematical methods.

The basic concept of NNs goes back to the concept of a "Perceptron", described by Rosenblatt in 1958 [22], which has been expanded on and optimized to great extent in the following decades.

In modern applications, the simplest commonly used type of NNs are Deep Neural Networks (DNNs), which are NNs with a large number of fully connected neuron layers. They have proven to often be superior to NNs with fewer large layers. In this work, we make use of DNNs to perform our SCA of Kyber.

The output of an NN is a vector of numbers, the length and interpretation of which may vary depending on the application. A popular choice for discrete problems are *classification networks*, using one output neuron for each possible *class* that an input can belong to. The resulting output vector $\mathbf{p}$ is processed using the *softmax* function, resulting in a probability distribution predicting the likelihood of the input belonging to each class.

$$\text{softmax}(\mathbf{p})_i = \frac{e^{\mathbf{p}_i}}{\sum_j e^{\mathbf{p}_j}} \quad (3)$$

2.3 Side Channel Analysis

SCA is a class of attacks on cryptographic systems which exploit weaknesses in the system's implementation in order to gain access to privileged information, e. g., cryptographic keys.

The idea behind SCA is that even if a cryptographic function or algorithm may be secure in theory, a real-world implementation may have exploitable flaws. An implementation of an encryption scheme may give the attacker additional information aside from the input/output data – for example, timing or power consumption. These additional attack vectors are called side channels.

In this work, we focus on one type of SCA: power analysis attacks. This is a (typically) passive and non-invasive type of attack, where the attacker is assumed to have physical access to the cryptographic hardware to be attacked, as well as some method to accurately measure the power consumption of this hardware.

The attacker measures and records the power consumption of the implementation while the system is running (in our case, during the decryption), usually for many repetitions of the underlying algorithm.

The basic principle for power analysis attacks is that the power consumption of transistor-based circuits varies based on the switching activity. Therefore, it is possible to correlate the power consumption to the secret values being processed. One such example is Differential Power Analysis (DPA) [14]. The attack makes use of a divide and conquer strategy and key guesses to sort power traces into two groups depending on a distinguisher. This distinguisher is itself dependent on the key, and if the sorting is correct (i. e., a correct key guess), then the power consumption is significantly different in both groups and the secret key can be retrieved. While this is a simple example of an attack, which was later extended, the idea remains the same for NN-based side channel attacks. In this case, the NN is doing the heavy lifting of the computation and characterizes the secret key based on the power consumption. The following section gives more details on such attacks.

Neural Network Based Power Analysis. Recently, there have been multiple studies on using machine learning methods for power analysis attacks, instead of traditional direct or statistical methods. For example, Hospodar et al. [8] describe a power analysis attack based on a Support Vector Machine learning algorithm. Later, Martinasek et al. [17,18] introduced and optimized an attack based on an NN, and there have been multiple works on the topic since then.

The advantage of using machine learning, in particular NNs, for power analysis is that this approach is more flexible regarding differences between implementations and different sources of information leakage. For traditional methods, it is necessary to know at least some details about the algorithm and implementation to be attacked – these must either be known to the attacker beforehand, or require reverse engineering. Also, depending on the implementation, a direct correlation between privileged information and power consumption may be more or less difficult to detect using these methods.

When using machine learning, this analysis step can automatically be optimized for the exact implementation to be attacked, using typical machine learning algorithms. Especially when it comes to popular methods like NNs, a lot of research on their optimization and use already exists, along with widely available, powerful, and easy to use implementations. On the other hand, the use of machine learning comes with a significant disadvantage, namely the requirement for a (usually large) set of known training data, consisting of power traces and their corresponding cryptographic information (including the privileged information that should be extracted). In the case of NN-based attacks, the training phase is comparable to profiling for template attacks. The attacker has access to an identical device and is free to set any secret key. During the attack phase, a different device using an unknown key is scrutinized.

NN-based power analysis has been used for a lot of recent SCA research, including a benchmarking effort for SCA resistance by Benadjila et al. [3], as well as prior SCAs on Kyber, e.g., by Ji et al. [12].

3 Method

In this section, the methods used in this work are outlined, starting with the power analysis setup and trace capture details, as a basis for a general Side Channel Analysis. Next, our Neural Network training and prediction methods are described, followed by further analysis, leading to a proposed attack.

3.1 Setup and Implementation

The goal of this work is to recover the secret key from a hardware implementation of `Kyber512` (from hereafter k is set to 2). Our proposed attack would scale to other Kyber variants, as only more coefficients would need to be recovered. Our chosen attack is a passive power analysis attack, with the goal of extracting information about the private key from a set of power traces. The corresponding ciphertext used for each trace is assumed to be chosen by the attacker.

The target is implemented on a Xilinx Artix-7 FPGA on a NewAE CW305 target board, which includes power measurement electronics. The FPGA bitstream is generated from C code using Vitis High-Level Synthesis (HLS), specifically from a modified, unprotected and hardware-adapted version of the Kyber reference implementation [1]. We use this implementation as it was provided by an industrial partner, who plans to further develop and use it, showcasing the practical real-world relevance of our attack. For measuring and capturing power traces, we use a LeCroy WaveSurfer 3104z Oscilloscope, bandwidth-limited to 20 MHz to suppress aliasing effects from high-frequency noise.

Aside from the cryptographic inputs/outputs, the FPGA implementation generates an additional trigger signal, either for the duration of the entire decryption, or only for a specific part of the decryption process (once a Point of Interest (POI) has been determined). This trigger signal is used by the oscilloscope to trigger a power trace capture, ensuring that multiple captured traces are synchronized with each other.

3.2 Power Trace Capture

In order to perform our attack, we measure the power consumption of our Kyber implementation. The power trace capture process is controlled by a Python script running on the connected PC. It handles the initialization and setup of the target and oscilloscope, reading or generating keys and ciphertexts for the decryption, running the hardware decryption and ensuring its correctness, as well as capturing and storing the resulting power traces.

Between trace captures, the target performs a dry run to reset all internal registers to a known fixed state, avoiding any dependence between consecutively captured traces.

Trace Preprocessing. The captured power traces in their raw form are not ideal for use in NNs because of their sensitivity to certain properties of the input data. We therefore pre-process the traces to improve the results of our NN-based attack. In short, we first normalize the traces to remove unwanted baseline components. Our measurement setup is also affected by low frequency interferences and we eliminate them by removing the mean of all traces (note that this can be done thanks to the normalization step, but it can also be performed by filtering). In addition, we downsample our traces to remove redundant data and we upscale the measurements into a more appropriate range for the network (e.g., $[-1, 1]$). Diverse methods for preprocessing input traces are commonly used (e.g., the cut-and-join technique used in [11]). They are out of scope for this work, so we do not provide more details on preprocessing here.

3.3 NN Training

Once some power traces have been captured, the traces need to be analyzed to extract the leaking information, which can then be used for our attack. As mentioned in Sect. 1, our approach is to perform Neural Network based analysis on our power traces, as described in Sect. 2.3.

For the implementation and training of these NNs, the TensorFlow Python library [26] is used, specifically with the Keras high-level interface. Training is performed on a computer with an Intel Core i7-11700 CPU and 64GB of RAM, using GPU acceleration on an NVIDIA RTX A4000 graphics card.

NN Structures. Benadjila et al. [3] present possible NN structures in their paper, describing how they arrived at certain hyperparameters for their use case. Our NN structures use their descriptions as a baseline, adapting and optimizing the exact hyperparameters for our use case, mostly by trial and error. For NN learning, we use the Adam optimizer introduced by Kingman and Ba [13].

For simplicity, we choose a basic DNN structure – we use n_{dense} equally sized layers of n_{units} neurons each, using the Rectified Linear Unit (ReLU) as their activation function:

$$\text{ReLU}(x) = \begin{cases} x \text{ if } x > 0 \\ 0 \text{ otherwise} \end{cases} \quad (4)$$

These layers are followed by a single output layer, designed as a classification network output, as described in Sect. 2.2.

To improve the NN training performance further, we use batch normalization [10], as well as dropout regularization [24] to combat overfitting.

Training Objective. As we intend to train a Neural Network to extract leaked privileged information from power traces, we must first choose exactly what information the NN should attempt to extract.

For our target, the most interesting power trace correlation is with the result of the polynomial multiplication (see Sect. 2.1). Since this result is a polynomial in R_q, attacking the entire product polynomial in one go is unrealistic. Instead, we aim to extract information about a single coefficient of that product polynomial from the power traces – specifically, the first coefficient (in the NTT domain). This first product coefficient is the coefficient we will be referring to from now on, unless specified otherwise.

There are two attractive options for information extraction: The value of the product coefficient itself, or its *Hamming weight*. Since the coefficients are represented using 12 bits in the Kyber implementation, their Hamming weights can have values in the range [0, 12].

Using the value itself has the advantage of extracting more information from the power traces, if predicted correctly. This allows for much more straightforward attacks based on the extracted information. However, since NN training requires many traces per possible output (typically thousands for good performance), with 3329 possible outputs, this leads to a requirement for extremely large training datasets and large networks, resulting in an infeasibly large training effort.

Hamming weights have the opposite advantages and disadvantages. A lot less information is extracted, as up to hundreds of coefficient values can have the same Hamming weight, requiring additional consideration for a subsequent attack to resolve this ambiguity. On the other hand, due to this reduction in possible options (13 instead of 3329), training a classification network for Hamming weights is much easier and requires much less training data. Another advantage of the Hamming weight approach is that a hardware implementation is likely to process all bits of a single value (such as this coefficient) simultaneously, leading to a possible direct correlation between the power consumption and the Hamming weight of the processed value, as described by Brier et al. [5].

NN Evaluation. Our classification NNs output vectors of class probabilities for a given input. For training purposes, we use the *Sparse Categorical Crossentropy (SCCE)* loss function, which is popular for classification problems. Additionally, we calculate three other metrics for a more intuitive estimation of the practical network performance:

- *Accuracy*: The proportion of evaluation inputs where the most likely predicted class is equal to the ground truth.
- *Mean ground truth probability*: Mean predicted probability of the ground truth class, similar to SCCE loss but more intuitive.
- *Mean predicted rank*: Mean position/rank of the ground truth in the class ranking defined by the predicted probability distribution.

3.4 Proposed Attack

With the previous steps of trace capture and NN-based power trace analysis established, we have the ability to measure the power consumption of our target during decryption, and to predict the corresponding product coefficients, or their Hamming weights. In this section, we propose methods to use this ability in order to perform a Side Channel Analysis on the target, specifically with the goal of extracting the private decryption key, or parts of it.

As mentioned in Sect. 3.1, we assume that the attacker is able to choose any ciphertexts and capture the power traces of their decryptions, all using the same unknown decryption key.

Implementation Analysis. The task of this attack stage is to "reverse" part of the decryption algorithm to derive information about the key from the known ciphertext and the predicted information about the product coefficient(s).

The relevant part of the algorithm can be seen in Listing 1.1. In short, the start of the algorithm (up to line 9) consists entirely of deterministic operations on the ciphertext (which is known to the attacker), and a trivial and reversible "unpacking" of the secret key. This means that we know b based on the ciphertext, and we have some NN-predicted information about the product polynomial mp.

The relationship between this known information and the secret key vector skpv is defined by the `polyvec_basemul_acc_montgomery` function in line 10 (from now on referred to as *vecmul*). Mathematically, the vecmul function in our implementation takes two polynomial vectors $\mathbf{a}, \mathbf{b}$ in NTT domain and calculates their dot product $\mathbf{a}^\top \mathbf{b}$ in NTT domain, using the NTT-domain polynomial multiplication at its center. As described in Sect. 2.1, each such multiplication consists of 128 separate polynomial multiplications in $\mathbb{Z}_q[X]/(X^2 + 1)$, which again results in 128 degree-1 polynomials, making up the product polynomial in the NTT domain.

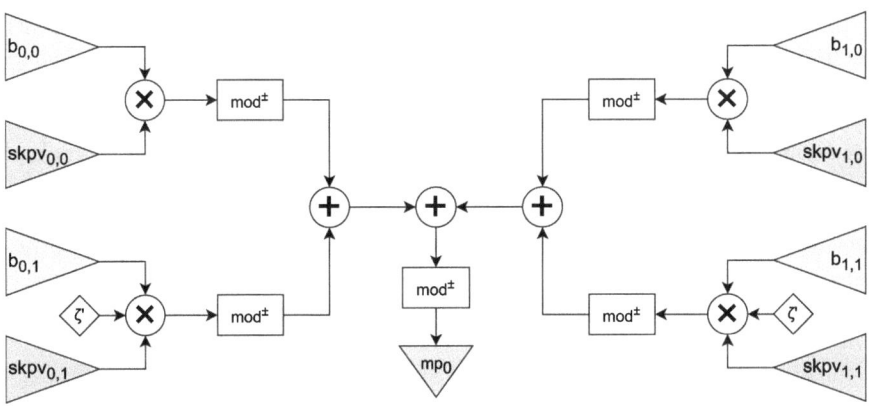

Fig. 1. First product coefficient calculation in our `Kyber512` implementation

Based on these definitions, Fig. 1 shows a visualization of the calculation of the first product coefficient using the `Kyber512` parameter set, which will be the initial attack target in the upcoming sections. Unfortunately, this product coefficient calculation is not reversible – even with full knowledge of b and the exact value of mp_0. However, we can construct ciphertexts where three out of four coefficients in the product calculation are zero, which eliminates the influence of the three corresponding key coefficients on the product coefficient. In such a chosen-ciphertext scenario, we can isolate a single key coefficient, resulting in the significantly simplified product coefficient calculation represented in Fig. 2. In this case, there is a unique (bijective) mapping between the known coefficient values (ciphertext and product) and the key coefficient value, for which we can create a simple lookup table.

While we may use this chosen-ciphertext construction to recover key coefficients, as mentioned in Sect. 3.3, training an NN to predict exact product coefficient values is likely not feasible – a Hamming weight prediction is much more realistic. We can therefore create Hamming weight prediction lookup tables for

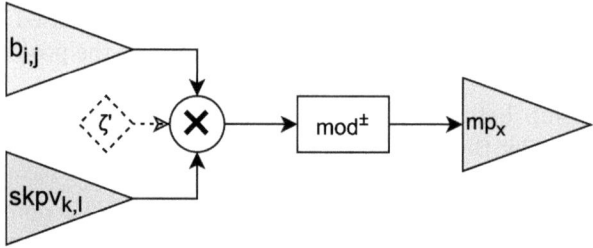

Fig. 2. Product coefficient calculation with key coefficient isolation

the multiplication instead. However, these tables no longer provide a bijective mapping, since many product coefficient values have the same Hamming weight.

In order to resolve this ambiguity, we can use the fact that we have control over the values of the nonzero ciphertext coefficients. Instead of just using four different ciphertexts with a single common value for their nonzero coefficients, we can use $4m$ ciphertexts, using m different values for their nonzero coefficients and four ciphertexts per value, in order to still isolate all key coefficients individually for each of the m values.

If we use such a set of $4m$ ciphertexts to collect power traces and predict the corresponding product coefficient Hamming weights, we get a vector of m such Hamming weights for each key coefficient, with one entry for each of the m chosen ciphertext values. Then, we can modify the lookup tables mentioned above, to show the Hamming weight vectors that result from all possible key coefficient values, instead of just single Hamming weights.

Since the Hamming weight mapping is different for each ciphertext value, for a good choice of m ciphertext values (for some $m > 1$), it is likely that we can create a unique (i.e., bijective) mapping between the key coefficient values and the resulting Hamming weight vectors. With this, assuming we can predict these $4m$ Hamming weights from our power traces for 128 product coefficients, we can use the (now bijective) lookup table to find the values of all key coefficients using their corresponding Hamming weight vectors.

Practical Attack. However, the Hamming weight predictions from our NNs will not be perfect, requiring further refinement of the attack. In particular, we can make use of the complete output of our classification NNs: Instead of just using the most likely prediction, we use the entire predicted probability distribution $\mathbf{p} \in [0, 1]^{13}$ of Hamming weight values for this coefficient. To improve prediction stability, we can optionally capture multiple traces per ciphertext and average their probability distributions.

Similar to above, we use a set of $4m'$ ciphertexts, as well as similar lookup tables containing the expected Hamming weights for each key coefficient value and each of the m' ciphertext coefficient values.

For each key coefficient, the NN predicts the probability $p(\mathbf{c}_i, w)$ of each Hamming weight value $w \in [0, 12]$, for each ciphertext coefficient value $\mathbf{c}_i$ ($i \in [1, m']$).

From this, we calculate a propagated probability[1] $q(v)$ of each key coefficient value $v \in [0, 3328]$ using the corresponding lookup table entries $L(v, \mathbf{c}_i) \in [0, 12]$:

$$q(v) = \prod_{i=1}^{m'} p(\mathbf{c}_i, L(v, \mathbf{c}_i)) \tag{5}$$

Next, we rank the possible values for each key coefficient using their propagated probabilities, in descending order. This gives us a search order for checking key candidates. If the attack performs well, the correct key coefficient values should be the at the top of these rankings.

To maximize the performance of this attack, the m' ciphertext coefficient values should be chosen such that the distances between Hamming weight vectors in the resulting lookup tables are as large as possible, for optimal differentiation between key coefficients. The required number of ciphertext values m' depends on the performance of the NN used, but is expected to be significantly larger than the number of values m required for a simple bijective mapping.

For a sufficiently large value of m' and acceptable NN performance, this attack is likely to succeed in predicting the correct key coefficients, given traces for the $4m'$ ciphertexts.

4 Results

In this section, we present our results, covering the methods presented in Sect. 3, insights gained from their use, and the rationale for their use, as well as the practicality and efficacy of the proposed attack ideas.

4.1 NN Training

The goal of our NN training, as described in Sect. 3.3, is the extraction of information about the result of the polynomial multiplication function.

Trace Capture and Processing. For optimal NN performance, we determine an ideal leakage point using standard Test Vector Leakage Assessment (TVLA) [6] methods, which we measure at a 500 MS/s sampling rate.

As described in Sect. 3.2, the captured traces are then preprocessed for further analysis, including normalization, centering, filtering, downsampling by a factor of 8 to remove redundant data, and upscaling by a factor of 2000.

For training, we cut the POI traces down to even smaller sections, depending on the exact location of the leakage.

---

[1] These 3329 propagated probabilities generally do not sum to 1, meaning they are not "true" probabilities, but off by a constant factor. This has no impact on the attack.

NN Hyperparameters. Considering the infeasibility of training well-performing NNs to predict exact product coefficient values, as described in Sect. 3.3, we focus on Hamming weight predictions for the purpose of this work. Table 1 shows two of our NN models developed for this task, as well as their performance on previously unseen validation data.

Considering our attack plan proposed in Sect. 3.4, the likely most important metric is the mean predicted rank, as the attack is essentially a "product" of the predicted rankings. Using this metric, these new NNs perform quite well, with `poi-hw-final` being significantly better than guessing (3.7). Therefore, we choose this network to perform information extraction for our attacks.

Table 1. Hamming weight based NNs

Name	poi-hw-single	poi-hw-final
NN type	DNN	
Input samples	25	75
Training traces	585000 (45000 per value)	
Evaluation traces	65000 (5000 per value)	
n_{dense}	5	6
n_{units}	512	1024
$p_{dropout}$ [2]	3	
Training batch size	200	
Training epochs	50	
Learning rate	$5 \cdot 10^{-4}$	
Classification accuracy	21%	25%
Ground truth probability	14%	18%
Mean predicted rank	4.2	3.7

[2] "Total" dropout, i.e., each layer has dropout probability $\frac{p_{dropout}}{n_{dense}}$.

4.2 Attack Results

With the ability to capture power traces and extract product coefficient Hamming weight information from them, we can now evaluate the attack method described in Sect. 3.4. A complete attack for the extraction of an entire unknown key requires the prediction of $k \cdot n = 512$ key coefficients, which requires the prediction of the Hamming weights of 128 product coefficients per ciphertext.

This complete attack may therefore require up to 128 different NNs to be trained for the extraction of this information. In this work, we focus on the first two product coefficients and the eight corresponding key coefficients, using these results to extrapolate the possible overall performance of the attack.

Ciphertext Choice. For a user-specified number m', of different values, we chose the values themselves using a greedy search algorithm that aims to maximize the Manhattan distances between the resulting Hamming weight vectors, as suggested in Sect. 3.4.

Attack Performance. With all prerequisites defined and NNs trained for the first two product coefficients, we perform our attack described in Sect. 3.4 on the corresponding eight key coefficients, in order to evaluate its performance and experimentally determine good values for the remaining attack parameters. In particular, we test ciphertext value counts $m' \in [10, 150]$ (in steps of 10), as well as 1–10 traces per ciphertext for NN prediction smoothing. To ensure statistical significance, we run the attack with 100 randomly generated secret keys.

Our main metric for the attack evaluation is the mean rank of the correct key coefficient, calculated over all keys and key coefficients for a given set of parameters. Running the attack with the aforementioned parameters on the first two product coefficients (indices 0 and 2) results in predictions for key coefficients 0, 1, 2, 3, 256, 257, 258 and 259 (i.e., 0 to 3 in both key polynomials), for each of the 100 keys. Figure 3 shows the mean ranks of the true values in these predictions, averaged over all 800 predicted coefficients.

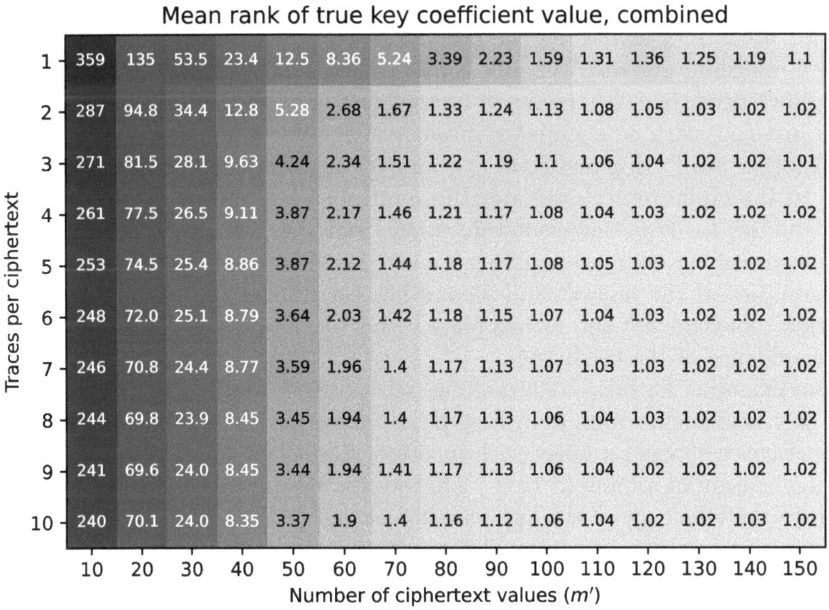

Mean rank of true key coefficient value, combined

Traces per ciphertext \ m'	10	20	30	40	50	60	70	80	90	100	110	120	130	140	150
1	359	135	53.5	23.4	12.5	8.36	5.24	3.39	2.23	1.59	1.31	1.36	1.25	1.19	1.1
2	287	94.8	34.4	12.8	5.28	2.68	1.67	1.33	1.24	1.13	1.08	1.05	1.03	1.02	1.02
3	271	81.5	28.1	9.63	4.24	2.34	1.51	1.22	1.19	1.1	1.06	1.04	1.02	1.02	1.01
4	261	77.5	26.5	9.11	3.87	2.17	1.46	1.21	1.17	1.08	1.04	1.03	1.02	1.02	1.02
5	253	74.5	25.4	8.86	3.87	2.12	1.44	1.18	1.17	1.08	1.05	1.03	1.02	1.02	1.02
6	248	72.0	25.1	8.79	3.64	2.03	1.42	1.18	1.15	1.07	1.04	1.03	1.02	1.02	1.02
7	246	70.8	24.4	8.77	3.59	1.96	1.4	1.17	1.13	1.07	1.03	1.03	1.02	1.02	1.02
8	244	69.8	23.9	8.45	3.45	1.94	1.4	1.17	1.13	1.06	1.04	1.03	1.02	1.02	1.02
9	241	69.6	24.0	8.45	3.44	1.94	1.41	1.17	1.13	1.06	1.04	1.02	1.02	1.02	1.02
10	240	70.1	24.0	8.35	3.37	1.9	1.4	1.16	1.12	1.06	1.04	1.02	1.02	1.03	1.02

Number of ciphertext values (m')

Fig. 3. Attack performance – first two coefficients

Clearly, with a large enough value for m', very good results are achievable, with a mean rank as good as 1.02 (i.e., on average, out of 50 key coefficients, the

Table 2. Attack parameter guidelines

Input samples	75–80
Training traces	≥ 585000 (45000 per value)
n_{dense}	6
n_{units}	1024
$p_{dropout}$[3]	3
Training batch size	200
Training epochs	50
Learning rate	$5 \cdot 10^{-4}$
Ciphertext value count m'	≥ 110
Traces per ciphertext	2–4

[3] "Total" dropout, i.e., each layer has dropout probability $\frac{p_{dropout}}{n_{dense}}$.

correct value is in first place on its ranking for 49 of them, and in second place for one). Considering that each key coefficient has 3329 possible values, this is quite a good result. If the same level of performance can be achieved for all key coefficients, a full key recovery attack is likely feasible.

A relatively large value for m' is required for such a near-perfect performance, but for $m' > 110$, increasing the number of ciphertext values further seems to have diminishing returns. When it comes to averaging predictions from multiple traces per ciphertext, 2–4 seems to be the ideal number, performing much better than just one, with no significant improvements above 4 traces per ciphertext.

Another interesting metric to consider is the confidence of these predictions. Due to the ciphertext choice and the multiplicative nature of the propagated probabilities for key coefficient values (see Sect. 3.4), we observe that each key coefficient value ranking generally has a very large factor between the propagated probabilities of the highest and second-highest ranked values. The size of this "margin" between first and second place seems to contain some information about the confidence of the prediction.

For example, for $m' = 120$, rankings with correct predictions (i.e., where the true key coefficient value is in first place) show such a relative margin of 2^{20} on average, whereas rankings with incorrect first-place prediction only have an average margin of around 2^5 to 2^7. This additional information could be used to improve the efficiency of the key search even further.

Summarizing these results, if we extrapolate the combined performance shown in Fig. 3, a full key recovery attack is likely to be feasible if similar performance can be achieved for the remaining key coefficients. Attack parameters that perform well in our experience are shown in Table 2, but may vary for some coefficients.

Due to the non-perfect performance of our key coefficient predictions, a search of the key space is still required to find the correct key, using the predicted key coefficient rankings to try keys in decreasing order of likelihood. For this purpose, at least one plaintext-ciphertext pair must be known to the attacker, to be able to test whether a key candidate is correct.

If we assume that our attack can predict key coefficient rankings with a mean true value rank of 1.02 (as achieved for some parameters in our attack), we can calculate an expected number of keys that need to be searched through using the predicted rankings as $1.02^{512} \approx 25300$. A search of this size is, of course, very easy to perform on modern computers. Even assuming a mean rank of 1.05, we have an expected search size of $1.05^{512} \approx 10^{11} \approx 2^{36}$, which is still feasible to perform on modern hardware. If we assume worse average performance of the final attack, like a mean rank of 1.1, the expected search size grows quickly to $1.1^{512} \approx 10^{21} \approx 2^{70}$, which is approaching the limits of what is practical on current computer hardware, at least in a reasonable time.

However, these numbers all assume that we use the predicted rankings themselves as the *only* information in our search (i.e., which position on the ranking each value has). If we improve the search algorithm by taking the prediction confidence into account (as discussed above), it is likely that the expected search size could be reduced significantly further in practice, making even worse-performing attacks feasible to execute.

4.3 Comparison to State-of-the-Art

There are currently few state-of-the art NN-based attacks on Kyber hardware implementations. Table 3 summarizes recent attacks on Kyber. However, most of them consider a microcontroller (MCU), running Kyber in software, as their target platform. Software targets are easier to attack because instructions are more isolated. Therefore, a direct comparison to our own attack is difficult and attacks against hardware platforms may require more traces. In addition, both the message and the secret key are common targets. In our case, we target the secret key, which means direct comparisons to message recovery attacks are once again difficult. In [11], which we consider related despite the message being the target, the authors also make use of fault injection in addition to SCA. This may explain the lower number of traces needed for the attack to be successful. To our knowledge, there are currently no NN-based attacks on hardware implementations of Kyber targeting the secret key. Nevertheless, we provide Table 3 as a general overview of the state-of-the-art attack landscape.

A CPA attack on the exact same platform and implementation can successfully recover the secret key within a few hours [28]. It would however require around 110k traces during the attack, as opposed to only 1000 for our proposed attack.

Table 3. Comparison to other state-of-the-art attacks

Reference	Target	Platform	NN Type	Counter Measure	Chosen Ciphertexts	Number of Traces: Training/Attack
Our Work	Key	FPGA	DNN	No	Yes	585k/$\geq$960
[7]	Key	MCU	CNN	No	No	500k/50
[27]	Key	MCU	DNN	Masking	Yes	10k/18
[16]	Key	MCU	CNN	No	Yes	9k/5
[12]	Message	FPGA	DNN	No	No	200k/5120
[11]	Message	FPGA	DNN	Masking	Yes	10k/299
[9]	Message	MCU	DNN	Masking	No	1000/1600

5 Conclusion

In this work, we have proposed a new NN-based SCA on the Kyber/ML-KEM encryption scheme. Specifically, we have targeted the decryption algorithm of Kyber512. Our analysis shows that there is an exploitable correlation between the power consumption and the Hamming weight of an intermediate product used during the decryption. We can then relate the Hamming weight information to the secret key part itself. To exploit this, we have trained a DNN to recover the corresponding Hamming weights. With these predictions, we are able to recover parts of the secret key with high accuracy, in a chosen-ciphertext scenario. We extrapolate from this partial recovery that our attack should be able to recover the complete key if extended to the remaining coefficients.

As future work, we plan to implement a full key recovery attack by training the appropriate number of NNs to evaluate the practical feasibility of the attack we proposed.

Disclosure of Interests. The authors have no competing interests to declare that are relevant to the content of this article.

References

1. Avanzi, R., et al.: CRYSTALS-Kyber - reference C implementation. https://github.com/pq-crystals/kyber/tree/main/ref
2. Avanzi, R., et al.: CRYSTALS-Kyber (version 3.02) (2021). https://pq-crystals.org/kyber/data/kyber-specification-round3-20210804.pdf
3. Benadjila, R., Prouff, E., Strullu, R., Cagli, E., Dumas, C.: Deep learning for side-channel analysis and introduction to ASCAD database. J. Cryptogr. Eng. **10**(2), 163–188 (2019). https://doi.org/10.1007/s13389-019-00220-8
4. Bos, J., et al.: CRYSTALS-Kyber: a CCA-secure module-lattice-based KEM. In: 2018 IEEE European Symposium on Security and Privacy (EuroS&P), pp. 353–367. IEEE (2018). https://doi.org/10.1109/EuroSP.2018.00032
5. Brier, E., Clavier, C., Olivier, F.: Correlation power analysis with a leakage model. In: Joye, M., Quisquater, J.-J. (eds.) CHES 2004. LNCS, vol. 3156, pp. 16–29. Springer, Heidelberg (2004). https://doi.org/10.1007/978-3-540-28632-5_2

6. Gilbert Goodwill, B.J., Jaffe, J., Rohatgi, P., et al.: A testing methodology for side-channel resistance validation. In: NIST Non-Invasive Attack Testing Workshop. vol. 7, pp. 115–136 (2011)
7. Hoang, A.T., et al.: Deep learning enhanced side channel analysis on CRYSTALS-Kyber. In: 2024 25th International Symposium on Quality Electronic Design (ISQED), pp. 1–8 (2024). https://doi.org/10.1109/ISQED60706.2024.10528674
8. Hospodar, G., Gierlichs, B., Mulder, E., Verbauwhede, I., Vandewalle, J.: Machine learning in side-channel analysis: a first study. J. Cryptographic Eng. **1**, 293–302 (2011). https://doi.org/10.1007/s13389-011-0023-x
9. Huang, Z., Wang, H., Cao, B., He, D., Wang, J.: A comprehensive side-channel leakage assessment of CRYSTALS-Kyber in IIoT. Internet Things **27** (2024)
10. Ioffe, S., Szegedy, C.: Batch normalization: accelerating deep network training by reducing internal covariate shift. In: Bach, F., Blei, D. (eds.) International Conference on Machine Learning. Proceedings of Machine Learning Research, vol. 37, pp. 448–456. PMLR (2015). https://proceedings.mlr.press/v37/ioffe15.html
11. Ji, Y., Dubrova, E.: A side-channel attack on a masked hardware implementation of CRYSTALS-Kyber. In: Workshop on Attacks and Solutions in Hardware Security, pp. 27–37. ASHES'23, Association for Computing Machinery (2023). https://doi.org/10.1145/3605769.3623992
12. Ji, Y., Wang, R., Ngo, K., Dubrova, E., Backlund, L.: A side-channel attack on a hardware implementation of CRYSTALS-Kyber. In: 2023 IEEE European Test Symposium (ETS) (2023). https://doi.org/10.1109/ETS56758.2023.10174000
13. Kingma, D.P., Ba, J.: Adam: A method for stochastic optimization (2017). https://doi.org/10.48550/arXiv.1412.6980
14. Kocher, P., Jaffe, J., Jun, B.: Differential power analysis. In: Wiener, M. (ed.) Advances in Cryptology — CRYPTO' 99, pp. 388–397. Springer Berlin Heidelberg, Berlin, Heidelberg (1999). https://doi.org/10.1007/3-540-48405-1_25
15. Langlois, A., Stehlé, D.: Worst-case to average-case reductions for module lattices. DCC **75**(3), 565–599 (2015). https://doi.org/10.1007/s10623-014-9938-4
16. Ma, Y., Yang, X., Wang, A., Wei, C., Chen, T., Xu, H.: Side-channel analysis on lattice-based KEM using multi-feature recognition - the case study of Kyber. In: Seo, H., Kim, S. (eds.) Information Security and Cryptology - ICISC 2023, pp. 221–239. Springer Nature Singapore, Singapore (2024)
17. Martinasek, Z., Hajny, J., Malina, L.: Optimization of power analysis using neural network. In: Francillon, A., Rohatgi, P. (eds.) Smart Card Research and Advanced Applications, pp. 94–107. Springer International Publishing, Cham (2014). https://doi.org/10.1007/978-3-319-08302-5_7
18. Martinasek, Z., Zeman, V.: Innovative method of the power analysis. Radioengineering **22**(2), 586–594 (2013). https://www.radioeng.cz/fulltexts/2013/13_02_0586_0594.pdf
19. Randolph, M., Diehl, W.: Power side-channel attack analysis: a review of 20 years of study for the layman. Cryptography **4**, 15 (2020). https://doi.org/10.3390/cryptography4020015
20. Regev, O.: New lattice based cryptographic constructions. In: 35th ACM STOC, pp. 407–416. ACM Press (2003). https://doi.org/10.1145/780542.780603
21. Regev, O.: On lattices, learning with errors, random linear codes, and cryptography. In: Proceedings of the Thirty-Seventh Annual ACM Symposium on Theory of Computing, pp. 84–93. STOC '05, Association for Computing Machinery, New York, NY, USA (2005). https://doi.org/10.1145/1060590.1060603

22. Rosenblatt, F.: The perceptron: a probabilistic model for information storage and organization in the brain. Psychol. Rev. **65**(6), 386 (1958). https://doi.org/10.1037/h0042519
23. Shor, P.W.: Algorithms for quantum computation: discrete logarithms and factoring. In: Proceedings 35th Annual Symposium on Foundations of Computer Science, pp. 124–134. IEEE (1994). https://doi.org/10.1109/SFCS.1994.365700
24. Srivastava, N., Hinton, G., Krizhevsky, A., Sutskever, I., Salakhutdinov, R.: Dropout: a simple way to prevent neural networks from overfitting. J. Mach. Learn. Res. **15**(1), 1929–1958 (2014)
25. Standaert, F.X.: Introduction to Side-Channel Attacks, pp. 27–42. Springer (2010). https://doi.org/10.1007/978-0-387-71829-3_2
26. TensorFlow, GoogleResearch: Large-scale machine learning on heterogeneous systems (2015)
27. Wang, R., Brisfors, M., Dubrova, E.: A side-channel attack on a higher-order masked CRYSTALS-Kyber implementation. In: Pöpper, C., Batina, L. (eds.) Applied Cryptography and Network Security, pp. 301–324. Springer Nature Switzerland, Cham (2024)
28. Welling, T., Gay, M., Polian, I.: Multi coefficient CPA on a black box hardware implementation of CRYSTALS-Kyber. In: 2025 IEEE European Test Symposium (ETS) (2025)

Jump, It Is Easy: JumpReLU Activation Function in Deep Learning-Based Side-Channel Analysis

Abraham Basurto-Becerra[1]([✉]), Azade Rezaeezade[2], and Stjepan Picek[1]

[1] Radboud University, Nijmegen, The Netherlands
abraham.basurto@ru.nl
[2] Delft University of Technology, Delft, The Netherlands

Abstract. Deep learning-based side-channel analysis has become a popular and powerful option for side-channel attacks in recent years. One of the main directions that the side-channel community explores is how to design efficient architectures that can break the targets with as little as possible attack traces, but also how to consistently build such architectures. In this work, we explore the usage of the JumpReLU activation function, which was designed to improve the robustness of neural networks. Intuitively speaking, improving the robustness seems a natural requirement for side-channel analysis, as hiding countermeasures could be considered adversarial attacks.

In our experiments, we explore three strategies: 1) exchanging the activation functions with JumpReLU at the inference phase, 2) training common side-channel architectures with JumpReLU, and 3) conducting hyperparameter search with JumpReLU as the activation function. While the first two options do not yield improvements in results (but also do not show worse performance), the third option brings advantages, especially considering the number of neural networks that break the target. As such, we conclude that using JumpReLU is a good option to improve the stability of attack results.

Keywords: Side-Channel Analysis · Deep Learning · JumpReLU

1 Introduction

Side-channel analysis (SCA) is a class of cryptanalytic attack techniques that exploit the physical implementation of cryptographic algorithms to extract sensitive information, such as cryptographic keys. Differing from traditional cryptanalysis that focuses on the mathematical properties of algorithms, side-channel attacks leverage unintentional information leakage from a device's physical characteristics during operation. These attacks can exploit different sources of leakage, including power consumption [18], electromagnetic emissions [11], timing [19], or even sound [12]. If a device is not sufficiently resistant to SCA, an adversary can measure its leakage and use statistical analysis methods to recover secrets.

SCA attacks can be divided into two categories [26]:

1. Non-profiling: also called direct attacks, where the adversary collects measurements from the device under attack and uses statistical methods to infer the secret information. Examples of this attack category include simple analysis, differential analysis [18], and mutual information analysis [13].
2. Profiling: also called two-stage attacks, the adversary has a clone (or very similar) device to the device to be attacked. Then, the attacker uses this clone device to perform multiple cryptographic executions with different keys and inputs to create a training set and learn a statistical model from side-channel leakages. Next, in the attack phase, this model is used against the target device. If the model provides satisfactory generalization, the attacker can recover secrets from the target device. The most well-known and powerful profiling method, from an information-theoretic perspective, is the template attack [4]. It is based on the Bayesian rule and the assumption that the measurements are mutually independent among the features given the target class [1,4].

In recent years, deep learning-based approaches have emerged as a powerful alternative that can often surpass template attacks in performance [25]. In particular, multilayer perceptron (MLP) and convolutional neural networks (CNNs) have been widely explored and shown to be effective in recovering secrets from implementations protected with countermeasures [2,34]. Finding high-performing neural network architectures is frequently challenging as it involves selecting from a long list of hyperparameters. From these hyperparameters, in the side-channel analysis domain, the activation function is normally selected to be either ReLU or SeLU. ReLU is the most commonly used activation function, mainly due to its simplicity and effectiveness. Despite research on novel activation functions specifically designed for side-channel analysis, such as the proposal by Knežević et al. [17], ReLU remains a standard choice. However, this does not mean that more suitable activation functions cannot be designed.

In the field of adversarial learning, Erichson et al. [8] presented the JumpReLU activation function. The authors describe it as a very simple and inexpensive strategy that can be used to "retrofit" a previously trained network to improve its resilience to adversarial attacks (i.e., attacks on machine learning that aim to cause misclassification of the machine learning algorithm). In deep learning side-channel analysis, traces capture noise, and implementation countermeasures can be seen as a manipulation to deceive the model into making incorrect predictions. Thus, the natural questions that arise are: Can JumpReLU be used to improve model accuracy in the SCA domain? Can JumpReLU be used as in [8] on already-trained models to enhance their accuracy? Which threshold value should be used? Can we expect randomly generated models to perform better using JumpReLU instead of ReLU and SeLU?

In this paper, we provide answers to these questions by performing a comprehensive list of experiments with the well-known SCA datasets.
In summary, our main contributions are:

1. We verify whether JumpReLU can be used in already-trained SCA models to increase their performance.
2. We show how performance is affected when an existing architecture is taken and its activation function is replaced with JumpReLU.
3. We provide experimental results of which threshold range provides the best performance.
4. We provide a benchmark between random models using ReLU, SeLU, and JumpReLU.

2 Background

2.1 Deep Learning SCA

Deep learning techniques, particularly neural networks, enhance SCA by eliminating the need for extensive pre-processing or manual feature engineering [3,15]. By training models on large datasets of captured leakages, attackers can improve their ability to recover secret keys even from countermeasure-protected (masking [20] and hiding [21]) devices, making this approach a growing concern [10].

Deep learning-based SCA (DLSCA) is a profiling attack defined as a classification problem. The output classes are specified using the target intermediate variable and leakage model. In the DLSCA profiling step, a set $\mathcal{X}$ contains N_p measurements along with their counterparts plain/ciphertexts and keys collected from the clone device and is used to train the deep neural network. In the attack phase, the trained model is used to classify N_a measurements from the target device. The output probabilities of the neural network for each class are used to rank the most probable key. For each key candidate, a score S_k is calculated using the formula:

$$S_k = \sum_{i=1}^{N_a} \log p(x_i, c_j). \quad (1)$$

Here, N_a is the number of measurements in the attack set, and $p(x_i, c_j)$ represents the probability that a measurement x_i belongs to class c_j. The keys are then sorted according to their scores. The key with the highest score is considered the most likely key used for the cryptographic operation on the target device. The guessing entropy (GE) and the required number of attack traces (NT) can be defined using the score vector in Eq. (1). Suppose the correct key $(k^\star)$ used in the cryptographic operation is ranked at the position r^{th} among all possible keys. This position is called the rank of $(k^\star)$. The guessing entropy is the average rank of $k^\star$ in multiple experiments. The required number of attack traces (NT) is the average minimum number of measurements needed for the model to place $k^\star$ in the first position (where $GE = 0$) [30].

2.2 Datasets

For this work, two well-known publicly available datasets were used, namely the ASCAD dataset [2] in its fixed-key and variable-key variants. These datasets were captured from EM measurements while executing a software-protected AES implementation running on an 8-bit AVR architecture microcontroller ATMega8415. The implementation is protected with the first-order masking, where the masks for the first two bytes in the AES state during the first round are fixed to 0, i.e., are not protected. As such, the target byte for this work is always the third byte. For the fixed-key version, the 700 points of interest preselected by the dataset authors are used. The dataset consists of a total of 60000 traces: 50000 training traces and 10000 test traces. For the variable-key version, the 1400 points of interest preselected by the dataset authors are used. The dataset consists of a total of 300000 traces: 200000 training traces and 100000 test traces.

2.3 Activation Functions

Activation functions are an essential component of neural networks, introducing non-linearity. They enable the learning of complex patterns and relationships in data. Without activation functions, a neural network would be equivalent to a single-layer model, regardless of the number of layers, limiting its ability to capture complicated dependencies. Activation functions help determine how neurons respond to inputs and control the flow of gradients during backpropagation, affecting convergence speed and overall training stability [6].

ReLU. The Rectified Linear Unit (ReLU) activation function is a widely used non-linear function in artificial neural networks [22,29], particularly in deep learning models. It is defined by:

$$g(z) = max\{0, z\}. \qquad (2)$$

ReLU is the default recommendation in modern neural networks [14].

SeLU. The Scaled Exponential Linear Units (SeLU) [16] activation function is defined by:

$$f(x) = \lambda \begin{cases} x, & \text{if } x > 0. \\ \alpha(e^x - 1), & \text{if } x \leq 0, \end{cases} \qquad (3)$$

with $\alpha \approx 1.6733$ and $\lambda \approx 1.0507$.

JumpReLU. The JumpReLU [9] (Jump Rectified Linear Unit) activation function is a variant of the standard ReLU function with a jump discontinuity, yielding piece-wise continuous functions. It introduces a positive threshold parameter

κ such that the neuron remains inactive until its input exceeds κ. The magnitude of the jump κ is a parameter the user must define.

$$J(z) = zH(z - \kappa) = \begin{cases} 0, & \text{if } z \leq \kappa. \\ z, & \text{if } z > \kappa. \end{cases} \quad (4)$$

Here, H denotes the discrete Heaviside unit step function. The JumpReLU activation function introduces robustness and an additional amount of sparsity, controlled via the jump value κ. Thus, JumpReLU suppresses small positive signals. We depict the operation of the JumpReLU activation function in Fig. 1.

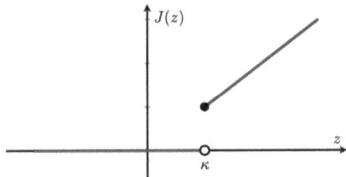

Fig. 1. JumpReLU activation function.

When presented, JumpReLU was proposed as a strategy to improve resilience to adversarial attacks. Moreover, it was concluded that it can be used in models already trained using ReLU. In this scenario, it provides a trade-off between robustness and classification accuracy, which the user can control in a post-training stage by tuning the threshold value κ.

Another application where JumpReLU has shown improved results versus other activation functions is in sparse autoencoders for language models. Here, JumpReLU enables more faithful reconstructions than competing methods, such as Gated or TopK Sparse AutoEncoders [27].

3 Related Work

Since the work of Maghrebi et al. [20], where the first published results of deep learning techniques applied to the domain of side-channel analysis are presented, multiple research works have been published. Those works showcase the importance of hyperparameter tuning and how identifying high-performing models can be challenging due to the large number of hyperparameters that must be considered. As such, multiple works considered how to find high-performing neural network architectures efficiently, see, e.g., [24, 30, 32–34].

Regarding the impact of activation functions, Benadjila et al. [2] have studied the effect of the activation function on the performance of the neural network, and they reported that their best results were obtained with ReLU, tanh, and softsign (a variation of tanh), but they chose ReLU due to its state-of-the-art results and because its computation time is lower than the other two functions.

Knežević et al. [17] used evolutionary algorithms to evolve new activation functions for side-channel analysis. Their experiments with the ASCAD database showed that this approach is highly effective compared to results obtained with standard activation functions and that it can match the state-of-the-art results from the literature. The authors evaluated two leakage models (the Hamming Weight (HW) and Identity (ID) models) and MLP and CNN architectures. Moreover, Do et al. [5] analyzed the effect of the activation function in MLP- and CNN-based deep learning models for non-profiled side-channel analysis. For their MLP-based models, using the ELU activation function provided better performance than ReLU in fighting against noise generation-based hiding countermeasures.

4 Experimental Setup

4.1 Neural Network Topologies

We use two well-known neural network topologies that are common choices in DLSCA: **Multilayer Perceptron (MLP)** is a basic type of neural network with an input layer, one or more hidden layers, and an output layer. The input layer receives training data that passes through fully connected hidden layers before reaching the output. In classification tasks, the output layer represents different classes. MLP learns patterns in the data by adjusting its weights using gradient descent and backpropagation.

Convolutional Neural Network (CNN) is another type of neural network designed to process structured data. It includes convolutional layers that detect important features using small filters (kernels). These layers are followed by activation functions and pooling layers, which help reduce complexity while keeping essential information. Finally, one or more fully connected layers process the extracted features for the final output.

4.2 Datasets and Leakage Model

In our experiments, we consider two publicly available datasets: **ASCAD-Fixed** and **ASCAD-Variable** and their **desynchronized 50 and 100** versions.[1] Both datasets are provided using measurements from a software implementation of AES-128. The implementation is protected with Boolean masking. Since the first and second bytes are masked with zero, and the sensitive variable leaks in the first order, we target the third byte. The target platform is an 8-bit AVR microcontroller (ATmega8515), and the measurements are the electromagnetic emanations (EM) from the target [2]. In ASCAD-Fixed, there are 50000 traces for training, all with the same key, and 10000 traces for attack. The traces have 700 features, an interval that includes most leaky time samples considering the Sbox output as a sensitive variable.

---

[1] The datasets can be found here.

In ASCAD-Variable, there are 200000 traces for training with the key changing randomly for every trace and 100000 traces for attack (we use 100000 traces for training and 10000 traces for attack from this dataset). The traces have 1400 features. The key is fixed when measuring the attack traces for both datasets. In the desynchronized versions of both datasets, each trace is shifted using a random variable of 0 to $N^{[0]}$, where $N^{[0]} = 50$ for ASCAD-Fixed and ASCAD-Variable denotes desynchronization of 50, and $N^{[0]} = 100$ for ASCAD-Fixed and ASCAD-Variable denotes desynchronization of 100.

We use the Identity (ID) leakage model, where we assume that the exact value of the sensitive variable is leaking. Using divide-and-conquer[2] strategy and targeting the Sbox output (8 bits) of the first round as the sensitive variable, there are 256 possible classes with the ID leakage model.

4.3 Analysis Methodology

This study examines how the use of JumpReLU affects the performance of DLSCA. To clarify this, we investigate two different scenarios.

1. We explore whether substituting the activation function in well-known architectures with JumpReLU can potentially enhance their performance. This is explored in two settings:
   - Substitution of the activation function on an already trained model, i.e., JumpReLU is used only at the inference phase.
   - Substitution of the activation function and training of the model, i.e., JumpReLU is employed during both the training and inference phases.
2. We investigate whether the average performance of random CNN and MLP models for DLSCA is better using JumpReLU compared to the other activation functions.

In the following, we introduce the steps required for each scenario.

In the **first scenario**, we would like to see if replacing the activation function of well-known architectures with JumpReLU results in improving the performance of those models. To verify this, our methodology is straightforward. We take the following steps:

- **Acquiring baseline models:** We start by training ten models using the architectures reported in previous works. Training is done using identical hyperparameters and datasets to ensure comparable results. The models we used are listed in Table 1. We call them "baseline models". The activation functions in these architectures are either ReLU or SeLU, but none use JumpReLU. The works listed in Table 1 reported one or more CNN and/or MLP neural networks for at least one of the datasets in Sect. 4.2. Table 1 shows what kind of model has been reported for which dataset in each work.

---

[2] Divide-and-conquer strategy is a strategy to recover a long key by retrieving its smaller parts separately.

Table 1. The list of works/architectures we consider in our experiments. We depict ∗ if the work reported a well-performing CNN and • if the work reported a well-performing MLP.

Covered datasets	ASCAD-Fixed			ASCAD-Variable		
	$N^{[0]} = 0$	$N^{[0]} = 50$	$N^{[0]} = 100$	$N^{[0]} = 0$	$N^{[0]} = 50$	$N^{[0]} = 100$
[2]	∗, •	∗, •	∗, •	∗, •	∗, •	∗, •
[34]	∗	∗	∗			
[32]	∗	∗	∗			

- **Record the baseline model's performance:** After training each model and using that model to attack, we use guessing entropy and the required number of traces (NT) to report that model's performance for the target dataset the model was developed for.
- **Re-training models with JumpReLU:** Once more, we need to train the baseline models. This time, we keep all the hyperparameters as before and only replace the models' activation function with JumpReLU. As mentioned in Sect. 2.3, JumpReLU has its own hyperparameter, κ, which should be tuned for each neural network. To do this tuning, we examine five thresholds for each baseline model. We train each model with five different values for κ, $\kappa \in \{0.001, 0.002, 0.003, 0.004, 0.005\}$. The tuned model with the best performance is denoted the "JumpReLU-equivalent model".
- **Report the JumpReLU-equivalent models performance:** The last step is to report the performance of the models with the JumpReLU activation function and compare it with the performance of the original ones. The hypothesis is to verify whether replacing previously found good models' activation functions with JumpReLU improves their performance.

In the **second scenario**, we would like to see if using JumpReLU can improve the performance of the models on average. To evaluate this, we compare the average performance of a number of neural networks using two common activation functions (ReLU and SeLU being randomly selected for each neural network combination of hyperparameters) against their performance when their activation function is fixed to JumpReLU. The methodology for comparing performance is described in the following steps.

- **Acquiring baseline models:** We generate 500 neural networks of the specific topology (MLP or CNN) using a random search. The searching ranges for hyperparameters of MLP and CNN are listed in Table 2. These ranges are chosen based on those reported in the previous works [7,23,34]. Since those 500 neural networks are generated randomly, many of them cannot decrease GE. Then, we only select the models that reached $GE = 0$ within 4000 attack traces as the "baseline models".
- **JumpReLU equivalent models:** With the same topologies generated for the baseline models we verify if by using JumpReLU would have provided

better results for this random model, and validate against five different values for κ, $\kappa \in \{0.001, 0.002, 0.003, 0.004, 0.005\}$.

Table 2. Searched range of MLP and CNN hyperparameters. For both MLP and CNN dense layers, we used the ranges shown in *dense layers* part of the table.

Hyperparameters	Range
MLP dense layers	
Number of neurons	[10, 30, 50, 70, 90, 120, 150, 200, 250, 300, 400, 500]
Number of layers	[2, 8], step = 1
CNN convolution and dense layers	
Number of neurons in dense layer	[50, 100, 150, 200, 300, 400, 500]
Number of dense layers	[2, 4], step = 1
Number of convolution layers	[2, 4], step = 1
Kernel size	[4, 20], step = 2
Number of filters	[4, 24], step = 4
i^{th} layer filter size	$((i-1)^{th} filter\_size)^2$
Pooling	"Average", "Max"
Pooling size	[2, 10], step = 2
Pooling stride	[2, 10], step = 2
Learning hyperparameters	
Optimizer	"Adam"
Weight initialization	"random_uniform", "he_uniform",
	"glorot_uniform",
Activation function	"ReLU", "SeLU"
Batch size	[128, 256, 512]
Learning rate	[1e-3, 5e-4, 1e-4, 5e-5, 1e-5]
Epochs	100

- **The average performance of baseline models:** We use "AVERAGE_GE" and "AVERAGE_NT" to represent the average performance of baseline models. The "AVERAGE_GE" is the average over GE that MLP or CNN baseline models can reach in an attack set with 4000 attack traces. The "AVERAGE_NT" is the average over the required number of attack traces that MLP or CNN baseline models need to reach $GE = 0$.
- **Re-training models with JumpReLU:** In step one, we generated two pools of MLP and CNN neural networks, each pool with 500 different models. Now, we replace the activation function of those models with JumpReLU and re-train them for $\kappa \in \{0.001, 0.002, 0.003, 0.004, 0.005\}$ jumping thresholds. Then, we consider the best-acquired performance as the performance of that model when using JumpReLU. Again, the considered metrics are GE

and NT. The tuned baseline model with the best performance is called the "JumpReLU-equivalent model."
- **The average performance of JumpReLU-equivalent models:** The AVERAGE_GE and the AVERAGE_NT are calculated as performance metrics for the models that reached $GE = 0$ in each pool. We compare the AVERAGE_GE and AVERAGE_NT of the baseline and the JumpReLU-equivalent models. This way, the influence of using JumpReLU on DLSCA performance can be observed.

5 Experimental Results

5.1 Baseline Models

Retrofit. To answer if the behavior observed by Erichson et al., where JumpReLU can be used to "retrofit" already trained models, is also true for SCA, we used two architectures described in [2]: MLP_{best} and CNN_{best}. For both architectures, ten models were trained for each dataset with each $N^{[0]}$ using its original activation function (ReLU), and at the inference moment, ReLU and JumpReLU were used. As there is no previous data on which threshold range κ would provide the best performance, three different sets of values were tested $S_a = \{0.001k \mid k \in [1..9]\}$, $S_b = \{0.01k \mid k \in [1..9]\}$ and $S_c = \{0.1k \mid k \in [1..9]\}$.

MLP_{best}-based models only achieved generalization on the ASCAD-Fixed dataset with $N^{[0]} = 0$. All CNN_{best}-based models achieved generalization on both datasets and with the three evaluated $N^{[0]}$ values.

The experimental results show that using JumpReLU at inference time with the already-trained models did not provide any relevant performance variation. When the value of κ was from S_a or S_b, the performance of the models was almost identical to that of ReLU; for κ values in S_c equal to or greater than 0.5, the performance was even slightly worse than with ReLU. These results are consistent across both datasets and the three $N^{[0]}$ corresponding values.

Substitution. Having seen that simply using JumReLU at inference time does not provide the desired performance gain, we investigate the impact of substituting the original activation function with JumpReLU. Again, we used MLP_{best} and CNN_{best} based models, but this time, these are trained using JumpReLU. Concerning model generalization, the results are the same as described in the previous experiments. However, in this scenario, the value of κ has a more pronounced impact on the performance of the models. Here, κ values from S_a provide a slight improvement for some models (see Figs. 2 and 3), while values from S_b generally provide worse performance, and finally, values from S_c mostly lead to models not generalizing. Note that the figures depict the average behavior in darker lines and the standard deviation by shaded area in the same color.

With the information that JumpReLu can provide a small performance gain on architectures that already have shown good performance, we proceed to evaluate the performance of other architectures that do not use the ReLU function but SeLU. The tested architectures are from [34] and [32]. Both works used a technique called One Cycle Policy [31] to choose the learning rate hyperparameter. However, as we want to isolate the effect of substituting the activation function to JumpReLU, this technique is not used in our experiments, and only three different learning rate values were used: $\{0.0005, 0.00025, 0.0001\}$. The experimental results show that for these architectures, SeLU presented the best results, and JumpReLU did not provide any improvement.

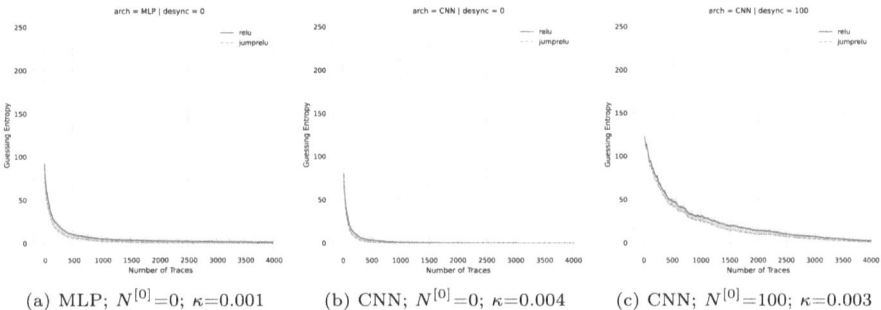

(a) MLP; $N^{[0]}{=}0$; $\kappa{=}0.001$ (b) CNN; $N^{[0]}{=}0$; $\kappa{=}0.004$ (c) CNN; $N^{[0]}{=}100$; $\kappa{=}0.003$

Fig. 2. ASCAD-Fixed observed performance improvement.

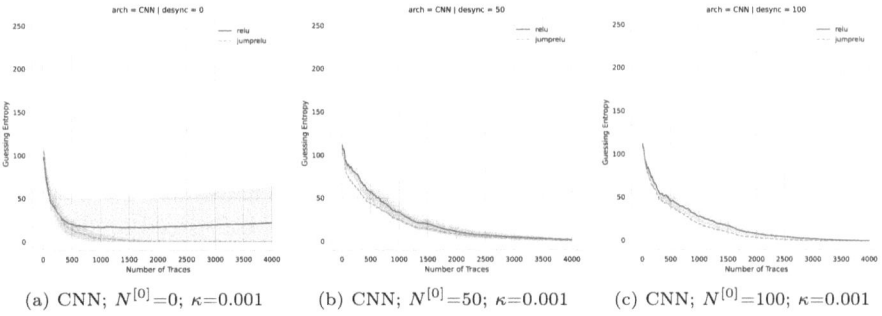

(a) CNN; $N^{[0]}{=}0$; $\kappa{=}0.001$ (b) CNN; $N^{[0]}{=}50$; $\kappa{=}0.001$ (c) CNN; $N^{[0]}{=}100$; $\kappa{=}0.001$

Fig. 3. ASCAD-Variable observed performance improvement.

5.2 Random Models

Our observations show that substituting the activation function of existing well-performing architectures with JumpReLU cannot provide a significant advantage. Thus, the remaining scenario where JumpReLU is considered is to find new well-performing architectures. We explore this scenario by performing a random model search.

ASCAD-Fixed. The results for the ASCAD-Fixed dataset are given in Table 3. For MLP-based models, $GE = 0$ was only reached with $N^{[0]} = 0$, with 163 models using ReLU and 104 using SeLU. CNN-based models did reach $GE = 0$ for all $N^{[0]}$, with 68 and 52 models for ReLU and SeLU activation functions, respectively. Note that we do not show any results with MLP and desynchronization as we could not find any architecture breaking the target with the given number of attack traces.

For JumpReLU, we see that both MLP and CNN architectures reach good results. More precisely, for CNNs, the threshold variations do not cause many differences, and all settings are stable: a similar number of models breaking the target and a similar minimal number of traces to break the target. Moreover, we observe that breaking a synchronized target is relatively simple, while after added desynchronization, the task becomes significantly more difficult (with only a handful of architectures breaking the target). An additional observation is that CNN with SeLU activation function actually reaches a better best result (only 2690 attack traces needed vs. 3990 for the case with JumpReLU). Still, CNNs with SeLU and ReLU do not manage to break the unsynchronized version with the 100 desynchronization level at all, showcasing that JumpReLU provides more robustness. On the other hand, for MLP, we see that using JumpReLU allows for the majority of the tested models to break the target, and the best results are comparable with the SeLU case (180 vs. 190 attack traces). To conclude, JumpReLU allows more architectures to break the target, with minimal influences from the selected threshold level, and allows comparable results on the minimal number of attack traces required to break the target.

ASCAD-Variable. The results for the ASCAD-Variable dataset are given in Table 4. With this dataset, for all $N^{[0]}$ values, at least one model reached $Ge = 0$. Considering JumpReLU, we can again observe that the threshold level does not play a significant role. Moreover, as before, JumpReLU allows more architectures to break the target than ReLU and SeLU. Still, with MLP-based models with desynchronization levels of 50 and 100, we break the target using SeLU, while we cannot do it with JumpReLU. However, since there is only one such architecture, it is difficult to assess the relevance of such a result. For CNNs without desynchronization, we also observe that JumpReLU reduces the minimal number of attack traces, giving additional advantage to the usage of JumpReLU.

Table 3. Experimental results for the ASCAD-Fixed dataset. The column Models denotes the number of models that reached GE equal to 0. $N^{[0]}$ denotes the desynchronization rate, Arch denotes the architecture type, and AF denotes the activation function used (in the last layer is always softmax).

$N^{[0]}$	Arch	AF	Threshold	Models	Avg NT	Min NT
0	cnn	SeLU	-	52	2202.7	460
0	cnn	ReLU	-	68	2682.8	570
0	cnn	JumpReLU	0.001	118	2289.2	440
0	cnn	JumpReLU	0.002	116	2430.6	390
0	cnn	JumpReLU	0.003	119	2457.7	430
0	cnn	JumpReLU	0.004	115	2437.2	420
0	cnn	JumpReLU	0.005	117	2494.5	490
50	cnn	SeLU	-	3	3123.3	2690
50	cnn	ReLU	-	1	4000.0	4000
50	cnn	JumpReLU	0.002	1	3990.0	3990
100	cnn	JumpReLU	0.001	2	3980.0	3970
100	cnn	JumpReLU	0.002	2	3860.0	3720
100	cnn	JumpReLU	0.005	2	3915.0	3830
0	mlp	ReLU	-	163	705.1	210
0	mlp	SeLU	-	104	902.0	180
0	mlp	jumpReLU	0.001	344	732.8	220
0	mlp	JumpReLU	0.002	344	754.6	210
0	mlp	JumpReLU	0.003	334	745.7	210
0	mlp	JumpReLU	0.004	337	729.6	230
0	mlp	JumpReLU	0.005	334	724.0	190

6 Conclusions and Future Work

This paper investigates how the JumpReLU activation function can improve the performance of DLSCA models. Finding performant models remains a significant challenge for DLSCA, and the process is still largely reliant on the designer's expertise and the computing resources at their disposal, as these factors determine how much experimentation and fine-tuning can be conducted within a given timeframe. Finding one model that shows good performance with a given combination of hyperparameters does not imply that small changes to any specific hyperparameter will lead to a predictable improvement or degradation in performance. Hyperparameter tuning is often highly context-dependent, with interactions between parameters influencing the overall model behavior. With this in mind and based on our experimental results, we can conclude that JumpReLU can be considered a promising option when constructing new architectures for DLSCA. More precisely, we see especially encouraging results when

Table 4. Experimental results for the ASCAD-Variable dataset. The column Models denotes the number of models that reached GE equal to 0. $N^{[0]}$ denotes the desynchronization rate, Arch denotes the architecture type, and AF denotes the activation function used (in the last layer is always softmax).

$N^{[0]}$	Arch	AF	Threshold	Models	Avg	Min
0	cnn	SeLU	-	17	2956.5	470
0	cnn	ReLU	-	29	2656.6	350
0	cnn	JumpReLU	0.001	71	2349.4	170
0	cnn	JumpReLU	0.002	70	2527.4	210
0	cnn	JumpReLU	0.003	69	2463.2	300
0	cnn	JumpReLU	0.004	69	2505.8	290
0	cnn	JumpReLU	0.005	66	2378.6	240
50	cnn	SeLU	-	1	3800.0	3800
50	cnn	JumpReLU	0.001	1	2930.0	2930
50	cnn	JumpReLU	0.003	1	3980.0	3980
100	cnn	SeLU	-	1	4000.0	4000
100	cnn	JumpReLU	0.003	1	4000.0	4000
0	mlp	ReLU	-	75	2333.2	710
0	mlp	SeLU	-	42	1670.7	340
0	mlp	JumpReLU	0.001	143	2153.7	420
0	mlp	JumpReLU	0.002	132	2249.5	480
0	mlp	JumpReLU	0.003	131	2346.5	600
0	mlp	JumpReLU	0.004	136	2515.8	560
0	mlp	JumpReLU	0.005	128	2333.0	700
50	mlp	SeLU	-	1	3990.0	3990
100	mlp	SeLU	-	1	4000.0	4000

the JumpReLU is given as one of the options during the hyperparameter tuning. The architectures with it seem to improve the performance from two aspects: 1) more architectures breaking the target and 2) fewer attack traces required to break the target for the most performant architectures.

In future work, we plan to explore whether JumpReLU can bring advantages against other hiding countermeasures like Gaussian noise or jitter. Moreover, JumpReLU showed very good performance when combined with sparse autoencoders [28], which could be another interesting research direction for DLSCA.

References

1. Batina, L., Djukanovic, M., Heuser, A., Picek, S.: It started with templates: the future of profiling in side-channel analysis. In: Avoine, G., Hernandez-Castro, J. (eds.) Security of Ubiquitous Computing Systems, pp. 133–145. Springer, Cham (2021). https://doi.org/10.1007/978-3-030-10591-4_8
2. Benadjila, R., Prouff, E., Strullu, R., Cagli, E., Dumas, C.: Deep learning for side-channel analysis and introduction to ASCAD database. J. Cryptogr. Eng. **10**(2), 163–188 (2020)
3. Cagli, E., Dumas, C., Prouff, E.: Convolutional neural networks with data augmentation against jitter-based countermeasures. In: Fischer, W., Homma, N. (eds.) CHES 2017. LNCS, vol. 10529, pp. 45–68. Springer, Cham (2017). https://doi.org/10.1007/978-3-319-66787-4_3
4. Chari, S., Rao, J.R., Rohatgi, P.: Template attacks. In: Kaliski, B.S., Koç, K., Paar, C. (eds.) CHES 2002. LNCS, vol. 2523, pp. 13–28. Springer, Heidelberg (2003). https://doi.org/10.1007/3-540-36400-5_3
5. Do, N., Hoang, V., Doan, V.S., Pham, C.: On the performance of nonâĂŘprofiled side channel attacks based on deep learning techniques. IET Inf. Secur. **17**(3), 377–393 (2022). https://doi.org/10.1049/ise2.12102
6. Dubey, S.R., Singh, S.K., Chaudhuri, B.B.: Activation functions in deep learning: a comprehensive survey and benchmark. Neurocomputing **503**, 92–108 (2022)
7. Emmanuel, P., Remi, S., Ryad, B., Eleonora, C., Cecile, D.: Study of deep learning techniques for side-channel analysis and introduction to ASCAD database. CoRR **53**, 1–45 (2018)
8. Erichson, N.B., Yao, Z., Mahoney, M.W.: JumpReLU: a retrofit defense strategy for adversarial attacks. arXiv preprint arXiv:1904.03750 (2019)
9. Erichson, N.B., Yao, Z., Mahoney, M.W.: JumpReLU: a retrofit defense strategy for adversarial attacks (2019). https://doi.org/10.48550/arXiv.1904.03750, http://arxiv.org/abs/1904.03750, arXiv:1904.03750
10. Federal Office for Information Security (BSI): Guidelines for evaluating machine-learning based side-channel attack resistance. https://www.bsi.bund.de/SharedDocs/Downloads/DE/BSI/Zertifizierung/Interpretationen/AIS_46_AI_guide.pdf?__blob=publicationFile&v=6 (2024). technical Report AIS 46
11. Gandolfi, K., Mourtel, C., Olivier, F.: Electromagnetic analysis: concrete results. In: Koç, Ç.K., Naccache, D., Paar, C. (eds.) CHES 2001. LNCS, vol. 2162, pp. 251–261. Springer, Heidelberg (2001). https://doi.org/10.1007/3-540-44709-1_21
12. Genkin, D., Shamir, A., Tromer, E.: Acoustic cryptanalysis. J. Cryptol. **30**(2), 392–443 (2017). https://doi.org/10.1007/s00145-015-9224-2
13. Gierlichs, B., Batina, L., Tuyls, P., Preneel, B.: Mutual information analysis. In: Oswald, E., Rohatgi, P. (eds.) CHES 2008. LNCS, vol. 5154, pp. 426–442. Springer, Heidelberg (2008). https://doi.org/10.1007/978-3-540-85053-3_27
14. Goodfellow, I., Bengio, Y., Courville, A.: Deep Learning. MIT Press (2016). http://www.deeplearningbook.org
15. Kim, J., Picek, S., Heuser, A., Bhasin, S., Hanjalic, A.: Make some noise unleashing the power of convolutional neural networks for profiled side-channel analysis. In: IACR Transactions on Cryptographic Hardware and Embedded Systems, pp. 148–179 (2019)
16. Klambauer, G., Unterthiner, T., Mayr, A., Hochreiter, S.: Self-normalizing neural networks. In: Advances in Neural Information Processing Systems, vol. 30 (2017)

17. Knežević, K., Fulir, J., Jakobović, D., Picek, S., Đurasević, M.: NeuroSCA: evolving activation functions for side-channel analysis. IEEE Access **11**, 284–299 (2023). https://doi.org/10.1109/ACCESS.2022.3232064, https://ieeexplore.ieee.org/document/9998512, conference Name: IEEE Access
18. Kocher, P., Jaffe, J., Jun, B.: Differential Power Analysis. In: Wiener, M. (ed.) Advances in Cryptology – CRYPTO 1999, pp. 388–397. Springer, Berlin Heidelberg, Berlin, Heidelberg (1999). https://doi.org/10.1007/3-540-48405-1
19. Kocher, P.C.: Timing attacks on implementations of Diffie-Hellman, RSA, DSS, and other systems. In: Koblitz, N. (ed.) CRYPTO 1996. LNCS, vol. 1109, pp. 104–113. Springer, Heidelberg (1996). https://doi.org/10.1007/3-540-68697-5_9
20. Maghrebi, H., Portigliatti, T., Prouff, E.: Breaking cryptographic implementations using deep learning techniques. In: Carlet, C., Hasan, M.A., Saraswat, V. (eds.) SPACE 2016. LNCS, vol. 10076, pp. 3–26. Springer, Cham (2016). https://doi.org/10.1007/978-3-319-49445-6_1
21. Masure, L., et al.: Deep learning side-channel analysis on large-scale traces. In: Chen, L., Li, N., Liang, K., Schneider, S. (eds.) ESORICS 2020. LNCS, vol. 12308, pp. 440–460. Springer, Cham (2020). https://doi.org/10.1007/978-3-030-58951-6_22
22. Nair, V., Hinton, G.E.: Rectified linear units improve restricted Boltzmann machines. In: Proceedings of the 27th International Conference on Machine Learning (ICML-10), pp. 807–814 (2010)
23. Perin, G., Picek, S.: On the influence of optimizers in deep learning-based side-channel analysis. In: Selected Areas in Cryptography: 27th International Conference, Halifax, NS, Canada (Virtual Event), 21-23 October 2020, Revised Selected Papers 27, pp. 615–636. Springer (2021). https://doi.org/10.1007/978-3-030-81652-0_24
24. Perin, G., Wu, L., Picek, S.: Exploring feature selection scenarios for deep learning-based side-channel analysis. In: IACR Transactions on Cryptographic Hardware and Embedded Systems, pp. 828–861 (2022)
25. Picek, S., Heuser, A., Perin, G., Guilley, S.: Profiled side-channel analysis in the efficient attacker framework. In: International Conference on Smart Card Research and Advanced Applications, pp. 44–63. Springer, Cham (2021). https://doi.org/10.1007/978-3-030-97348-3_3
26. Picek, S., Perin, G., Mariot, L., Wu, L., Batina, L.: Sok: deep learning-based physical side-channel analysis. ACM Comput. Surv. **55**(11), 1–35 (2023)
27. Rajamanoharan, S., et al.: Jumping ahead: improving reconstruction fidelity with JumpReLU sparse autoencoders (2024). https://doi.org/10.48550/arXiv.2407.14435, http://arxiv.org/abs/2407.14435, arXiv:2407.14435 [cs]
28. Rajamanoharan, S., et al.: Jumping ahead: improving reconstruction fidelity with JumpReLU sparse autoencoders (2024). https://arxiv.org/abs/2407.14435
29. Ramachandran, P., Zoph, B., Le, Q.V.: Searching for activation functions. arXiv preprint arXiv:1710.05941 (2017)
30. Rijsdijk, J., Wu, L., Perin, G., Picek, S.: Reinforcement learning for hyperparameter tuning in deep learning-based side-channel analysis. In: IACR Transactions on Cryptographic Hardware and Embedded Systems, pp. 677–707 (2021)
31. Smith, L.N.: Cyclical learning rates for training neural networks. In: 2017 IEEE Winter Conference on Applications of Computer Vision (WACV), pp. 464–472 (2017). https://doi.org/10.1109/WACV.2017.58
32. Wouters, L., Arribas, V., Gierlichs, B., Preneel, B.: Revisiting a methodology for efficient CNN architectures in profiling attacks. In; IACR Transactions on Cryptographic Hardware and Embedded Systems, pp. 147–168 (2020)

33. Wu, L., Perin, G., Picek, S.: I choose you: automated hyperparameter tuning for deep learning-based side-channel analysis. IEEE Trans. Emerg. Top. Comput. **12**(2), 546–557 (2024). https://doi.org/10.1109/TETC.2022.3218372
34. Zaid, G., Bossuet, L., Habrard, A., Venelli, A.: Methodology for efficient CNN architectures in profiling attacks. In: IACR Transactions on Cryptographic Hardware and Embedded Systems, pp. 1–36 (2020)

Arithmetic Masking Countermeasure to Mitigate Side-Channel-Based Model Extraction Attack on DNN Accelerator

Hirokatsu Yamasaki[1], Kota Yoshida[1(✉)], Yuta Fukuda[1,2], and Takeshi Fujino[1]

[1] Ritsumeikan University, 1-1-1 Noji-higashi, Kusatsu, Shiga, Japan
y0sh1d4@fc.ritsumei.ac.jp
[2] National Institute of Advanced Industrial Science and Technology, 1-1-1, Umezono, Tsukuba, Ibaraki, Japan

Abstract. Trained deep neural networks (DNNs) are valuable intellectual property because they require huge costs for data, computation, and expertise to develop. Because the trained DNN models can be exploited for attacks to induce malfunctions and privacy violations, protecting them is crucial from a security perspective. Especially for edge devices, considering physical attacks on hardware, such as side-channel attacks (SCAs) is necessary. For instance, DNN model parameters can be encrypted and stored in the memory of the device, but they are vulnerable to SCAs because they are decrypted during computation. This paper proposes an arithmetic masking countermeasure to mitigate model extraction attacks using correlation power analysis on the wavefront array, one of the matrix multiplication accelerators. This countermeasure adds rows and columns with random numbers on the input and weight matrix; these random numbers make a register transition unpredictable. It can be implemented without any circuit modification and with only two additional clock cycles. We evaluated it using simulation and power traces acquired from FPGA implementation.

Keywords: Systolic array · Side-channel attacks · Deep neural networks · Arithmetic masking

1 Introduction

Deep neural networks (DNNs), one of the machine learning techniques, are widely used in cloud and edge computing. There is a wide range of model sizes, from large-scale language models and generative models executed in the cloud server to task-specific small models executed on edge devices. Among these, DNNs implemented on edge devices are superior to cloud ones in terms of latency, communication costs, confidentiality, and privacy. Because inference of DNN process mainly consists of matrix multiplication, edge devices can be equipped with hardware to accelerate that [9, 11].

Because training DNN models requires huge datasets, computational resources, and expertise, trained models are valuable intellectual property. Consequently, trained DNN models are highly attractive to attackers, providing them with a strong motivation to steal them. Additionally, the stolen model can be exploited to cause malfunctions [16] and training data violations [5].

Unlike cloud computing, edge devices are deployed in local environments. Therefore, hardware security that assumes attackers may have physical access to the device is important. Side-channel attacks, especially using a device's power consumption or leaked electromagnetic emissions, are one of the threats to hardware security. These attacks have traditionally targeted cryptographic systems; however, recent research has extended these attacks to target DNN inference processes to extract DNN model parameters. Batina et al. reported that a side-channel attack using electromagnetic analysis identifies the model architecture and parameters of multilayer perceptron (MLP) executed on an MCU [2]. We demonstrated that model parameters can be revealed using electromagnetic analysis against a DNN accelerator that equips a single processing element (PE) implemented on an FPGA [21]. Furthermore, we demonstrated that model parameters can be revealed through power analysis against FPGA implementations of systolic arrays, which are equipped with multiple PEs, such as the wavefront array and tensor processing unit (TPU [9]) [20,22]. Similarly, Li et al. [12] performed a power analysis on a systolic array and successfully revealed model parameters.

In this paper, we propose a masking countermeasure to mitigate SCA vulnerabilities on systolic arrays reported by us. [20,22]. Hereafter, the proposed masking is referred to as arithmetic masking because it uses addition and subtraction. In this attack, an attacker exploits the correlation between a target register transition and power consumption. Our countermeasure extends matrices to be computed with random values, and these random values randomize the transition of registers that store intermediate results. Because these random values are finally subtracted from the intermediate result, they do not affect the computational result. We conduct evaluations with simulation and FPGA implementation on a wavefront array, one of the previously attacked systolic array architectures.

The contributions of this paper are summarized as follows.

- We propose arithmetic masking to mitigate model parameter extraction attacks that analyze the power consumption of a wavefront array. Because the countermeasure is implemented by adding random numbers to the input and weight parameter matrices before computation, no modifications to the circuit are required. Moreover, the execution time overhead is only two clock cycles compared to the unprotected implementation.
- We simulated power consumption traces of the systolic array and conducted SCA using these traces. The simulation was performed using an ideal power consumption model where power consumption increases with increased Hamming distance (HD) of the register transition. The attack results show that

the proposed countermeasure randomizes the relation between the attacker-expected intermediate value and power consumption.
- We collected power consumption traces from the wavefront array with our countermeasure implemented in the FPGA and demonstrated that model parameters could not be revealed even when the attacker used 500,000 traces.

2 Preliminarly

2.1 Computation of DNNs

MLP, a representative architecture of DNNs, has an architecture where nodes are connected layer-by-layer, as shown in Fig. 1. Each node applies an activation function (such as ReLU) to the weighted sum of its inputs and propagates the output to each node in the subsequent layer. In other words, for a given node, the output y is defined as

$$u = \sum_{i=0}^{I-1} w_i x_i + \beta, \qquad (1)$$

$$y = f(u), \qquad (2)$$

where x represents the inputs to the node, I is the total number of inputs, w_i is the weight parameter corresponding to each input x_i, β is the bias parameter for each node, and the function f is an activation function. The inputs to a node are the outputs from the previous layer's nodes of the previous layer; the total number of inputs I is equivalent to the number of nodes in the previous layer. The weights w and bias β parameters, which are called model parameters, are determined during the training of the DNN.

The pre-activation output value, u, of a node can be expressed as the sum of the product with the input and weight matrices. Similarly, operations in other DNN architectures (e.g., convolution and attention) can largely be represented as matrix multiplications. Therefore, matrix multiplication hardware, such as systolic arrays, can be used for DNN accelerators.

2.2 Wavefront Array

Wavefront array [11], one of the systolic array architectures [10], is designed for matrix multiplication. This circuit consists of PEs arranged in a tiled structure, and they are connected to adjacent ones. When elements of the input matrix are provided sequentially, each PE performs computations in parallel, and finally, the results are output. Each PE performs multiply-accumulate (MAC) operations on the given inputs a and b. Figure 2 shows an overview of the wavefront array configured with a three-by-three arrangement of PEs. Please note that an 8-bit integer format represents the inputs and weight parameters because we assume an accelerator for lightweight DNNs for edge devices. Furthermore, the results

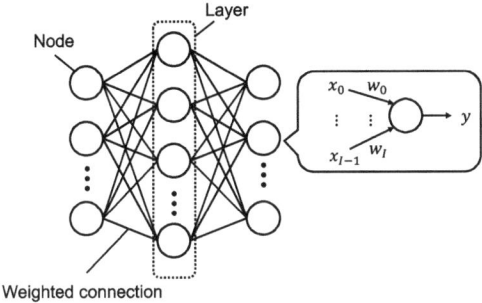

Fig. 1. MLP architecture

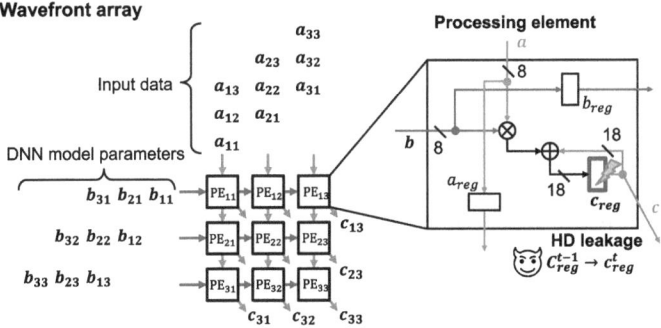

Fig. 2. Overview of 3 × 3-sized wavefront array

of the MAC operations are handled as 18-bit integers to prevent overflow during computations.

This circuit computes the product of a $3 \times N$-sized input matrix A and an $N \times 3$-sized weight parameter matrix B, and outputs a 3×3-sized matrix C like

$$\begin{pmatrix} c_{11} & c_{12} & c_{13} \\ c_{21} & c_{22} & c_{23} \\ c_{31} & c_{32} & c_{33} \end{pmatrix} = \begin{pmatrix} a_{11} & \cdots & a_{1N} \\ a_{21} & \cdots & a_{2N} \\ a_{31} & \cdots & a_{3N} \end{pmatrix} \begin{pmatrix} b_{11} & b_{12} & b_{13} \\ \vdots & \vdots & \vdots \\ b_{N1} & b_{N2} & b_{N3} \end{pmatrix}. \quad (3)$$

Here, a, b, and c with subscriptions denote the elements and their positions of matrices A, B, and C, respectively. Moreover, N is an arbitrary positive integer representing the matrix size.

When the elements of matrices A and B are input sequentially as shown in Fig. 2, the PE_{11} computes c_{11} by $c_{11} = a_{11}b_{11} + a_{12}b_{21} + \cdots + a_{1N}b_{N1}$. Each PE is composed of a multiplier, an adder, and registers. The registers a_{reg} and b_{reg} receive the 8-bit input a and weight b from the top and left, respectively, and forward them to the adjacent PEs on the bottom and right. The 18-bit register c_{reg} accumulates the result of multiplication $a \times b$.

Here, we consider the computation procedure of c_{11} on the PE_{11}. First, the register c_{reg} that stores the intermediate result is initialized by 0 at the time

$t = 0^1$. The PE_{11} receives the input $a_{11}, ..., a_{1N}$ and weight parameter $b_{11}, ..., b_{N1}$ from the time $t = 1$ sequentially, and the stored value in c_reg is transitioned at each time t as;

$$c_\text{reg}^t = \begin{cases} 0 & (t = 0) \\ a_{1t}b_{t1} + c_\text{reg}^{t-1} & (t = 1, \cdots, N) \end{cases} \quad (4)$$

3 Threat Model

3.1 Attack Scenario

In this paper, we define a target device and an attacker as follows.

Target device: Figure 3 shows an overview of the edge device assumed in this paper. The DNN model parameters are stored in non-volatile memory, where they are encrypted and handled except during calculation. Therefore, the attacker cannot steal the parameters by using other techniques such as reading non-volatile memory and tapping the data bus. Moreover, the cryptographic circuits in the device are designed to be tamper-resistant, so the cryptographic key cannot be revealed by attacking the encryption circuit. The DNN accelerator reads the encrypted parameters and decrypts them on the fly.

Attacker: The objective of the attacker is to reveal the model parameters via power-based SCAs by exploiting the knowledge that decrypted model parameters are used in each PE during computation. Here, we assume that the wavefront array shown in Fig. 2 is used for the DNN accelerator. The attacker is considered to know the structure of the wavefront array and the DNN model architecture[2]. The weight parameter b is used for computations in multiple PEs, for example, weight parameter b_{11} is used in $PE_{11}, PE_{12}, PE_{13}$ and is multiplied by a_{11}, a_{21}, a_{31} on these PEs, respectively. Consequently, the attacker can observe leakage corresponding to a single weight parameter multiple times by focusing on the timing when the parameter is used at each PE. The attacker is capable of providing arbitrary inputs to the edge device.

3.2 Correlation Power Analysis on Wavefront Array

Correlation power analysis (CPA) [4] is a technique used to reveal cryptographic keys by exploiting the correlation between the intermediate values and the power consumption during cryptographic processing. We applied this to extract DNN model parameters from the wavefront array and demonstrated using FPGA implementation [20, 22].

It is known that the power consumption when register transitions (i.e., 0 to 1 or 1 to 0) consumes larger power than when the value remains unchanged (i.e.,

---

[1] The time corresponds to clock cycles.
[2] In the case of open-source hardware, the attacker can know the circuit structure of the accelerator. Depending on the application, adopting a specific DNN model architecture may be disclosed as a specification, allowing the attacker to know the model architecture.

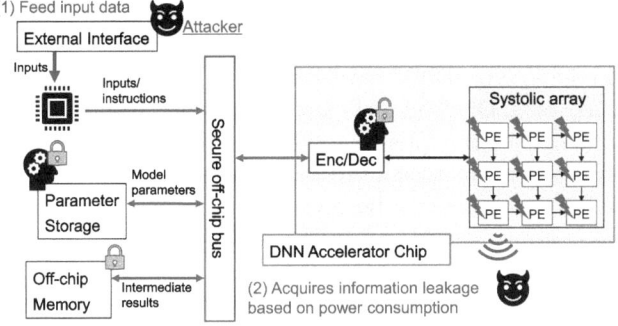

Fig. 3. Overview of assumed target device structure and attack procedure.

0 to 0 or 1 to 1). Consequently, there is a correlation between the Hamming distance of the register value transition and the power consumed. CPA against wavefront array focuses on the value transition of c_{reg} in each PE. When we focus on the register transition from the time $t-1$ to t, the HD of the register transition is given as $\text{HD}(c_{reg}^{t-1}, c_{reg}^{t})$, where the function HD calculates HD of the given input.

The detailed attack procedure is as follows. Here, we consider a specific PE, weight (secret) b used in the PE, and input a multiplied by the b on the PE. The attacker feeds 8-bit known values a^k ($k \in \{0, 1, \cdots, K-1\}$) into the wavefront array K times and measures the circuit's power consumption traces p^k corresponding to the calculation timing of the multiplication of a^k and b. The attacker lists 256 candidates of the secret as $\hat{b} \in \{-128, \cdots, 127\}$. For each candidate $\hat{b}$, the attacker calculates the expected value transition of the register c_{reg} by following Eq. (4) and computes the expected HD $H_{k,\hat{b}}$ for all candidates and given inputs a, where $H_{a^k,\hat{b}}$ is the HD of the target register transition by assuming the given input a^k and candidate $\hat{b}$. The attacker then calculates the correlation between the HD $H_{a^k,\hat{b}}$ and the corresponding power trace p^k using Eq. (5), and the candidate $\hat{b}$ that achieves the highest correlation coefficient is assumed to be the target model parameter b.

$$\rho(\hat{b}) = \frac{\sum_{k=0}^{K-1}(p^k - \bar{p})(H_{a^k,\hat{b}} - \overline{H_{\hat{b}}})}{\sqrt{\sum_{k=0}^{K-1}(p^k - \bar{p})^2}\sqrt{\sum_{k=0}^{K-1}(H_{a^k,\hat{b}} - \overline{H_{\hat{b}}})^2}}. \tag{5}$$

Here, $\bar{p}$ is the average power consumption, and $\overline{H_{\hat{b}}}$ is the average Hamming distance.

4 Related Works

Side-channel attack threats against DNN computations can be classified as follows [3].

Architecture recovery is an attack aimed at stealing a DNN model architecture, such as the number of layers and nodes and the type of layers and activation functions. The DNN model architecture is an element that affects the performance of a DNN model, along with the training data and weight parameters. Attackers can exploit the extracted architecture to train their models or perform subsequent weight recovery attacks. Hua et al. demonstrated that the model architecture can be revealed from memory access patterns in a CNN accelerator implemented on an FPGA [8]. When focusing on power consumption traces, similar to the memory access patterns, the architecture can be revealed by observing the characteristic trace patterns corresponding to the layer types and the number of layers. Such attacks have been reported for various targets, including software [2] and hardware implementations (e.g., NVDLA [7] and BNN [23]). Additionally, attacks targeting multi-tenant FPGAs via remote side-channel attacks have also been reported [17,19,24].

Weight recovery is an attack aimed at stealing the weights of a DNN model. A typical scenario assumes that the attacker has knowledge of the model architecture (such as the number and types of layers). Weights are an important element of knowledge obtained from the training data and training process, and they are valuable. Attackers can exploit the extracted weights to generate adversarial examples [16] or to violate the privacy of the training data [5]. Evaluations targeting software implementations have reported that weight parameters in floating-point format can be revealed [2,14]. Furthermore, evaluations targeting FPGA implementations have reported that 8-bit quantized weight parameters can be extracted. This attack has been reported not only for implementation with a single PE but also with multiple PEs, including systolic arrays [12,20–22]. Combined with the architecture recovery attacks, attacks that reveal the model architecture and the weights from side-channel information during inference on MCU [2] or FPGA-implemented DNN accelerators [6] have been reported.

Input recovery is an attack aimed at recovering the inputs to a DNN model [13]. The basic approach is similar to the weight recovery attacks, but it is characterized by recovering the inputs by exploiting known weight parameters or model architectures.

Countermeasures for these attacks have also been reported. Yan et al. [18] proposed a countermeasure against remote side-channel attacks on multi-tenant FPGAs. They obfuscated the side-channel traces by generating adversarial noise using ring oscillators. Nozaki et al. [15] implemented and evaluated a mitigation technique against CPA-based side-channel attacks by shuffling the order of MAC operations in an MLP implemented on an MCU. Amano et al. [1] proposed a countermeasure against CPA-based side-channel attacks that utilizes the loss of significance (LoS) trick. In this countermeasure, a sufficiently large constant is multiplied by each multiplication in the MAC operation. The intermediate result is finally multiplied by the reciprocal of the constant so that the computation result is unchanged. In the float32 format, adding numbers with significantly different exponent bits causes a large shift in the mantissa, thereby reducing the SNR of leakage based on the HD. This countermeasure assumes float32 operations and cannot be applied to accelerators based on integer operations, which are widely used in edge devices. Our countermeasure introduced in the next section is based on addition and subtraction, and it can be applied to accelerators based on integer operations.

5 Proposed Method

5.1 Arithmetic Masking

We propose an arithmetic masking countermeasure to mitigate CPA-based side-channel analysis on the wavefront array [20,22]. In matrix operations using a 3×3 wavefront array, 8-bit integer random numbers m are inserted to the first and $(N+2)$-th columns of the input matrix, and 8-bit integer random numbers n and $-n$ are inserted to the first and $(N+2)$-th rows of the model parameter matrix.

$$\begin{pmatrix} c_{11} & c_{12} & c_{13} \\ c_{21} & c_{22} & c_{23} \\ c_{31} & c_{32} & c_{33} \end{pmatrix} = \begin{pmatrix} m_1 & a_{11} & \cdots & a_{1N} & m_1 \\ m_2 & a_{21} & \cdots & a_{2N} & m_2 \\ m_3 & a_{31} & \cdots & a_{3N} & m_3 \end{pmatrix} \begin{pmatrix} n_1 & n_2 & n_3 \\ b_{11} & b_{12} & b_{13} \\ \vdots & \vdots & \vdots \\ b_{N1} & b_{N2} & b_{N3} \\ -n_1 & -n_2 & -n_3 \end{pmatrix}. \quad (6)$$

Figure 4 illustrates the data flow of a 3×3 wavefront array with our arithmetic masking countermeasure. For example, in PE_{11}, c_{11} is calculated as follows.

$$c_{11} = m_1 n_1 + a_{11} b_{11} + \cdots + a_{1N} b_{N1} - m_1 n_1 \quad (7)$$

Because the product of the random numbers n_1 and m_1 is finally subtracted, it does not change the result c_{11}.

By inserting random numbers n and m into the matrices as described above, the intermediate value that is stored in c_reg in PE_{11} at each time t is given by

$$c_\text{reg}^t = \begin{cases} 0 & (t=0) \\ m_1 n_1 & (t=1) \\ a_{1t} b_{t1} + c_\text{reg}^{t-1} & (t=2, \cdots, N) \\ -m_1 n_1 + c_\text{reg}^{t-1} & (t=N+2) \end{cases} \quad (8)$$

In the wavefront array without our countermeasure (Eq. (4)), the c_reg transitions from 0 to $a_{11}b_{11}$ at $t=1$. However, in the wavefront array with our countermeasure (Eq. (8)), the c_reg transitions from $m_1 n_1$ to $a_{11}b_{11} + m_1 n_1$ at $t=2$. Because the attacker does not know the random numbers n and m, the transitions of c_reg are unpredictable for the attacker. The mask value $m_1 n_1$ is finally subtracted at $t=N+2$.

To ensure the randomness of the register transition of the c_reg, the probability of occurrence of 0 s and 1 s in each bit position of the mask value at $t=1$ ($m_1 n_1$)

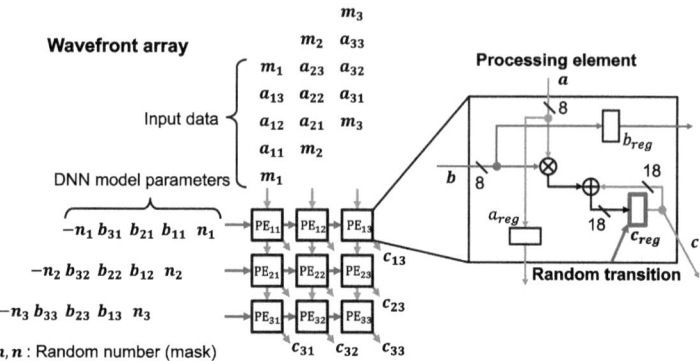

Fig. 4. Overview of data flow of 3×3 wavefront array with our arithmetic masking countermeasure

is required to be uniform. In the following section, we introduce the sampling technique of the random value n to achieve the requirement.

Our proposed countermeasure requires two additional costs. For the first one, it increases the computation time by only two clock cycles by comparing Eq. (4) and (8). The second one requires a random number generator (RNG) to securely generate the random values and insert them into the matrices. A dedicated RNG on the wavefront array can securely insert random numbers into matrices, but it requires an additional implementation cost. Most modern CPUs have built-in hardware RNGs to satisfy security standards; thus, we can reduce the implementation cost by using them. Because the inference software embeds random numbers generated by the RNG on the CPU into matrices and transfers them to the wavefront array, this countermeasure can be applied without modifying the hardware architecture of the wavefront array.

5.2 Sampling Technique for Random Mask

In this countermeasure, it is necessary to impose two constraints on the value range of n. The first constraint is to sample n from the range $[-127, 127]$. This is required so that $-n$ exists for every n.

The second constraint is to require n to be odd. For two unsigned integers m and n, the probability that the l-th bit of $m \cdot n$ is 0 is given[3] by $\frac{2^l+1}{2^{l+1}}$. This indicates that the distribution of 0s and 1s in each bit position of $m \cdot n$ stored in c_{reg} is biased. By requiring n to be odd, the probability becomes $1/2$ for every bit position[3], guaranteeing the randomized register transition.

Although these assume the unsigned integers m and n, we can see similar trends in the signed integers. Figure 5 shows the probability of a 0 appearing in each bit of the product of 8-bit signed integers n and m. The blue line represents the case where n is sampled from the range $[-127, 127]$ (w/o odd selection).

---

[3] Proofs for these probabilities are provided in the Appendix.

The orange line represents the case where n is sampled from $[-127, 127]$ and is restricted to odd values (w/ odd selection); it indicates that 0 and 1 appear with equal probability in every bit position.

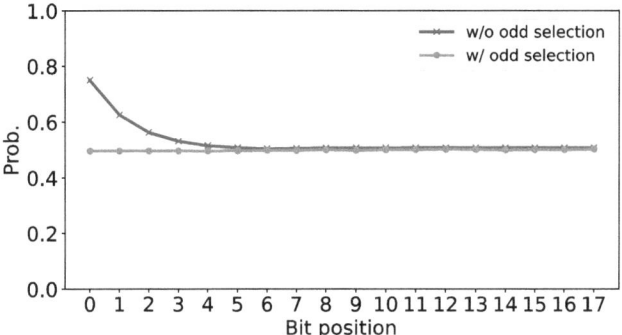

Fig. 5. Proportion that 0 appears in each bit position. The blue line indicates sampling without odd selection, showing a bias towards 0 s near the LSB. The orange line indicates the proposed sampling (odd selection), which results in uniform proportions of 0 s and 1 s per bit position. (Color figure online)

5.3 Evaluation Using HD Leakage Simulation

To evaluate the correlation between power consumption and transition of c_{reg} with and without our countermeasure, we conducted a CPA simulation on a PE shown in Fig. 2. We assume a circuit with only one PE, and its power consumption is assumed to be equal to the HD of the actual transitions of c_{reg}. Please note that we do not include any effects from other circuits or measurement noise. This is an advantageous condition for the attacker exploiting an HD leakage model.

Figure 6 shows the results of CPA performed using 500,000 simulated traces with random inputs a for all 256 possible values of the model parameter b. This figure arranges all combinations of the actual (target) model parameter (horizontal axis) and the candidate model parameter (vertical axis) in a tiled format. For each target model parameter, the cell corresponding to the candidate with the highest correlation value in CPA is colored. If the target and estimated parameters match, the cell is colored red; if they do not match, it is colored black.

Figure 6a shows the unprotected case, assuming that CPA is performed at the $t = 1$ timing in Eq. (4). Because the simulated power consumption is the HD of the transition of c_{reg}, the correct parameter candidates achieved a correlation value of 1.0, which is the highest. Therefore, the estimated model parameter matched the target parameter, and the diagonal cells are colored red. It indicates that the attacker can reveal all parameters from unprotected implementations.

Figure 6b shows the result with our arithmetic masking countermeasure. The attacker's estimations had been divided into -127 or 127, and all cells were colored black (incorrect estimation) except for the cases where the target parameter is one of these values. This result indicates that the register transition is unpredictable for the attacker.

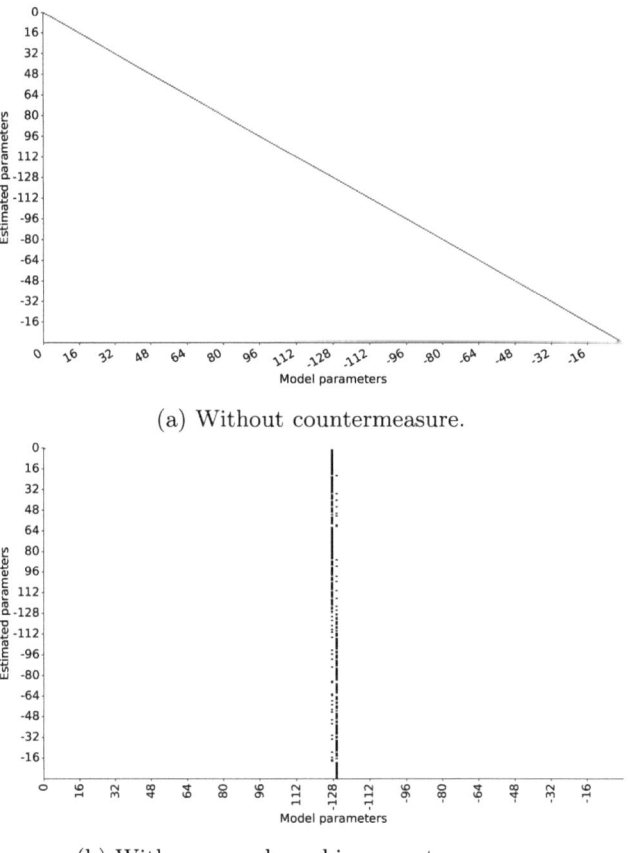

(a) Without countermeasure.

(b) With proposed masking countermeasure.

Fig. 6. Result of CPA simulation for all possible values of model parameters. Red cells indicate that the attacker successfully revealed, and black cells indicate that the attacker failed to estimate. (Color figure online)

6 Experiments

6.1 Experimental Setup

We implemented the 3×3 wavefront array on an FPGA and measured power consumption (supply voltage drops) traces to evaluate our proposed countermeasure. Our experimental setups are shown in Fig. 7, where the evaluation board is the side-channel attack evaluation standard board ZUIHO, which is equipped with a Xilinx Spartan3A FPGA operating at 2MHz, developed by the National Institute of Advanced Industrial Science and Technology (AIST), Japan. We used an oscilloscope DSOX6004A (maximum sampling rate 20 GSa/s, bandwidth 2.5 GHz) from Keysight Technologies. We followed the previous works [20, 22], the DNN model parameters were set as a 3×3 weight parameter matrix B given in Eq. (9).

$$B = \begin{pmatrix} -92 & 122 & 22 \\ -20 & -16 & 46 \\ -104 & -73 & 73 \end{pmatrix} \quad (9)$$

Please note that we focused only on the parameters in the first row ($-92, 122,$ and 22). These elements are used in the multiplication at time $t = 1$ (without countermeasure) and $t = 2$ (with countermeasure) for each of the nine PEs, whereas the remaining parameters are used at the subsequent computation. The register c_{reg} accumulates the intermediate results sequentially. Therefore, if the attacker estimates incorrect parameters at first, the attacker makes incorrect assumptions about subsequent register transitions and estimates the wrong parameters for subsequent weight parameters. That is, revealing the parameters of the first row $b_{11} = -92, b_{12} = 122, b_{13} = 22$ is the initial step that the attacker succeeds in the attack; In this study, we evaluate whether this step can be prevented.

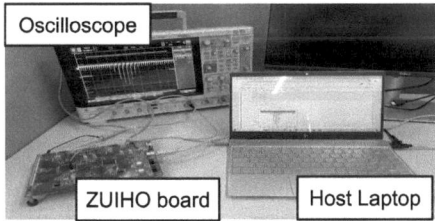

Fig. 7. Experimental setup.

For the unprotected setup, the 3×3 input matrix A and weight parameter matrix B are provided to the wavefront array. For the protected setup, which equips our countermeasure, the random numbers m, n are inserted into the matrices; the 3×5 input matrix A and 5×3 weight parameter matrix B are provided to the wavefront array. We acquired 500,000 power traces while varying the input matrix A. Figure 8 shows the average power traces from the wavefront array with and without our countermeasure. We noted examples of calculations performed at the timing of specific voltage drops in the figure; Please note that the calculations performed at each timing are not limited to those shown because each PE operates in parallel. When the attacker conducts CPA, the points of interest (PoI) are set near the timing at which the target parameter b is used in the multiplication.

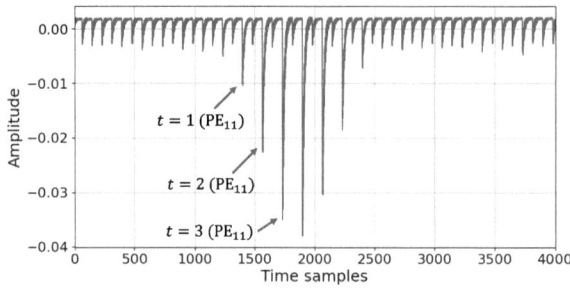

(a) Without countermeasure.

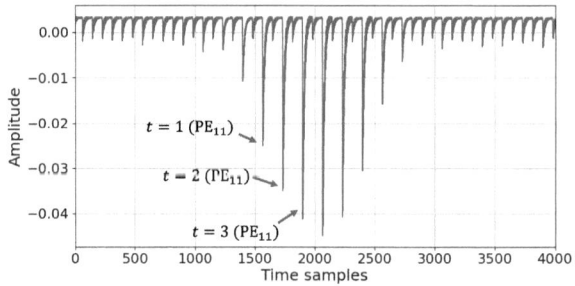

(b) With countermeasure.

Fig. 8. Mean traces of power supply voltage.

6.2 Results

Figure 9 lists the results of the CPA conducted at time $t = 1$ on each PE. The horizontal axis represents the number of traces used for the attack, and the vertical axis represents the correlation value. Each plot corresponds to each candidate of the model parameter; red indicates the correct (target) parameter, and gray indicates the other (incorrect) parameter. The attack succeeds when the correct candidate (red) achieves the highest correlation; the corresponding PEs are titled in red and bold.

Figure 9a shows the results of the unprotected implementation. For the model parameters -92 and 122, the correct parameter achieved the highest correlation value in two PEs, specifically in PE_{21} and PE_{31} for -92, and in PE_{12} and PE_{32} for 122. Furthermore, the model parameter 22 was successfully revealed in PE_{13}. Even if PEs that the attacker estimated incorrect parameters, the correct parameter achieved a high correlation value. These results are almost equivalent to those of previous works [20, 22]. The reason the attack failed in some PEs can be considered that measurement noise affects the rank of the correlation values between the target (correct) parameter and its bit-shifted variants. We have described that CPA on the multiplication observes high correlation coefficients not only for the target parameter but also for its bit-shifted variants [20, 22].

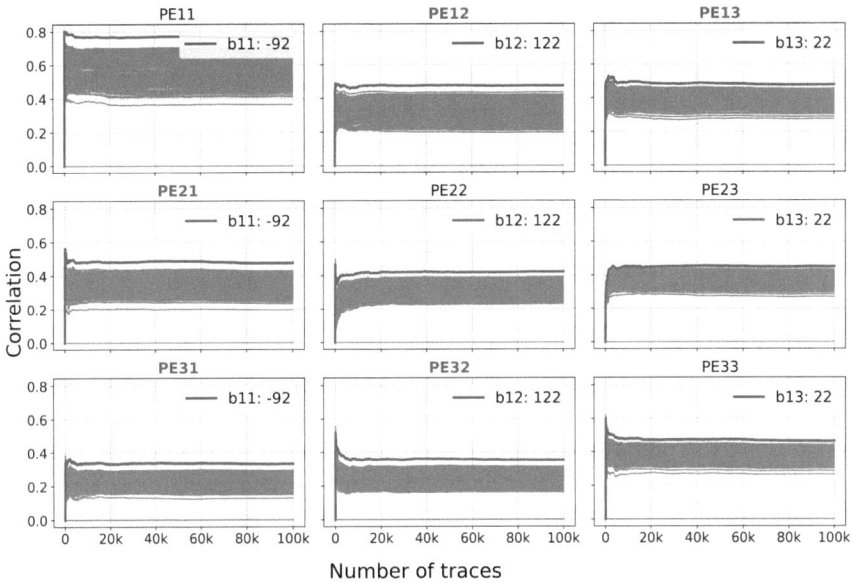

(a) Without countermeasure.

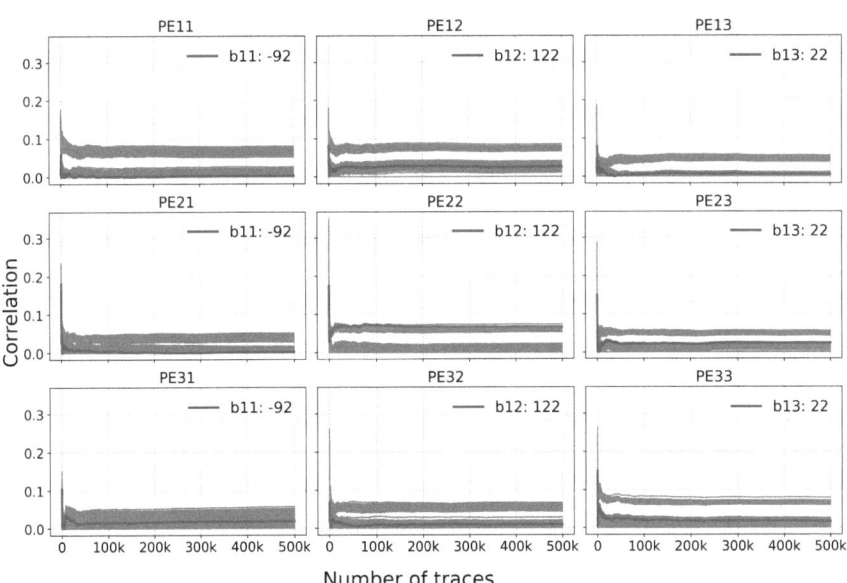

(b) With masking countermeasure.

Fig. 9. Correlation coefficient over the number of traces for all candidates. (Color figure online)

Namely, the measurement noise affected the correlation coefficients between the target parameter and its bit-shifted variants, and their rank changed.

Figure 9b shows the results of the protected implementation, which adopts our arithmetic masking countermeasure. In this case, the parameters could not be revealed in all the PEs, and the correct parameter (red) correlation represented a significantly lower value than the unprotected case. This indicates that our masking countermeasure successfully randomizes the transition of the register that the attacker focused on, and it decreases the correlation significantly.

7 Conclusion

In this paper, we proposed an arithmetic masking countermeasure to mitigate CPA on a wavefront array, part of DNN accelerators. This countermeasure inserts random values into matrices before they are multiplied; it does not require any modifications to the circuit implementation and consumes only two additional clock cycles. We evaluated this countermeasure through simulation and FPGA implementation. Simulation results based on a theoretical HD leakage model without noise demonstrate that even with 500,000 traces, the attacker could not reveal any parameters. Experimental results using the power traces from the FPGA similarly showed that the model parameters could not be revealed under 500,000 traces. These results indicate that the proposed arithmetic masking countermeasure mitigated the threat of CPA on the wavefront array.

Acknowledgements. This research was funded by JST AIP Acceleration Research grant number JPMJCR23U3.

Appendix

Theorem 1. *Let l be a positive integer and let $m, n \in \{0, 1, \ldots, 2^l - 1\}$. Then the proportion that the l-th binary digit (i.e., the coefficient of 2^{l-1}) of the product $m \cdot n$ is 0 (equivalently, $m \cdot n \mod 2^l < 2^{l-1}$) is*

$$\frac{2^l + 1}{2^{l+1}}. \tag{10}$$

Proof. Because $m, n \in \{0, 1, \ldots, 2^l - 1\}$, the total number of pairs is $2^l \cdot 2^l = 2^{2l}$.

We count the number of pairs (m, n) satisfying

$$m \cdot n \mod 2^l < 2^{l-1}, \tag{11}$$

by considering three cases based on the value of n.

Case 1. $n = 0$. In this case, $m \cdot n = 0$ for all m, so Eq. (11) holds on $N_0 = 2^l$ pairs.

Case 2. n is odd. Because $\gcd(n, 2^l) = 1$, it has a multiplicative inverse element modulo 2^l. Therefore, the mapping

$$m \mapsto m \cdot n \mod 2^l \tag{12}$$

is a bijection on $\{0, 1, \ldots, 2^l - 1\}$, and exactly half of the values of m satisfy Eq. (11); that is, for each odd n, there are 2^{l-1} choices for m. As there are 2^{l-1} odd numbers in $\{0, 1, \ldots, 2^l - 1\}$, the total number in this case is

$$N_{\text{odd}} = 2^{l-1} \cdot 2^{l-1} = 2^{2l-2}. \tag{13}$$

Case 3. n is even and nonzero. We can write $n = 2^r \cdot n'$, $(1 \leq r \leq l-1)$ where n' is an odd integer in $\{0, 1, \ldots, 2^{l-r} - 1\}$. For a fixed r, the number of choices for n' is 2^{l-r-1}, because half of the numbers in $\{0, 1, \ldots, 2^{l-r} - 1\}$ are odd. Because $m \cdot n \mod 2^l = 2^r \cdot (m \cdot n') \mod 2^l$, condition Eq. (11) becomes

$$2^r \cdot (m \cdot n') \mod 2^l < 2^{l-1}, \tag{14}$$

which is equivalent to

$$m \cdot n' \mod 2^{l-r} < 2^{l-1-r}. \tag{15}$$

Because n' is odd, for fixed n, the number of $m \in \{0, 1, \ldots, 2^l - 1\}$ satisfying Eq. (11) is 2^{l-1-r} on modulo 2^{l-r}, and each occurs 2^r times. Hence, for a fixed n, the number of m is

$$2^{l-1-r} \cdot 2^r = 2^{l-1}. \tag{16}$$

Thus, for fixed r, the total number of pairs is

$$2^{l-r-1} \cdot 2^{l-1} = 2^{2l-r-2}. \tag{17}$$

Summing over $r = 1, \ldots, l-1$, we obtain

$$N_{\text{even}} = \sum_{r=1}^{l-1} 2^{2l-r-2} = 2^{l-1}(2^{l-1} - 1). \tag{18}$$

Adding the combinations for all three cases, the total number of pairs satisfying Eq. (11) is

$$\begin{aligned} N_{\text{cond}} &= N_0 + N_{\text{odd}} + N_{\text{even}} \\ &= 2^{l-1}(2^l + 1). \end{aligned}$$

Thus, the proportion of (m, n) satisfying Eq. (11) in all combinations is

$$\frac{2^{l-1}(2^l + 1)}{2^{2l}} = \frac{2^l + 1}{2^{l+1}}. \tag{19}$$

□

Theorem 2. *Let l be a positive integer and consider $m, n \in \{0, 1, \ldots, 2^l - 1\}$ with the restriction that n is odd. The proportion that the l-th binary digit (i.e., the coefficient of 2^{l-1}) of the product $m \cdot n$ is 0 (equivalently, $m \cdot n \mod 2^l < 2^{l-1}$) is $\frac{1}{2}$.*

Proof. By Eq. 13, the total number of pairs satisfying condition Eq. (11) when n is odd is
$$N_{\text{odd}} = 2^{2l-2}. \tag{20}$$
The total number of pairs, when n is odd, is 2^{2l-1}. Hence, the proportion of (m, n) satisfying Eq. (11) in all combinations is
$$\frac{2^{2l-2}}{2^{2l-1}} = \frac{1}{2}. \tag{21}$$
□

References

1. Amano, R., Sakiyama, K., Miyahara, D., Li, Y.: Los trick: countermeasure against CPA for DNN models using loss of significance in multiply-accumulate operations. In: Twelfth International Symposium on Computing and Networking, CANDAR 2024 - Workshops, Naha, Japan, 26-29 November 2024, pp. 240–246. IEEE (2024). https://doi.org/10.1109/CANDARW64572.2024.00046
2. Batina, L., Bhasin, S., Jap, D., Picek, S.: CSI NN: reverse engineering of neural network architectures through electromagnetic side channel. In: 28th USENIX Security Symposium, USENIX Security 2019, Santa Clara, CA, USA, 14-16 August 2019, pp. 515–532. USENIX Association (2019)
3. Bhasin, S., Jap, D., Picek, S.: On (in)security of edge-based machine learning against electromagnetic side-channels. In: 2022 IEEE International Symposium on Electromagnetic Compatibility & Signal/Power Integrity (EMCSI), pp. 262–267 (2022). https://doi.org/10.1109/EMCSI39492.2022.9889639
4. Brier, E., Clavier, C., Olivier, F.: Correlation power analysis with a leakage model. In: Cryptographic Hardware and Embedded Systems - CHES 2004: 6th International Workshop Cambridge, MA, USA, 11-13 August 2004. Proceedings. LNCS, vol. 3156, pp. 16–29. Springer (2004). https://doi.org/10.1007/978-3-540-28632-5_2
5. Fredrikson, M., Lantz, E., Jha, S., Lin, S.M., Page, D., Ristenpart, T.: Privacy in pharmacogenetics: an end-to-end case study of personalized warfarin dosing. In: Proceedings of the 23rd USENIX Security Symposium, San Diego, CA, USA, 20-22 August 2014, pp. 17–32. USENIX Association (2014)
6. Gao, Y., Ma, H., Yan, M., He, J., Zhao, Y., Jin, Y.: NNLEAK: an AI-oriented DNN model extraction attack through multi-stage side channel analysis. In: Asian Hardware Oriented Security and Trust Symposium, AsianHOST 2023, Tianjin, China, 13-15 December 2023, pp. 1–6. IEEE (2023). https://doi.org/10.1109/ASIANHOST59942.2023.10409396
7. Gupta, N., Jati, A., Chattopadhyay, A.: AI attacks AI: recovering neural network architecture from NVDLA using ai-assisted side channel attack. IACR Cryptol. ePrint Arch, p. 368 (2023)

8. Hua, W., Zhang, Z., Suh, G.E.: Reverse engineering convolutional neural networks through side-channel information leaks. In: Proceedings of the 55th Annual Design Automation Conference, DAC 2018, San Francisco, CA, USA, 24-29 June 2018, pp. 4:1–4:6. ACM (2018). https://doi.org/10.1145/3195970.3196105
9. Jouppi, N.P., et al.: In-datacenter performance analysis of a tensor processing unit. In: Proceedings of the 44th Annual International Symposium on Computer Architecture, ISCA 2017, Toronto, ON, Canada, 24-28 June 2017. pp. 1–12. ACM (2017). https://doi.org/10.1145/3079856.3080246
10. Kung, H.T.: Why systolic architectures? Computer **15**(1), 37–46 (1982). https://doi.org/10.1109/MC.1982.1653825
11. Kung, S., Arun, K.S., Gal-Ezer, R.J., Rao, D.V.B.: Wavefront array processor: language, architecture, and applications. IEEE Trans. Comput. **31**(11), 1054–1066 (1982). https://doi.org/10.1109/TC.1982.1675922
12. Li, G., Tiwari, M., Orshansky, M.: Power-based attacks on spatial DNN accelerators. ACM J. Emerg. Technol. Comput. Syst. **18**(3), 58:1–58:18 (2022). https://doi.org/10.1145/3491219
13. Moini, S., Tian, S., Holcomb, D.E., Szefer, J., Tessier, R.: Power side-channel attacks on BNN accelerators in remote fpgas. IEEE J. Emerg. Sel. Topics Circuits Syst. **11**(2), 357–370 (2021). https://doi.org/10.1109/JETCAS.2021.3074608
14. Nozaki, H., Kobara, K.: Power analysis of floating-point operations for leakage resistance evaluation of neural network model parameters. IEICE Trans. Fundam. Electron. Commun. Comput. Sci. **107**(3), 331–343 (2024). https://doi.org/10.1587/TRANSFUN.2023CIP0012
15. Nozaki, Y., Yoshikawa, M.: Shuffling countermeasure against power side-channel attack for MLP with software implementation. In: 2021 IEEE 4th International Conference on Electronics and Communication Engineering (ICECE), pp. 39–42 (2021). https://doi.org/10.1109/ICECE54449.2021.9674668
16. Szegedy, C., et al.: Intriguing properties of neural networks. In: 2nd International Conference on Learning Representations, ICLR 2014, Banff, AB, Canada, 14-16 April 2014, Conference Track Proceedings (2014)
17. Tian, S., Moini, S., Wolnikowski, A., Holcomb, D.E., Tessier, R., Szefer, J.: Remote power attacks on the versatile tensor accelerator in multi-tenant FPGAS. In: 29th IEEE Annual International Symposium on Field-Programmable Custom Computing Machines, FCCM 2021, Orlando, FL, USA, 9-12 May 2021, pp. 242–246. IEEE (2021). https://doi.org/10.1109/FCCM51124.2021.00037
18. Yan, X., Chang, C., Zhang, T.: Defense against ml-based power side-channel attacks on DNN accelerators with adversarial attacks. CoRR abs/2312.04035 (2023). https://doi.org/10.48550/ARXIV.2312.04035
19. Yan, X., et al.: MERCURY: an automated remote side-channel attack to nvidia deep learning accelerator. In: International Conference on Field Programmable Technology, ICFPT 2023, Yokohama, Japan, 12-14 December 2023, pp. 188–197. IEEE (2023). https://doi.org/10.1109/ICFPT59805.2023.00026
20. Yoshida, K., Kubota, T., Okura, S., Shiozaki, M., Fujino, T.: Model reverse-engineering attack using correlation power analysis against systolic array based neural network accelerator. In: IEEE International Symposium on Circuits and Systems, ISCAS 2020, Sevilla, Spain, 10-21 October 2020, pp. 1–5. IEEE (2020). https://doi.org/10.1109/ISCAS45731.2020.9180580
21. Yoshida, K., Kubota, T., Shiozaki, M., Fujino, T.: Model-extraction attack against FPGA-DNN accelerator utilizing correlation electromagnetic analysis. In: 27th

IEEE Annual International Symposium on Field-Programmable Custom Computing Machines, FCCM 2019, San Diego, CA, USA, April 28 - May 1, 2019, p. 318. IEEE (2019). https://doi.org/10.1109/FCCM.2019.00059
22. Yoshida, K., Shiozaki, M., Okura, S., Kubota, T., Fujino, T.: Model reverse-engineering attack against systolic-array-based DNN accelerator using correlation power analysis. IEICE Trans. Fundam. Electron. Commun. Comput. Sci. **104-A**(1), 152–161 (2021). https://doi.org/10.1587/TRANSFUN.2020CIP0024
23. Yu, H., Ma, H., Yang, K., Zhao, Y., Jin, Y.: DeepEM: deep neural networks model recovery through EM side-channel information leakage. In: 2020 IEEE International Symposium on Hardware Oriented Security and Trust, HOST 2020, San Jose, CA, USA, 7-11 December 2020, pp. 209–218. IEEE (2020). https://doi.org/10.1109/HOST45689.2020.9300274
24. Zhang, Y., Yasaei, R., Chen, H., Li, Z., Faruque, M.A.A.: Stealing neural network structure through remote FPGA side-channel analysis. IEEE Trans. Inf. Forensics Secur. **16**, 4377–4388 (2021). https://doi.org/10.1109/TIFS.2021.3106169

Investigation of EM Fault Injection on Emerging Lightweight Neural Network Hardware

Bhanprakash Goswami[ID], Reejit Chetry, Chithambara Moorthii J[ID], and Manan Suri[✉][ID]

Indian Institute of Technology Delhi, New Delhi, India
manansuri@ee.iitd.ac.in

Abstract. This study investigates electromagnetic fault injection (EMFI) on lightweight neural networks hardware. Three compact neural networks (MobileNet, ResNet, EfficientNet) were trained first on Fashion-MNIST and later with CIFAR-10 datasets, then implemented on a custom NVM-based lightweight tinyML hardware platform for EMFI susceptibility testing. We demonstrate that the stored model weights on NVM, can be corrupted by EM injection on the NVM chip during network loading. Further, we demonstrate that the EMFI corrupted weights can lead upto 40% reduction in inference accuracy in case of highly sensitive lightweight models.

Keywords: Hardware Security · Electromagnetic Fault Injection · Lightweight Neural Networks · FRAM · Neural Networks · TinyML Hardware · Embedded AI

1 Introduction

Deploying Deep Neural Network (DNN) models has become ubiquitous, powering various applications across industries and devices. DNNs are now integral to computer vision, natural language processing, healthcare diagnostics, finance, agriculture, and cybersecurity, enabling machines to interpret images, understand language, detect fraud, optimize crop yields, and identify security threats in real-time. Highly accurate DNN models are generally larger because achieving better performance requires more complex architectures with more parameters, layers, and operations.

The DNNs exhibit a certain level of resistance to fault-injection attacks. The lower fault vulnerability of bigger models is closely linked to their increased model capacity and redundancy [1]. This redundancy means that even if parts of the model are compromised or exposed to adversarial attacks, other parts can compensate, thereby reducing the overall vulnerability. However, this increase in size comes at the cost of greater memory usage, longer inference time, and higher energy consumption, which can limit deployment on resource-constrained devices.

The rise of lightweight or low resource edge neural networks or tinyML networks, a subset of artificial neural networks (NNs) optimized for low-power edge devices, has enabled the deployment of neural networks in resource-constrained environments such as IoT devices, wearables, and embedded systems. Where low weight refers to networks with parameter size of less than 5MB. These models are typically trained off-chip, and the generated weights are stored in Non-Volatile Memory (NVM) chips for inference tasks. NVM in general, Ferroelectric Random Access Memory (FRAM) in particular has emerged as a promising candidate for such applications due to its low power consumption, high endurance, and fast read/write speeds [2,3]. However, the security of NVM-based emerging hardware systems has come under scrutiny due to their susceptibility to hardware-based attacks, particularly fault injection (FI) techniques [4–7].

Electromagnetic Fault Injection (EMFI) is a powerful non-invasive attack method that exploits the sensitivity of electronic components to electromagnetic interference. By inducing transient faults in the system, adversaries can manipulate the behavior of memory chips and corrupt stored data. While previous research has explored the impact of voltage and temperature-based FI on NVM chips, the effects of EMFI on NVM-based lightweight tinyML hardware remain largely unexplored.

In this work, we experimentally analyze the susceptibility of emerging NVM-based tinyML hardware to EMFI attacks. We target NVM chip and evaluate its resilience to EM pulses during memory read operations. Our key contributions are:

- Setup of NVM-based hardware platform for EMFI susceptibility testing.
- EMFI characterization of commerical FRAM chips.
- Analysis of weight corruption and its impact on the inference accuracy of lightweight models.

2 Experiments and Results

2.1 Threat Model

Advanced tinyML hardware neural networks utilizing emerging non-volatile memory (NVM) introduces critical security vulnerabilities through electromagnetic fault-injection (EMFI) attacks, particularly during the network loading i.e. transfer of neural network model from NVM to SRAM of the computing unit.

Attackers may target these NVM-based tinyML hardware implementations through weaknesses stemming from three critical factors: (1) architectural separation between NVM storing model weights and processing units creates localized attack surfaces, enabling electromagnetic side-channel and EMFI exploitation during model transfers; (2) physical accessibility of these edge devices allows direct hardware probing for EMFI or side channel analysis (SCA); and (3) frequent model reloading by authorized users generates recurring possibility of additional current/voltage through EM flux injection. Figure 1 illustrates the threat model proposed in this study for tinyML hardware.

We assume the following conditions for our threat model:

Table 1. Lightweight NN Models Studied

Model	MobileNet	ResNet	EfficientNet
Model depth	55	8	132
Training/Test data	FMNIST (60k/10k)		
Test accuracy(%)	89–91.5	85–90.8	84–91.7
Total weights	3.24 MB	58.3 KB	4.06 MB
Weights discrete representation = 8 bits			

- The adversary has physical access to the edge hardware device and can generate EM pulses in close proximity to the device.
- The attack is launched during the memory read operation of trained weights, with the goal of corrupting the weights and reducing inference accuracy.
- The adversary operates in a black-box setting, with no prior knowledge of the NN model architecture or weights.

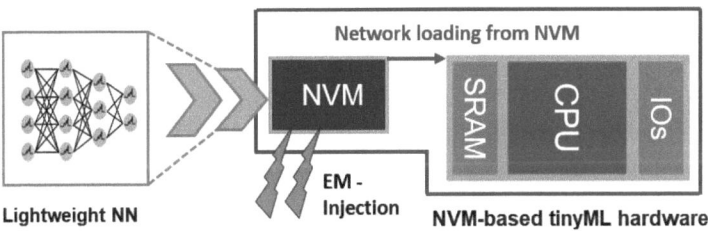

Fig. 1. Threat model of the NVM-based edge tinyML hardware.

2.2 Model Mapping to Experimental Setup

Three different tinyML models were used: MobileNet [9], ResNet [10], and EfficientNet [11]. Each model was trained using the standard Fashion-MNIST (FMNIST) [12] dataset, and later experiments were performed with CIFAR-10 dataset. The details of these used models are summarized in Table 1. Off-chip training is used to get the model weights because of the resource limitations on the tinyML edge devices. In order to facilitate inference procedures, the resulting model weights are subsequently stored on hardware as discrete numerical values (8 bits format in this case).

The models were trained using the TensorFlow framework. The ResNet architecture uses residual blocks to reduce the vanishing gradient problem i.e. learning is slow or none. Each residual block in our model consists of two convolutional

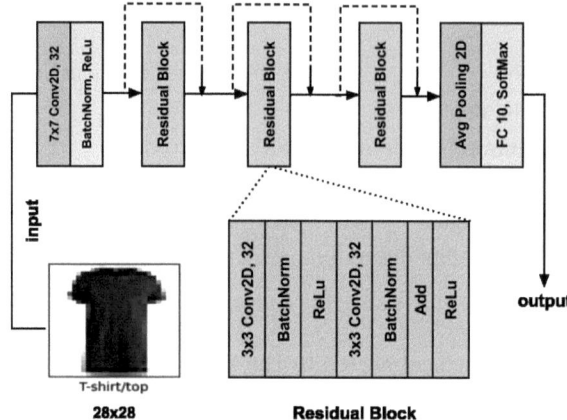

Fig. 2. Architecture of ResNet Neural Network implemented for our experiments.

layers with 32 filters of size 3 × 3 and a stride of (1,1). Figure 2 depicts the architecture of the ResNet model. The Conv2D layer is followed by batch normalisation and ReLU activation functions. The Residual blocks consist of shortcut connections which enables the network to learn identity mappings. The input shape of the images is (28,28,1) and the model starts with an initial convolutional layer with 32 7 × 7 filters, followed by batch normalisation and ReLU activation. Then we further reduce the spatial dimensions of the feature maps by a max pooling layer with a pool size of (3,3).

The overall structure of the model consists of three residual blocks, each containing two convolution layers. These layers are constrained using Min-Max normalisation to ensure weight stability and regularized using L2 regularization. A global average pooling layer is used after the stack of residual blocks to reduce feature maps. After that, a fully connected dense layer with a softmax activation function produces the final class probabilities. The dense layer is also regularized and limited.

2.3 Custom FPGA-NVM Based EMFI Setup

Figure 3(a) depicts a concise image of the EMFI experimental setup. The setup consists of an EM pulse generator, control circuitry for synchronization, an FPGA-based interface for FRAM chip communication, and a host PC to provide necessary input and control parameters. The EM pulse generator is used to induce controlled electromagnetic interference during weight transfer from NVM to the local SRAM of the computing unit. The parallel interface between the computing unit (in FPGA) and the FRAM (or FeRAM) chip allow programming, erase, and memory read operations. The block diagram of the setup is shown in Fig. 3(b). The edge tinyML hardware implementation utilizes a parallel FRAM chip (1-Mbit capacity, organized as 64K × 16-bit words) [8] for model storage, interfaced through the Zedboard's built-in FMC connector.

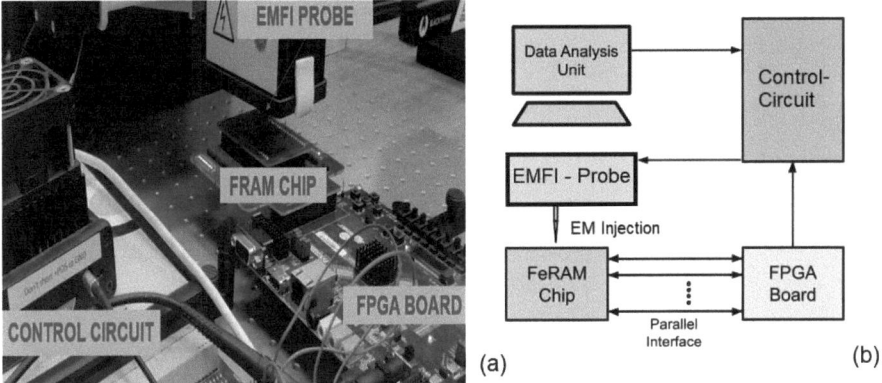

Fig. 3. (a) The custom FPGA-NVM experimental setup for EMFI. (b) Illustrative block diagram of the setup.

2.4 EMFI Characterization of FRAM

Prior to performing EM injection, we need to determine the region of interest (RoI) on top of the FRAM chip surface. One method could be hit and trial, i.e., we move the EMFI probe to each point on the chip top surface and see the effect of EMFI at every point. This hit-and-trial method is time-consuming. Instead of probing every point on the chip top surface, we use the X-Y EM intensity plots to probe a few distinct points. The X-Y EM intensity plots for any memory chip depict the magnitude of EM emanations from every point of that chip surface during memory operations.

As discussed in [13], there are two different types of points such as P1 and P2 on the FRAM chip surface, depicted in Fig. 4 (a), (b). At points similar to P1, EM emanations remains unchanged during any change in memory operations. On the other side, points similar to P2, called as hotspot in [13], provides varying EM emission with change in memory operations. Therefore, we analyze the characteristics of the FRAM chip towards EM injection at both types of points or regions near these points. For better clarity, we named regions near P1 and P2 as RoI-1 and RoI-2, respectively.

We use fully controlled EMFI probe for EM injection, its maximum voltage over coil is 450 V ($+/-10\%$) and we keep EM pulse power at 100%. We inject EM intensity at RoI-1, while performing memory read operation, and observed that the data values are getting replaced with faulty data values. The newly added data value in the memory due to EM injection, posses random value. However, we have observed that the count of the data value "0x00" among newly added data values remains high. Therefore, we target the RoI-1 to increase the 0x00 fault data value in the stored memory data. On the other hand, injecting the EM intensity at the RoI-2, leads to high data value fault. Mostly, count of 0xFF, 0x74, 0x7C faulty data values remains high, apart from other added faulty random values. This EM fault behavior has been depicted in Fig. 4(c).

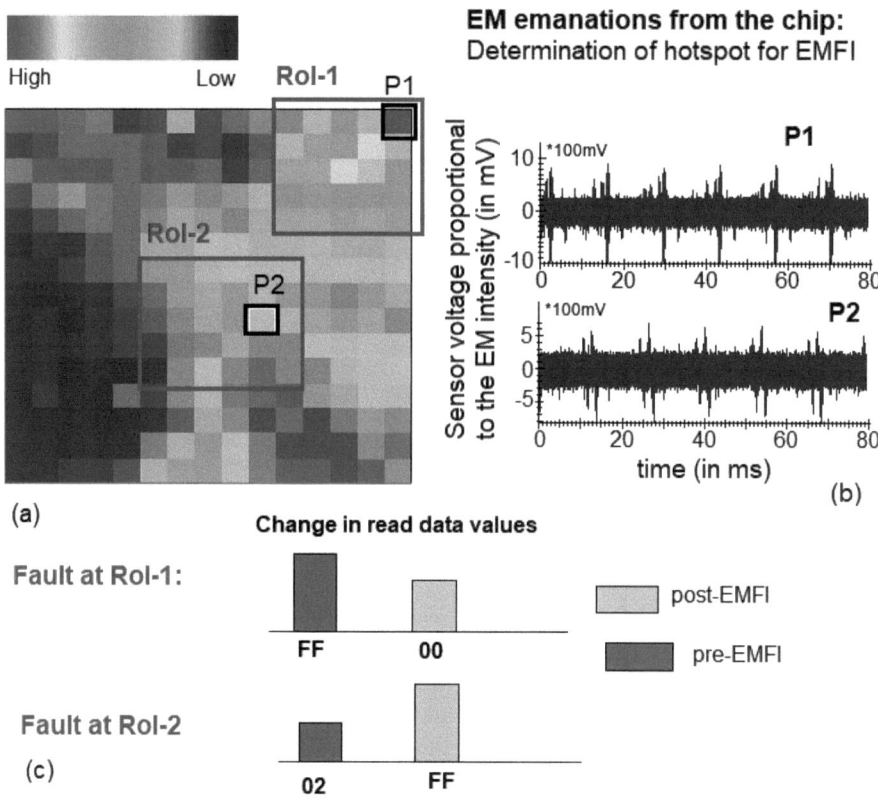

Fig. 4. (a) X-Y EM intensity plot while scanning the top surface of the FRAM chip during write operation, adopted from [13]. (b) Sample of EM emanations collected from P1 and P2 location on the chip surface using EM-probe. (c) Effect of EMFI on the read data values at RoI-1, and RoI-2

Further, we store the weights of the pre-trained ResNet model in the FRAM chip, and inject the EM intensity at both RoIs, one at a time, during network loading. The change in weights, corresponding to the EMFI at both RoIs has been depicted in Fig. 5. This confirms the trend that EMFI regions like RoI-1 leads to increase the count of low data values/weights such as 0x00. Also, we should target the regions such as RoI-2, with intention to increase the count of high data values/weights (i.e. 0xFF).

2.5 EMFI Results

Algorithmic description of the procedure for the proposed EMFI attack on the edge tinyML hardware has been shown in Fig. 6. First we generate the NN weights by training the off-chip training. The generated analog weights are then discretized to 8-bit format, and stored in the NVM. While loading the model

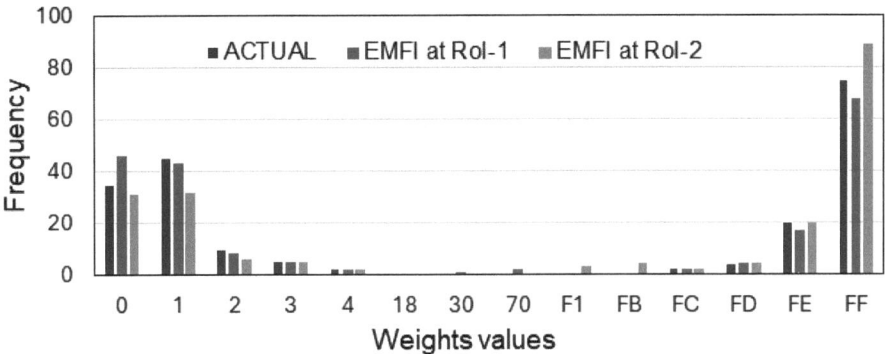

Fig. 5. A sample of 200 weights from layer-2 of the pre-trained ResNet model, and change in count of weights post-EMFI at RoI-1 and RoI-2.

from the NVM to the processor, EM is injected at the RoI. We perform the EMFI experiments again, after mapping the Lightweight NN models to FPGA-FRAM setup, one model at a time, for multiple cycles. Note that adversary is assumed to have no information about the layout design of the target chip.

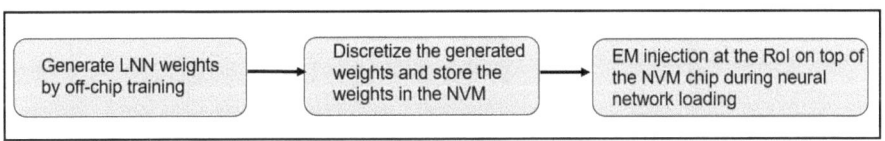

Fig. 6. Attack methodology.

Figure 7 shows change in inference accuracy post-EMFI attack at RoI-2 on various sensitive layers of ResNet model for 100 cycles. Layer-1 (convolution) is much sensitive to weight change that even single weight change causes upto 40% decrease in inference accuracy of the ResNet model. We have also shown that to obtain a consistent decrease in inference by 30%, we need to inject fault such that 32 number of different weights in this layer-1 gets altered.

We also observed that there are some less sensitive convolution layers in the ResNet model such as layer-2 and layer-4. Even changing 32 number of weights in these layers hardly reduces inference accuracy of the model by 20%. Figure 8 shows EMFI results for the ResNet model trained and validated with CIFAR-10 dataset. Again attack was carried out at RoI-2 on layer-1 of the model for 100 cycles.

Similarly, we also performed the EMFI attack at RoI-2 for the EfficientNet model, results are depicted in Fig. 9. In order to achieve 30% reduction in inference accuracy for this model consistently, we require to replace at least 90 number of weights by a high value faulty weight.

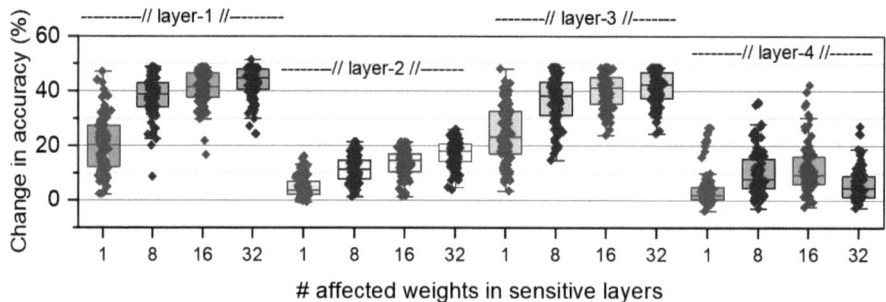

Fig. 7. EMFI results for ResNet: change in inference accuracy post-EMFI attack at RoI-2 on various sensitive layers of the model for 100 cycles in each case for FMNIST dataset.

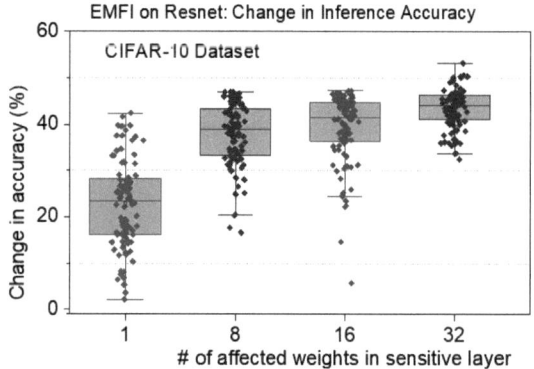

Fig. 8. EMFI result for ResNet: change in inference accuracy post-EMFI attack at RoI-2 on layer-1 of the model for 100 cycles for CIFAR-10 dataset.

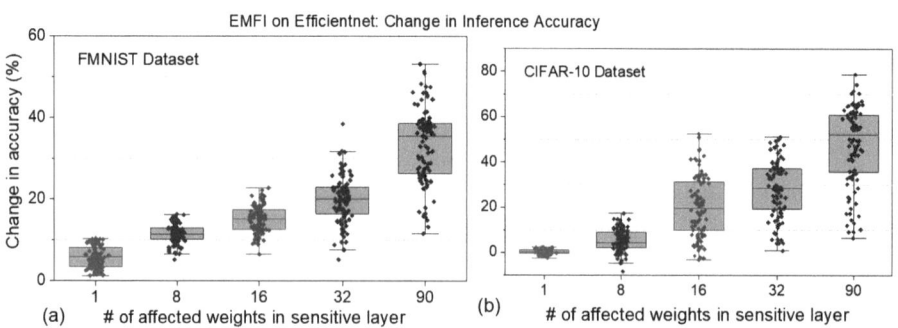

Fig. 9. EMFI results for EfficientNet: change in inference accuracy post-EMFI attack at RoI-2 on a sensitive layer of the model for 100 cycles in each case for (a) FMNIST (b) CIFAR-10 datasets.

Compared to the EfficientNet, the MobileNet model was found more fault tolerant. Even altering 32 number of weights in a sensitive layer of the MobileNet could reduce the inference accuracy by 10%. We had to run EMFI attack multiple times to bring changes in the 128 number of weights. Even for the case of 128 number of weights change, the inference accuracy reduction in the MobileNet model was not consistent, it varies from 10 to 40% as shown in Fig. 10.

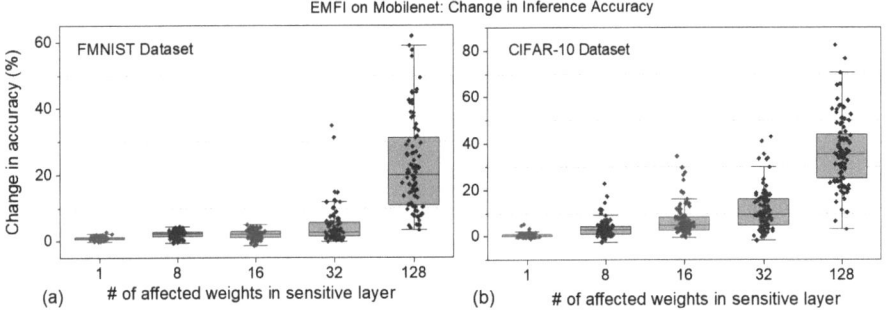

Fig. 10. EMFI results for MobileNet: change in inference accuracy post-EMFI attack at RoI-2 on a sensitive layer of the model for 100 cycles in each case for (a) FMNIST (b) CIFAR-10 datasets.

3   Discussion and Analysis

The innovative features of this work have been compared against existing literature in Table 2. In [4] author investigate Voltage Fault Injection (VFI) attack on NVM chips, and could reduce the inference accuracy by 14% with this invading the power supply. However, in this work, we achieve much higher reduction in inference accuracy without disturbing the power line. Authors in [15] employ laser to induce faults in the activation functions of the DNN networks running on the Micro-controller unit (MCU); however, handling the laser is not easy for some practical applications and environments. On the other hand, authors in [14] exploit temperature side channel for inducing fault in a relatively simpler neural network running on NAND flash. In this work, we have shown that we targeted EM injection on sensitive layers of the lightweight model during network loading can result upto 40% reduction in the inference accuracy. The method in [16] move the EMFI probe to scan each point on the Intel Neural Compute Stick-2 chip top surface and see the effect of EMFI at every point on the chip. Compared to the method in [16] we make use of X-Y EM intensity plots and target specific spatial locations on the chip for EMFI.

Table 2. Comparison of our proposed approach with recent relevant literature works

References	This work	APCCAS'23 [4]	CCS'18 [15]	TDMR'20 [14]
Attack Surface	FRAM	NOR Flash, RRAM	MCU	NAND Flash
Attack Target	tinyML models	MLP, AlexNet	DNN	MLP weights
Attack Channel	EM	Power supply	Laser	Temperature
Invasive attack	No	No	Yes	No
# of networks	3	2	1	1
Accuracy reduction	upto 40%	14%	-	-

4 Conclusion

This study investigates the vulnerabilities of future generation NVM-powered edge tinyML hardware to EM fault-injection attacks. We implemented three different lightweight trained neural networks; MobileNet, ResNet, and EfficientNet, on to a custom FPGA-FRAM setup for EMFI susceptibility testing. We demonstrated that the model weights can be corrupted through EM-fault injection. Further, we demonstrate that the EMFI corrupted weights can lead upto 40% reduction in validation accuracy in case the EMFI targets highly sensitive layers of the lightweight model.

Acknowledgements. This study is partially supported by MoE-IoE, IIT-Delhi Grant and MeiTY AI for Cyber Security Grant under NSM.

Disclosure of Interests. The authors have no competing interests to declare that are relevant to the content of this article.

References

1. Mittal, S., Gupta, H., Srivastava, S.: A survey on hardware security of DNN models and accelerators. J. Syst. Archit. **117**, 102163 (2021)
2. Boku, K., et al.: FRAM memory technology - advantages for low power, fast write, high endurance applications. In: Proceedings. 2005 International Conference on Computer Design, San Jose, CA, USA, pp. 485 (2005). https://doi.org/10.1109/ICCD.2005.60.
3. https://www.globenewswire.com/news-release/2021/06/23/2252222/0/en/FRAM-Market-is-Projected-to-Reach-USD-343-2-Million-By-2025-Growing-at-a-3-78-CAGR-Report-by-Market-Research-Future-MRFR.html
4. Chakraborty, S., Das, T., Suri, M.: Investigation of voltage fault injection attacks on NN inference utilizing NVM based weight storage. In: 2023 IEEE Asia Pacific Conference on Circuits and Systems (APCCAS), Hyderabad, India, pp. 26–30 (2023). https://doi.org/10.1109/APCCAS60141.2023.00018.
5. Bozzato, C., Focardi, R., Palmarini, F.: Shaping the glitch: optimizing voltage fault injection attacks. TCHES **2019**(2), 199–224 (2019). https://doi.org/10.13154/tches.v2019.i2.199-224

6. Khan, M.N.I., Ghosh, S.: Fault injection attacks on emerging non-volatile memory and countermeasures. In: Proceedings of the 7th International Workshop on Hardware and Architectural Support for Security and Privacy (HASP 2018), 2018, Association for Computing Machinery, New York, NY, USA, Article 10, pp. 1–8 (2018). https://doi.org/10.1145/3214292.3214302
7. Goswami, B., Suri, M.: Experimental investigation of EM side channel and FI attacks on commercial FRAM Chips. In: 8th IEEE Electron Devices Technology & Manufacturing Conference (EDTM). Bangalore, India, vol. 2024, 1–3 (2024). https://doi.org/10.1109/EDTM58488.2024.10511546
8. Fujitsu Semiconductor Memory Solution Data Sheet, Memory FeRAM, MB85R1002A, doc. Number: DS501-00004-6v1E Rev. H, dated May (2023)
9. Howard, A.G., et al.: MobileNets: efficient convolutional neural networks for mobile vision applications. arXiv:1704.04861 (2017)
10. He, K., Zhang, X., Ren, S., Sun, J.: Deep residual learning for image recognition. In: 2016 IEEE Conference on Computer Vision and Pattern Recognition (CVPR), Las Vegas, NV, USA, pp. 770–778 (2016). https://doi.org/10.1109/CVPR.2016.90.
11. Tan, M., Le, Q.: EfficientNet: rethinking model scaling for convolutional neural networks. In: Proceedings of the International Conference on the Machine Learning, pp. 6105–6114 (2019)
12. Xiao, H., Rasul, K., Vollgraf, R.: Fashion-MNIST: a novel image dataset for benchmarking machine learning algorithms. arXiv preprint arXiv:1708.07747 (2017)
13. Goswami, B., Moorthii J, C., Bansal, H., Sajwan, A., Suri, M.: Investigation of security vulnerabilities in NVM based persistent TinyML hardware. In: IEEE Embedded Systems Letters, Early Access (2024) https://doi.org/10.1109/LES.2024.3496508
14. Hasan, M.M., Ray, B.: Reliability of NAND flash memory as a weight storage device of artificial neural network. IEEE Trans. Device Mater. Reliab. **20**(3), 596–603 (2020). https://doi.org/10.1109/TDMR.2020.3012430
15. Breier, J., Hou, X., Jap, D., Ma, L., Bhasin, S., Liu, Y.: Practical fault attack on deep neural networks. In: Proceedings ACM SIGSAC Conference Computer and Communications Security, pp. 2204–2206 (2018)
16. Bhasin, S., Jap, D., Krček, M., Picek, S., Ravi, P.: Practical electromagnetic fault injection on intel neural compute stick 2, Cryptology ePrint Archive, Paper 2025/192 (2025). https://eprint.iacr.org/2025/192

μSCAN: Deep Learning Detection of Faulty Micro-architecture States and Patterns from Scan-Chain Data

Dillibabu Shanmugam(✉)[iD], Zhenyuan Liu[iD], Andrew Malnicof[iD], and Patrick Schaumont[iD]

Worcester Polytechnic Institute, Worcester, MA 01609, USA
`{dshanmugam,zliu12,armalnicof,pschaumont}@wpi.edu`

Abstract. Hardware Fault injection can leave processors in *weird* micro-architecture states that evade detection by conventional software-level monitors, jeopardizing system reliability. We propose μSCAN, a deep learning framework that leverages scan-chain observability to detect such anomalous states. μSCAN fine-tunes a large language model (LLM) to classify single-cycle processor states as *weird* or *sane*, achieving an average classification accuracy of 92% and maintaining robust performance across different CPU architectures (MSP430, PICO (RV32IC), IBEX (RV32IMC)). We further refine this LLM classifier with reinforcement learning, which sharpens its decision boundaries and improves detection of borderline anomalies. μSCAN also employs a graph neural network (GNN) to analyze multi-cycle fault patterns, capturing complex temporal dependencies that single-cycle analysis might miss. This GNN-based analysis successfully identifies recurring fault sequences and maps them to known Common Weakness Enumeration (CWE) vulnerability classes, revealing potential hardware design flaws. μSCAN demonstrates scalability and generalization on multiple processor architectures (including micro-coded and pipelined cores) and is evaluated with both pre-silicon simulation data and a post-silicon prototype. Our results show that μSCAN enables early detection of micro-architecture vulnerabilities in the design phase and provides a robust post-silicon anomaly detection mechanism.

Keywords: Hardware Fault Analysis · Weird State Machine · Large Language Models

1 Introduction

Silent Data Corruption, a recently observed and quantified phenomenon [2], causes one out of every one thousand central processing units to silently produce incorrect results without triggering any obvious malfunction. Although the precise rate can vary according to architecture and workload, this concern applies just as critically to embedded processors, which often operate in safety-critical settings. A minor fault at the micro-architectural level can jeopardize an entire system, especially under constraints of limited power, tight cost targets, and demanding environmental conditions. This phenomenon underscores the need for

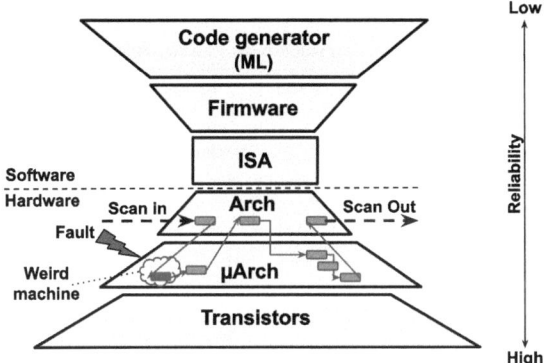

Fig. 1. Overview of the hardware–software abstraction layers—starting at code generation and firmware, passing through the ISA and architectural registers, and reaching down to the micro-architecture and transistors. A micro-architectural fault can create a "weird machine," so scan-chain instrumentation ("scan in/scan out") is used to spot errors otherwise hidden at the micro-architectural level.

robust fault-detection mechanisms throughout the hardware–software abstraction layers, ensuring that latent errors are discovered early, and that reliability remains intact. In this paper, we propose an ML based mechanism to detect errors that affect the runtime hardware state of a processor. Since the hardware state can cover thousands of bits, the state space is enormous, and the challenge is to reliably distinguish anomalous (faulty) states from the normal states.

Problem Statement: Understanding a fault at the micro-architectural level requires analysis of a massive state space, which remains hidden from software. Under these circumstances, a key question emerges: How can one determine if a micro-architecture state is faulty or not? A second question is how can one determine if a given fault behavior is catastrophic for the firmware's execution or not, in the sense that a fault may lead to extended anomalous behavior. The second question cannot be answered from a single faulty state, but rather requires observation of a sequence of weird and sane states. To the best of our knowledge, no systematic methodology exists to answer either of these questions. The solution proposed in μSCAN is to rely on machine learning techniques that leverage micro-architectural state information obtained through the scan chain of hardware-software system. We aim to show that the classification of single faulty states, as well as the classification of faulty sequences, can be solved adequately using machine learning.

Hardware-Software Abstraction Layers: In modern processor design, the instruction set architecture (ISA) acts as both the interface and a limiting factor as highlighted in the Fig. 1. From the software perspective, the ISA acts as a gateway because firmware and higher-level applications cannot directly access every flip-flop within the processor. Meanwhile, from a hardware perspective, the ISA provides essential protection by preventing users from inadvertently manip-

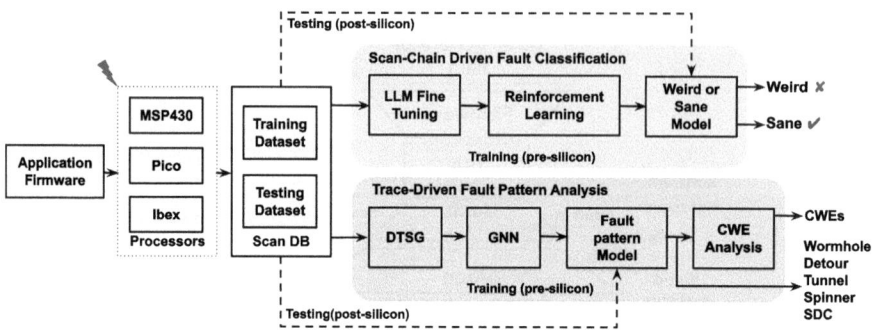

Fig. 2. Overall framework for micro-architectural fault classification and analysis. Micro-architectural data from MSP430, PICO, or IBEX processors is collected via scan chain and divided into training and testing datasets. The upper part uses LLM fine-tuning and reinforcement learning to classify processor states as weird or sane, while the lower part employs graph neural networks for fault pattern analysis, ultimately mapping anomalies to relevant CWE categories.

ulating micro-architectural registers. This separation is beneficial under normal circumstances, but it becomes problematic in fault scenarios. In particular, each layer in the hardware–software abstraction layer tends to mask faults, thereby making it difficult to pinpoint error sources.

Observability Through Scan Chain: Under normal circumstances, firmware developers have no straightforward means of detecting micro-architecture level faults via the usual architectural registers, as the ISA does not expose micro-architectural state. However, the scan-chain, a structure present in many complex chip designs, gives us a handle on this problem. The idea of a scan-chain is to organize every register of the processor, regardless of the abstraction level, into a sequential data structure. By stopping the program and scanning out the contents of the scan-chain, full observability of the processor state becomes possible. Thus, the scan-chain offers the means to detect faulty processor states even before they are able to affect the behavior of the firmware. The faulty state obtained from the scan-chain can be combined with simulation of the processor structure, to obtain a full and detailed trace of a fault effect in the processor hardware. Faulty scan-chain data is a key to the proposed ML based framework that classifies the processor status.

Weird vs Sane Machine: The software community has struggled with precisely defining a faulted processor, in part because the high-level architecture state alone is clearly not enough to capture the fault impact in its entirety. Dullien's [3] proposal defines a *weird machine* as a software state machine that deviates from its intended execution specification. But he does not address how to detect such anomalies in practice. However, using the scan-chain, the state of a weird machine becomes known as a scan-state where one or more registers in the processor are faulted. FaultDetective [8] demonstrates this idea as a proof-of-concept, and examines the classification of *weird machine* and fault patterns at the hardware level using scan-chain instrumentation. FaultDetective traces short sequences of faulty states and represents them in a data structure called a Dynamic State Transition Graph (DSTG). However, the approach in FaultDetective is application-specific, requiring an exact comparison between a non-faulted ground truth (sane state) and the weird state.

Given the high dimensionality and sequential nature of scan-chain data, we require models capable of capturing long-range dependencies to detect subtle anomalies. Hence, we propose an LLM-based solution that recognises when a given micro-architectural state deviates from normal execution. Furthermore, hardware faults manifest as a *chain* of state changes, rather than a single weird state. For this reason, we also explore a graph-based approach to identify evolving fault patterns over multiple clock cycles. Building on these foundations, this paper introduces two complementary methods. First, *Scan-Chain Driven Fault Classification* leverages scan-chain data and a fine-tuned large language model (LLM) [6] to classify processor states as *weird* or *sane* in real time (Fig. 2, top flow). Second, *Trace-Driven Fault Pattern Analysis* applies a graph neural network to DSTGs for detailed fault pattern identification (Fig. 2, bottom flow). Together, these methods improve the scalability of fault detection across different abstraction layers.

Technique 1 - Scan-Chain Driven Fault Classification: The primary objective is to determine whether a micro-architectural state is weird or sane. Because real-time observation of every state is impractical, we adopt a two-phase strategy. In the profiling phase (pre-silicon), we simulate both faulty and non-faulty program executions and collect each state using scan-chain. We then fine-tune a large language model (LLM) to capture deviations from the intended semantics. In the deployment phase (post-silicon), we extract a single state from the device via scan chain and classify it as weird or sane based on the trained model. Any state that diverges from the intended behavior is labeled weird, designating a weird machine.

Technique 2 - Trace-Driven Fault Pattern Analysis: This technique employs a graph neural network (GNN) to interpret multi-cycle data and observe a fault pattern. Its primary objective is to analyze the DSTG and to identify recurring fault patterns thereby revealing where a fault originates in the control/data flow of the application. The approach uses a profiling phase (pre-silicon), which simulates both faulty and non-faulty program executions, collects micro-architectural states via scan chain, and constructs the DSTG for GNN training. Because GNNs excel at modeling relational dependencies in graph-based structures, they are well-suited to capturing the complex interactions of fault-induced transitions. In the deployment phase, the trained model detects fault patterns in from observed DSTGs for a large number of applications. Frequent re-occurrences of a given pattern can signify heightened vulnerability, prompting further netlist analysis to map the identified fault category to a specific Common Weakness Enumeration (CWE). The μSCAN implementation and all datasets used in this paper are available at https://github.com/Secure-Embedded-Systems/microscan.git.

Contributions of the Paper. We demonstrate the proposed ML-based techniques to classify faults on several processor architectures, including a micro-coded MSP430, a micro-coded PICORV32, and a pipelined IBEX. We construct a dataset consisting of faulty and non-faulty executions for several sample applications on these processors, and capture the micro-architectural register state by gate-level simulation. We then develop a classification framework by fine-tuning a large language model (LLM) to recognize weird or sane patterns within the pre-silicon dataset, validating the approach with both pre-silicon and post-silicon data. We further enhance inference through a reinforcement learning strategy, achieving improved classification accuracy under real-world conditions. At the architectural level, we employ a graph neural network (GNN) for pattern classification. Finally, we attempt to map the discovered vulnerabilities to relevant CWE categories.

Outline of the Paper. The rest of this paper is organized as follows: Sect. 2 reviews background and related work. Section 3 shares the preliminaries and the dataset. Section 4 presents the methodology for micro-architectural fault classification and pattern analysis. Section 5 details the experimental results. Finally, Sect. 6 concludes the paper.

2 Background and Related Work

A fault injection attack on a processor aims to extract secret data, to escalate privilege, or to induce failures. Although multiple fault injection mechanisms exist, we focus on transient faults created through three injection mechanisms: electromagnetic fault injection (EMFI), laser fault injection (LFI), and clock-glitch injection (CGI). Each fault injection technique causes one or more temporary bit-flips in the processor hardware, and these bit-flips eventually affect the software's behavior. Commonly reported effects include instruction-skip [11] and blocking the execution of a branch [9].

Anomaly Detection Using ML. A first area of related work is in the area of detecting faults using machine-learning techniques. At the software level, machine-learning techniques have been used to assess multicore soft error reliability [12], to locate faults [10], and to find bugs through large language models [17]. These methods observe run-time states, recognizing patterns that suggest anomalies. At the hardware level, machine-learning techniques have been used for fault characterisation [13], for multisource injection detection [16], and for clock-glitch detection [5]. Our proposed method crosses the hardware/software boundary, by using the low-level machine state observed through a scan chain to infer future anomalous behavior.

Fault Modeling. A fault simulation stands or falls with the accuracy of the fault model [1]. The intrinsic characteristics of physical faults must be appropriately translated into a simulation model, reflecting complex phenomena such as multibit flips and timing violations. This is a known hard problem, frequently relying on probabilistic assumptions. In our approach, we avoid fault modeling because we observe fault effects immediately after fault injection by reading out the scan chain of the post-silicon prototype. We then use the faulty bits observed to seed the pre-silicon fault simulation model.

Scan Chain and Dynamic State Transition Graphs. Scan chains allow direct access to the register of a hardware design, enabling an external observer to record the processor state. Using such a recorded (and possibly faulty) state, subsequent processor states can be simulated over time using a pre-silicon model. This simulation provides a precise cycle-by-cycle record of processor states. An Architectural Dynamic State Transition Graph (ADSTG) captures programmer-visible architectural bits by mapping state changes at instruction boundaries [8]. In contrast, the Micro-architectural Dynamic State Transition Graph (MDSTG) logs per-clock-cycle register snapshots—including both ISA-visible and internal micro-architectural bits—to reveal and analyze pipeline-level fault behaviors. By analyzing these state-transition graphs under fault conditions, one can detect patterns that compromise normal operation. A graph neural network (GNN) [14] often supports pattern recognition in these scenarios, highlighting anomalies that arise from injected faults.

Fault Patterns. The following fault patterns, identified through FSMRED firmware experiments, characterize distinct deviations observed in the microarchitecture; graphical representations appear in Appendix Sect. A. The *Sane* pattern denotes fault-free microarchitectural execution, with pipeline and control-flow transitions occurring without disruption. The *Detour* pattern signifies transient deviations, briefly diverging from the intended execution path before recovering, implying temporary signal or timing disturbances. The *Tunnel* pattern involves skipped or delayed state transitions, introducing subtle shortcuts that disrupt expected control-flow progression. The *Wormhole* pattern describes an abrupt, high-impact jump from valid to anomalous states, bypassing sequential progression. Finally, the *Spinner* pattern reflects indefinite looping within a limited set of states due to compromised control-flow management, effectively halting normal processor operation.

3 Preliminaries and Dataset

In this section, we explain the experimental setup, and the programs we have analyzed using μSCAN.

Fault Simulation Setup. Capturing every glitch or laser-induced fault at the microarchitectural level demands a carefully orchestrated simulation flow that configures, compiles, and logs hardware states in one cohesive pipeline. The fault simulation setup begins with a configuration stage, where parameters such as the target processor core (PICO, MSP430, or IBEX), fault type (glitch or laser), fault injection offset from trigger or start of a program in clock cycles, and compiler optimizations are chosen. Next, a code generator creates a set of test cases that each combine a randomized input vector into the firmware C

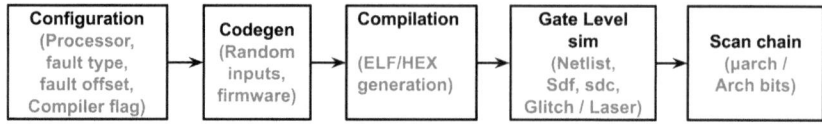

Fig. 3. Block diagram of the integrated fault simulation flow, where the chosen parameters (processor core, fault type, offset, etc.) closely approximate real-world fault conditions. The process moves from firmware generation through gate-level netlist simulation, finally capturing micro-architecture states for anomaly classification.

code under test. Each of these programs is then compiled into memory images (ELF/HEX). These memory images then become inputs to a gate-level simulation (ModelSim/Verilator) that combines the netlist, delay constraints, and a test script to inject faults by global clock glitching or layout-local laser fault injection. During the gate-level simulation, every clock cycle triggers a scan-chain capture of microarchitectural registers, allowing precise logging of internal state transitions. If a laser fault is configured, the simulator toggles the specified registers at the indicated clock offset, using layout-level information to select the precise register(s) to be faulted. For glitch-based faults, the test script modifies the global clock signal. Each simulation run thus produces a trace of clock-by-clock register states, enabling subsequent analysis—such as anomaly detection via large language models or graph neural networks. We perform all fault simulation experiments on an Intel Xeon Gold 6248 server (Fig. 3).

Listing 1 Partial assembly (left) and bitslice C implementation (right) for the ASCON Sbox. The red-highlighted instruction (f0b8: cmp r14, r9) was targeted by a laser fault.

```
 1  f086: mov   #128,  &0x001a         1  Input: x[0..4],Output: y[0..4]
 2  f08c: mov   r1,    r14             2  for(j = 0; j < WORD_SIZE; ++j){
 3  f08e: add   #16,   r14             3    q0[j]=!(x3[j]^x4[j]);
 4  f092: mov   r1,    r15             4    q1[j]=!x4[j];
 5  f094: add   #24,   r15             5    t0[j]=q0[j]&q1[j];
 6  f098: mov   r1,    r10             6    q2[j]=x0[j]^x2[j]^x4[j];
 7  f09a: mov   r1,    r11             7    q3[j]=x1[j];
 8  f09c: add   #8,    r11             8    t1[j]=q2[j]&q3[j];
 9  f09e: mov   r15,   r9              9    q4[j]=x0[j]^x1[j]^x4[j];
10  f0a0: mov   @r15+, r13            10    q5[j]=x1[j];
11  f0a2: mov   r13,   r12            11    t2[j]=q4[j]&q5[j];
12  f0a4: xor   @r10+, r12            12    q6[j]=x3[j]^x4[j];
13  f0a6: mov   @r11+, r8             13    q7[j]=x0[j];
14  f0a8: bic   r12,   r8             14    t3[j]=q6[j]&q7[j];
15  f0aa: mov   r8,    r12            15    q8[j]=x3[j]^t1[j]^t2[j];
16  f0ac: xor   @r14+, r13            16    q9[j]=x1[j]^x2[j];
17  f0ae: xor   r13,   r12            17    t4[j]=q8[j]&q9[j];
18  f0b0: and   #511,  r12            18    y0[j]=x0[j]^x1[j]^x2[j]^x3[j]^t1[j];
19  f0b4: mov   r12,   &0x0028        19    y1[j]=x0[j]^x2[j]^x3[j]^x4[j]^t4[j];
20  f0b8: cmp   r14,   r9             20    y2[j]=x1[j]^x2[j]^x3[j]^t0[j];
21  f0ba: jnz   $-26                  21    y3[j]=x0[j]^x1[j]^x2[j]^x3[j]^x4[j]^t3[j];
22  f0bc: mov   #0,    &0x001a        22    y4[j]=x3[j]^x4[j]^t2[j]; }
```

Example: Simulation of Micro-architecture Faults on ASCON Sbox. We apply our fault-injection workflow to CAPRI6, an SoC with six openMSP430 cores in lockstep and scan-chain observability. The ASCON Sbox bitslice routine starts at clock cycle 67 and ends at cycle 155, with each cycle paused to log microarchitecture registers using scan chain. Under normal conditions, the 89 states (cycles 67–155) remain *sane*. However, clock glitches or laser pulses may cause one or more *weird* states. In one campaign, a laser fault occurred in cycle 122 at instruction target f0b8: cmp r14, r9. The fault flipped inst_sa_reg_2_ from 0 to 1 in core3 and this *weird* state persisted until jnz $-26 restored normal operation in cycle 125. Although no *architectural* registers changed, such faults may leak cryptographic data or cause malfunctions. Listing 1 and Fig. 4 refer to this same experiment, showing a partial assembly snippet and potential weird-state transitions using the MD-STG. In another MSP430 design, a corrupted ADD instruction became XOR, converting $b + (w \times a)$ into $b \oplus (w \times a)$, thereby breaking arithmetic correctness. Integrating these results with pre-silicon simulations yields a comprehensive set of *sane* and *weird* states for subsequent training in our framework.

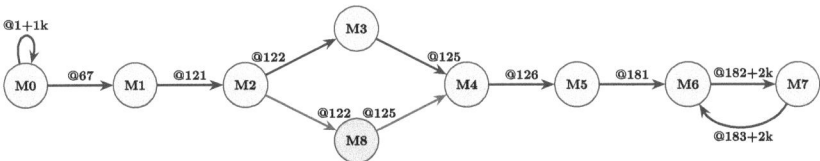

Fig. 4. MD-STG of the ASCON Sbox showing potential weird-state transitions (red color) under fault injection. (Color figure online)

Dataset. Building upon the weird and sane states observed in these campaigns, we now systematically compile them into a dataset. We generated random-instruction tests for *PICO* (RV32IC) and *IBEX* (RV32IMC), each covering more than 40 types of ISA instruction (load / store, branching, arithmetic, logic) to exercise all CPU registers. In our post-silicon evaluation on CAPRI6, we specifically targeted the MOV, ADD, and MUL instructions under two fault-injection campaigns (laser-based and clock-glitch-based), collecting 517 *weird* states in total (265 from laser, 252 from clock glitches). Table 1 summarizes the *weird* and *sane* states from these experiments alongside the ASCON Sbox runs.

4 Methodology: Fault Classification and Pattern Analysis

Our approach consists of two complementary models: (*i*) an LLM-based classifier to flag individual weird states, and (*ii*) a GNN-based analyzer to identify patterns of faults across multiple states. We describe each in turn.

4.1 LLM-Based Classifier

We arrive at a robust mathematical model that classifies microarchitectural states as weird or sane.

Table 1. Each processor exhibits distinct architecture and microarchitecture register counts (Columns 2 and 3). Microarchitectural registers are typically not directly accessible by programmers. Column 4 indicates the firmware scenario, while Columns 5 and 6 show the sane and weird state counts, respectively. The last row lists instructions (MOV/ADD/MUL) used on CAPRI6.

Processors	Arch. Reg	μarch. Reg	Firmware	Sane	Weird
MSP430	385	275	FSMRed	28	627
			ASCON Sbox [18]	89	3120
			PinVerify5 [4]	248	22576
PICO	1024	1265	Random Instr.	80	480
			ASCON Sbox	24	350
IBEX	993	1013	Random Instr.	486	1013
			ASCON Sbox	402	1000
Post-Silicon (CAPRI6)			MOV/ADD/MUL [15]	517	517

Fine Tuning LLM Models. We treat the classification task as a pattern-recognition problem, leveraging a large language model capable of detecting subtle semantic relationships within high-dimensional scan-chain data. Such models excel at capturing long-range dependencies, making them especially effective for distributed fault scenarios in which anomalies span thousands of bits. We employ *DeepSeek-R1-Distill-Qwen-1.5B* as our base model due to its open-source.

Profiling and Deployment Phase. We represent the microarchitectural register dump as a sequence of tokens (bits or groups of bits) that the LLM can ingest via its tokenizer. To reduce computational overhead while maintaining accuracy, we adopt Quantized Low-Rank Adaptation (QLoRA). This method quantizes the base model's weights to 4-bit precision and inserts low-rank adapters that learn task-specific features. During fine-tuning, we freeze the main LLM parameters and update only the LoRA components [7], allowing the model to capture essential directions of variance via a low-rank decomposition. After training, the low-rank matrices merge back into the base model, resulting in a final classifier

Hyperparameter	Value
EPOCHS	4/16
Learning Rate	$1 \times 10^{-5} / 2 \times 10^{-5}$
LoRA Rank	4/8/16
LoRA Alpha	64/128
LoRA Dropout	0.1/0.2
Batch Size	4/8/16
Warmup Steps	50/200
Threshold	0.48/0.5/0.52

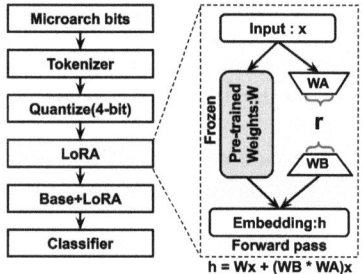

Fig. 5. (Left) Key hyperparameters used in LoRA fine-tuning. (Right) LoRA + Base Model architecture, illustrating how LoRA adapters integrate with the frozen pre-trained weights.

that infers *weird* or *sane* states on test data. Figure 5 shows the block diagram (Right) and the network hyperparameters (Left) used for the model.

Mathematical Model for Anomaly Detection. Let $\mathbf{x} \in \mathbb{R}^d$ represent the microarchitectural state captured via scan-chain, where d denotes the dimensionality (the number of micro-architecture bits). We employ a large language model (LLM) with QLoRA to classify $\mathbf{x}$ as either *weird* (faulty) or *sane* (non-faulty). Formally, we define

$$y = \text{LLM}_{\theta + \Delta}(\mathbf{x}), \tag{1}$$

where θ are the frozen weights of the base pre-trained model, and Δ represents the low-rank updates learned during fine-tuning. The output y is a logit or score that reflects the likelihood of $\mathbf{x}$ being a *weird* state.

For a binary classification task, we apply a sigmoid function $\sigma(\cdot)$ to convert y into a probability:

$$p(\text{weird} \mid \mathbf{x}) = \sigma\bigl(y(\mathbf{x})\bigr). \tag{2}$$

A decision boundary $\tau \in [0, 1]$ determines the final label:

$$\text{Class}(\mathbf{x}) = \begin{cases} \text{weird,} & \text{if } p(\text{weird} \mid \mathbf{x}) \geq \tau, \\ \text{sane,} & \text{otherwise.} \end{cases} \tag{3}$$

During fine-tuning, we minimise a supervised loss (e.g., cross-entropy) over labelled states $\{(\mathbf{x}_i, y_i)\}$, where $y_i \in \{\text{weird}, \text{sane}\}$. Notably, only the LoRA parameters Δ receive gradient updates, while the base weights θ remain fixed. This strategy ensures that the essential directions of variation in the data are captured in the low-rank subspace, thus allowing efficient adaptation of the large model to our anomaly detection task.

Reinforcement Learning on Top of LLM Fine-Tuning. Although supervised fine-tuning equips an LLM with broad discriminative features for *weird* vs. *sane* states, borderline or outlier cases may remain problematic. Reinforcement learning refines decision boundaries by rewarding correct classifications and penalising errors, prompting the model to adapt to ambiguous samples. Over repeated updates, it strengthens effective classification strategies and better detects subtle anomalies. This iterative process is especially valuable for microarchitectural data, where faults can span thousands of bits.

Mathematical Model. Let $\mathbf{x} \in \mathbb{R}^d$ denote the extracted microarchitectural state, and let $a \in \{\text{weird}, \text{sane}\}$ be the classification action. The LLM parameters, initially tuned via supervised learning, define a policy $\pi_\theta(a \mid \mathbf{x})$ that assigns a probability to each action. After an action a is chosen, a reward function $r(\mathbf{x}, a)$ is provided: for example,

$$r(\mathbf{x}, \text{weird}) = p(\text{weird} \mid \mathbf{x}) \quad \text{and} \quad r(\mathbf{x}, \text{sane}) = p(\text{sane} \mid \mathbf{x}),$$

where $p(\cdot \mid \mathbf{x})$ corresponds to the model's confidence for each label. The RL objective is to maximize the expected return,

$$\max_\theta \ \mathbb{E}_{\mathbf{x} \sim \mathcal{D}}\bigl[\mathbb{E}_{a \sim \pi_\theta}\bigl(r(\mathbf{x}, a)\bigr)\bigr],$$

where $\mathcal{D}$ is the distribution of microarchitectural states. Intuitively, correct classifications (matching ground truth) yield higher rewards, nudging the policy to strengthen those decisions. As the model repeatedly observes states where it previously misclassified, the updated reward feedback guides it to adjust its predictions. Thus, the policy gradually converges to an improved discriminator for weird versus sane states, leveraging both the representation learned by fine-tuning and the adaptive reward-driven updates of RL.

4.2 GNN-Based Analyzer

Next, we leverage graph neural networks to classify fault patterns over time.

Motivation and DSTG Representation. While single-state classification can identify anomalies at a single clock cycle, many hardware faults emerge across multiple cycles and transitions. To capture these multi-cycle behaviours, we adopted a *Dynamic State Transition Graph* (DSTG), in which each node represents a microarchitectural state (the set of registers at a given cycle), and each directed edge denotes a transition triggered by instruction execution or a fault injection. For instance, Fig. 4 shows an assembly snippet from the ASCON SBox where a fault changes the instruction register, causing a weird state that lasts for three clock cycles before returning to normal. Because this anomaly spans multiple cycles, a graph-based model is more effective than per-cycle analysis at capturing the fault's evolution over time.

Profiling and Deployment Phase. In the profiling phase, we simulate both normal and faulty executions for each target application (e.g. ASCON SBox, FSMRED, VP5). These simulations yield DSTGs that record normal transitions as well as fault-induced deviations. We label each DSTG according to the observed pattern among six known fault classes (e.g. wormhole, tunnel, spinner, detour, silent data corruption, or crash). The GNN is then trained on these labelled graphs, learning to recognise topological and feature-based indicators of each fault category. In practice, we store node attributes (such as instruction type, clock cycle index, or register usage) and edge attributes (timing differences, potential glitch sites, etc.) in a graph database, ensuring the GNN has sufficient context to learn discriminative patterns. Once trained, the GNN is deployed on device traces collected *post-silicon* via the scan chain. As new microarchitectural states are read, the corresponding DSTG is constructed in batches and fed to the GNN. The model then predicts which of the six patterns best describes the transitions within that graph.

Mathematical Model for Fault Pattern Classification. Formally, let $G = (V, E)$ be a DSTG where each node $i \in V$ has features $\mathbf{x}_i$ (e.g. instruction label, cycle index) and each edge $(i, j) \in E$ has features $\mathbf{e}_{ij}$ (e.g. time deltas, potential glitch). A GNN iteratively updates node embeddings $\mathbf{h}_i^{(l)}$:

$$\mathbf{h}_i^{(l)} = \sigma\Big(\sum_{j \in \mathcal{N}(i)} \alpha_{ij}^{(l)} \, \mathbf{W}^{(l)} \, \mathbf{h}_j^{(l-1)} \Big),$$

where $\alpha_{ij}^{(l)}$ is an attention coefficient (potentially derived from $\mathbf{e}_{ij}$) and $\mathbf{W}^{(l)}$ are learnable parameters. After L layers, the graph-level embedding emerges from pooling the final node embeddings:

$$\mathbf{z} = \text{Pool}(\{\mathbf{h}_i^{(L)} : i \in V\}),$$

which is then fed into a classifier MLP($\mathbf{z}$) that outputs a fault-pattern label among the six categories. This GNN-based method scales well to large DSTGs and offers efficient inference, as the local connectivity constrains the amount of message passing per node. Consequently, it provides an effective framework for multi-cycle fault analysis, bridging the gap between low-level transitions and high-level categorisation of fault behaviour.

5 Experimental Evaluation and Analysis

In this section, we present a comprehensive evaluation of our fault detection framework, which integrates an LLM-based classifier enhanced through reinforcement learning (RL) and a graph neural network (GNN) for fault pattern analysis. The experiments are designed to validate our hypothesis that RL-enhanced classification can significantly improve the detection of anomalous states, while the GNN-based approach effectively identifies multi-cycle fault patterns. Evaluation metrics include classification accuracy, convergence speed, and fault pattern recognition precision.

5.1 Classification Performance with LLM

Table 2 shows a progressive improvement in classification accuracy and offers insight into the trade-offs between model performance and training cost. In Case 1, the classifier obtains a modest accuracy (77%), which reflects a relatively small training set and limited coverage of fault scenarios. Moving to Case 2, a more extensive dataset yields higher accuracy (94%), but the training phase grows proportionally longer. In Case 3, augmenting the data further elevates the accuracy (98%) yet incurs an even greater training time, underscoring the overhead of large-scale learning. PICO and IBEX confirm that the approach generalizes across distinct processor architectures, PICO and IBEX, while preserving strong precision (94% and 97%, respectively). Finally, CAPRI6 achieves a precision 90%, demonstrating the viability of the method under realistic constraints, but also highlighting the computational demands of increased data diversity.

Comparison. Figure 6 presents a head-to-head comparison of six detectors on the 365-state test subset from Case 1. The QLoRA fine-tuned classifier—using 4-bit weight quantization and rank-8 adapters—requires 99% fewer trainable parameters and 80% less GPU memory than conventional full-model tuning, yet achieves the highest accuracy (79.00%), substantially outperforming both

Table 2. Classification performance of the LLM-based fault-state classifier evaluated across six distinct experimental cases. Case 1 (Balanced): Dataset with equal numbers of sane and weird states (365 each) from three MSP430 firmware, evenly split for training and testing. Case 2 (Imbalanced): Full MSP430 dataset (365 sane, 26,273 weird) divided into 80% training and 20% testing subsets. Case 3 (Augmented): Entire MSP430 dataset used for training (100%) and expanded testing dataset by 50% (approximately 150% total states). Case 4 (Cross-firmware, PICO): Classifier trained on random-instruction firmware, evaluated on ASCON firmware states (PICO platform). Case 5 (Cross-firmware, IBEX): Same approach as Case 4 but on IBEX platform, using a smaller GPU (NVIDIA T4, 16GB RAM) compared to other experiments (NVIDIA A100, 40 GB RAM). Case 6 (Cross-platform, CAPRI6): Classifier trained on MSP430 firmware states, tested on MOV/ADD/MUL instruction states of CAPRI6 processor. Results highlight progressive improvements in accuracy with increasing data size and demonstrate computational trade-offs in scaling and cross-platform evaluation.

Test Case	Target	FSMRed	ASCON Sbox	VP5	Random Inst	MOV/ADD/MUL	Dataset		Train		Test		Acc.	Time (min)
							Sane	Weird	Sane	Weird	Sane	Weird	(%)	(Train+Test)
1	MSP430	•	•	•			365	365	183	183	182	182	79	6 + 1
2	MSP430	•	•	•			365	26,273	292	21,019	73	5,254	94	460 + 8
3	MSP430	•	•	•			365	26,273	365	26,273	564	39,085	98	620 + 25
4	PICO		•		•		104	830	80	480	24	350	94	60 + 5
5	IBEX		•		•		1499	1,402	486	1,013	402	1,000	97	370 + 15
6	CAPRI6					•	365	26,273	292	21,019	517	517	90	460 + 6

transformer baselines (BERT-base: 51.00%; RoBERTa-base: 57.00%) and three non-LLM approaches (Isolation Forest: 49.45%; Autoencoder: 50.55%; 1D-CNN: 55.22%). This significant performance margin indicates that low-rank adapters, when applied to domain-specific "bit tokens," capture subtle microarchitecture-level fault signatures that generic language models and unsupervised detectors fail to discern.

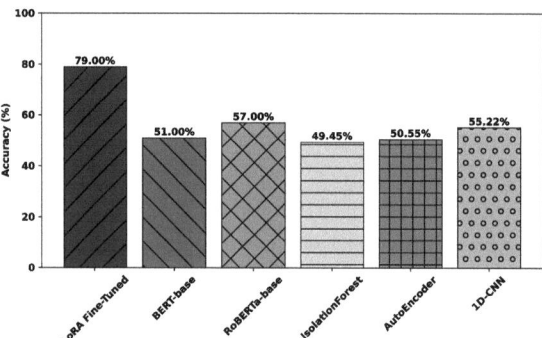

Fig. 6. Comparison of model accuracies.

LLM Classification and RL Enhancements In Test Case 1, the SFT LLM shows limited success in distinguishing weird from sane states, resulting in lower

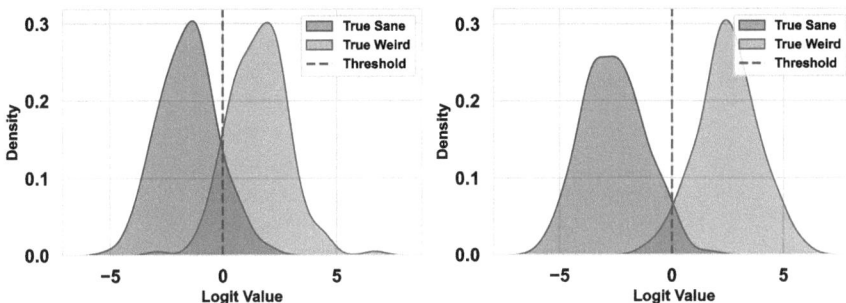

Fig. 7. This figure shows the distribution of predicted logits for two true labels (sane vs. weird) for the SFT model (left) and for the RL_SFT model (right). The vertical dashed line at logit = 0 corresponds to a probability of 0.5, illustrating how borderline anomalies arise where the two distributions overlap.

accuracy. We incorporate the MSP430 case 1 LoRA adapter into the model and then apply RL to 30% of the data, following Sect. 4.2. The resulting RL model is evaluated on the same test samples to measure improvements over the SFT baseline. Figure 7 compares the logit distributions for the SFT model (left) and the RL+SFT model (right). The left distribution, with 79.12% accuracy, shows moderate overlap between sane and weird classes, revealing borderline cases that the SFT model struggles to classify. The right distribution, produced after RL on top of SFT, presents fewer borderline cases and an accuracy of 90.22%, indicating that RL refines the model's ability to distinguish weird from sane states. This improvement suggests that combining RL with SFT yields more effective separation of borderline samples and enhances overall classification accuracy.

5.2 GNN-Based Multi-cycle Pattern Detection

Dataset and Methodology. We generated multi-cycle fault datasets on MSP430 using three firmware scenarios (FSMRED, ASCON, and VP5) under clock-glitch and laser injections. Each *campaign* yielded an MDSTG capturing micro-architectural state transitions across full execution: FSMRED (28 cycles), ASCON (89 cycles), and VP5 (293 cycles). Training utilized states from cores $\{0,1,2,4,5\}$, reserving core 3 exclusively for testing. The GNN classifier processed MDSTGs, predicting fault patterns (e.g., *wormhole*, *spinner*, *detour*). We employed a multi-layer attention-based architecture with ReLU activation and assessed classification accuracy.

Results and Discussion. Table 3 summarizes experimental results across injection types and firmware. Glitch-based scenarios achieved around 80% accuracy, with ASCON significantly outperforming FSMRED, attributed to more distinguishable fault patterns. Laser injections yielded accuracies above 98%, demonstrating GNN efficacy under varied fault mechanisms. The combined scenario confirmed robustness with 99% accuracy, highlighting strong generalization. The confusion matrix (Table 4) shows precise classification across fault types, confirming

Table 3. GNN classification accuracy for multi-cycle fault pattern detection on MSP430. Training utilized cores {0,1,2,4,5}; testing on core 3 to verify cross-core generalization.

Injection	Firmware	Campaigns		Clock	GNN
		Train	Test	Cycles	Acc.
Glitch	FSMRED	140	28	28	67.86%
	ASCON	480	96	89	96.88%
Laser	ASCON	2171	435	89	98.62%
	VP5	2171	435	293	99.70%
-	All	4962	994	293	99.80%

Table 4. Confusion matrix (combined scenario). Rows represent true fault patterns, columns show predictions.

	sane	wormhole_imp	wormhole_noimp	spinner	tunnel	detour
sane	117	0	0	0	0	0
wormhole_imp	0	98	0	0	0	0
wormhole_noimp	0	0	420	0	0	0
spinner	0	0	0	17	0	0
tunnel	0	0	0	2	47	0
detour	0	0	0	0	0	293

the GNN's effectiveness in capturing distinctive multi-cycle fault patterns. To identify recurring fault motifs, we first assign each MDSTG the class with the highest softmax score and extract its penultimate-layer embedding. We then cluster these embeddings via agglomerative clustering with cosine affinity and flag any cluster exceeding a user-defined size threshold as a recurring motif. Finally, each identified motif is manually mapped to its corresponding CWE category. This methodology is scalable to large SoCs and enables validation of complex applications via periodic scan-out.

5.3 Correlating Fault Patterns with CWEs

Fault patterns observed in experiments closely align with CWE classifications, highlighting hardware control-flow vulnerabilities.

Tunnel Fault: Program Counter (PC) Advance. Figure 8a depicts a tunnel fault induced by laser injection at instruction f0ac (xor @r14+, r13). This injection prematurely advances the program counter (PC), bypassing three critical instructions (f0ac, f0ae, f0b0). Consequently, the ASCON SBox computation omits an entire iteration, failing to update register data correctly. While immediate erroneous states are not evident, the final output incorrectly resolves to 0x0018 instead of 0x00E5. This behavior precisely aligns with **CWE-1332** (Skipped Valid Transitions), wherein valid, necessary transitions are unintentionally skipped due to faults, causing incorrect system states.

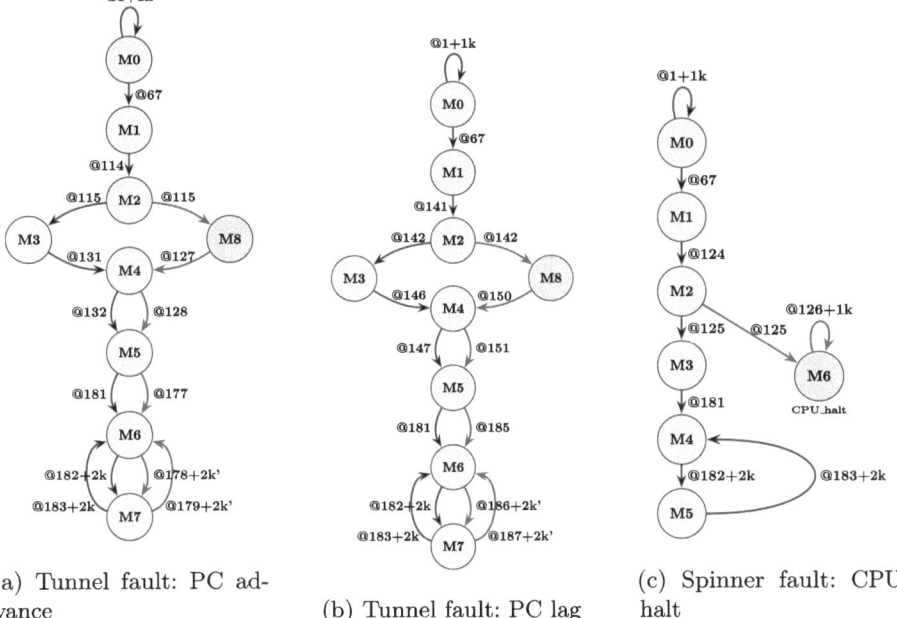

Fig. 8. Micro-architectural state-transition graphs illustrating sane (green nodes, black edges) versus weird/fault-induced (red nodes, red edges) execution paths. (Color figure online)

Tunnel Fault: Program Counter (PC) Lag. Figure 8b illustrates another tunnel fault scenario introduced by laser injection at instruction f0b4 (mov r12, &0x0028). This fault introduces a delay of four clock cycles without skipping instructions. After these additional cycles, the processor's micro-architectural state realigns, preserving the correctness of final output data. Nonetheless, the internal timing disturbance remains undetected by the CPU, indicative of insufficient hardware-level control flow management. This critical fault effect maps directly to **CWE-691** (Insufficient Control Flow Management), where transient timing disturbances in the execution path go unnoticed due to inadequate checking mechanisms.

Repeated Tunnel Fault Patterns and Vulnerability Analysis. Repeated occurrences of tunnel faults were observed consistently within experiments on core 3, highlighting underlying vulnerabilities in the program counter logic. Netlist analysis revealed that PC registers (e.g., pc_reg_2, pc_reg_3, pc_reg_4) sample memory address bus signals directly without protective synchronization. Mid-cycle glitches in these registers thus lead to unintended forward or backward jumps in instruction flow. The absence of dedicated synchronization or protective logic facilitates recurrent tunnel faults, further reinforcing the identified vulnerabilities associated with CWE mappings **CWE-1332** and **CWE-691**.

Spinner Fault in ASCON Computation. Figure 8c illustrates a spinner fault observed during laser-based fault injection experiments on the ASCON bitslice implementation. A targeted laser pulse at coordinates (2788, 2176) at clock cycle 125 triggered this fault. Detailed layout-level analysis confirmed that all relevant pipeline registers maintained their correct state prior to fault injection. Immediately after the laser pulse, the signal dbg_0.cpu_ctl_reg_4_.Q transitioned from 0 to 1. This transition activated the debug halt/reset logic within the processor's control circuitry, propagating through a dedicated debug pathway to assert a global CPU halt signal (evidenced by the subsequent assertion of clock_module_0.dbg_rst_noscan_reg.Q). The global halt condition forced the frontend pipeline logic, particularly the program counter registers (frontend_0.pc_reg_[15..0].Q), to reset to zero. Consequently, the processor immediately ceased executing further instructions, becoming trapped in an unresponsive halted state.

The spinner fault emerged repeatedly, observed in 17 out of 994 campaigns conducted under similar injection parameters. This recurrent behavior directly corresponds to **CWE-835** (Loop with Unreachable Exit Condition). Specifically, the debug halt path creates an internal state from which no recovery is possible without external intervention or reset. This fault demonstrates a critical vulnerability in the processor's debug and control-flow logic, underscoring the necessity for enhanced protection mechanisms against targeted physical fault injections, such as precise laser strikes, capable of exploiting sensitive internal debug signals.

Limitations. The proposed methodology relies on scan-chain data collected primarily during pre-silicon stages, which may not be feasible or permitted post-silicon due to restricted access in authorized environments. In cases where scan-chain or memory-based access to micro-architectural states is unavailable, partial visibility can still be obtained through alternative methods such as JTAG interfaces, performance counters, or firmware-based debug instructions. Furthermore, dimensionality-reduction techniques (e.g., PCA or t-SNE) were intentionally not explored in this study to preserve subtle yet critical fault signatures that could otherwise be diluted. Future research may investigate suitable approaches to dimensionality reduction that maintain diagnostic precision while enhancing computational efficiency. The scan-chain implementation requires four dedicated I/O pins and imposes a 2–4% overhead in scan flip-flop area and critical-path delay. A full scan capture operation completes in under one second.

6 Conclusion

A Deep-Learning-based framework for micro-architecture fault detection uses scan-chain data to expose hidden anomalies in embedded processors. Our experiments achieved 92% detection accuracy across multiple architectures and fault injection methods, indicating that direct microarchitecture observability can substantially mitigate reliability and security risks. By systematically correlating recurring hardware fault patterns with established CWE categories, the proposed approach facilitates a deeper understanding of potential vulnerabilities and enables standardized mitigation strategies. These findings underscore the value of early, cross-layer detection in safety-critical and cryptographic contexts. Future work includes targeted fault analysis of memory modules under realistic application workloads, the development of hybrid techniques that integrate hardware trace data with software profiling, and the evaluation of on-chip inference accelerators for real-time fault detection. Utimately, this methodology can help formalize hardware-level fault detection.

Acknowledgements. This research was supported in part by NSF Award 2219810.

A Appendix

See (Fig. 9).

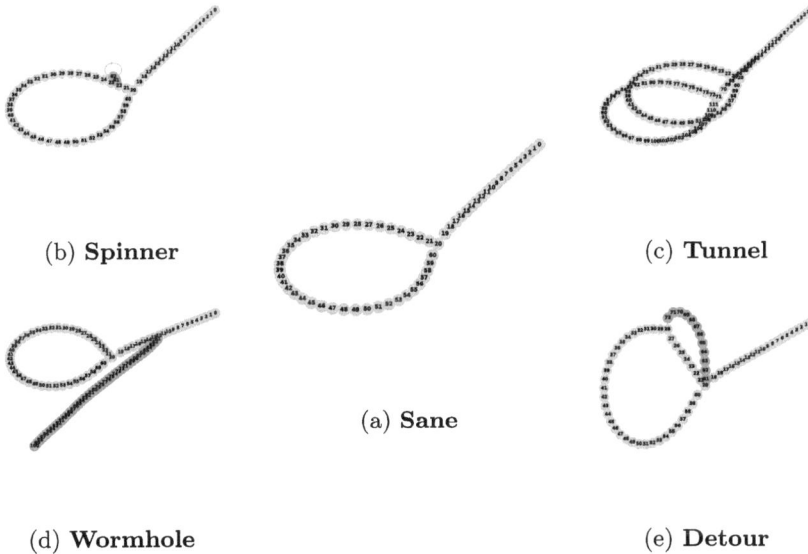

Fig. 9. Five principal fault patterns derived from FSMRED firmware experiments. Each subfigure illustrates a distinct micro-architectural path: (a) Sane: The nominal, fault-free execution in which all microarchitectural state transitions occur strictly according to the design specification. (b) Spinner: A fault pattern in which execution becomes trapped within a confined subset of microarchitectural states, endlessly cycling without advancing the control-flow. (c) Tunnel: A fault-induced anomaly that bypasses one or more intended intermediate states, creating a direct shortcut through the state sequence. (d) Wormhole: A high-impact fault event characterized by an instantaneous jump to a distant, non-sequential microarchitectural state, circumventing all intermediate transitions. (e) Detour: A transient fault pattern whereby execution momentarily diverges along an alternate sequence of microarchitectural states before reconverging with the intended progression.

References

1. Adhikary, A., Petrucci, G.T., Tanguy, P., Lapôtre, V., Buhan, I.: SoK: the apprentice guide to automated fault injection simulation for security evaluation. Cryptology ePrint Archive, Paper 2024/1944 (2024). https://eprint.iacr.org/2024/1944
2. Dixit, H.D., et al.: Silent data corruptions at scale (2021). https://arxiv.org/abs/2102.11245
3. Dullien, T.: Weird machines, exploitability, and provable unexploitability. IEEE Trans. Emerg. Top. Comput. **8**(2), 391–403 (2020). https://doi.org/10.1109/TETC.2017.2785299
4. Dureuil, L., Petiot, G., Potet, M., Le, T., Crohen, A., de Choudens, P.: FISSC: a fault injection and simulation secure collection. In: Skavhaug, A., Guiochet, J., Bitsch, F. (eds.) Computer Safety, Reliability, and Security - 35th International Conference, SAFECOMP 2016, Trondheim, Norway, 21-23 September 2016, Proceedings. LNCS, vol. 9922, pp. 3–11. Springer (2016). https://doi.org/10.1007/978-3-319-45477-1_1, https://doi.org/10.1007/978-3-319-45477-1_1
5. Gambra, A., Chatterjee, D., Rioja, U., Armendariz, I., Batina, L.: Machine learning-based detection of glitch attacks in clock signal data. IACR Cryptol. ePrint Arch, p. 1939 (2024). https://eprint.iacr.org/2024/1939
6. Howard, J., Ruder, S.: Fine-tuned language models for text classification. CoRR abs/1801.06146 (2018). http://arxiv.org/abs/1801.06146
7. Hu, E.J., et al.: LORA: low-rank adaptation of large language models (2021). https://arxiv.org/abs/2106.09685
8. Liu, Z., Shanmugam, D., Schaumont, P.: FaultDetective: explainable to a fault, from the design layout to the software. In: IACR Transactions on Cryptographic Hardware and Embedded Systems, vol. 2024, pp. 610–632 (2024). https://doi.org/10.46586/tches.v2024.i4.610-632, https://tches.iacr.org/index.php/TCHES/article/view/11804
9. Moore, S., Anderson, R., Cunningham, P., Mullins, R., Taylor, G.: Improving smart card security using self-timed circuits. In: Proceedings Eighth International Symposium on Asynchronous Circuits and Systems, pp. 211–218 (2002). https://doi.org/10.1109/ASYNC.2002.1000311
10. Rafi, M.N., Kim, D.J., Chen, T.H., Wang, S.: Enhancing fault localization through ordered code analysis with LLM agents and self-reflection (2024). https://arxiv.org/abs/2409.13642
11. Rivière, L., Najm, Z., Rauzy, P., Danger, J.L., Bringer, J., Sauvage, L.: High precision fault injections on the instruction cache of ARMv7-M architectures. In: IEEE International Symposium on Hardware-Oriented Security and Trust (2015). https://doi.org/10.1109/HST.2015.7140238
12. da Rosa, F.R., Garibotti, R., Ost, L., Reis, R.: Using machine learning techniques to evaluate multicore soft error reliability. IEEE Trans. Circuits Syst. I Regul. Pap. **66**(6), 2151–2164 (2019). https://doi.org/10.1109/TCSI.2019.2906155
13. Saha, S., Jap, D., Patranabis, S., Mukhopadhyay, D., Bhasin, S., Dasgupta, P.: Automatic characterization of exploitable faults: a machine learning approach. IEEE Trans. Inf. Forensics Secur. **14**(4), 954–968 (2019). https://doi.org/10.1109/TIFS.2018.2868245
14. Scarselli, F., Gori, M., Tsoi, A.C., Hagenbuchner, M., Monfardini, G.: The graph neural network model. IEEE Trans. Neural Networks **20**(1), 61–80 (2009). https://doi.org/10.1109/TNN.2008.2005605

15. Shanmugam, D., Liu, Z., Schaumont, P.: CAPRI6: a solution for fault root cause detection. In: Proceedings of the 34th Microelectronics Design and Test Symposium (IEEE MDTS 2025), Accepted for publication (2025). https://mdts.ieee.org/full-agenda-2025/
16. Shrivastwa, R.R., Guilley, S., Danger, J.L.: Multi-source fault injection detection using machine learning and sensor fusion. In: Stănică, P., Mesnager, S., Debnath, S.K. (eds.) Security and Privacy, pp. 93–107. Springer International Publishing, Cham (2021). https://doi.org/10.1007/978-3-030-90553-8_7
17. Stein, A., Wayne, A., Naik, A., Naik, M., Wong, E.: Where's the bug? attention probing for scalable fault localization (2025). https://arxiv.org/abs/2502.13966
18. Stoffelen, K.: Optimizing s-box implementations for several criteria using sat solvers. In: Peyrin, T. (ed.) Fast Software Encryption, pp. 140–160. Springer, Berlin Heidelberg, Berlin, Heidelberg (2016). https://doi.org/10.1007/978-3-662-52993-5_8

Let's Share a Secret: Share-Reduced Design of M&M for the AES S-Box

Haruka Hirata[1]✉ , Daiki Miyahara[1] , Yuko Hara[2] , Kazuo Sakiyama[1] , and Yang Li[1]✉

[1] The University of Electro-Communications, Tokyo, Japan
{h.haruka,miyahara,sakiyama,liyang}@uec.ac.jp
[2] Institute of Science Tokyo, Tokyo, Japan
hara@cad.ict.e.titech.ac.jp

Abstract. Masks and Macs (M&M), proposed at TCHES 2019, is a powerful countermeasure against physical attacks. This scheme combines masking and circuit duplication with information-theoretic MAC tags. Specifically, masking mitigates side-channel analysis, while circuit redundancy protects against fault analysis. However, it was reported that the AES encryption circuit protected by M&M is vulnerable to zero-value attacks, and an extended countermeasure was proposed to address this issue. Counteracting the attacks is mandatory due to their ease of execution, but this proposed method requires additional circuits to detect faults. While the implementation cost remains reasonable for lower-security-order designs, it becomes considerable for higher-security-order implementations. In this paper, we propose an area-efficient implementation of M&M that reduces the number of shares while preserving its functionality. We focus on the S-box and compare our approach's security and implementation cost to the original M&M. Furthermore, we discuss the limitations of share reduction in maintaining the security of the original M&M scheme.

Keywords: AES · M&M · side-channel analysis · fault analysis · combined countermeasure

1 Introduction

Side-channel analysis exploits physical information leaked during cryptographic operations, such as power consumption, electromagnetic emissions, or processing time [13,14]. On the other hand, in fault analysis, an attacker intentionally induces faults in cryptographic devices and then analyzes the resulting ciphertext [4]. Since such attacks that exploit physical information or faults do not rely on the mathematical strength of cryptographic algorithms, countermeasures at the implementation level are crucial. However, countermeasures for these physical attacks are often discussed separately, and research on comprehensive and efficient countermeasures remains limited.

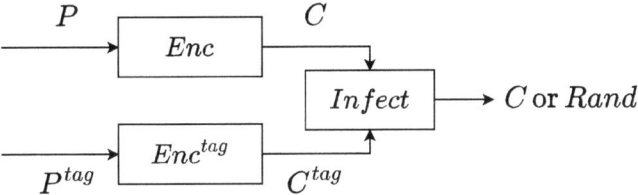

Fig. 1. An overview of M&M. The circuits are duplicated for plaintext and tag, and encryptions are performed in parallel.

Masks and Macs proposed by De Meyer et al. at TCHES 2019 [8] provides resistance to side-channel and fault analysis by combining masking with circuit redundancy using information-theoretic message authentication code (MAC) tags used for verifying the output. This scheme can be implemented with reasonable costs compared to other countermeasures [19,21], which were state-of-the-art at the time. However, it was reported that the AES encryption circuit protected by M&M (hereafter referred to as M&M-AES) is vulnerable to zero-value attacks at TCHES 2022 [10]. This vulnerability is caused by Canright's design for AES S-box [5], and the tag corresponding to zero is also zero in the M&M scheme. As a result, faults remain undetected on both value and tag circuits, and a correct ciphertext is obtained, i.e., the fault is ineffective. To counteract zero-value attacks, the authors of [10] added detection circuits to the intermediate calculations of the S-box, enabling fine-grained fault detection. While the implementation costs of their schemes for second-order security are reasonable, they would be considerable for higher-order security implementations because the added circuits for detection are nonlinear operations. The costs increase as $(d+1)^2$ with the security order d. Despite the considerable costs, counteracting zero-value attacks is inevitable due to their ease of execution.

In this paper, we take on this challenge and attempt to design a share-reduced version of M&M-AES to suppress the implementation cost overhead. Specifically, we focus on reducing the number of shares in the masking implementation of the S-box, thereby achieving a more efficient M&M-AES. This paper proposes a share-reduced implementation of the S-box and discusses the trade-off between effectiveness and security against probing attacks and differential fault analysis (DFA) attacks. To the best of our knowledge, this is the first work to reduce the number of shares on the redundant circuit while maintaining its security.

The rest of the paper is organized as follows. Section 2 provides previous work, an overview of M&M, zero-value attacks, and their countermeasure. Section 3 describes a methodology to implement the share-reduced S-box. In Sect. 4, we compare implementation costs and analyze security. Finally, we conclude this paper in Sect. 5.

Algorithm 1. $Infect$

Input: c, τ^c, α
Output: c or $rand$

$R \xleftarrow{\$} GF(2^k)\backslash\{0\}$
$\tilde{c} \leftarrow c + R \cdot (\alpha \cdot c + \tau^c)$
Output $\tilde{c}$

2 Previous Work

This section provides an overview of previous works, the M&M technique, and describes zero-value attacks on M&M-AES and their countermeasures, extending the original M&M scheme.

2.1 Masks and Macs

Redundant Circuits Using MAC Tag. In the M&M scheme, the value circuit, which receives the plaintext, and the tag circuit for the MAC tag of the plaintext are implemented in parallel, as shown in Fig. 1. The tag τ^x corresponding to the value $x \in GF(2^k)$ is obtained using the tag key $\alpha \in GF(2^k)$ as $\tau^x := \alpha x$, and is used to verify the correctness of the output. Simply redundantly implementing the value circuit allows an attacker to bypass the fault detection by causing the same fault in the replicated circuits. In contrast, M&M makes bypassing fault detection more difficult by redundantly implementing the tag circuit instead of the value circuit, a countermeasure against Differential Fault Analysis (DFA) attacks. Fault detection is performed by comparing the outputs of each circuit using the $Infect$ function. The calculation method for $Infect$ is described in Algorithm 1. If the ciphertext c or the tag τ^c contains a fault, then $\alpha \cdot c + \tau^c \neq 0$, meaning that the faulty ciphertext masked with random values will be output. The $Infect$ calculation is typically performed at the block size level. For example, spreading a one-byte fault across 16 bytes is required as a countermeasure against DFA attacks. However, the multiplication cost for 16 bytes is very high, which is a significant issue. Therefore, in the M&M-AES implementation, following the method by Lomné et al. [15], one-byte computation is performed 16 times instead of a 128-bit multiplication.

Masking Against Side-Channel Analysis. Masking [11] is a well-studied technique to counteract the side-channel analysis, originated from Ishai, Sahai, and Wagner, where the secret data is encoded into multiple values, called shares, using random numbers. The circuit keeps the value in a shared form until the computation ends. Thus, the encryption is performed in a shared form. When the number of shares is $d + 1$, the scheme is resistant to observation using d probes (known as d-probing attacks), and d is referred to as the security order. In addition to circuit redundancy for the Countermeasure against DFA, the M&M scheme implements masking for both the value and tag circuits. Therefore,

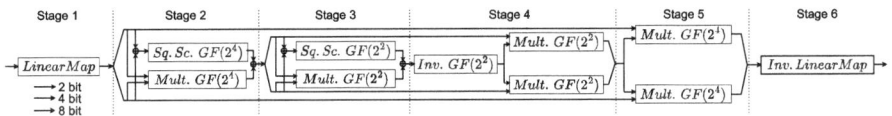

Fig. 2. The pipelined AES S-box with six stages proposed by De Cnudde et al. [7].

the implementation cost of the circuit countermeasures by M&M increases by approximately $2(d+1)^2$.

While M&M allows the use of arbitrary masking methods, M&M-AES [8] employs a Consolidating Masking Scheme [18], hereafter referred to as CMS, which extends threshold implementation [17] as a case study implementation.

2.2 Zero-Value Attacks Against M&M-AES

The calculation of the multiplicative inverse has a high implementation cost. Canright proposed a compact inversion algorithm [5], and the inversion of zero is defined as zero. The inverse circuit for M&M-AES is shown in Fig. 2. In the following, we explain the vulnerability in Canright's design, exploiting zero-value input.

First, the mapping λ_n from $GF((2^n)^2)$ to $GF(2^n)$ is defined as follows:

$$\lambda_n((a,b)) := ab + (a+b)^2 \nu, \quad (1)$$

where $\nu \in GF(2^n)$ is a constant. The elements of $GF((2^n)^2)$ are represented in the form $a\beta^{2^n} + b\beta$, where $a, b \in GF(2^n)$, with β being a root of an irreducible polynomial, and $[\beta^{2^n}, \beta]$ denoting the normal basis. Still, this paper represents it as a pair (a, b) for simplicity.

The multiplicative inverse in $GF((2^n)^2)$ is given by

$$(c, d) = (b\, \lambda_n((a,b))^{-1}, a\, \lambda_n((a,b))^{-1}), \quad (2)$$

and the inverse $y = x^{-1}$ is computed as follows:

$$c = \left[ab + (a+b)^2 \nu\right]^{-1} b, \quad (3)$$

$$d = \left[ab + (a+b)^2 \nu\right]^{-1} a. \quad (4)$$

The computation within the brackets corresponds to Stage 2 of the circuit shown in Fig. 2, which is λ_4. When the input x is zero, the outputs c and d will also be zero. The value in Stage 1 after applying the field isomorphism to $GF((2^4)^2)$ is $(a, b) = (0, 0)$, and thus the final multiplication of inversion multiplies by zero if and only if $x = 0$. Multiplying by zero is the key point of the zero-value attack; even if an attacker injects faults during the computation inside the brackets (i.e., inversion over $GF(2^4)$), these errors are nullified by multiplication with zero, resulting in a correct output value. Such faults that do not affect the output are called ineffective faults.

2.3 Countermeasure Against Zero-Value Attacks

As mentioned, M&M is ineffective against ineffective faults caused at the algorithm level, and zero-value attacks can be easily conducted. To counter zero-value attacks, Hirata et al. [10] added detection circuits to the susceptible stages, i.e., Stages 2, 3, and 4, to achieve fine-grained detection. Fault detection is performed by utilizing the intermediate values of the inversion on the value and tag circuits, i.e., the output of each stage.

Hirata et al. [10] showed that the map λ has multiplicative homomorphic properties. By this property, the faults can be detected before they are nullified by multiplying by zero. The outputs of Stage 2–4 can be written as $\lambda_4(x)$, $\lambda_2(x)$, and $\lambda_4(x)^{-1}$, respectively. Since the outputs of each stage in the value and tag circuits are $\lambda_n(x)$ and $\lambda_n(\alpha x)$, the following equation always holds for any x and α due to the homomorphism property of λ:

$$\lambda_n(x)\lambda_n(\alpha) + \lambda_n(\alpha x) = 0. \tag{5}$$

Therefore, faults can be detected by comparing the product of outputs of the value and the α circuits at each stage with the output of the tag circuit as in Eq. (5). Furthermore, a masked OR-accumulator accumulates the calculation results of λ to prevent attackers from determining the timing of fault occurrence.

The fault detection technique described above requires three multiplication circuits, a comparator (for calculating Eq. (5)), and an OR-accumulator register. After the encryption, the circuit computes *Match check* described in Algorithm 2 instead of *Infect*, then applies Kronecker's δ-function to check whether the fault has been injected or not. The additional modules are summarized as follows:

- Multiplication,
- OR-accumulator,
- δ-function.

These functions and accumulators are nonlinear operations and implemented in a shared form; thus, their costs are estimated as $(d+1)^2$ with a security order d. The second-order λ-detection M&M cost overhead factor is 1.33×, comparing with the original M&M, as reported in [10]. While this overhead remains reasonable for second-order implementation, higher security orders would significantly increase implementation costs.

Moreover, the amount of randomness required for refreshing increases as the security order increases. Despite this, the rise in cost is inevitable as a countermeasure against zero-value attacks, which are easy to execute. Therefore, in the following sections, we aim to reduce the implementation cost of M&M-AES while balancing robustness and cost efficiency.

3 Implementation of a Share-Reduced S-Box

In this section, we explore the implementation of M&M-AES with a reduced number of shares, focusing on the S-box.

Algorithm 2. *Match check*

Input: c, τ^c, α
Output: z
$z = 0$
for $i = 1$ to 16 **do**
    $z_i \leftarrow \alpha \cdot c_i \oplus \tau_i^c$ // just compare
    $z \leftarrow$ shared-OR(z, z_i) // then accumulate
end for
Output z

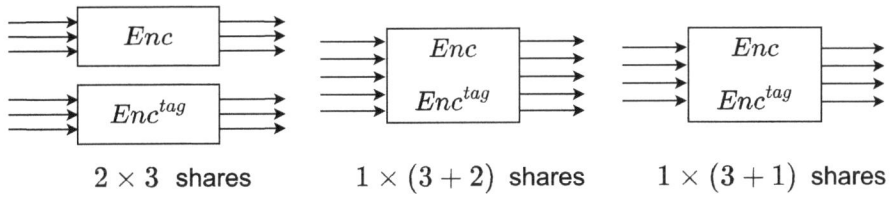

Fig. 3. The countermeasure circuit based on spatial redundancy, such as M&M (left), and the share-reduced M&Ms proposed in this paper (middle and right).

3.1 Overview of the Share-Reduced Implementation

The conceptual diagram of the circuit is shown in Fig. 3. In duplication-based countermeasures such as M&M, the total number of shares, $d + 1$, increases with the number of redundant circuit components. For example, as illustrated in Fig. 3, adding one redundant circuit doubles the total number of shares to $2(d + 1)$. In contrast, we propose a share-reduced variant of M&M to lower implementation costs. We consolidate the value and the tag circuit, where several shares are literally *shared* among the circuits, and indicate the number of shares that can be reduced.

$$\underbrace{(x_0,\quad r_0,}_{S_{\text{indep}}}\quad \underbrace{r_1,}_{S_{\text{dep}}}\quad \underbrace{r_2,\quad y_0)}_{S_{\text{indep}}} \qquad \underbrace{(x_0,\quad r_0,}_{S_{\text{indep}}}\quad \underbrace{r_1,}_{S_{\text{dep}}}\quad \underbrace{y_0)}_{S_{\text{indep}}}$$

Fig. 4. (In)dependent shares of five-share (left) and four-share (right) implementation.

As depicted in Fig. 4, we reuse the random value(s) in the value circuit and the tag circuit, and we name the resued shares *dependent share* S_{dep} and the others shares *independent share* S_{indep}. Hereafter, we refer to S_{dep} and S_{indep} as the number of shares, not the share value.

This paper describes an implementation methodology for a four-share implementation as an example. However, the five-share version can be implemented in the same way. Hence, partial summations of the shares indicate x and τ^x, respectively, and r_0 and r_1 are common:

$$x = x_0 + r_0 + r_1,$$
$$\tau^x = r_0 + r_1 + y_0.$$

3.2 Implementing a Share-Reduced S-Box

As already mentioned in Sect. 2.2, the inversion of M&M-AES S-box is implemented based on Canright's algorithm and the proposal by De Cnudde et al. (shown in Fig. 2). The implementation comprises the following four operations, explaining Canright's algorithm in detail.

- Field isomorphism $\phi\colon GF(2^8) \to GF((2^4)^2)$, and its inverse ϕ^{-1},
- Squaring and scaling over $GF(2^4)$, $GF(2^2)$,
- Inversion over $GF(2^2)$,
- Multiplication over $GF(2^4)$, $GF(2^2)$.

Except for multiplication, the operations above are additively holomorphic. We show that each operation is an additively homomorphic map and describe the method for performing multiplication for this design.

Field Isomorphism. The map ϕ and its inverse map ϕ^{-1} are defined as field automorphisms. Therefore, for any $a, b \in GF(2^8)$, the operation is trivially homomorphic for both addition and multiplication, i.e., $\phi(a) + \phi(b) = \phi(a+b)$ and $\phi(a)\phi(b) = \phi(ab)$ holds (the same holds for ϕ^{-1}).

Squaring and Scaling. The sum of two inputs is squared and scaled by a constant value. The function $f_n\colon (a,b) \mapsto (a+b)^2 \nu$, where $a, b, \nu \in GF(2^n)$, can be similarly defined for any n.

$$f_n((a,b)) + f_n((c,d)) = (a+b)^2\nu + (c+d)^2\nu \tag{6}$$
$$= (a^2 + b^2 + c^2 + d^2)\nu, \tag{7}$$

$$f_n((a,b) + (c,d)) = f_n((a+c, b+d)) \tag{8}$$
$$= ((a+b) + (c+d))^2 \nu \tag{9}$$
$$= (a^2 + b^2 + c^2 + d^2)\nu. \tag{10}$$

The function has additive homomorphic properties, as shown in Eqs. (7) and (10).

Inversion Over $GF(2^2)$. This computation is just a bit-swapping and is denoted as $g\colon (a,b) \mapsto (b,a)$ for $a, b \in GF(2)$.

$$g((a,b)) + g((c,d)) = (b,a) + (d,c) \tag{11}$$
$$= (b+d, a+c), \tag{12}$$

$$g((a,b) + (c,d)) = g((a+c, b+d)) \tag{13}$$
$$= (b+d, a+c). \tag{14}$$

As with squaring and scaling, from Eqs. (12) and (14), it can be seen that the multiplication inversion over $GF(2^2)$ exhibits additively homomorphic properties.

Again, we note that all of the above calculations are additive homomorphic. Therefore, calculations can be performed share-wise, and the output share can thus be obtained with the additively homomorphic function F.

$$(z_0, z_1, z_2, z_3) \leftarrow (F(x_0), F(r_0), F(r_1), F(y_0)).$$

Multiplication. As mentioned, multiplication is not a homomorphic function, and independent calculations for each share cannot be performed. Therefore, we calculate them with all shares. Here, we take the multiplication on Stage 2 as an example. The upper and lower four bits of x are denoted as x^{top} and x^{bot}, respectively (applied for y as well). We compute $x^{top}x^{bot} = (x_0^{top} + r_0^{top} + r_1^{top})(x_0^{bot} + r_0^{bot} + r_1^{bot})$ and $y^{top}y^{bot} = (y_0^{top} + r_0^{top} + r_1^{top})(y_0^{bot} + r_0^{bot} + r_1^{bot})$. The resulting terms for the value $(x^{top}x^{bot})$ and the tag $(x^{top}x^{bot})$ are as follows:

$$
\begin{aligned}
x^{top}x^{bot} &= x_0^{top}x_0^{bot} + x_0^{top}r_0^{bot} + x_0^{top}r_1^{bot} \\
&+ r_0^{top}x_0^{bot} + \boldsymbol{r_0^{top}r_0^{bot}} + \boldsymbol{r_0^{top}r_1^{bot}} \\
&+ r_1^{top}x_0^{bot} + \boldsymbol{r_1^{top}r_0^{bot}} + \boldsymbol{r_1^{top}r_1^{bot}},
\end{aligned} \tag{15}
$$

$$
\begin{aligned}
y^{top}y^{bot} &= y_0^{top}y_0^{bot} + y_0^{top}r_0^{bot} + y_0^{top}r_1^{bot} \\
&+ r_0^{top}y_0^{bot} + \boldsymbol{r_0^{top}r_0^{bot}} + \boldsymbol{r_0^{top}r_1^{bot}} \\
&+ r_1^{top}y_0^{bot} + \boldsymbol{r_1^{top}r_0^{bot}} + \boldsymbol{r_1^{top}r_1^{bot}}.
\end{aligned} \tag{16}
$$

As shown in Eqs. (15) and (16), the terms in bold $r_0^{top}r_0^{bot}$, $r_0^{top}r_1^{bot}$, $r_1^{top}r_0^{bot}$, and $r_1^{top}r_1^{bot}$ are overlapping between the value and tag calculations; thus we can omit these computations. In general, the number of overlapping multiplications is represented as $(d_{\text{dep}})^2$. Therefore, the 18 ($= 2 \times (3^2)$) multiplications are reduced to 14 for $d_{\text{dep}} = 2$.

Then, we combine the terms relating x_0 to the share of z_0 (the same as for y_0) to satisfy the correctness of the output shares, namely, ensuring $x_0 + r_0 + r_1 = x$ and $y_0 + r_0 + r_1 = \tau^x$. Hence, the output share is computed as follows, where registers are denoted as $[\cdot]_{reg}$, and R_i represents a random value for refreshing:

$$
\begin{aligned}
t_0 &= x_0^{top}x_0^{bot} + R_0 + R_1 \\
t_1 &= x_0^{top}r_0^{bot} + R_1 + R_2 \\
t_2 &= x_0^{top}r_1^{bot} + R_2 + R_3 \\
t_3 &= r_0^{top}x_0^{bot} + R_3 + R_4 \\
t_4 &= r_1^{top}x_0^{bot} + R_4 + R_5
\end{aligned}
\qquad z_0 = [t_0]_{reg} + [t_1]_{reg} + [t_2]_{reg} + [t_3]_{reg} + [t_4]_{reg}
$$

$$t_5 = r_0^{top} r_0^{bot} + R_5 + R_6$$
$$t_6 = r_0^{top} r_1^{bot} + R_6 + R_7 \qquad z_1 = [t_5]_{reg} + [t_6]_{reg}$$
$$t_7 = r_1^{top} r_0^{bot} + R_7 + R_8$$
$$t_8 = r_1^{top} r_1^{bot} + R_8 + R_0 \qquad z_2 = [t_7]_{reg} + [t_8]_{reg}$$
$$t_9 = y_0^{top} y_0^{bot} + R_0 + R_9$$
$$t_{10} = y_0^{top} r_0^{bot} + R_9 + R_{10}$$
$$t_{11} = y_0^{top} r_1^{bot} + R_{10} + R_{11}$$
$$t_{12} = r_0^{top} y_0^{bot} + R_{11} + R_{12}$$
$$t_{13} = r_1^{top} y_0^{bot} + R_{12} + R_5 \qquad z_3 = [t_9]_{reg} + [t_{10}]_{reg} + [t_{11}]_{reg} + [t_{12}]_{reg} + [t_{13}]_{reg}$$

Based on the CMS scheme, we refresh shares with the ring-refreshing approach of [7]. We discuss the security for the probing model of the implementation in Sect. 4.3.

Multplying α^2 to the Tag Shares. The multiplicative inverses obtained from the calculations are x^{-1} and $(\alpha x)^{-1}$, but the value and tag do not match ($\because$ $(\alpha x)^{-1} \neq \tau^{x^{-1}}$). By multiplying the tag share by α^2, the tag corresponding to x^{-1} is obtained $(\alpha^2(\alpha x)^{-1} = \alpha x^{-1})$. However, the share after multiplying by α^2 becomes $(x_0, \alpha^2 r_0, \alpha^2 r_1, \alpha^2 y_0)$, and the shares for x no longer satisfies the correctness, i.e., $x_0 + \alpha^2 r_0 + \alpha^2 r_1 \neq x$. To tweak this, we add r_0 and r_1 to the x_0 share, and $\alpha^2 r_0$ and $\alpha^2 r_1$ to the y_0 share. Thus, the share for the inversion output is as follows.

$$z_0 \leftarrow x_0 + \alpha^2 r_0 + \alpha^2 r_1,$$
$$z_1 \leftarrow \alpha^2 r_0 + r_0,$$
$$z_2 \leftarrow \alpha^2 r_1 + r_1,$$
$$z_3 \leftarrow \alpha^2 y_0 + r_0 + r_1.$$

Affine Transformations. We compute an affine transformation with the inversions to obtain the S-box outputs. The calculation for the value circuit is straightforward: $A(x) = L(x) + c$, where L is a linear transformation and $c = $ 0x63 is a constant value, while the tag shares require another matrix for the tag circuit.

From [8], the matrix $\mathbf{M_{tag}}$ for a transformation of the tag is obtained as follows;

$$\mathbf{M_{tag}} = [\psi(\alpha L(128\alpha^{-1})) \quad \psi(\alpha L(64\alpha^{-1})) \quad \cdots \quad \psi(\alpha L(\alpha^{-1}))],$$

where ψ is the isomorphism between $GF(2^8)$ and $GF(2)^8$. The matrix depends on the tag key α and can be precomputed; hence, it is represented as a constant value. The affine transformation for the tag is computed as $A_{tag}(t) = \mathbf{M}_\alpha \psi(t) + c_{tag}$, where $c_{tag} = \alpha c$. Thus, the output shares of the S-box are as follows;

Table 1. Area comparison. The column of the original M&M includes two S-boxes.

	Original M&M	This work	
	6 shares	5 shares	4 shares
Area [μm^2]	8854.61	8192.80	6717.032
Reduction ratio	–	0.075	0.24

$$z_0 \leftarrow A(x_0) + A_{tag}(r_0) + A_{tag}(r_1),$$
$$z_1 \leftarrow A_{tag}(r_0) + A(r_0),$$
$$z_2 \leftarrow A_{tag}(r_1) + A(r_1),$$
$$z_3 \leftarrow A_{tag}(y_0) + A(r_0) + A(r_1).$$

Moreover, for the latency optimization, we could compute the matrix $\mathbf{M_{tag}}$ as

$$\mathbf{M_{tag}} = [\psi(\alpha L(128\alpha)) \quad \psi(\alpha L(64\alpha)) \quad \cdots \quad \psi(\alpha L(\alpha))],$$

and this allows us to omit multiplying α^2 to the tag shares after calculating the inversion. Therefore, we can directly apply the affine transformation to the inversion outputs.

The tag key α is a secret; thus, computations regarding the matrix and the tag key are performed in shared form.

4 Implementation Cost and Security Evaluation

We compare the implementation costs of the second-order secure S-box of M&M-AES and the share-reduced S-box and analyze the security of the share-reduced implementation against Differential Fault Analysis (DFA) and probing attacks.

4.1 Implementation Cost

We implemented the S-box in Verilog-HDL and compared its circuit area and randomness implementation costs.

Area. We synthesize them with the open-source tool Yosys [22] and the Nangate 45 nm Open Cell Library [16]. Circuit areas for both the M&M-AES S-box and the share-reduced S-box are shown in Table 1. The circuit area[1] was reduced by approximately 24 % for four-share and 7.5 % for five-share compared to two M&M-AES S-boxes.

While the number of shares in the M&M circuit was reduced from 6 to 4, the multiplications in the S-box were only reduced from 18 to 14 (a reduction rate of approximately 22 %).

---
[1] An area of 0.798 μm^2 corresponds to one 2-input, 1-output NAND gate.

Table 2. Implementation cost for S-box with security order d and reducing level S_{dep} (register bit).

	Original M&M-AES	Share-reduced design
Stage 1	$16(d+1)$	$16(d+1) - 8S_{\text{dep}}$
Stage 2	$8(d+1)^2 + 16(d+1)$	$8(d+1)^2 + 16(d+1) - (8S_{\text{dep}} + 4S_{\text{dep}}^2)$
Stage 3	$4(d+1)^2 + 24(d+1)$	$4(d+1)^2 + 24(d+1) - (12S_{\text{dep}} + 2S_{\text{dep}}^2)$
Stage 4	$8(d+1)^2 + 16(d+1)$	$8(d+1)^2 + 16(d+1) - (8S_{\text{dep}} + 4S_{\text{dep}}^2)$
Stage 5	$16(d+1)^2$	$16(d+1)^2 - 8S_{\text{dep}}^2$
Stage 6	$16(d+1)$	$16(d+1) - 8S_{\text{dep}}$
Total	$36(d+1)^2 + 88(d+1)$	$36(d+1)^2 + 88(d+1) - (44S_{\text{dep}} + 18S_{\text{dep}}^2)$

Table 3. Comparison of randomness for S-box ([bit/cycle]). The columns of the original M&M include two S-boxes.

	Original M&M	This work	
	6 shares	5 shares	4 shares
Stage 1	0	0	0
Stage 2	72	64	52
Stage 3	36	32	26
Stage 4	72	64	52
Stage 5	144	128	104
Stage 6	0	0	0
Total	324	288	234

To compare implementation costs for higher security orders d, Table 2 summarizes the number of register bits required for the S-box implementation at each stage. According to the table, a ratio of required bits (obtained by share-reduced/original M&M-AES) is expected to increase as the share reduction level d_{dep} increases. Thus, the share-reduced implementation contributes significantly to cost efficiency when a higher reduction level is available.

Randomness. The number of random bits consumed during the S-box computation is summarized in Table 3. Multiplications requiring refreshing are reduced from 18 to 14. Thus, the overall randomness consumption is also decreased. The implementation is based on the original M&M-AES from [8] and utilizes the ring-refreshing [18]. The use of randomness can be optimized by employing Domain-Oriented Masking [9], which refreshes only the cross products between different domains (e.g., $x_0^{top} \cdot r_1^{bot}$).

4.2 Security Against Differential Fault Analysis

In this section, we discuss the resistance of the proposed share-reduced S-box against Differential Fault Analysis (DFA) under two scenarios: when different faults occur independently in the value and tag circuits, and when an identical fault occurs in both circuits.

We note that the share-reduced implementation is vulnerable to zero-value attacks as provided by Hirata [10] since it is based on the original M&M-AES. We do not consider the zero-value attacks in this paper, and the share-reduced implementation must integrate λ-detection M&M to counteract the attacks.

Different Faults in the Circuits. We assume that faults Δ_c and Δ_τ occur independently in the value and tag circuit. This includes the case where $\Delta_c = \Delta_\tau$. A calculation for the fault detection in $Infect$ is performed as follows:

$$(c + \Delta_c)\alpha + (\tau^c + \Delta_\tau) = c\alpha + \Delta_c\alpha + c\alpha + \Delta_\tau$$
$$= \Delta_c\alpha + \Delta_\tau. \qquad (17)$$

When Δ_c and Δ_τ are random, the probability that Eq. (17) equals zero is $2^{-8} = 0.00392$. Even if the faults are constant, the probability remains 0.00392 because α takes uniformly random values. Thus, the fault detection probability of M&M is very high. Then, if $\alpha = 0$ and a fault occurs only in the value circuit (i.e., $\Delta_\tau = 0$), Eq. (17) will always equal zero. However, the probability $\Pr[\alpha = 0]$ is 0.00392 since the tag key α is randomly generated for each encryption operation, and this corresponds to injecting proper faults Δ_c and Δ_τ into the circuit such that Eq. (17) holds. Therefore, this implementation guarantees the same security as the original M&M-AES for different circuit faults.

Identical Faults in the Circuits. In our proposed share-reduced S-box circuit, the shares r_0 and r_1 are literally "shared" between the value and tag circuits. As a result, when faults occur in both or one of the shares, identical faults are easily introduced into both the value circuit and the tag circuit. This means $\Delta_c = \Delta_\tau \neq 0$, which, for simplicity, is denoted as Δ. Under this condition, the computation in $Infect$ is given by

$$(c + \Delta)\alpha + (\tau^c + \Delta) = c\alpha + \Delta\alpha + c\alpha + \Delta \qquad (18)$$
$$= \Delta\alpha + \Delta, \qquad (19)$$

and Eq. (19) equals zero only when $\alpha = 1$.

Therefore, faults that occur in both the value circuit and the tag circuit can be detected with a high probability, unlike faults that occur independently in each circuit. However, when $\alpha = 1$, Eq. (19) is always zero for any fault Δ, resulting in a vulnerability to DFA attacks, and the attacker needs just a single fault on the circuit. Consequently, this tag key $\alpha = 1$ would be a flaw in the share-reduced S-box. It remains as long as the shares are "shared"; thus, the flaw is inevitable in the share-reduced implementation.

Vulnerable Tag Key $\alpha = 1$. As described in the previous section, the critical tag key $\alpha = 1$ exists for which M&M always fails to detect faults, making DFA attacks easily executable. This issue can be addressed by ensuring the tag key α does not take the value 1. However, if $\alpha \in GF(2^8)$ is not uniformly distributed, the output of $Infect$ becomes biased. Moreover, it has already been pointed out that this bias can be exploited for attacks [2].

De Meyer et al. [8] noted that when α is not uniform in $GF(2^8)$, output randomization using $Infect$ becomes insecure due to the biased outputs. Therefore, we use $Match\,check$ to detect faults instead of $Infect$, following $Match\,check$ method proposed in [10], This approach does not randomize the output but merely checks for faults. If a fault is detected, all output bits are set to 0. Consequently, the bias observed in the output does not occur. Hence, DFA attacks caused by the critical key can be mitigated.

4.3 Security Against Probing Attacks

The security order of the original M&M-AES is $d - 2$, and this guarantees that both the value circuit and the tag circuit withstand up to two probing[2]. On the other hand, we integrate these into a single circuit in our design. Hence, we consider an attacker obtaining share(s) across the value and tag circuits.

The attacker is allowed to observe up to $d = 2$ shares in the second-order attack scenario, and the joint distribution $\Pr[\text{Probe} = \{x_0, y_0\}]$, where x_0 and y_0 are independent shares, is as follows;

$$\Pr[\text{Probe} = \{x_0, y_0\}] = \frac{254}{65024}. \tag{20}$$

To guarantee second-order security against probing attacks, the conditional probability below must hold;

$$\Pr[\text{Probe} = \{x_0, y_0\} \mid x] = \Pr[\text{Probe} = \{x_0, y_0\}], \tag{21}$$

with the given unmasked, namely, the secret value x. This equation means the probing does not leak information regarding x.

However, from the following lemma, Eq. (21) does not hold when $x = 0$ for the four-share implementation.

Lemma 1. $x_0 = y_0$ *if and only if* $x = 0$, *for any tag key* α.

Proof. (1) $x = 0 \Rightarrow x_0 = y_0$.
If $x = 0$, then $x_0 = 0 + r_0 + r_1$ and $y_0 = \alpha \cdot 0 + r_0 + r_1$. Thus, $x_0 = y_0$.
(2) $x = 0 \Leftarrow x_0 = y_0$.
If $x + r_0 + r_1 = \alpha x + r_0 + r_1$, then it follows that $x = \alpha x$. Since $\alpha \notin \{0, 1\}$, this equation holds only when $x = 0$. □

---

[2] The authors proposed the first- and second-order implementation, but we take only the second-order version in this paper.

Hence, the conditional probability is obtained as follows;

$$\Pr[\text{Probe} = \{x_0, y_0\} \mid x = 0] = \begin{cases} 1, & x_0 = y_0, \\ 0, & x_0 \neq y_0. \end{cases} \quad (22)$$

Furthermore, when the observed values are identical, i.e., $x_0 = y_0$, the attacker would obtain information that the secret value x is zero. This observation indicates a potential for other zero-value attacks; the attacker knows whether the value processed is zero, despite the implementation must withstand up to two probes. Therefore, the security order of the four-share implementation is towards the first-order, implying that at least three shares must be independent to prevent second-order attacks.

Theorem 1. *The maximum allowable share reduction, S_{dep}, must be less than $\frac{d+1}{2}$ to ensure dth-order security.*

Proof. To ensure dth-order probing security, the number of independent shares, S_{indep}, must be at least $d + 1$. Therefore,

$$S_{\text{indep}} = 2(d+1) - 2S_{\text{dep}} \geq d+1, \quad (23)$$
$$\Rightarrow d + 1 - 2S_{\text{dep}} \geq 0, \quad (24)$$
$$\Rightarrow S_{\text{dep}} \leq \frac{d+1}{2}. \quad (25)$$

Thus, the maximum allowable share reduction is given by $S_{\text{dep}} \leq \frac{d+1}{2}$. □

From Theorem 1, the five-share implementation (i.e., $S_{\text{dep}} = 1$) ensures second-order probing security. The original M&M-AES, i.e., six-share implementation, follows this theorem, and any two probing reveals neither secret value x nor the tag αx, withstanding the second-order attacks.

Verification of Refreshing Gadgets by SILVER. In our design, the refreshing of shares is performed as follows: the left side corresponds to the five-share implementation, while the right side represents the four-share implementation.

$$\begin{aligned} z'_0 &= z_0 + R_0 + R_1 \\ z'_1 &= z_1 + R_1 + R_2 \\ z'_2 &= z_2 + R_2 + R_0 \\ z'_3 &= z_3 + R_0 + R_3 \\ z'_4 &= z_4 + R_3 + R_2 \end{aligned} \qquad \begin{aligned} z'_0 &= z_0 + R_0 + R_1 \\ z'_1 &= z_1 + R_1 + R_2 \\ z'_2 &= z_2 + R_2 + R_0 \\ z'_3 &= z_3 + R_0 + R_1 \end{aligned}$$

As discussed above, the security of the design has the potential to be downgraded due to the reuse of randomness despite the reduction in implementation cost. To confirm whether the number of dependent shares, $S_{\text{dep}} = 1$, ensures security equivalent to that of the original M&M-AES, we conduct a leakage evaluation using the formal verification tool SILVER [12]. Not only did we identify a potential flaw against another type of zero-value attack, but we also observed a reduction in the security level of SNI (Strong Non-Interference) [1] in the four-share implementation due to the reuse of randomness, as shown in Table 4. On the other hand, the five-share implementation has the 2-SNI security equivalent to the $d+1$ masking scheme from [7], which is used in the M&M-AES implementation.

Table 4. Verification results of refreshing gadgets by SILVER.

Model	Result		
	$d+1$ Masking [7]	This work	
	3 shares	5 shares	4 shares
Probing	PASS ($d \leq 2$)	PASS ($d \leq 4$)	PASS ($d \leq 3$)
NI	PASS ($d \leq 2$)	PASS ($d \leq 4$)	PASS ($d \leq 3$)
SNI	**PASS** ($d \leq 2$)	**PASS** ($d \leq 2$)	**PASS** ($d \leq 1$)
PINI	PASS ($d \leq 2$)	PASS ($d \leq 4$)	PASS ($d \leq 3$)
Uniformity	PASS	PASS	PASS

These refreshing operations are performed independently on each share, ensuring that all shares remain isolated and do not interfere. Consequently, the results of the probing, NI, and PINI [6] models indicate that the implementation can withstand up to the total number of shares minus one probing.

Here, we note that the security order of the share-reduced implementation must be less than three, i.e., $d \leq 2$, because probing x_0, r_0, and r_1 reveals a secret value x. Furthermore, the security against the probing model decreases when the value is zero, as previously mentioned. However, SILVER does not recognize this condition, leading to "PASS" results with security levels greater than two for both the five-share and four-share implementations, as shown in Table 4. Nevertheless, the verification results confirm that the design achieves at least second-order security in the probing, NI, and PINI models. Therefore, we focus on the SNI model to ensure security equivalent to the original M&M-AES.

5 Conclusion

Based on our findings, we proposed a share-reduced implementation of M&M-AES to improve area efficiency while maintaining security. By reducing the number of shares in the masking implementation of the S-box, our approach mitigates the increase in the implementation cost associated with higher-security-order designs.

We practically confirmed that the proposed design achieves reductions of area and randomness for both five-share and four-share implementations. Our analysis demonstrated that the five-share design is comparable to the original M&M-AES

in terms of security against probing and DFA attacks. In contrast, the four-share design reduces the security level. Then, we identified general limitations in share reduction to guarantee the required security order.

In future work, it is essential to evaluate the security of its application to the entire AES encryption process. This study focuses on only the S-box and explores the share-reduced implementation. We will extend our new design to the entire AES encryption circuit and conduct evaluations using power consumption traces for leakage analysis based on TVLA [3,20] and fault injection experiments for further investigation.

Acknowledgements. This work was supported by JST CREST (grant number JPMJCR23M2), JSPS Bilateral Joint Research Projects (grant number JPJSBP120242301), and JSPS Research Fellows (grant number JP25KJ1291). We would like to express our deepest gratitude to Svetla Nikova for granting permission to use the M&M source code to implement the S-box.

References

1. Barthe, G., et al.: Strong non-interference and type-directed higher-order masking. In: Proceedings of the 2016 ACM SIGSAC Conference on Computer and Communications Security, pp. 116–129. CCS '16, Association for Computing Machinery, New York, NY, USA (2016)
2. Battistello, A., Giraud, C.: Fault analysis of infective AES computations. In: 2013 Workshop on Fault Diagnosis and Tolerance in Cryptography, pp. 101–107 (2013)
3. Becker, G.T., et al.: Test vector leakage assessment (TVLA) methodology in practice. In: International Cryptographic Module Conference (2013)
4. Biham, E., Shamir, A.: Differential fault analysis of secret key cryptosystems. In: Advances in Cryptology — CRYPTO '97. LNCS, vol. 1294, pp. 513–525. Springer (1997)
5. Canright, D.: A very compact S-Box for AES. In: Cryptographic Hardware and Embedded Systems — CHES 2005. LNCS, vol. 3659, pp. 441–455. Springer (2005)
6. Cassiers, G., Standaert, F.X.: Trivially and efficiently composing masked gadgets with probe isolating non-interference. IEEE Trans. Inf. Forensics Secur. **15**, 2542–2555 (2020)
7. De Cnudde, T., Reparaz, O., Bilgin, B., Nikova, S., Nikov, V., Rijmen, V.: Masking AES with d+1 shares in hardware. In: Bilgin, B., Nikova, S., Rijmen, V. (eds.) Proceedings of the ACM Workshop on Theory of Implementation Security, TIS@CCS 2016 Vienna, Austria, October, 2016, p. 43. ACM (2016)
8. De Meyer, L., Arribas, V., Nikova, S., Nikov, V., Rijmen, V.: M&M: masks and macs against physical attacks. IACR Trans. Cryptographic Hardware Embedded Syst. **2019**(1), 25–50 (2019)
9. Groß, H., Mangard, S., Korak, T.: Domain-oriented masking: compact masked hardware implementations with arbitrary protection order. In: Proceedings of the ACM Workshop on Theory of Implementation Security, p. 3. ACM (2016)
10. Hirata, H., et al.: All you need is fault: zero-value attacks on AES and a new λ-detection M&M. IACR Trans. Cryptographic Hardware Embedded Syst. **2024**(1), 133–156 (2023)

11. Ishai, Y., Sahai, A., Wagner, D.A.: Private circuits: securing hardware against probing attacks. In: Advances in Cryptology — CRYPTO 2003. LNCS, vol. 2729, pp. 463–481. Springer (2003)
12. Knichel, D., Sasdrich, P., Moradi, A.: SILVER - statistical independence and leakage verification. In: Advances in Cryptology — ASIACRYPT 2020, pp. 787—816 (2020)
13. Kocher, P.C.: Timing attacks on implementations of Diffie-Hellman, RSA, DSS, and other systems. In: Advances in Cryptology — CRYPTO '96. LNCS, vol. 1109, pp. 104–113. Springer (1996)
14. Kocher, P.C., Jaffe, J., Jun, B.: Differential power analysis. In: Wiener, M.J. (ed.) Advances in Cryptology — CRYPTO '99. LNCS, vol. 1666, pp. 388–397. Springer (1999)
15. Lomné, V., Roche, T., Thillard, A.: On the need of randomness in fault attack countermeasures - application to AES. In: 2012 Workshop on Fault Diagnosis and Tolerance in Cryptography, pp. 85–94 (2012)
16. NANGATE. The Nangate 45nm Open Cell Library. https://www.nangate.com/
17. Nikova, S., Rechberger, C., Rijmen, V.: Threshold implementations against sidechannel attacks and glitches. In: Information and Communications Security. LNCS, vol. 4307, pp. 529–545. Springer (2006)
18. Reparaz, O., Bilgin, B., Nikova, S., Gierlichs, B., Verbauwhede, I.: Consolidating masking schemes. In: Advances in Cryptology — CRYPTO 2015. LNCS, vol. 9215, pp. 764–783. Springer (2015)
19. Reparaz, O., et al.: CAPA: the spirit of beaver against physical attacks **10991**, 121–151 (2018)
20. Schneider, T., Moradi, A.: Leakage assessment methodology - a clear roadmap for side-channel evaluations. In: Güneysu, T., Handschuh, H. (eds.) Cryptographic Hardware and Embedded Systems — CHES 2015. LNCS, vol. 9293, pp. 495–513. Springer (2015)
21. Schneider, T., Moradi, A., Güneysu, T.: ParTI: towards combined hardware countermeasures against side-channel and fault-injection attacks. In: Bilgin, B., Nikova, S., Rijmen, V. (eds.) Proceedings of the ACM Workshop on Theory of Implementation Security, TIS@CCS 2016 Vienna, Austria, October, 2016, p. 39. ACM (2016)
22. Wolf, C.: Yosys Open SYnthesis Suite. https://yosyshq.net/yosys/

AIoTS – Artificial Intelligence and Industrial IoT Security

Protecting Privacy in IoT-Based Deep Learning: State-of-the-Art Methods and Challenges

Martin Nocker(✉)[iD], Florian Merkle[iD], Pascal Schöttle[iD], and Matthias Janetschek[iD]

Josef Ressel Centre for Security Analysis of IoT Devices, MCI The Entrepreneurial School, Innsbruck, Austria
{martin.nocker,florian.merkle,pascal.schoettle, matthias.janetschek}@mci.edu

Abstract. The expansion of Internet of Things (IoT) devices across diverse domains has led to the generation of an enormous amount of sensitive data. While IoT networks have been extensively studied for their security vulnerabilities, privacy concerns have emerged as a critical issue, particularly in scenarios involving sensitive data, such as smart healthcare. Simultaneously, the rich data ecosystem of IoT devices has enabled their integration with machine learning (ML) and deep learning (DL), adding obstacles to protecting private data. This paper investigates the state-of-the-art methods for privacy-preserving deep learning (PPDL) in IoT systems, focusing on two key scenarios: DL-as-a-Service and collaborative learning. We evaluate existing privacy-preserving technologies regarding their practical applicability for IoT devices. Our study identifies strengths, limitations, and gaps in the current methods, offering insights into their deployment feasibility in resource-constrained environments. Our analysis highlights the underrepresentation of PPDL technologies tailored to IoT applications and key challenges to overcome, such as stalled research efforts and suboptimal privacy-utility tradeoffs. We also highlight future research directions to address these challenges, ensuring the development of robust and scalable PPDL solutions.

Keywords: Privacy-Preserving Technologies · Internet of Things · Deep Learning

1 Introduction

The rapid growth of Internet of Things (IoT) devices across various domains, ranging from consumer technologies [58] to industrial applications [20], and military use cases [33], has led to the collection of vast amounts of heterogeneous data. This data is typically stored centrally in the cloud, creating opportunities for advanced analytics but also raising concerns about privacy and security. Deep learning (DL) has revolutionized data processing and analysis, outperforming traditional statistical methods in processing both structured and unstructured data [55]. Consequently, DL has been applied in IoT applications like agriculture, healthcare, and smart homes [51].

However, DL relies on large-scale datasets, entailing privacy challenges. Data owners must trust model providers when sharing sensitive data for evaluation, while deploying models on IoT devices allows data owners to retain control but puts model owners at risk of exposing proprietary information or intellectual property. Besides IoT, these privacy challenges also exist in application areas like healthcare [70]. Sensitive data collected by IoT devices, such as in medical IoT or smart home, highlights the importance of data privacy in IoT applications [60].

To address these challenges, privacy-preserving technologies (PPTs), such as federated learning, homomorphic encryption, secure multi-party computation, and differential privacy, have emerged to minimize trust dependencies between data and model providers [13]. However, the unique constraints of IoT devices, being limited computational power, restricted memory, constrained power supply, and low data transmission rates, pose additional barriers to implementing PPTs [19]. For example, the computational overhead of homomorphic encryption and the communication demands of secure multi-party computation are often infeasible for resource-limited IoT devices.

This paper focuses on two key use cases of privacy-preserving deep learning (PPDL) in the IoT context: Deep-Learning-as-a-Service (DLaaS) and collaborative learning. In DLaaS, inference is outsourced to external servers when IoT devices lack the computational capacity to process complex models. Collaborative learning enables the use of sensitive data for training models without exposing user data to external entities. Practical applications of these use cases exist in the industry, such as predictive maintenance [9]. In consumer IoT, it has been shown that security and privacy concerns influence purchase decisions, with consumers willing to pay for improved privacy measures [24].

We propose a framework to address PPDL in IoT applications and identify gaps through a comprehensive literature review. By unifying the DL workflow, i.e., training and inference, with the computational resources of IoT devices and PPTs, we offer a structured mapping of applicable methods to specific use cases and challenges. Our findings include the underrepresentation of PPTs specifically tailored for DL in IoT. Most existing approaches demand substantial computational resources, which are typically beyond the capabilities of IoT devices. Furthermore, dedicated PPDL technologies designed for IoT often suffer from either a lack of ongoing development or a suboptimal privacy-utility tradeoff. This framework serves as a practical guide for researchers and practitioners, providing valuable insights into the intersection of DL, privacy, and IoT.

The rest of this paper is organized as follows. Section 2 introduces the relevant background. Section 3 presents the threat model we consider in Sects. 4 and 5, where we analyze the privacy for the two use cases, DLaaS and collaborative learning. We discuss our findings in Sect. 6 and conclude in Sect. 7.

2 Background

The rapid growth of IoT devices has substantially increased data volume and transformed data creation, collection, and usage. Advances in DL are crucial for analyzing this data and enabling innovative IoT features. However, application areas of IoT often generate and process sensitive data, raising privacy concerns. PPTs protect the privacy interests of data owners while simultaneously enabling the exploitation of vast amounts of data for intelligent applications.

2.1 Deep Learning in IoT Applications

In their survey, Ma et al. [51] identified four broader categories of IoT applications that benefit from implementing DL: smart healthcare, smart homes, smart transportation, and smart industry.

DL plays an important role in smart healthcare, e.g., in detecting COVID-19 outbreaks by analyzing data from smart home devices [64]. In medical imaging, DL methods facilitate tumor detection in ultrasound scans [82] and automated segmentation of CT images, improving diagnostic workflows [79]. Additionally, wearable IoT devices utilize DL to monitor physiological signals to detect sleep apnea [34].

In smart homes, DL enhances functionalities such as surveillance, with intruder detection systems leveraging facial recognition [49]. Patel et al. [62] address the privacy challenges of video-based intelligent doorbell systems by proposing a federated learning approach. ML models are also applied in energy management systems to improve resource utilization and energy efficiency [23].

DL enhances infrastructure and services in smart transportation and smart city applications. It provides timely alerts for earthquake early warning systems [2], optimizes waste management via object detection and classification [69], and improves traffic control [16]. Privacy implications of such use cases are addressed on the application of federated learning in smart cities [5].

In the smart industry context, also called industrial IoT, DL is applied in predictive maintenance to anticipate equipment failures, minimize downtime, and improve operational efficiency [43]. Farahani and Monsefi [26] propose a federated learning approach for collaborative predictive maintenance, addressing multiple data owners. DL is also employed in quality control processes, such as ensuring precision in tile manufacturing [45].

2.2 Privacy-Preserving Technologies

Reviewing the application areas outlined above, it is evident that IoT devices often generate and process sensitive data. This information can include personal health data, home surveillance image data, traffic and mobility patterns, or industrial operational data, which may raise notable privacy implications. In the following, we discuss PPTs that have been developed to address these concerns.

Homomorphic Encryption (HE) enables computations on encrypted data without decryption, allowing for secure processing while preserving privacy. Given plaintexts m_1 and m_2 and their corresponding encrypted ciphertexts c_1 and c_2, it is possible to compute a ciphertext c_3 that decrypts to $f(m_1, m_2)$ for some function f. Formally, if $E(m)$ denotes the encryption of a plaintext m and $D(c)$ denotes the decryption of a ciphertext c, for FHE: $D\left(f\left(E(m_1), E(m_2)\right)\right) = f(m_1, m_2)$. Fully homomorphic encryption (FHE) schemes support additions and multiplications on encrypted data, theoretically enabling arbitrary function computation.

Modern HE schemes rely on the ring-learning-with-errors (RLWE) hardness assumption [50]. Random noise is added to the ciphertext during encryption, increasing with operations on ciphertexts. Additions increase noise negligibly, while multiplications raise it substantially. Correct decryption requires that the noise remains below a certain threshold, limiting the multiplicative depth of computations. To manage noise, an operation called bootstrapping resets the noise level [31]. However, bootstrapping is computationally expensive. Schemes like BFV [25] and CKKS [17] configure encryption parameters to avoid bootstrapping, though this reduces computational efficiency. These schemes also support packing multiple data elements into a single ciphertext for parallel processing, called batching. This is particularly useful for operations such as matrix multiplications in ML. Meanwhile, schemes like TFHE [18] focus on Boolean circuits with fast bootstrapping and extensions for arithmetic operations and programmable bootstrapping, enabling efficient evaluation of complex functions like activation layers in neural networks. Despite these advancements, HE introduces considerable memory and runtime overhead compared to cleartext computations, making its application a non-trivial challenge.

Secure Multi-Party Computation (MPC) is a cryptographic technique that enables multiple parties to jointly compute a function over their private inputs without disclosing their inputs to each other. MPC employs cryptographic primitives, rounds of communication between parties, and a (offline) preliminary processing phase. The main bottleneck of MPC is the communication required between parties.

Additive secret sharing (SS) splits a secret $x \in \mathbb{Z}_p$ into n shares within the ring $\mathbb{Z}_p$, i.e., the integers mod p. For example, for $n = 2$ and a random number r, the two shares are $\langle x \rangle_0 = r$ and $\langle x \rangle_1 = x - r$ mod p. This means the message x is perfectly hidden. Additions between secrets and multiplications with constants can be performed by the shareholders individually. Multiplications between two secret shares, represented by $\langle x \cdot y \rangle$ with $\langle x \rangle_i$ and $\langle y \rangle_i$ at party i, require a round of communication and the use of Beaver triplets [10], which must be precomputed. Garbled circuits (GC) [81] constitute a two-party protocol for evaluating functions on private inputs with a fixed number of communication rounds. The function is represented as a Boolean circuit, which grows exponentially in accordance with the computational complexity.

In the context of PPDL, enhancing the protocol efficiency of DL computations, such as convolutional layers and activation functions, is of high priority. The architecture of DNNs is disclosed in MPC, as the network is known to all parties. However, the model weights are private inputs within the protocol.

Differential Privacy (DP) quantifies privacy preservation of individuals in a dataset when releasing outputs of data analysis algorithms [22]. It ensures that for adjacent datasets, i.e., datasets that differ by only one entry, the information gain for adversaries is minimized, regardless of their side knowledge. A randomized algorithm $\mathcal{M}$, satisfies (ϵ, δ)-DP if, for any pair of adjacent datasets d and d', and any possible output subset S, it holds that:

$$Pr[M(d) \in S] \leq e^\epsilon Pr[M(d') \in S] + \delta \quad (1)$$

Smaller ϵ-values correspond to stronger privacy, and δ denotes the probability that the privacy guarantee may not hold, allowing for a small chance of error. To achieve DP, random noise is added to the algorithm's output, determined by the function's sensitivity $S_f = |f(d) - f(d')|$, over all adjacent datasets d and d'. Adding noise enhances privacy but reduces accuracy, requiring noise mechanisms that balance this tradeoff [30].

In DL, DP involves randomizing inputs, outputs, or the training process to prevent inference of private data from model parameters or outputs. Differentially private stochastic gradient descent (DP-SGD) perturbs gradients by adding noise during training [1], which is large enough to obscure the influence of any single record within a batch. Excessive noise could lead to large gradient changes, making the model ineffective. Therefore, gradients are clipped, but this is computationally intensive for individual gradients and eliminates the benefits of parallel GPU processing. Goodfellow [32] proposed an efficient gradient clipping method for fully connected networks, while newer methods extend support to diverse architectures [41] or optimize gradient norm computation [73].

Federated Learning (FL) [52] is a distributed approach for training a shared ML model M on decentralized data owned by n users. Unlike centralized learning, which aggregates data at a central location, FL enables users to keep their data locally. This mitigates the costs and privacy risks associated with centralized data collection, allowing participants to collaboratively build a model without exposing their private datasets. McMahan et al. [52] initially explore mobile devices collaboratively training a model for next-word prediction for keyboards.

The FL process is coordinated by a central server, which initializes the model at iteration $t = 0$. In each subsequent iteration t, a subset of m users ($m \ll n$) participate in the training, download the current model $M^{(t)}$ and compute gradients ∇ using batches from their local datasets. The gradients from the participating users are then sent back to the central server, which aggregates them using an averaging approach to compute an updated model $M^{(t+1)}$. This process resembles a decentralized extension of batch stochastic gradient descent (SGD), where model updates are computed across distributed parties.

FL was viewed as privacy-preserving, but recent research showed that sensitive data can be reconstructed by a passive attacker with access to model updates [12]. Hence, DP has been incorporated into FL to address these privacy risks, commonly referred to as DP-FL. It introduces calibrated noise to the model updates before sharing them, limiting the amount of information an attacker can infer about any single user's data while preserving the utility of the global model.

FL faces additional challenges, such as managing non-independent and identically distributed data, ensuring fairness among participants, and safeguarding the system against malicious users who may submit harmful model updates to compromise the integrity of the resulting model. These challenges, however, lie beyond the scope of this paper, and we refer to the literature for further details.

2.3 Related Work

Privacy in IoT systems has been the focus of several surveys. Zheng et al. [83] discuss the challenges of PPDL in IoT. The authors provide a taxonomy of privacy-preserving ML approaches and propose a hybrid approach combining data obfuscation and encryption. In contrast to their work, we provide a more in-depth analysis of several technologies while focusing on DL. Briggs et al. [14] review FL for privacy protection and focus on IoT contexts. Li and Palanisamy [44] discuss how PPTs can support legal privacy laws for different architectures of IoT. Ogonji et al. [59] offer a detailed taxonomy of privacy and security threats in IoT, focusing on human-centric threats. Unlike prior studies, our work specifically addresses the privacy of DL applications within the IoT ecosystem. We offer a comprehensive analysis of state-of-the-art PPTs, including HE, MPC, DP, FL, and others, evaluating their applicability in resource-constrained IoT environments. Additionally, we map these PPTs to corresponding IoT devices based on their computational resources, providing a clear understanding of their practical deployment feasibility.

3 Threat Model

We consider the following scenarios of IoT-based PPDL: In the DLaaS setting, an IoT device (client or data owner) holds data x, while a model owner (server) possesses a pre-trained model M. The objective is to privately compute the inference result $M(x)$ without revealing x to the server or M to the client. In the second scenario, multiple IoT devices, each acting as a data owner, collaboratively train a model. The privacy goals are twofold: First, to ensure that training data remains confidential, and second, to make the resulting model resilient to privacy attacks that attempt to extract sensitive information. We impose no assumptions on the distribution of data across the participating devices.

In the context of PPDL, adversaries are typically classified as passive or active [42]. Passive adversaries are honest-but-curious, meaning they follow the protocol but seek to extract as much sensitive information as possible. These adversaries can intercept and analyze data exchanged between parties and perform analyses to infer private information. In contrast, active adversaries are malicious and may deviate from the protocol, e.g., by injecting false or manipulated data. Protecting against active adversaries is more challenging due to their disruptive and adaptable nature.

In n-party protocols with t adversaries, two scenarios can be distinguished: honest majority ($t < n/2$) and dishonest majority ($t \geq n/2$). Honest majority protocols are more efficient, whereas dishonest majority scenarios require more resource-intensive and complex schemes to ensure security [39]. The non-colluding assumption, often linked to helper servers, presumes that parties do not share their secrets with others. If collusion occurs, parties can combine their knowledge to reveal sensitive information, compromising the system's integrity [54].

Attacks on ML systems can be broadly categorized as security or privacy attacks. Security attacks aim to disrupt the model's integrity, availability, or functionality [11]. Privacy attacks target the confidentiality of training data, model parameters, or inferences while leaving model functionality intact. We focus on privacy attacks as defined in [65]. Membership inference attacks aim to determine whether a specific sample was part of the training dataset [71]. These attacks exploit the overfitting tendencies of ML models, which cause them to respond differently to training data compared to unseen samples. Model extraction attacks, also known as model stealing, seek to obtain the model by querying it extensively and using the responses to reconstruct its parameters or architecture [75]. Models with low overfitting and low generalization error are especially susceptible to extraction. Reconstruction attacks focus on inferring sensitive features of training samples and their respective training labels [28]. These attacks leverage the predictive power of models, especially those with high accuracy, to reverse-engineer private information. Property inference attacks aim to extract global properties of the training dataset that are not explicitly encoded as features. For instance, an attacker could determine demographic distributions such as the gender ratio in datasets used to train a model [8].

Adversaries are classified based on their knowledge and access to the model and training data. These categories include white-, gray-, or black-box scenarios [11]. In the context of privacy attacks, adversaries typically operate with limited knowledge, often restricted to the model's architecture or the black-box setting, as their primary goal is to exploit the model's parameters or training data.

4 Privacy-Preserving DL-as-a-Service

This section addresses privacy-preserving inference within the IoT context. Specifically, we consider the scenario where an IoT device evaluates its sensitive data using a DL model owned by another party. More formally, a data owner (also called client) holds sensitive data denoted as x, while a model owner (server) maintains a DL model M and offers inference service. This setup is typically referred to as DLaaS, as illustrated in Fig. 1.

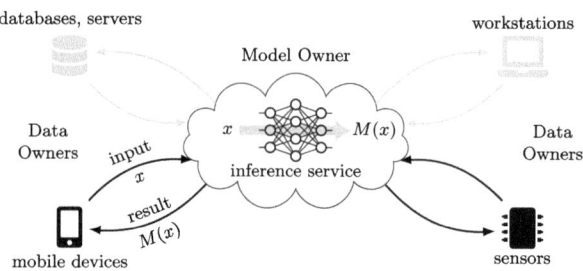

Fig. 1. DLaaS scenarios (IoT highlighted). Inputs x are sent to the model owner, who performs inference using the model M and returns the result $M(x)$. Arrows to the model owner denote inputs x, arrows from the model owner denote $M(x)$.

This approach is commonly applied when the computation is too expensive for resource-restricted devices or model providers do not want to disclose their model. Training powerful models is not trivial and involves costs. Hence, these models are often considered intellectual property and not shared. Moreover, exposing the model facilitates the computation of security attacks. The primary objective is to compute $M(x)$ for the client while protecting x and $M(x)$ from disclosure to the server, and M should not be disclosed to the client.

Use Case Example: A smart home security camera captures video data x to detect unusual activities or intrusions. The camera cannot locally run the DL models required for real-time analysis due to hardware limitations. Thus, it sends video frames to a cloud-based inference service hosting a proprietary DL model M for evaluation. The model processes the input and returns predictions $M(x)$ to the camera. The data collected by the camera is sensitive as it reveals extensive information about the users, such as recurring patterns in their daily routines or social contacts.

4.1 Homomorphic Encryption

HE emerges as a suitable approach for private inference. Under this approach, the IoT device encrypts its data and sends it to the model owner, who then performs inference on the encrypted input using local unencrypted model parameters. However, HE exhibits substantial computational and memory overhead, which conflicts with the resource limitations inherent to IoT devices.

Efforts to make HE viable on IoT devices have led to lightweight HE library implementations, such as SEAL-embedded [56]. However, SEAL-embedded is no longer actively maintained, and alternative implementations are scarce. Many available libraries support only partially homomorphic encryption schemes [68], which are insufficient for private inference using HE only.

If IoT devices can securely transfer data to a more powerful, trusted device, they can utilize standard HE libraries for inference. Computational speed and accuracy in these scenarios depend primarily on the efficiency of nonlinear function implementations, model compression techniques (e.g., pruning or quantization), and the availability of specialized hardware (e.g., GPUs or FPGAs).

Implementing nonlinear functions, such as ReLU, sigmoid, or max pooling, poses additional challenges under HE constraints. Most implementations rely on polynomial approximations, such as Taylor series expansions, minimax techniques to minimize maximum error, or Chebyshev approximations [63]. By contrast, the TFHE library allows more flexible approximations by utilizing table lookups or leveraging high-degree polynomials, enabling more accurate approximations compared to low-degree polynomials. AutoFHE uses mixed-degree polynomial activations to optimize bootstrapping placement for optimal CNN inference [7]. However, this flexibility comes at the expense of increased runtime, and TFHE lacks support for batching, which would allow simultaneous processing of multiple inputs. Therefore, switching between HE schemes to leverage batching for linear layers and TFHE for activation functions and other nonlinear operations uses the strengths of the respective schemes [48].

Pruning and quantization enhance the latency, accuracy, or throughput of DL inference. Pruning sets certain network weights, reducing the number of operations [3]. In the extreme case of quantization, weights and inputs of linear layers are reduced to the binary set $\{\pm 1\}$, enabling efficient computations using Boolean circuits in so-called binarized neural networks [84]. The sign function is a frequently employed activation within this context.

4.2 Secure Multi-party Computation

MPC protocols are more efficient concerning memory and computational overhead than HE but require communication among parties. This online communication poses a considerable challenge for IoT devices due to their limited bandwidth. The frequent exchanges required by MPC protocols can lead to delays and degraded performance in IoT scenarios, especially where network reliability is inconsistent. Additionally, IoT devices often have constrained processing power and energy resources, which increases the difficulty of implementing computationally intensive protocols or handling high-frequency data exchanges efficiently.

An important distinction between HE and MPC is that parties involved in MPC protocols possess knowledge of the computation, i.e., the architecture of the ML model. The standard MPC approach involves the execution of a protocol with collaboration between client and server comprising the exchange of SS [21], the execution of GC [76], or a hybrid approach [35].

Similar to HE, leveraging standard MPC protocols in IoT applications often requires offloading data from the IoT device to a more powerful, trusted device within the owner's infrastructure. This auxiliary device then performs the computationally demanding aspects of the MPC protocol, effectively bridging the gap between the IoT device's capabilities and the protocol's resource requirements.

Besides the classical approach where a data owner and a model owner engage in an MPC protocol, many works use n external non-colluding servers, abbreviated nPC, typically with two [54], three [74], or four servers [39].

Inference inputs and the model are split into SS and distributed across these servers, which then collectively execute the MPC protocol. Using more servers allows for more flexible protocols, improving efficiency. However, it offers a larger attack surface as it suffices to compromise two servers to produce a dishonest majority for frameworks with up to four servers.

4.3 Other Technologies

DP is a lightweight solution executable on IoT devices, but using DP alone for privacy protection in the context of PPDL has shown suboptimal results. The level of noise required to obscure sensitive information effectively degrades the utility of the results substantially, rendering them unusable.

Trusted execution environments (TEEs) are isolated areas within a processor that protect sensitive data and computations from unauthorized access, even by privileged software like the operating system. TEEs are well-established among mixed solutions, however face challenges when used as standalone solutions in PPDL. Using TEEs requires strong trust in chip manufacturers, i.e., using TEEs represents a shift of trust from the model owner to the chip manufacturer. Moreover, the computation is commonly divided, and only parts of the model evaluation are conducted within the TEE [36].

4.4 Mixed Frameworks

Different techniques have advantages for various types of computations, e.g., FHE is well-suited for (batched) linear operations like matrix-vector multiplication, whereas MPC handles nonlinear functions more efficiently. These methods also allow for balancing tradeoffs, such as introducing DP noise to enhance privacy at the cost of reduced accuracy, while DP impacts efficiency only slightly compared to HE and MPC. As a result, mixed frameworks have been developed to combine the strengths of these various approaches. Notable solutions include combinations of HE with MPC [42] and integrations of HE with TEE [57].

4.5 Privacy Analysis

The aforementioned technologies enable inference without exposing the input data or the model to the other party, thus addressing the core privacy concerns in a DLaaS setup. However, it is essential to note that these protections do not eliminate the risk of privacy attacks against the model. Privacy attacks can exploit the model's query outputs, which remain largely unaltered or are only minimally obfuscated, such as in scenarios using HE.

To counteract such attacks, model owners should adopt additional protective measures. During inference, defenses include adding carefully calibrated noise to the model's outputs and enforcing strict query rate limits, thereby mitigating the risk of privacy attacks that exploit the model's responses. These query-time strategies can be complemented by robust training methods such as DP and regularization. These techniques help limit the model's tendency to memorize specific data points, reducing its vulnerability to membership inference and other privacy attacks.

5 Privacy-Preserving Collaborative Model Training

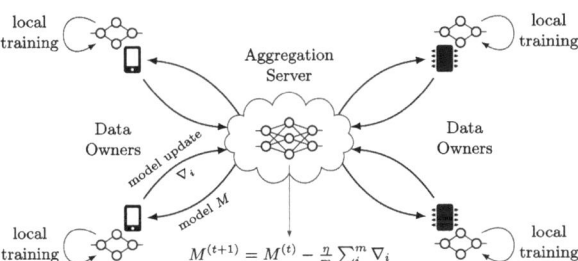

Fig. 2. Collaborative training in the IoT domain using FL. Data owners train a model using their local data and the global model $M^{(t)}$ at time t. Model updates (gradients ∇_i) are sent to the aggregation server, which updates the model to $M^{(t+1)}$ by aggregating the updates, scaled by the learning rate η. The updated model is distributed back to the data owners. Arrows to the server denote gradients ∇_i, and arrows from the server denote models M.

This section examines privacy-preserving model training in the context of distributed IoT devices. These devices generate data that is collaboratively used to train a DL model, leveraging the collective knowledge embedded in the aggregated dataset. In cases where datasets are distributed across IoT devices, collaborative learning techniques enable the creation of more accurate models. Upon completion of the training process, all data owners receive the model automatically through the protocol or explicitly via transmission. In this scenario, the primary objective is to protect the training data of each data owner, as it often contains sensitive or proprietary information such as personal data, business intelligence, or IoT sensor measurements. An auxiliary computation server, which may be untrusted, often facilitates this process by serving roles such as a communication coordinator, model aggregation server, or encryption manager. Including such a server introduces efficiencies but necessitates robust mechanisms to safeguard against data leakage or malicious interference. Figure 2 illustrates collaborative training using FL.

Use Case Example: In a healthcare setting, wearable health devices, such as fitness trackers or smartwatches, collect sensitive data from individual users, including heart rate, activity levels, and sleep patterns. These devices are owned by different individuals, each with their private health data. To develop a more accurate DL model that can predict potential health risks or provide personalized health recommendations, the data from multiple wearables needs to be collaboratively used for training. However, it is crucial that the health data from one individual is not shared with others, as it contains highly sensitive personal information. In this scenario, wearable devices train a DL model collaboratively without revealing their individual datasets.

5.1 Differential Privacy

To defend against privacy attacks, it is essential to apply protections during model training, not just inference. DP offers a principled approach by introducing calibrated noise to obscure sensitive data. For deep neural networks, the most effective method is DP-SGD, which perturbs gradients during training. This approach avoids the limitations of input, output, and objective function perturbation, which are less effective for non-convex objectives and offer poorer privacy-utility tradeoffs [38].

Balancing the tradeoff between privacy and utility in DP-SGD remains a core challenge when perturbing the training process with DP. The goal is to inject the minimum necessary noise to provide strong privacy guarantees while maintaining high model accuracy. Several approaches try to improve this tradeoff, targeting different aspects: First, a set of works modify activation and loss functions to be more privacy-friendly [61]. Another line of research applies DP to gradient embeddings [27]. As networks with more parameters require proportionally stronger perturbations, some implementations leverage gradient sparsity [37]. Several works address key bottlenecks of DP-SGD, specifically gradient clipping and noise addition [46]. Sharpness-aware training exploits the geometric properties of the objective function, seeking flat minima that are more robust to DP noise during training [29]. If available, using a non-sensitive dataset to pre-train a model enhances the accuracy of the final model, which is subsequently trained on sensitive data using DP [29].

5.2 Homomorphic Encryption

Using HE, devices encrypt their data before engaging in collaborative model training, either by sending it to a central server or exchanging it directly among devices. HE provides three principal approaches: (1) All data owners encrypt and decrypt using a shared key. While straightforward, this method bears risks. If the server or communication channels are compromised, an attacker possessing the shared key could decrypt all data. This approach supports flexible participant inclusion and is robust to participants dropping out. (2) In multi-key HE (MKHE) [47], each party independently generates their public and private key pairs, simplifying key generation. Data inputs are encrypted using all parties' public keys, i.e., $[[x]_{pk_A}]_{pk_B}$. While this extended encryption impacts performance, MKHE dynamically enables parties to join the protocol. (3) Multi-party HE (MPHE) employs a shared public key generated by summing individual public keys $pk = \sum_i pk_i$. Data is encrypted using this shared key $[x]_{pk}$, resulting in ciphertext sizes comparable to single-key HE. MPHE achieves efficient runtime performance but requires the participant set to be fixed during the initial setup.

Both concepts, MKHE and MPHE, use a multi-party protocol for decryption to recover the plaintext. In summary, MPHE offers better efficiency in terms of ciphertext size and computational cost but restricts new parties from joining after initialization. Conversely, MKHE allows for flexible participation at the expense of higher computational overhead, though recent advancements have achieved a runtime complexity that is linear in the number of involved parties [4]. Despite these theoretical advancements, practical implementations and evaluations of MPHE and MKHE remain underexplored, not only in the IoT domain, highlighting the need for further real-world investigations. Both MKHE and MPHE are computationally more expensive than standard HE. As a result, their implementation requires resource-rich devices capable of managing the increased computational and memory demands, rendering these technologies unsuitable for IoT devices. For practical implementations, the snu-mghe project [72] provides the most efficient known MKHE scheme [40].

5.3 Secure Multi-party Computation

Given the potentially large number of IoT devices contributing to the training of a joint model, conventional MPC protocols are not inherently designed to scale to hundreds or thousands of participants. Consequently, the typical approach involves distributing the training data as secret shares among n independent, non-colluding servers. These servers then engage in an n-party computation (nPC) protocol, which produces secret shares of the final model. The model can subsequently be reconstructed by aggregating these shares. While such frameworks often demonstrate strong performance, they rely on the assumption that data owners trust the operators of the non-colluding servers. Establishing such a trusted environment, however, is not always straightforward.

Frameworks for training DNNs using n non-colluding servers that execute MPC protocols are distinguished based on the provided security from passive [74] to active [15] and implementations that support both adversarial models [39].

5.4 Federated Learning

FL enables collaborative model training across multiple data owners without sharing raw data. However, standard FL is vulnerable to privacy breaches, as discussed in Sect. 2.2. Gradients exchanged during training can inadvertently reveal sensitive information about the underlying data. To address this, various advanced PPTs have been developed.

One effective method to mitigate information leakage is gradient pruning, which involves transmitting only a selected subset of gradient updates to the central server. By reducing the amount of shared information, gradient pruning not only diminishes the potential for privacy breaches but also has the added benefit of lowering communication costs between clients and the server [65]. Additionally, DP ensures privacy by introducing controlled noise to the gradients during training (via DP-SGD) or to the gradient updates before they are shared. This integration, referred to as DP-FL, offers robust privacy guarantees by ensuring that the added noise effectively obscures private information in the gradient updates. However, this comes at the expense of reduced model accuracy, requiring careful tuning of privacy parameters to achieve an optimal tradeoff between privacy and utility [53].

The integration of DP into FL and the development of gradient pruning have received notable research interest [78]. Cryptographic techniques like HE and MPC can provide strong privacy guarantees, however introduce considerable computational and communication overhead. Lightweight solutions use HE to enable encrypted aggregation at the server [77]. In this scenario, all clients have to encrypt using the same HE keys. Hence, either a secure channel between the server and each client or another layer of encryption is necessary to ensure security. FL frameworks using MPC for secure aggregation add communication overhead in return for robust privacy guarantees. Another approach to enhance privacy and efficiency involves selectively aggregating updates from a subset of clients [6]. This can limit exposure to potentially malicious or low-quality data sources, focusing instead on high-quality updates. This selective aggregation not only strengthens privacy by minimizing the number of updates processed but can also improve overall model performance by emphasizing reliable contributions.

Decentralized approaches eliminate the need for a central aggregation server, thereby removing a single point of failure and mitigating trust concerns associated with centralized entities. In these frameworks, model updates are communicated directly among data owners, ensuring efficient and secure collaboration. However, this design typically results in increased communication overhead compared to centralized systems. The POSEIDON framework [66] addresses this challenge by employing a hierarchical, tree-based structure where data owners communicate updates to their parent nodes until aggregation is completed at the root node. To safeguard sensitive information during this process, an MPHE scheme is utilized, enabling secure aggregation while preserving privacy. In fully peer-to-peer systems, such as the NeuroCrypt framework [67], model updates are exchanged directly among all participants, removing the reliance on a central server. To manage the substantial communication costs inherent to this approach, NeuroCrypt employs a transfer learning paradigm. Specifically, it fine-tunes only the final layers of a pre-trained model (trained on non-sensitive data) using local, sensitive data from each client. This method reduces the computational and communication overhead, making it suitable for lightweight applications while still preserving the privacy and independence of individual participants.

5.5 Privacy Analysis

The utility-privacy tradeoff is a central concern in privacy-preserving collaborative model training, particularly in the resource-constrained context of IoT devices. Greater privacy typically comes at the cost of reduced utility, as techniques like DP introduce noise to protect sensitive data, reducing the accuracy of the resulting model. However, the integration of DP into training frameworks suffers from the difficulty of interpreting privacy parameters ϵ and δ for end-users. MPC, as well as MPHE and MKHE schemes, provide robust privacy guarantees but demand substantial computational and communication resources, which can exceed the capabilities of many IoT devices. This creates a fundamental challenge: The low-resource nature of IoT devices inherently limits their ability to achieve high levels of privacy. Effective privacy-preserving methods require at least minimal resources to implement safeguards such as secure aggregation or noise addition. FL is a common technique that reduces the need for direct data sharing but still relies on computationally intensive techniques like HE and MPC for secure aggregation. Consequently, in IoT ecosystems, protecting privacy requires balancing the resources available and the level of privacy needed. Devices with limited resources may struggle to provide strong privacy protections, making it essential to design solutions that consider these limitations.

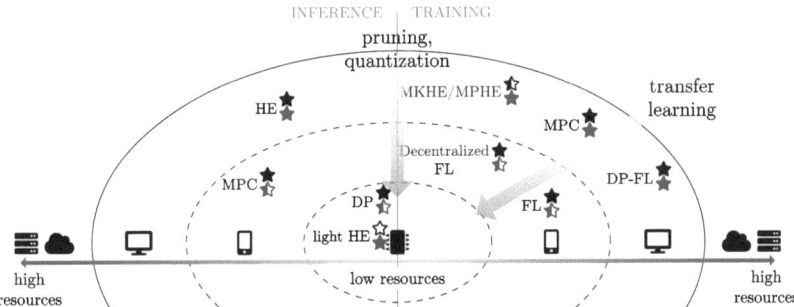

Fig. 3. Classification of PPTs by IoT device resources for private inference (left) and collaborative learning (right). Concentric ellipses represent increasing device resources, from low-resource sensors (inner dashed ellipse) to resource-rich mobile devices (middle) and high-performance workstations (outer solid ellipse). Technologies are mapped to suitable devices, with applicability extending outward to higher-resource categories. The upper black star indicates maturity (empty: early-stage, half-filled: partial readiness, filled: established), and the lower blue star shows privacy protection (filled: strong, half-filled: suboptimal). Purple arrows indicate methods to adapt technologies for low-resource devices.

6 Discussion

Within the IoT domain, PPDL can ensure data confidentiality and protect intellectual property in inference and training processes. The suitability of different PPTs depends heavily on the available resources of the IoT device, which vary from low-resource and poorly connected sensors to more resource-rich mobile or embedded devices. In this section, we discuss how the mentioned technologies can be applied in practical IoT scenarios, i.e., DLaaS and collaborative learning, considering their resource requirements and maturity for deployment.

Our analysis is summarized in Fig. 3, where we relate PPTs based on the resource capabilities and IoT devices in the two use cases: DLaaS on the left and collaborative model training on the right. The diagram's concentric ellipses represent devices with increasing computational resources, from low-resource devices like basic sensors (inner dashed ellipse) to resource-rich mobile or embedded devices (middle dashed ellipse) and high-performance workstations (outer solid ellipse). Devices within this last category are not necessarily IoT devices but can still support PPTs when connected to IoT devices within a trusted network environment. Technologies are hierarchically mapped to the device category best suited for their computational demands. Therefore, a technology's applicability extends to devices in higher-resource categories outward in the diagram. Each technology is equipped with two star-based labels. The upper black star indicates maturity: An empty star means the technology is in the early research stages, a half-filled star suggests partial readiness, and a filled star denotes a practical, established solution. The lower blue star reflects privacy protection: A filled star indicates strong privacy guarantees, while a half-filled star highlights suboptimal protection. Auxiliary methods, shown in purple, enhance the applicability of PPTs for lower-resource devices. This classification offers a concise framework for understanding the interplay between IoT resources, privacy technologies, and their practical application.

6.1 Inference

For resource-constrained devices, privacy-preserving inference is particularly challenging. HE offers strong privacy guarantees by allowing computations directly on encrypted data, but its computational and memory overhead makes it impractical for these devices. Lightweight implementations like SEAL-embedded have been explored, but limited support and active development hinder their applicability. DP is computationally efficient and can be deployed on resource-limited IoT devices. However, relying solely on DP for privacy protection has produced suboptimal outcomes. MPC provides an alternative with lower computational overhead than HE but requires frequent communication, which is constrained by low bandwidth and unreliable networks typical of sensors. While more powerful IoT devices may be capable of handling the computational demands of MPC protocols, they must also be able to manage the associated communication load. Stable connectivity and sufficient bandwidth are crucial for ensuring the feasibility of MPC-based PPTs on these devices. We put MPC towards the edge between powerful workstations and resource-richer IoT devices.

To further enable PPTs on resource-constrained devices, methods like pruning and quantization can be employed to reduce the computational and memory requirements [80]. For example, using quantized (or even binarized) inputs and model weights or pruning the model, medium-resource devices such as mobile devices could execute HE or MPC protocols more efficiently.

6.2 Training

The challenge of privacy-preserving training for DL models on low-resource devices, such as IoT sensors, is even more complex than inference. Since DL model training is inherently resource-intensive, combining it with PPTs like HE or MPC is impractical for devices with limited computational capabilities. As a result, low-resource IoT devices typically transfer their data to more powerful local devices within a trusted environment for processing and training.

Medium-resource devices like mobile devices can support certain PPTs for collaborative model training, especially FL, which was introduced in this case. Techniques such as secure aggregation ensure that updates are shared without revealing individual data points. When a central aggregation server is not used, decentralized FL solutions provide an alternative. These decentralized approaches demand more resources, as they not only require local training but also increase communication overhead compared to traditional FL methods.

Technologies like MPC and MKHE or MPHE are restricted to resource-rich devices, as their computational and memory demands exceed the capabilities of most current IoT devices. Incorporating DP during model updates can further enhance privacy. However, the noise levels must be carefully calibrated to balance accuracy and privacy, a fundamental and ongoing challenge in privacy-preserving model training. State-of-the-art DP-FL frameworks typically utilize DP-SGD. While DP-SGD is effective at providing privacy guarantees, it comes with its computational overhead, as it requires the introduction of calibrated noise based on gradients and gradient clipping to avoid exploding gradients.

As with inference, model compression techniques such as pruning and quantization can reduce the computational demands of privacy-preserving training, making these technologies more feasible for resource-constrained devices. With further research, FL might soon be practical for low-resource IoT devices, enabling more efficient privacy-preserving collaborative model training in these environments. Additionally, transfer learning, which involves fine-tuning the final layers of a pre-trained DNN, reduces the computational load in privacy-preserving training. By leveraging a pre-trained model trained on non-sensitive data, IoT devices can perform privacy-preserving training on smaller datasets with lower computational and memory requirements, thereby enabling the practical application of PPTs even on resource-limited devices.

7 Conclusion

In this work, we explored the critical role of PPDL in the rapidly growing IoT ecosystem, where devices frequently handle sensitive data. While DL is well-suited to process the vast and diverse datasets generated by IoT devices, ensuring the privacy of both data and models remains a challenge.

We review state-of-the-art PPDL and map these methods to IoT-specific challenges by analyzing two representative key use cases of privacy-sensitive DL in IoT: DLaaS and collaborative learning. We propose a structured framework mapping PPTs to IoT devices based on their resource capabilities and evaluate each technology's maturity and practicality. Our analysis underscores a key finding: "no power, no privacy". IoT devices with limited computational and memory resources are currently ill-suited to implement most PPDL technologies effectively. This results in discrepancies between privacy needs and PPDL methods that are viable in the IoT context. In other words, a possible approach to realizing PPDL in IoT with the currently available technologies involves a "leveled approach" based on computational power. This entails establishing trustworthy connections between resource-constrained devices and more resource-rich intermediary devices capable of managing and executing PPTs.

This work contributes to the IoT research community, providing an overview of the methods available for different devices and use cases and pointing towards the limitations of these methods. It further informs future research directions for the field of PPDL, highlighting the need for lightweight approaches and optimizing the tradeoff between privacy and requirements in terms of computation, memory, and communication bandwidth.

References

1. Abadi, M., et al.: Deep learning with differential privacy. In: ACM Conference on Computer and Communications Security (CCS), pp. 308–318 (2016)
2. Abdalzaher, M.S., Elsayed, H.A., Fouda, M.M., Salim, M.M.: Employing machine learning and IoT for earthquake early warning system in smart cities. Energies **16**(1), 495 (2023)
3. Aharoni, E., et al.: Efficient pruning for machine learning under homomorphic encryption. In: European Symposium on Research in Computer Security, pp. 204–225. Springer (2023)
4. Akın, Y., Klemsa, J., Önen, M.: A practical TFHE-based multi-key homomorphic encryption with linear complexity and low noise growth. In: European Symposium on Research in Computer Security, pp. 3–23. Springer (2023)
5. Al-Huthaifi, R., Li, T., Huang, W., Gu, J., Li, C.: Federated learning in smart cities: privacy and security survey. Inf. Sci. **632**, 833–857 (2023)
6. Annamalai, M.S.M.S., Bilogrevic, I., De Cristofaro, E.: FP-Fed: privacy-preserving federated detection of browser fingerprinting. In: Symposium on Network and Distributed System Security (2024)
7. Ao, W., Boddeti, V.N.: AutoFHE: automated adaption of CNNs for efficient evaluation over FHE. In: 33rd USENIX Security Symposium (USENIX Security 24), pp. 2173–2190 (2024)
8. Ateniese, G., Mancini, L.V., Spognardi, A., Villani, A., Vitali, D., Felici, G.: Hacking smart machines with smarter ones: how to extract meaningful data from machine learning classifiers. Int. J. Secure. Network. **10**(3), 137–150 (2015)
9. Bagheri, B., Rezapoor, M., Lee, J.: A unified data security framework for federated prognostics and health management in smart manufacturing. Manufact. Lett. **24**, 136–139 (2020)
10. Beaver, D.: Efficient multiparty protocols using circuit randomization. In: Advances in Cryptology – CRYPTO '92, pp. 420–432. Springer (1992)
11. Biggio, B., Roli, F.: Wild patterns: ten years after the rise of adversarial machine learning. In: ACM Conference on Computer and Communications Security (CCS), pp. 2154–2156 (2018)
12. Boenisch, F., Dziedzic, A., Schuster, R., Shamsabadi, A.S., Shumailov, I., Papernot, N.: When the curious abandon honesty: federated learning is not private. In: IEEE European Symposium on Security and Privacy (EuroS&P), pp. 175–199 (2023)
13. Boulemtafes, A., Derhab, A., Challal, Y.: A review of privacy-preserving techniques for deep learning. Neurocomputing **384**, 21–45 (2020)

14. Briggs, C., Fan, Z., Andras, P.: A review of privacy-preserving federated learning for the internet-of-things. Federated Learning Systems: Towards Next-Generation AI, pp. 21–50 (2021)
15. Chaudhari, H., Rachuri, R., Suresh, A.: Trident: efficient 4PC framework for privacy preserving machine learning. In: Symposium on Network and Distributed System Security (2020)
16. Chen, M., Hao, Y., Lin, K., Yuan, Z., Hu, L.: Label-less learning for traffic control in an edge network. IEEE Network **32**(6), 8–14 (2018)
17. Cheon, J.H., Kim, A., Kim, M., Song, Y.: Homomorphic encryption for arithmetic of approximate numbers. In: International Conference on the Theory and Application of Cryptology and Information Security, pp. 409–437. Springer (2017)
18. Chillotti, I., Gama, N., Georgieva, M., Izabachène, M.: TFHE: fast fully homomorphic encryption over the torus. J. Cryptol. **33**(1), 34–91 (2020)
19. Čolaković, A., Hadžialić, M.: Internet of things (IoT): a review of enabling technologies, challenges, and open research issues. Comput. Netw. **144**, 17–39 (2018)
20. Daji, D., Ghule, K., Gagdani, S., Butala, A., Talele, P., Kamat, H.: Cloud-based asset monitoring and predictive maintenance in an industrial IoT system. In: 2020 International Conference for Emerging Technology (INCET), pp. 1–5. IEEE (2020)
21. Diaa, A., et al.: Fast and private inference of deep neural networks by co-designing activation functions. In: 33rd USENIX Security Symposium (USENIX Security 24), pp. 2191–2208 (2024)
22. Dwork, C., Kenthapadi, K., McSherry, F., Mironov, I., Naor, M.: Our data, ourselves: privacy via distributed noise generation. In: Vaudenay, S. (ed.) EUROCRYPT 2006. LNCS, vol. 4004, pp. 486–503. Springer, Heidelberg (2006). https://doi.org/10.1007/11761679_29
23. Elsisi, M., Amer, M., Su, C.L., et al.: A comprehensive review of machine learning and IoT solutions for demand side energy management, conservation, and resilient operation. Energy 128256 (2023)
24. Emami-Naeini, P., Dheenadhayalan, J., Agarwal, Y., Cranor, L.F.: Are consumers willing to pay for security and privacy of IoT devices? In: 32nd USENIX Security Symposium (USENIX Security 23), pp. 1505–1522 (2023)
25. Fan, J., Vercauteren, F.: Somewhat practical fully homomorphic encryption. Cryptology ePrint Archive (2012)
26. Farahani, B., Monsefi, A.K.: Smart and collaborative industrial IoT: a federated learning and data space approach. Digital Commun. Netw. **9**(2), 436–447 (2023)
27. Feng, C., Xu, N., Wen, W., Venkitasubramaniam, P., Ding, C.: Spectral-DP: Differentially private deep learning through spectral perturbation and filtering. In: IEEE Symposium on Security and Privacy (SP), pp. 1944–1960 (2023)
28. Fredrikson, M., Jha, S., Ristenpart, T.: Model inversion attacks that exploit confidence information and basic countermeasures. In: ACM Conference on Computer and Communications Security (CCS), pp. 1322–1333 (2015)
29. Ganesh, A., et al.: Why is public pretraining necessary for private model training? In: Proceedings of the 40th International Conference on Machine Learning. vol. 202, pp. 10611–10627 (2023)
30. Geng, Q., Viswanath, P.: The optimal noise-adding mechanism in differential privacy. IEEE Trans. Inf. Theory **62**(2), 925–951 (2016)
31. Gentry, C.: Fully homomorphic encryption using ideal lattices. In: Proceedings of the Forty-First Annual ACM Symposium on Theory of Computing, pp. 169–178 (2009)
32. Goodfellow, I.: Efficient per-example gradient computations. arXiv preprint arXiv:1510.01799 **2015** (2015)

33. Gotarane, V., Raskar, S.: IoT practices in military applications. In: 3rd International Conference on Trends in Electronics and Informatics, pp. 891–894 (2019)
34. Haoyu, L., Jianxing, L., Arunkumar, N., Hussein, A.F., Jaber, M.M.: An IoMT cloud-based real time sleep apnea detection scheme by using the SpO2 estimation supported by heart rate variability. Futur. Gener. Comput. Syst. **98**, 69–77 (2019)
35. Hussain, S.U., Javaheripi, M., Samragh, M., Koushanfar, F.: COINN: Crypto/ML codesign for oblivious inference via neural networks. In: ACM Conference on Computer and Communications Security (CCS), pp. 3266–3281 (2021)
36. Islam, M.S., Zamani, M., Kim, C.H., Khan, L., Hamlen, K.W.: Confidential execution of deep learning inference at the untrusted edge with arm TrustZone. In: Proceedings of the Thirteenth ACM Conference on Data and Application Security and Privacy, pp. 153–164 (2023)
37. Ito, R., Liew, S.P., Takahashi, T., Sasaki, Y., Onizuka, M.: Scaling private deep learning with low-rank and sparse gradients. J. Inf. Process. **31**, 748–757 (2023)
38. Jarin, I., Eshete, B.: DP-UTIL: comprehensive utility analysis of differential privacy in machine learning. In: Proceedings of the Twelfth ACM Conference on Data and Application Security and Privacy, pp. 41–52 (2022)
39. Keller, M., Sun, K.: Secure quantized training for deep learning. In: International Conference on Machine Learning (ICML), pp. 10912–10938. PMLR (2022)
40. Kim, T., Kwak, H., Lee, D., Seo, J., Song, Y.: Asymptotically faster multi-key homomorphic encryption from homomorphic gadget decomposition. Cryptology ePrint Archive, Paper 2022/347 (2022). https://eprint.iacr.org/2022/347
41. Lee, J., Kifer, D.: Scaling up differentially private deep learning with fast per-example gradient clipping. Proc. Priv. Enhancing Technol. **2021**(1) (2021)
42. Lehmkuhl, R., Mishra, P., Srinivasan, A., Popa, R.A.: MUSE: secure inference resilient to malicious clients. In: 30th USENIX Security Symposium (USENIX Security 21), pp. 2201–2218 (2021)
43. Lei, Y., Jia, F., Lin, J., Xing, S., Ding, S.X.: An intelligent fault diagnosis method using unsupervised feature learning towards mechanical big data. IEEE Trans. Industr. Electron. **63**(5), 3137–3147 (2016)
44. Li, C., Palanisamy, B.: Privacy in Internet of Things: from principles to technologies. IEEE Internet Things J. **6**(1), 488–505 (2019)
45. Li, L., Ota, K., Dong, M.: Deep learning for smart industry: efficient manufacture inspection system with fog computing. IEEE Trans. Industr. Inf. **14**(10), 4665–4673 (2018)
46. Liu, H., Li, C., Liu, B., Wang, P., Ge, S., Wang, W.: Differentially private learning with grouped gradient clipping. In: ACM Multimedia Asia (MMAsia) (2022)
47. López-Alt, A., Tromer, E., Vaikuntanathan, V.: On-the-fly multiparty computation on the cloud via multikey fully homomorphic encryption. In: Proceedings of the Forty-Fourth Annual ACM Symposium on Theory of Computing, pp. 1219–1234 (2012)
48. Lou, Q., Feng, B., Charles Fox, G., Jiang, L.: Glyph: Fast and accurately training deep neural networks on encrypted data. Adv. Neural Inf. Process. Syst. (NeurIPS) **33**, 9193–9202 (2020)
49. Lulla, G., Kumar, A., Pole, G., Deshmukh, G.: IoT based smart security and surveillance system. In: 2021 International Conference on Emerging Smart Computing and Informatics (ESCI), pp. 385–390. IEEE (2021)
50. Lyubashevsky, V., Peikert, C., Regev, O.: On ideal lattices and learning with errors over rings. In: Annual International Conference on the Theory and Applications of Cryptographic Techniques, pp. 1–23. Springer (2010)

51. Ma, X., et al.: A survey on deep learning empowered IoT applications. IEEE Access **7**, 181721–181732 (2019)
52. McMahan, B., Moore, E., Ramage, D., Hampson, S., y Arcas, B.A.: Communication-efficient learning of deep networks from decentralized data. In: International Conference on Artificial Intelligence and Statistics, pp. 1273–1282. PMLR (2017)
53. Melis, L., Song, C., De Cristofaro, E., Shmatikov, V.: Exploiting unintended feature leakage in collaborative learning. In: IEEE Symposium on Security and Privacy (SP), pp. 691–706. IEEE (2019)
54. Mohassel, P., Zhang, Y.: SecureML: a system for scalable privacy-preserving machine learning. In: IEEE Symposium on Security and Privacy (SP), pp. 19–38. IEEE (2017)
55. Najafabadi, M.M., Villanustre, F., Khoshgoftaar, T.M., Seliya, N., Wald, R., Muharemagic, E.: Deep learning applications and challenges in big data analytics. J. Big Data **2**(1), 1–21 (2015). https://doi.org/10.1186/s40537-014-0007-7
56. Natarajan, D., Dai, W.: SEAL-embedded: a homomorphic encryption library for the Internet of Things. IACR Trans. Cryptographic Hardware Embedded Syst. **2021**(3), 756–779 (2021)
57. Natarajan, D., Loveless, A., Dai, W., Dreslinski, R.: CHEX-MIX: combining homomorphic encryption with trusted execution environments for oblivious inference in the cloud. In: IEEE European Symposium on Security and Privacy (EuroS&P), pp. 73–91. IEEE (2023)
58. Ngu, A.H., Tseng, P.T., Paliwal, M., Carpenter, C., Stipe, W.: Smartwatch-based IoT fall detection application. Open J. Internet Things (OJIOT) **4**(1), 87–98 (2018)
59. Ogonji, M.M., Okeyo, G., Wafula, J.M.: A survey on privacy and security of internet of things. Comput. Sci. Rev. **38**, 100312 (2020)
60. Ogunniye, G., Kokciyan, N.: A survey on understanding and representing privacy requirements in the Internet-of-Things. J. Artif. Intell. Res. **76**, 163–192 (2023)
61. Papernot, N., Thakurta, A., Song, S., Chien, S., Erlingsson, Ú.: Tempered sigmoid activations for deep learning with differential privacy. In: AAAI Conference on Artificial Intelligence. vol. 35, pp. 9312–9321 (2021)
62. Patel, V., Kanani, S., Pathak, T., Patel, P., Ali, M.I., Breslin, J.: An intelligent doorbell design using federated deep learning. In: Proceedings of the 3rd ACM India Joint International Conference on Data Science & Management of Data, pp. 380–384 (2021)
63. Qian, J., Zhang, P., Zhu, H., Liu, M., Wang, J., Ma, X.: LHDNN: maintaining high precision and low latency inference of deep neural networks on encrypted data. Appl. Sci. **13**(8), 4815 (2023)
64. Rahman, M.A., Hossain, M.S.: An internet-of-medical-things-enabled edge computing framework for tackling COVID-19. IEEE Internet Things J. **8**(21), 15847–15854 (2021)
65. Rigaki, M., Garcia, S.: A survey of privacy attacks in machine learning. ACM Comput. Surv. **56**(4) (2023)
66. Sav, S., et al.: POSEIDON: privacy-preserving federated neural network learning. In: Symposium on Network and Distributed System Security (2021)
67. Senanayake, N., Podschwadt, R., Takabi, D., Calhoun, V.D., Plis, S.M.: NeuroCrypt: machine learning over encrypted distributed neuroimaging data. Neuroinformatics **20**(1), 91–108 (2022)
68. Serengil, S.I., Ozpinar, A.: LightPHE: Integrating partially homomorphic encryption into python with extensive cloud environment evaluations (2024)

69. Sheng, T.J., et al.: An internet of things based smart waste management system using LoRa and TensorFlow deep learning model. IEEE Access **8**, 148793–148811 (2020)
70. Shokri, R., Shmatikov, V.: Privacy-preserving deep learning. In: 22nd ACM SIGSAC Conference on Computer and Communications Security, pp. 1310–1321 (2015)
71. Shokri, R., Stronati, M., Song, C., Shmatikov, V.: Membership inference attacks against machine learning models. In: IEEE Symposium on Security and Privacy (SP), pp. 3–18. IEEE (2017)
72. SNU Cryptography & Privacy Lab, S.N.U.: SNU-MGHE. Online: https://github.com/SNUCP/snu-mghe
73. Subramani, P., Vadivelu, N., Kamath, G.: Enabling fast differentially private SGD via just-in-time compilation and vectorization. Adv. Neural Inf. Process. Syst. (NeurIPS) **34**, 26409–26421 (2021)
74. Tan, S., Knott, B., Tian, Y., Wu, D.J.: CRYPTGPU: fast privacy-preserving machine learning on the GPU. In: IEEE Symposium on Security and Privacy (SP), pp. 1021–1038. IEEE (2021)
75. Tramèr, F., Zhang, F., Juels, A., Reiter, M.K., Ristenpart, T.: Stealing machine learning models via prediction APIs. In: 25th USENIX Security Symposium (USENIX Security 16), pp. 601–618 (2016)
76. Treiber, A., Molina, A., Weinert, C., Schneider, T., Kersting, K.: CryptoSPN: Privacy-preserving sum-product network inference (2020)
77. Trieu Phong, L., Aono, Y., Hayashi, T., Wang, L., Moriai, S.: Privacy-preserving deep learning via additively homomorphic encryption. IEEE Trans. Inf. Forensics Secur. **13**(5), 1333–1345 (2017)
78. Varun, M., Feng, S., Wang, H., Sural, S., Hong, Y.: Towards accurate and stronger local differential privacy for federated learning with staircase randomized response. In: Proceedings of the Fourteenth ACM Conference on Data and Application Security and Privacy, pp. 307–318 (2024)
79. Wang, E.K., Chen, C.M., Hassan, M.M., Almogren, A.: A deep learning based medical image segmentation technique in internet-of-medical-things domain. Futur. Gener. Comput. Syst. **108**, 135–144 (2020)
80. Widmann, T., Merkle, F., Nocker, M., Schöttle, P.: Pruning for power: optimizing energy efficiency in IoT with neural network pruning. In: International Conference on Engineering Applications of Neural Networks, pp. 251–263. Springer (2023)
81. Yao, A.C.C.: How to generate and exchange secrets. In: Symposium on Foundations of Computer Science, pp. 162–167. IEEE (1986)
82. Zhang, Z., Han, Y.: Detection of ovarian tumors in obstetric ultrasound imaging using logistic regression classifier with an advanced machine learning approach. IEEE Access **8**, 44999–45008 (2020)
83. Zheng, M., Xu, D., Jiang, L., Gu, C., Tan, R., Cheng, P.: Challenges of privacy-preserving machine learning in IoT. In: Proceedings of the First International Workshop on Challenges in Artificial Intelligence and Machine Learning for Internet of Things, pp. 1–7 (2019)
84. Zhou, J., Li, J., Panaousis, E., Liang, K.: Deep binarized convolutional neural network inferences over encrypted data. In: IEEE International Conference on Cyber Security and Cloud Computing (CSCloud)/IEEE International Conference on Edge Computing and Scalable Cloud (EdgeCom), pp. 160–167. IEEE (2020)

Using Traditional Image Kernels and Image Processing Techniques to Harden Convolutional Neural Networks Against Adversarial Attacks

Andrew Kiggins[✉] and Jide Edu

School of Computer and Information Sciences, University of Strathclyde, Glasgow, UK
andrewkiggins2000@gmail.com, jide.edu@strath.ac.uk

Abstract. Convolutional Neural Networks (CNNs) are the primary image classification method, especially in safety-critical physical environments such as autonomous driving and industrial automation. However, CNNs are vulnerable to adversarial attacks in which noise could be added to an image to deceive the classifier. This can lead CNN to make incorrect predictions with high confidence, posing significant threats to physical systems. Although there are various defense mechanisms against adversarial attacks, many are unsuitable for safety-critical applications due to possible image degradation or high computational costs. In this research, we investigate the use of traditional image denoising techniques as a defense against adversarial attacks in environments with limited computational resources. We evaluated three denoising methods: Median filtering, Gaussian filtering, and the Markov chain Monte Carlo (MCMC) method, under "real-world conditions". The results demonstrate that these three methods not only reduce the impact of adversarial attacks but also surpass the state-of-the-art defense technique, APE-GAN, in speed while preserving prediction accuracy. Our findings show that traditional denoising techniques could provide a practical and efficient defense against adversarial attacks in low-power, safety-critical systems.

Keywords: Convolutional Neural Networks · Physical Systems · Adversarial Patch Attacks · Adversarial Attack Defense · Image Classification · Low Powered Computing

1 Introduction

Image classification is a crucial element of computer vision that leverages artificial intelligence (AI) to identify and label objects or scenes within images [1–4]. This fundamental process now relies on deep convolutional neural networks (CNNs), which have achieved state-of-the-art accuracy in image classification tasks [5,6]. CNNs have been widely implemented in various real-world applications, from explicit image filtering to autonomous vehicles [1]. The increasing use of these models has exposed vulnerabilities, especially to adversarial attacks. Such attacks can cause models to make incorrect classifications, potentially leading to severe misinterpretations.

Adversarial attacks are intentional manipulations of inputs designed to mislead machine learning classifiers [7–9]. In image classification, two main types of adversarial attacks can easily deceive a typical CNN architecture that uses a gradient-based method. These are the standard adversarial attacks [10] and adversarial patch-based attacks [11,12]. Standard attacks involve generating noise to introduce imperceptible perturbations that can trick the classifier into making incorrect predictions. On the other hand, patch attacks involve placing small, sticker-like perturbations in the image (or on physical objects) to cause misclassifications. Patch attacks come in various styles that include changes in the number of patches, shape, and orientation of the patches. Unlike traditional adversarial attacks, patch attacks have the possibility of being able to influence physical systems, such as self-driving cars. This opens up potential new attack vectors for adversarial attacks.

The need for robust defenses against adversarial attacks is becoming increasingly apparent, with more than twenty billion connected physical devices worldwide engaged in mission-critical classification tasks in sectors such as autonomous vehicles and robotic-assisted surgery [13]. These systems require rapid and accurate decision-making to ensure user safety. Although these physical systems are growing in computational power, we can no longer rely on the exponential growth of microprocessors [14] to accommodate the growth of computationally intensive algorithms into physical systems. Scaling machine learning models to meet the computational limitations of physical systems is already a challenge. However, integrating a scaled convolutional neural network with an existing defense technique presents significant complexity.

Defense techniques such as adversarial training can fail under non-adversarial conditions [15] and most input transformation techniques are computationally intensive. Moreover, existing defense solutions suffer from limited adaptably or insufficient applicability in a highly dynamic environment [16]. For example, APE-GANs [10], for mitigating standard adversarial attacks, have demonstrated effectiveness in countering adversarial noise; however, they are characterized by high computational demands. Likewise, the Segment and Complete method [17] for patch attacks can degrade image quality, negatively affecting performance. As the reliance on convolutional neural networks for image classification grows and given that these methods are increasingly used in safety-critical systems, it is important to develop a defensive approach that is both computationally efficient and robust against potential adversarial attacks.

Defense methods must effectively reduce or eliminate adversarial noise [18]. Traditional image filters [19], commonly used for denoising and sharpening, may offer computationally feasible solutions, as these filters apply mathematical operations to transform pixel values, suggesting the potential for low-latency scalable defenses that can be tailored for mission-critical systems. A physical image classification system typically starts by capturing pixel data using a sensor, such as a camera. Once the data is acquired, it is fed into a deep learning model where the pixel information is processed. This generates a set of class probabilities that influence the actions of the physical system [20]. This paper explores innovative methods for image classification systems that operate with limited computational resources, with the goal of enhancing the security of critical safety systems. Drawing inspiration from traditional classification systems that used image kernels for pixel data processing, we demonstrate the value of incorporating a conventional input processing layer into low power image classification systems.

In this work, we propose a defense mechanism that utilizes traditional image kernels to effectively counter adversarial patch attacks. Our approach shows strong resilience against adversarial modifications while maintaining image quality. Our proposed method significantly improves computational efficiency compared to the current state-of-the-art defense model, APE-GANs. By incorporating traditional image kernels, we effectively reduce computational overhead, making our approach suitable for real-time applications and those with resource constraints.

2 Background

2.1 Image Classification and CNNs

Image classification is a task in computer vision that involves labeling objects within images. The early methods relied on raw pixel data and predesigned image kernels to detect objects, using fixed statistical approaches for classification [21]. The introduction of the LeNet architecture [22] marked a significant change in this approach, as it effectively leveraged convolutional neural networks (CNN). LeNet used multiple convolutional layers, pooling layers, and activation functions to identify features in images [23]. LeNet and other similar methods have some shortcomings, which led to the development of the ResNet architecture (Residual Neural Network). ResNet introduced shortcut pathways between the input and activation layers, allowing error backpropagation through multiple pathways and alleviating the vanishing gradient problem [23].

2.2 Adversarial Attacks

The traditional adversarial attack involves adding noise to an image to deceive a classifier to predict an incorrect label while the human perception of the image remains unchanged [23]. Common methods for training traditional adversarial attacks include the Fast Gradient Sign Method, the Basic Iterative Method, and the Carlini-Wagner Method [10]. These methods aim to maximize the effectiveness of misclassification while minimizing image degradation. Fast Gradient Sign Method (FGSM) is the easiest attack method to implement and the most widely used. FGSM operates inversely to the traditional gradient descent algorithm; instead of minimizing an error function, it moves up the gradient to maximize the error. FGSM performs a single-step update to prevent image degradation, making it the most computationally efficient attack method.

Basic Iterative Method (BIM) is based on FGSM by generating an adversarial image through a predetermined number of iterative steps. If FGSM were applied continuously without modifications, the resulting image would be significantly degraded. To address this, BIM employs gradient clipping, which scales down the gradient during updates if it exceeds a predefined threshold. Properly defined clipping helps to maintain the image quality.

2.3 Adversarial Threat Model

Attacker's Knowledge: In adversarial attacks, attackers can operate under three different levels of knowledge about their target systems: Zero Knowledge (black box attack), Perfect Knowledge (white box attack) and Limited Knowledge. These levels indicate the extent of the attacker's awareness regarding the architecture of CNNs and their defense mechanisms. In the Zero-Knowledge scenario, the attacker has no information about the CNN or defense mechanisms. As a result, they often create a generic attack model or develop an attack misaligned with the defense due to differences in architecture. In contrast, Perfect Knowledge refers to a scenario in which the attacker has complete knowledge of the defense mechanisms and CNN architecture. Lastly, limited Knowledge falls between Zero Knowledge and Perfect Knowledge. It often leads to the most effective attacks in real-world scenarios [10]. This variation in knowledge levels results in various attack methods, making it challenging for training hardening to compile an ideal dataset that represents all possible architectural variations.

2.4 Real World Systems and Patch Attacks

Traditional adversarial attacks have limited attack vectors. Patch attacks are an example of an adversarial attack in which visible noise is injected into a subset of the image, effectively forming a patch. This opens the door to more attack vectors, most notably real-world systems, such as deceiving autonomous driving systems. Patch attacks are trained using a method similar to FGSM; however, unlike FGSM, the training is only done on a select few pixels. During training, the attacker decides on a label class that they want to deceive the image as [11]. By cyclic rotation and patch placement, the attacker can make the attack more robust. Unlike FGSM, the attacker does not need to try to hide the patch, so larger gradients can be followed to make the patch more effective.

An extension of the patch attack is the multi-patch attack. Many varieties of multi-patch attacks involve training multiple different patches and their optimal placements. The process of generating optimal placements is done through Boundary Space Search [13]. Boundary Space Search is achieved by moving N patches around the border of an image in synchrony until an optimal placement is reached. Boundary Space Search is only practical for attacking digital systems, as trying to recreate placing the patches in a given format by hand is not practical. These multi-patch attacks are highly effective; however, the Mono-Multi

Patch Attack is the simplest and involves training just one patch and randomly placing multiples of the trained patch. The mono-multi-patch attack is significantly more difficult to defend against compared to a single-patch attack [13].

2.5 Existing Defense Methods

Defense methods vary widely in their techniques, and some apply only to specific types of attack. Among the most general current defense strategies are training hardening and Adversarial Perturbation Elimination Generative Adversarial Networks (APE-GANs). Training hardening involves modifying the CNN training data set by injecting examples of various adversarial attacks into the training data, along with their correct labels [24]. Although training hardening can provide robust defense, it requires a broad and diverse selection of attack types and architectures to ensure adequate protection.

APE-GANs are one of the most recent breakthroughs in adversarial attack defense [10]. The main goal of an APE-GAN is to optimize a generator function to denoise a given adversarial image input [25]. As shown in Fig. 1, APE-GANs follow a modified architecture of a traditional GAN. The traditional GAN architecture consists of "two models: a generative model G that captures the data distribution and a discriminative model D that estimates the probability that a sample came from the training data rather than G' [26]. APE-GANs often incorporate techniques from Deep Convolutional GANs (DCGANs). DCGANs provide more stable output by including transposed convolutional layers in the generator to up-sample images [27]. However, APE-GANs differ significantly from traditional GANs and DCGANs in their approach to training data. APE-GANs have two training sets, one of the unattacked images and one of the attacked images. The goal is to optimize a generator so that a discriminator cannot tell if the input image came from attacked or unattacked sets. This is achieved by optimizing the denoising abilities of the generator.

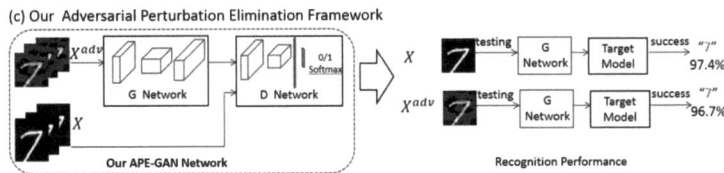

Fig. 1. APE-GAN Framework [26]

When appropriately trained and combined with training hardening, APE-GANs demonstrate strong defense benchmarks against targeted attack models. However, their performance declines when defending against non-targeted attack models (unseen models), resulting in a higher error rate. Furthermore, APE-GANs may slightly degrade the quality of the images [26].

For defense mechanisms specifically for patch attacks, the most effective defense mechanism is the Segment and Complete(SAC) method [17]. The SAC method works by first detecting a patch's location, finding the patch shape's dimension, and then removing the patch by filling the patch with black pixels. SAC is highly effective at handling a variety of patch sizes and shapes; however, this versatility can lead to image degradation proportional to the patches' size. Although this may not be problematic in some cases, physical systems, such as those described by Huang [28], may encounter difficulties due to the limited data available for edge detection. As the number of patches increases, the area of lost pixels also expands, further impacting the system.

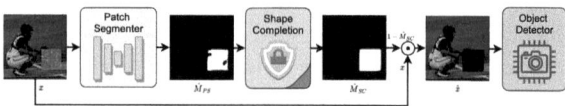

Fig. 2. SAC Framework [17]

2.6 Other Lesser Used Defense Methods

All the methods mentioned earlier use the entire image as a single input. A differing defense method for adversarial patch attacks is Local logits. Local logit is a method that takes small subsets of the original image and feeds the subsets into a classifier. Local logits then take the aggregation of the classifier's predictions for the subsets to decide on the whole image. The decision is made by picking the label with the highest aggregated prediction confidence. The logic is that the majority of features that the classifier makes decisions on are unobstructed by the patch, thus the majority of the decisions made are accurate. In practice, the Local logit method does not defend against adversarial attacks robustly, since by taking the simple average, the classifier cannot accurately weigh features correctly in making a decision [29]. Patchguard is a framework that extends the use of image subsets (slices). Patchguard takes all the aggregation matrices for each label and performs a "robust mask" to mute the high values in the patch label matrix (the slice that contains the patch). Patchguard framework uses robust mask algorithm."

However, the Patchguard framework has multiple drawbacks. The most significant drawback is that as the number of labels for a classifier increases, the successful defense rate drops. The dropoff rate is the reduction in the percentage of successful classification. The successful classification rate for Patchguard goes from a success rate of approximately 87% for 10 labels to 26% for 1000 labels [29]. Another drawback is computational complexity. The Patchguard framework had two steps. The first step, generating the logit map (the prediction matrix for the slices), runs in $O(N)$, where N is the desired number of image slices. The second step, running the "robust mask" algorithm, runs in $O(M*K)$, where M is the number of labels for a given classifier and K is the number of pixels in an image slice. These drawbacks make the Patchguard framework unsuitable for low-powered safety critical physical systems, especially if the classifier has many labels.

Recent studies have explored the integration of Gabor layers into CNNs. Gabor layers are characterized by convolutional filters parameterized with learnable Gabor functions. These layers have consistently demonstrated enhanced robustness across various CNN architectures. However, research validating the efficacy of Gabor networks has not examined their performance against patch attacks, despite the potential of Gabor layers as a defensible technique for constrained physical systems [30].

2.7 Traditional Denoising Techniques

Upon thorough analysis of standard defense methodologies, it is clear that these approaches are fundamentally focusing on denoising. Image denoising has been heavily researched, with traditional denoising techniques being used for decades. Among traditional denoising techniques, the two most common are the Median Filter and the Gaussian Filter. The Median Filter works by assigning pixels as a new value. The new value is the median value from the surrounding $N \times N$ neighbors of a given pixel, this avoids skew which results in better preservation in smaller details [31]. The Gaussian filter is a denoising technique that uses a Gaussian hump of size $N \times N$ and σ as the kernel to build a convolution matrix, which is used to assign new weighted averages as the value to a given pixel [32]. Both of these filters are spatial filters. The Gaussian filter does a good job at reducing areas of high noise, while the median filter does a good job at reducing large magnitude jumps [33]. The characteristics of these filters could make them a good candidate for a low computationally intensive approach to reduce the noise in patches and other adversarial images.

A non-spatial image denoising algorithm is Markov-Chain Monte Carlo Sampling Denoising (MCMC). MCMC typically performs better on images with a high noise level compared to spatial filters since "the local information redundancy is insufficient to provide a good noise-free image estimate" when using spatial filters [34]. MCMC combines two algorithms, a Markov-Chain, and a Monte Carlo Simulation.MCMC denoising is very flexible when dealing with a variety of noise distributions and relatively computationally efficient compared to other denoising techniques of similar styles.

3 Methodology

3.1 Dataset and Preparations

For this work, we used a labeled dataset known as ImageNet [29]. Specifically, a pre-processed subset of ImageNet was utilized, consisting of 5 images for each of 1,000 labels, totaling 5,000 images. This selection aligns with the data required for a pre-trained CNN used in this study [23]. ImageNet was selected because of its extensive repository, which includes millions of images associated with more than 100,000 unique labels. ImageNet is known for its exceptional labeling accuracy, boasting a correct label rate exceeding 99.7%. This high level of precision is achieved through the human validation of candidate labels. Multiple human annotators participate in the labeling process, and an image is included in the dataset only when a "convincing majority" of the votes supports a particular label [29]. The concept of "convincing majority" is determined using various statistical methods to minimize human bias [29].

This correctness and diversity of the data ensure that models trained on ImageNet have reduced training bias [35]. This reduction in training bias increases the reliability of the experiment's results, as the results are more likely to be derived from the success rate of defense and not bias introduced from the classification model.

3.2 Training Steps

Before the experiment can run, the conductor must train two Convolutional Neural Networks (CNNs). One of the CNNs will be used as a benchmark to assess the success rate of the adversarial attacks and defense methods. The other CNN will be used to generate an APE-GAN and adversarial attacks. Two CNNs are needed to simulate a black-box attack [36]. A black box attack occurs when the attacker has a minimal idea (or they do not know) about the inner workings of the classifiers: this lack of knowledge results in the attacker and the defender training their models on separate CNN architectures. Using two different CNNs of different architectures, the experiment can effectively simulate a black-box attack.

For the first CNN, this experiment used a pre-trained model, ResNet34. This model was chosen because it used modern architectural standards and was trained on ImageNet dataset. Resnet34 also has a prediction accuracy of 99.2%. The accuracy of ResNet34's prediction reduces the additional error in the results, allowing the classification error to be safely accredited to the attack model and failed defense. In addition, ResNet is more computationally and memory efficient than similar cutting-edge models, such as DenseNet.

The second model is a plain CNN trained locally using specifications from an implementation of the paper by Jin et al. [25]. This architectural difference aligns with black-box simulation, as mentioned above. In addition, the plain CNN is a simpler architecture than ResNet34. This also simulates more real-world attacks, as the attacker often lacks the same research and funding to develop the same level of sophisticated classifiers as companies that build low-powered physical systems.

Before the experiment can be run, the conductor must first install the required Python packages and a Docker file[1]. Containerization is needed to ensure that resources are capped and consistent between runs. This allows the

---

[1] The requirement list and Docker file can be found on the project at https://gitfront.io/r/anon12345/BT8GFuKhhvCx/ImageKernelsForPatchAttackDefence/.

conductor to apply the findings to various computational levels depending on the cap set when launching the docker image. This limitation on computational levels helps the conductor determine the effectiveness of a defense method's viability for low-powered machines. For example, would a low-powered IoT device have enough time to run the defense method and still make a classification in a sufficient time frame?

3.3 Experiment Setup

Python 3 was chosen for this experiment due to its status as the industry standard for machine learning, supported by robust frameworks like PyTorch and TensorFlow. Its extensive libraries streamline development and reduce errors, making it the ideal choice given the substantial machine learning requirements.

Containerization was used to simulate low-powered machines, with Docker selected as the industry-standard tool for ensuring consistent performance across different hardware. It offers advantages over competitors in simulating constrained physical systems.

Four defense methods were selected on the basis of computational efficiency, APE-GANs and traditional techniques. APE-GANs were chosen for their effectiveness against adversarial attacks, though their performance on physical machines with limited resources remains uncertain.

For traditional image processing, median and Gaussian filters were used as spatial denoising techniques. These local filters suppress noise by leveraging spatial redundancy, but struggle with varied noise. They were included for their low computational cost at small kernel sizes. To offset their limitations, Markov Chain Monte Carlo (MCMC) sampling was incorporated, offering a more computationally intensive but viable alternative with optimized parameters.

Three adversarial attacks were tested: the fast gradient sign method, the singular patch attack, and the mono multi-patch attack.

Once the conductor executes the launch command, the Docker container starts. By using Docker, the conductor can set limits on the RAM and CPU cores; for this experiment, the hard limits were set to 4 CPU cores and 8 GB of RAM. Algorithm 1 outlines the steps to carry out the experiment.

4 Analysis

4.1 Prediction Results

In this experiment, the measure of prediction accuracy was represented by the prediction confidence of the CNN for the correct label. Across all the attack methods, the single patch method was defended at the highest rate.

Table 1 presents the prediction confidence levels for the models. The Median filter method achieved an average correct prediction confidence of 31.67%, with a range from 0% to 99.99%. In particular, the median filter performed better with smaller kernel sizes. Larger kernel sizes caused significant blurring, making

Algorithm 1. Adversarial Attack Evaluation and Defense Benchmarking

1: Run the ImageNet dataset through the ResNet34 classifier to obtain baseline classification accuracy.
2: Run the ImageNet dataset through the attack models to generate three adversarial image sets:
   – Traditional adversarial attack set (Fast Gradient Sign Method)
   – Single patch adversarial attack set
   – Mono multi-patch adversarial attack set
3: Pass the generated adversarial image sets through the ResNet34 classifier to benchmark the effectiveness of the attack methods.
4: **for** each adversarial image set **do**
5:     Start timer (initiated in the Python script).
6:     Apply the APE-GAN defense method on the adversarial image set, saving the resulting images.
7:     Stop the timer and record the time.
8:     Pass the resulting images through the ResNet34 classifier and record the prediction accuracy.
9: **end for**
10: **for** each adversarial image set and each defense method **do**
11:     **for** each defense method (Median denoising, Gaussian denoising, Markov Chain Monte Carlo) **do**
12:         Repeat steps 4 through 7 for the remaining defense methods.
13:     **end for**
14: **end for**
15: **for** each defense method **do**
16:     **for** each set of parameters (Kernel sizes, Sigma values, Beta values) **do**
17:         Vary parameter values and repeat the defense and classification process.
18:     **end for**
19: **end for**
20: Write the results to CSV for analysis.

the images unrecognizable, which hindered CNN's ability to make accurate predictions, regardless of the attack method used. In terms of performance against traditional adversarial attacks, the Median filter demonstrated a 31-fold improvement compared to an undefended model. However, for single patch attacks, there was only a 1% increase in classification accuracy compared to the undefended model. In the case of multipatch attacks, no significant differences were observed between the median filter model and the undefended model.

The Gaussian filter method had an average correct prediction confidence of 27.02% with a span of 0% to 99.99%. The Gaussian defense rate improved performance when using a smaller sigma value. This is likely caused by a lesser blur effect, which helps preserve the character of the image while cleaning up spikes in high noise. For traditional adversarial attacks, the Gaussian denoising method had no significant difference in performance compared to the undefended model. For the single patch attack method, the Gaussian denoising method had a roughly 18% increase in performance compared to the undefended model. For the multi-patch attack method, the Gaussian denoising method had no significant difference in performance compared to the undefended model.

The Markov Chain Monte Carlo denoising had an average performance of 29.32% with a spread from 0% to 99%. MCMC performed 10 times better than the undefended model for traditional adversarial attacks. This was somewhat surprising, as MCMC's ability to take more global information than spatial denoising techniques should have lent itself to denoise FGSM at a more successful rate than the spatial methods discussed above (Median filter drastically outperformed MCMC). MCMC performed slightly better than the undefended model for the single-patch attack method. MCMC performed at no significant difference from the undefended model for the multi-patched attack method.

The GAN Defense Method for defending against Adversarial Perturbation Elimination had an average performance of 24.03% with a spread of 0% to 99.99%. For the traditional attack method, the APE-GAN performed roughly 24 times better than the undefended model; however, it is worth noting that the CNN could classify with over 90% accuracy for a few tests. This confidence was only seen with one other method, the median filter method. For the single-patch attack method, the APE-GAN method had no difference in defense compared to the undefended model.

Table 1. Prediction Accuracy for the models

Attacks	Undefended	Median	Gaussian	MCMC	APE-GAN
Traditional	0.96%	31.91%	0.96%	10.29%	24.98%
Single-Patch	37.57%	38.76%	55.06%	52.39%	24.18%
Multi-Patch	25.11%	24.34%	25.03%	25.28%	22.97%

In conclusion, the Median filter effectively mitigates various forms of adversarial attacks. The Gaussian technique exhibits optimal performance against the single-patch attack method. The Gaussian method removes noise in confined regions with high intensity [32], rendering it particularly effective in blurring patches, which constitute meticulously devised noise. However, no method consistently defends against the Multi-patch attack methodology.

4.2 Computational Performance

In this experiment, the measure of computational intensity was represented as the time it took to defend an image. Across all defense methods, Gaussian denoising was the most computationally efficient in the selected range. Gaussian denoising had an average compute time of roughly 0.0673 s with a spread from 0.0262 to 0.1723 s. This result is most likely driven by the fact that changing the sigma value only affects the significance of the blur and not the input for the number of pixels. The same cannot be said for the median filter algorithm, the other spatial filter in this experiment. The median filter had the largest average out of all the techniques used in the experiment. As shown in Fig. 3, the average compute time for the median filter algorithm was roughly 20.2758 s, with a spread from 0.4527 to 91.5563 s. This enormous spread is a result of the time efficiency of median filters, $O(N^2)$, where N is the kernel size.

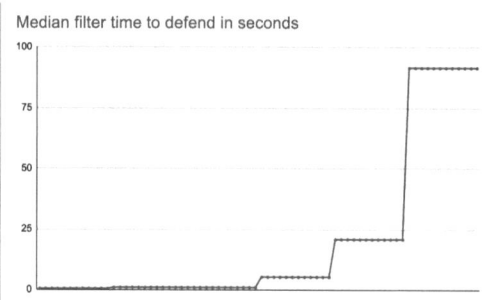

Fig. 3. Graph of Median Filter Performance in Seconds

This highlights the importance of choosing an optimal kernel size. This could be done with a naive optimization technique to find the optimal balance between prediction accuracy and computation time. The Markov chain Monte Carlo had nearly the same average as APE-GAN. As shown in Fig. 4, the average time to defend for MCMC was 3.1501 s and spread from 2.8871 to 3.6844 s.

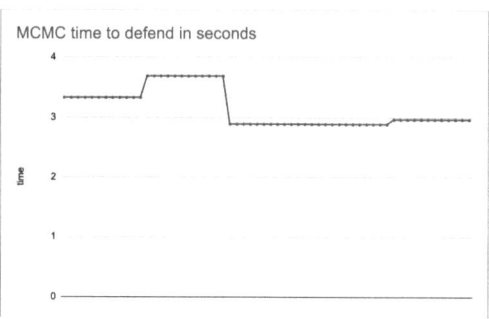

Fig. 4. Graph of MCMC Denoising Performance in Seconds

Each bump is an increase in beta size of .2 starting at .2 (creating a range from .2 to .8). A larger beta could create a more concentrated posterior, which would decrease the number of computed pixels in the denoised images. A larger variety for MCMC (not tested in this experiment) would be to increase/decrease the number of iterations. This increase/decrease would have a significantly stronger impact on compute time.

The APE-GAN had an average compute time of 2.7383 s and a spread from 2.7383 to 2.7383 s. The APE-GAN had no variables to change in the experiment and, thus, was the most consistent against the attacked images in terms of computation time. A key factor for APE-GANs is training time, which varies by method and hardware and can be time-consuming.

4.3 Computational Intensity

In safety-critical systems with on-board computing, the computation speed and prediction accuracy are crucial. Among the defense methods analyzed, median denoising performed best when picking an optimal kernel size is picked; however, patch attacks are a more likely attack vector for physical systems. The Gaussian denoising method performs best on patches in speed and prediction accuracy. A key factor is how much image degradation occurs during the defense method. Figures 5, 6, 7, 8, show examples of defended attacks along with the original image and the top five predictions from the classifier (the green bar is the correct label).

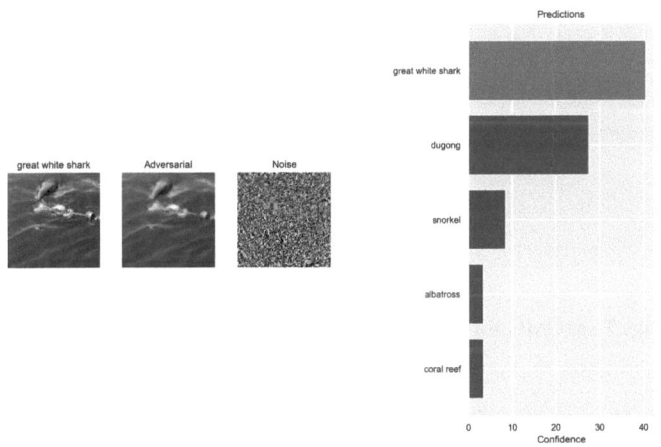

Fig. 5. Median filter (7 × 7) successfully defending FGSM attack

We can see that MCMC and Gaussian filters have minimal image degrading and provide enough denoising to defend against that attack. The Median filter successfully defends the image but applies a noticeable blur to the image (even at a reasonable kernel size). The APE-GAN defense failed to protect the attack; however, the patch label was not the top result. The classifier failed to correctly classify the image because the image had significant degrading in color and features. This is likely due to the APE-GAN being overfitted to the training

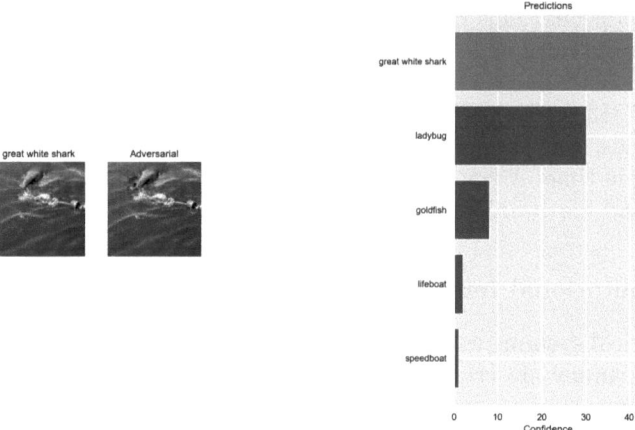

Fig. 6. Gaussian Filter successfully defending standard single patch attack

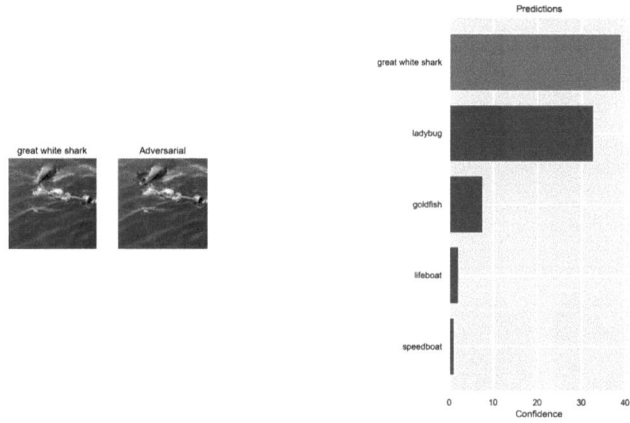

Fig. 7. MCMC filter successfully defending single patch attack

data it was subjected to. This implies that APE-GANs are less fitted to the wild, as APE-GANs are not as easily trained to be a jack-of-all-trades defense method.

After analyzing prediction accuracy, computation time, and image degradation, the Gaussian filter emerged as the most optimal defense method in this experiment, as it is the best candidate to defend lower power physical systems. In addition, Gaussian filters require much less setup compared to APE-GANs, as no training is required. It is worth noting that even a successful defense does not guarantee a high confidence percentage, but it ensures that the most confident label is correct.

It is important to note that for the tuneable parameters, there was a clear optimal point for creating the best results in terms of retaining accurate pre-

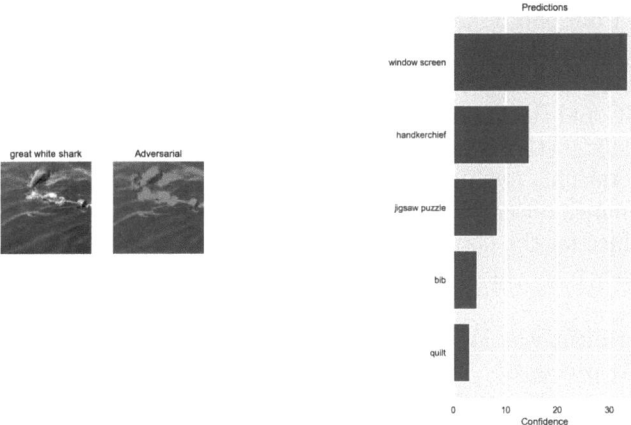

Fig. 8. APE-GAN failing to defend single patch attack

dictions. Figure 9 illustrates the regression of prediction confidence versus kernel size for the median filter. Similarly, the other two filters also exhibited clear optimal points. This suggests that many traditional denoising techniques could enhance a model's robustness by adding an additional input layer that represents a tunable filter.

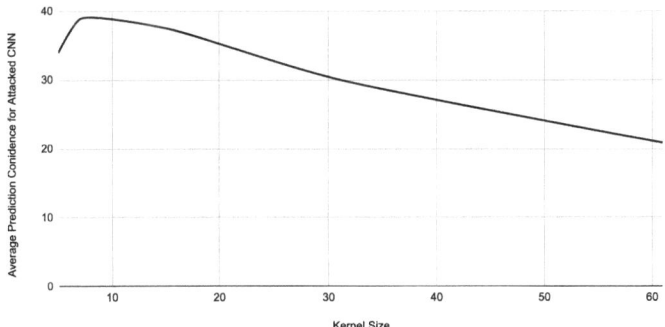

Fig. 9. Median Filter: Kernel Size vs Prediction Confidence

5 Limitations

Although the study has successfully demonstrated that traditional image denoising techniques can effectively reduce the impact of adversarial attacks and perform better than existing defense techniques in terms of speed, it also has certain limitations. First, the small sample size of the labels is a limitation. Our results were derived from only four "goal" labels, which limits our ability to fully evaluate the effectiveness of the attack vectors in a larger and more diverse sample. Secondly, there was a deficiency in variability regarding the parameters utilized for the MCMC and the Gaussian filter. In the case of MCMC, modifications were restricted solely to the beta values. Consequently, critical factors, such as the number of iterations, remained constant, potentially contributing to the suboptimal performance observed in MCMC. Similarly, alterations were restricted to the sigma values for the Gaussian filter method. This constraint limits the scope of the outcomes from this experimental approach concerning the Gaussian filter method.

The experiment was also conducted on an M1 MacBook with an eight-core 3.2 GHz ARM processor. Although most low-powered physical systems employ ARM processors, their processing capabilities are substantially inferior to those of the M1 MacBook. Despite Docker's configuration limiting the number of CPU cores, the notable speed advantage of the M1 MacBook may have circumvented performance bottlenecks typically encountered on genuine low-powered machines. Finally, our proof-of-concepts focus exclusively on square patches. Given the square kernel configuration of Median and Gaussian filters, their efficacy could potentially vary when applied to non-square patch shapes. Furthermore, the lack of variation in patch size may have further impacted the performance of the defensive mechanisms evaluated.

6 Related Studies

In the past few years, there has been an increase in the number of state-of-the-art defense methods. These methods enhance defense in one aspect but often weaken it in others.

A possible robust and lightweight defense method is using Denoising Auto Encoders (DAE). The traditional use of DAEs to defend against adversarial attacks suffers from computational limitations; however, if orthogonality is enforced, better computation performance is achieved [37]. While the initial results for orthogonality enforced DAE are promising implement explore a variety of attack methods and only used black and white images. This raises the question of how well orthogonality-enforced DAE could be applied to real-world systems. The experiment confirms that adequate denoising is all that is needed to defend an adversarial attack successfully. The work carried out in this study has proven to be successful in creating a lightweight defense method. Unlike orthogonality-enforced DAE, our method has been shown to be able to generalize to different attack methods, as well as extend results found in [30] (traditional denoising methods could be used as a first trainable layer like a Gabor layer). There has been some research evaluating the effectiveness of traditional denoising algorithms' performance compared to deep learning alternatives [18]. Limshuebchuey et al. [18] found that naive noise (salt and pepper, as well as Gaussian noise) was removed more successfully by deep learning models. While this research [18] provides insights on how deep learning techniques might outperform traditional denoising methods (when using peak signal-to-noise ratio as a benchmark) on naive noise, the research does not provide insight to how deep learning models and traditional denoising methods would perform on more sophisticated noise (such as an adversarial attack), nor does this research provide insight to how these methods would perform in a computationally limited space.

7 Conclusion and Future Work

Image classification has experienced a substantial increase in the application of convolutional neural networks (CNNs). These networks present several challenges, including the need to defend against adversarial attacks. Mitigating such attacks requires the implementation of denoising techniques. However, these defense mechanisms can result in high computational costs and may compromise the integrity of the input image. Such limitations of existing defense strategies can pose significant issues for low-power physical systems that are safety-critical. Consequently, there is an imperative need to develop appropriate defense methods for such physical systems.

In this study, a variety of traditional image kernels were used as defensive mechanisms against various adversarial attacks. The image kernels utilized in this experiment encompassed both spatial and non-spatial filtering types. These kernels exhibited a superior ability to defend against various adversarial attacks with greater accuracy than the prevailing industry standard defense method, APE-GAN. These findings, coupled with previous results that demonstrate the efficacy of integrating Gabor layers, suggest the need for further investigation into low-power alternative defense methodologies against adversarial attacks.

Future work could investigate the integration of these computationally efficient defense techniques with a training-hardened CNN. Previous research [25], has shown that fortifying CNN with an APE-GAN as a defensive layer leads to highly robust classifiers, in contrast to a standard CNN used with an APE-GAN alone.

In addition, APE-GANs have consistently demonstrated superior performance in numerous studies [38]. In simulations involving low-power physical systems, they have been shown to be capable of processing an image in less than three seconds. Future research could investigate the feasibility of miniaturizing APE-GANs to facilitate rapid image processing. Established techniques for scaling down GAN architectures, such as pruning-based methods for generator compression, suggest that applying these approaches to the APE-GAN framework should be feasible.

References

1. Rawat, W., Wang, Z.: Deep convolutional neural networks for image classification: a comprehensive review. Neural Comput. **29**(9), 2352–2449 (2017)
2. Sharma, N., Jain, V., Mishra, A.: An analysis of convolutional neural networks for image classification. Procedia Comput. Sci. **132**, 377–384 (2018)

3. Lu, D., Weng, Q.: A survey of image classification methods and techniques for improving classification performance. Int. J. Remote Sens. **28**(5), 823–870 (2007)
4. Chen, L., Li, S., Bai, Q., Yang, J., Jiang, S., Miao, Y.: Review of image classification algorithms based on convolutional neural networks. Remote Sens. **13**(22), 4712 (2021)
5. He, K., Zhang, X., Ren, S., Sun, J.: Deep residual learning for image recognition. In: Proceedings of the IEEE conference on Computer Vision and Pattern Recognition, pp. 770–778 (2016)
6. Gu, J., et al.: Recent advances in convolutional neural networks. Pattern Recogn. **77**, 354–377 (2018)
7. Goodfellow, I.J., Shlens, J., Szegedy, C.: Explaining and harnessing adversarial examples. arXiv preprint arXiv:1412.6572 (2014)
8. Chakraborty, A., Alam, M., Dey, V., Chattopadhyay, A., Mukhopadhyay, D.: A survey on adversarial attacks and defences. CAAI Trans. Intell. Technol. **6**(1), 25–45 (2021)
9. Akhtar, N., Mian, A.: Threat of adversarial attacks on deep learning in computer vision: a survey. IEEE Access **6**, 14:410–14:430 (2018)
10. Short, A., et al.: Defending against adversarial examples. Tech. Rep, Sandia National Laboratories, Albuquerque, New Mexico (2019)
11. Brown, T.B., Mané, D., Roy, A., Abadi, M., Gilmer, J.: Adversarial patch. arXiv preprint arXiv:1712.09665 (2017)
12. Liu, X., Yang, H., Liu, Z., Song, L., Li, H., Chen, Y.: DPatch: An adversarial patch attack on object detectors. arXiv preprint arXiv:1806.02299 (2018)
13. Sharma, A., Bian, Y., Nanda, V., Munz, P., Narayan, A.: Vulnerability of CNNs against multi-patch attacks. In: Proceedings of the 2023 ACM Workshop on Secure and Trustworthy Cyber-Physical Systems, pp. 23–32 (2023)
14. Abdel Magid, S., Petrini, F., Dezfouli, B.: Image classification on IoT edge devices: profiling and modeling. Cluster Comput. **23**(2), 1025–1043 (2020)
15. Ren, K., Zheng, T., Qin, Z., Liu, X.: Adversarial attacks and defenses in deep learning. Engineering **6**(3), 346–360 (2020). https://www.sciencedirect.com/science/article/pii/S209580991930503X
16. Liu, Q., Wen, W.: Model compression hardens deep neural networks: a new perspective to prevent adversarial attacks. IEEE Trans. Neural Netw. Learn. Syst. **34**(1), 3–14 (2023)
17. Liu, J., Levine, A., Lau, C.P., Chellappa, R., Feizi, S.: Segment and complete: defending object detectors against adversarial patch attacks with robust patch detection. In: Proceedings of the IEEE/CVF Conference on Computer Vision and Pattern Recognition, pp. 14:973–14:982 (2022)
18. Limshuebchuey, A., Duangsoithong, R., Saejia, M.: Comparison of image denoising using traditional filter and deep learning methods. In: 2020 17th International Conference on Electrical Engineering/Electronics, Computer, Telecommunications and Information Technology (ECTI-CON), pp. 193–196. IEEE (2020)
19. Milanfar, P.: A tour of modern image filtering: new insights and methods, both practical and theoretical. IEEE Signal Process. Mag. **30**(1), 106–128 (2012)
20. Fujiyoshi, H., Hirakawa, T., Yamashita, T.: Deep learning-based image recognition for autonomous driving. IATSS Res. **43**(4), 244–252 (2019). https://www.sciencedirect.com/science/article/pii/S0386111219301566
21. Fang, W., Love, P.E., Luo, H., Ding, L.: Computer vision for behaviour-based safety in construction: a review and future directions. Adv. Eng. Inform. **43**, 100980 (2020)

22. Crowley, J.L.: Convolutional neural networks. In: ECCAI Advanced Course on Artificial Intelligence. Springer, pp. 67–80 (2021)
23. Lippe, P.: Tutorial 10: Adversarial attacks. https://uvadlc-notebooks.readthedocs.io/en/latest/tutorial_notebooks/tutorial10/Adversarial_Attacks.html, 2022, university of Amsterdam, UvA DL Notebooks v1.2 Documentation
24. Gupta, V., Narayan, A.: Do we need entire training data for adversarial training? arXiv preprint arXiv:2303.06241 (2023)
25. Jin, G., Shen, S., Zhang, D., Dai, F., Zhang, Y.: APE-GAN: adversarial perturbation elimination with GAN. In: ICASSP 2019-2019 IEEE International Conference on Acoustics, Speech and Signal Processing (ICASSP), pp. 3842–3846. IEEE (2019)
26. Goodfellow, I., et al.: Generative adversarial nets. Adv. Neural Inf. Process. Syst. **27** (2014)
27. Radford, A.: Unsupervised representation learning with deep convolutional generative adversarial networks. arXiv preprint arXiv:1511.06434 (2015)
28. Huang, H., Liu, X., Yang, R.: Image style transfer for autonomous multi-robot systems. Inf. Sci. **576**, 274–287 (2021)
29. Deng, J., Dong, W., Socher, R., Li, L.-J., Li, K., Fei-Fei, L.: ImageNet: a large-scale hierarchical image database. In: IEEE Conference on Computer Vision and Pattern Recognition, pp. 248–255. IEEE (2009)
30. Pérez, J.C., et al.: Gabor layers enhance network robustness. European Computer Vision Association (2020). https://arxiv.org/abs/1912.05661
31. Narendra, P.M.: A separable median filter for image noise smoothing. IEEE Trans. Pattern Anal. Mach. Intell. **1**, 20–29 (1981)
32. Kopparapu, S.K., Satish, M.: Identifying optimal gaussian filter for gaussian noise removal. In: 2011 Third National Conference on Computer Vision, Pattern Recognition, Image Processing and Graphics, pp. 126–129. IEEE (2011)
33. Budhiraja, S., Goyal, B., Dogra, A., Agrawal, S., et al.: An efficient image denoising scheme for higher noise levels using spatial domain filters. Biomed. Pharmacol. J. **11**(2), 625–634 (2018)
34. Wong, A., Mishra, A., Zhang, W., Fieguth, P., Clausi, D.A.: Stochastic image denoising based on Markov-chain monte Carlo sampling. Signal Process. **91**(8), 2112–2120 (2011)
35. Arora, A., et al.: The value of standards for health datasets in artificial intelligence-based applications. Nat. Med. **29**(11), 2929–2938 (2023)
36. Ilyas, A., Engstrom, L., Athalye, A., Lin, J.: Black-box adversarial attacks with limited queries and information. In: International Conference on Machine Learning, pp. 2137–2146. PMLR (2018)
37. Bifis, A., Psarakis, E.Z., Kosmopoulos, D.: Developing robust and lightweight adversarial defenders by enforcing orthogonality on attack-agnostic denoising autoencoders. In: Proceedings of the IEEE/CVF International Conference on Computer Vision, pp. 1272–1281 (2023)
38. Shen, S., Jin, G., Gao, K., Zhang, Y.: APE-GAN: Adversarial perturbation elimination with GAN (2017). https://arxiv.org/abs/1707.05474

LAPIS: Layered Anomaly Detection System for IoT Security

Cheng Wang[1], Yan Lin Aung[2(✉)], Ye Dong[3], Trupil Limbasiya[4], and Jianying Zhou[1]

[1] Singapore University of Technology and Design, Singapore, Singapore
jianying_zhou@sutd.edu.sg
[2] University of Derby, Derby, UK
y.aung@derby.ac.uk
[3] National University of Singapore, Singapore, Singapore
dongye@nus.edu.sg
[4] Desay SV Automotive Singapore Pte Ltd., Singapore, Singapore

Abstract. Internet of Things (IoT) is a rapidly growing technology that significantly benefits and impacts our daily lives. However, with the rise of IoT, new challenges in security have emerged. A formidable challenge to tackle new threats arises as a result of the constantly evolving nature of malware. In this paper, we present an anomaly detection system that has been integrated with a honeypot infrastructure to facilitate real-time data capture and anomaly detection. The two-layer anomaly detection system, named LAPIS, is capable of detecting malicious network traffic and identifying novel attacks. This integration aims to enhance security measures by providing a sophisticated mechanism for monitoring and analyzing network flows with precision and efficiency. We evaluated LAPIS using realistic network traffic collected by the honeypot during 12 months of operation. The experimental results show that the overall F1 score of LAPIS reaches 0.91 and 0.84 for detecting malicious network flows and zero-day attacks, respectively outperforming the closest state-of-the-art work. Compared to VirusTotal, which analyzes suspicious files and URLs to detect malware and malicious content, 61% of novel attacks are detected earlier by our system or yet to be available in VirusTotal.

Keywords: Anomaly Detection · IoT Honeypot · Machine Learning · Cyber Security

1 Introduction

The Internet of Things (IoT) has emerged as an expanding technology field, attracting significant research interest in recent years [21]. The number of IoT

C. Wang and Y. L. Aung—Both authors contributed equally.
Y. L. Aung, Y. Dong and T. Limbasiya —This work was done while the authors were at iTrust, Singapore University of Technology and Design.

devices has been estimated at around 7 billion in 2018, and its growth is expected to increase by 3 times by 2025 [10]. Amidst the advancement of Industry 4.0 revolution and the evolution of 5G technology, IoT devices are expected to play a key role in improving the quality of daily life.

IoT Security Vulnerabilities and Threats: However, many existing IoT devices are often designed and produced in a low-cost industrial process. This raises concerns about insecure network services, unsafe default settings, and outdated device components. In addition, most consumers pay little attention to the configuration of IoT products and lack security awareness. These factors have led to increased security concerns and exposure to vulnerabilities, leading to critical security incidents [12]. For example, in 2016, Mirai malware demonstrated its devastating potential by infecting hundreds of thousands of IoT devices, using weak and default passwords to gain unauthorized access. With an unprecedented offensive capability of approximately 1.2 terabits per second, the Mirai malware not only highlighted the inherent vulnerabilities in IoT devices, but also underscored the potential for widespread disruption in digital services and the Internet infrastructure [14].

In addition, the continuously evolving nature of malware exacerbates its long-term impacts, leading to further expansion of the potential harm it can cause to society and the economy. Since Mirai source code became available in 2017, variants and adaptations from it have continued to spread and infect devices to date. In 2019, the number of Mirai family malware samples doubled. In 2020, the number of samples captured increased by 150,000 and by 7%. Malware variants have even more samples than the original Mirai malware. The occurrence of Mirai and the disruptive damages caused by it became a wake-up call for the industry to secure IoT devices [1,10].

Trends of Threat Intelligence and Anomaly Detection: To deal with these arising challenges and risks, researchers have addressed the applicability of machine learning (ML) approaches to detect security breaches and attacks on IoT networks. In traditional approaches such as signature-based detection [2], the rules are established and maintained by certain domain experts. Such traditional methods are less efficient compared to automated learning and identification based on ML models. Therefore, ML-based approaches have become more popular in recent years. At the same time, honeypot, which is set as bait to divert attention from critical systems and attract potential attackers, is known to be a promising approach to collecting attack data and threat intelligence in the wild [13,24].

Challenges and Motivations: Although ML-based methods have played an important role in IoT security, they are still facing several challenges:

- Firstly, many of the existing datasets utilized for training and evaluation often derive from simulation experiments or historical data collections. These simulations do not fully replicate the complexity and nuances of the real-world attack and methods, resulting in a lack of fidelity to reality [17,20]. Moreover, such dataset scarcely encompass more contemporary attack vectors, leading

to a gap in the representation of the latest attack behaviors. This discrepancy underscores a challenge in dataset construction that limits the effectiveness of ML models to identify and mitigate current and emerging threats.
- Honeypots serve as a valuable supplement to these limitations by capturing data that are timely and diverse, presenting an enriched source of attack data. However, the second challenge lies in the effective labeling, analysis, and utilization of these raw and first-hand attack data [22]. Unlike controlled experimental setups where attack types and methods are predefined, extracting insights, information, and defensive measures from the vast and continuously accumulated data collected by honeypots represents a significant hurdle. Our paper addresses this challenge, exploring methodologies to harness the potential of honeypot data to enhance the security defenses of IoT devices.
- Thirdly, many of the ML-based detection methods target classifying known attack families and pay less attention to detecting potentially zero-day attacks.

Our Contributions: To address these challenges, we advocate for a hybrid system leveraging honeypot infrastructure [5]. Our approach involves constructing ground-truth data from the information captured by honeypots, which serves as the training input for our anomaly detection system. By harnessing the honeypots' ability to capture cutting-edge attacks and combining it with the power of ML models for training detection systems, we effectively merge the complementary strengths of both methodologies. This synergy enables the development of a network anomaly detection system that offers comprehensive coverage for identifying and detecting malicious intrusions. Our contributions in this work are summarized as follows:

- We propose a methodology to create ground truth from substantial network traffic data collected by a honeypot infrastructure with IoT devices during 12 months of operation. The methodology makes use of attack attribution to process raw network traffic data, so that processed network flows are labeled for both binary labeling (i.e., benign or malicious) and various malware families. In addition, we integrate benign activity data collected from IoT devices and other public datasets into our collected data to construct the dataset. Compared with many existing datasets, our dataset comprises the latest attack data collected by the IoT honeypot.
- We propose and implement an ML-based two-layer anomaly detection system, named LAPIS, for IoT devices, which performs i) anomaly detection using attack classifiers based on supervised learning to classify benign and malicious traffic, and ii) a novel adaptive clustering algorithm to detect potential zero-day attacks. In our experimental evaluations, the overall F1 score of anomaly detection and zero-day attack detection reach 0.91 and 0.84, respectively.
- Finally, we integrate the anomaly detection system with the honeypot infrastructure setup as a lightweight real-time detection system, which is capable of detecting malicious attack attempts and zero-day IoT attacks. Compared

to VirusTotal, the system detected 61% of novel attacks that were not previously known to VirusTotal or were recorded by the system, indicating the system's ability to detect new and unknown threats.

Organization: We first provide an overview of the design of the IoT honeypot system and the two-layer anomaly detection system in Sect. 2. Section 3 presents the concrete design of our anomaly detection system, including the IoT honeypot deployed on real devices and an ML-based two-layer anomaly detection method. Next, experimental evaluations are analyzed in Sect. 4 to determine the accuracy of malware detection. Finally, we discuss related work in Sect. 5 and conclude this work in Sect. 6.

2 Overview of System Design

This section describes the design considerations taken into account for developing the anomaly detection system. We compare different methodologies for the implementation of each component and select the suitable choice for our anomaly detection task.

2.1 IoT Honeypot Categories and Design Considerations

A honeypot is designed and implemented to collect up-to-date data, especially malicious attack data. It attracts attackers and captures the details of malicious behavior attempt. Subsequently, the corresponding network flows are stored in packet capture (PCAP) files for further analysis. Based on the interactivity level, there are two types of honeypots:

Low-interaction honeypots mainly contain simulations of services that have security vulnerabilities and usually do not generate real information traffic. Virtualization technologies are usually applied in the setup and running process of a low-interaction honeypot. The attackers cannot access physical devices directly and the risk of hijacking is low. Therefore, less detailed information about the attack is gathered. In addition, errors that occurred during the simulation process could help the attacker detect the honeypot. The recognition of honeypots by attackers could create other unexpected potential risks. The honeypot setup could not fulfill its function and design purpose in such cases.

In contrast, high-interaction counterparts include real services and devices to lure attackers. Having real devices maximizes the attack surface for the attackers, allowing full access to the underlying system. The data and traffic information captured by high-interaction honeypots tend to be richer and more realistic. As a result, we deploy high-interaction honeypots in our system.

2.2 Machine Learning Categories

Machine learning algorithms can be broadly classified into supervised and unsupervised learning methods.

Supervised learning methods require labeled data during the training process, where the algorithm learns to predict the label associated with a set of input features. For example, in the context of anomaly detection, supervised learning algorithms can be trained on labeled datasets to classify network flows into malicious and benign categories based on known patterns of attacks.

Unsupervised learning methods, on the other hand, do not require labeled data, instead rely on similarities between data to identify patterns and group them into clusters. In the context of anomaly detection, unsupervised learning algorithms can be used to identify unknown or novel attacks by grouping them into clusters that are different from known benign and malicious clusters. This approach is more robust to novel types of attacks, as the algorithm could learn to recognize new patterns and group them accordingly.

To address the intricacies of intrusion detection and the identification of zero-day attacks, we propose a comprehensive two-layer ML-based detection system. In the first layer dedicated to intrusion detection, the use of supervised learning techniques becomes paramount. These methods leverage labeled datasets that contain instances of known attacks, enabling them to adeptly classify network flows into malicious or benign categories. This approach is highly effective in rapid detection and real-time response that provides robust defense [25].

Furthermore, the second layer, which specializes in zero-day attack detection, requires the application of unsupervised learning methodologies. This layer thrives on its ability to discover new and emerging threats that have not been previously encountered. Unsupervised algorithms excel in grouping unknown attacks into distinct clusters based on shared feature patterns. By comparing these clusters with existing ones, the system can quickly identify potential zero-day attacks. This approach acts as a proactive shield against previously unidentified threats and plays a pivotal role in mitigating the ever-evolving risks posed by emerging security breaches.

In summary, the selection of the appropriate machine learning algorithms for anomaly detection depends on the specific demands of the task at hand. Supervised learning methods excel in the detection of well-established attacks, providing a robust defense against known threats. In contrast, unsupervised learning techniques shine when it comes to discovering new and emerging threats. The synergy achieved by employing a two-layer system that seamlessly combines both supervised and unsupervised learning methodologies culminates in a highly effective and resilient anomaly detection system tailored for the unique challenges of IoT security. Further insights into the intricacies of this algorithmic approach will be expounded on in Sect. 3.3.

3 Details of System Design

In this section, we first describe the design of the honeypot infrastructure, which is the main data source used for training and shown in Fig. 1. Then, we provide the information and labeling method of the final dataset. Finally, we present the structure and implementation of the ML-based two-layer anomaly detection system.

3.1 IoT Honeypot Infrastructure

Based on the considerations (see Sect. 2), our anomaly detection system is implemented based on a hybrid and high-interaction VPN-forwarded IoT honeypot infrastructure as proposed in [4,5,23], which is shown in Fig. 1. In our implementation, 17 real IoT devices are deployed, which include IP cameras, printer, smart plug, smart bulb, industrial control system devices such as programmable logic controller (PLC), remote terminal unit (RTU), human-machine interface (HMI) as well as industrial control system (ICS) emulators based on *conpot*[1]. This provides a rich attack surface and geographical diversity for data collection.

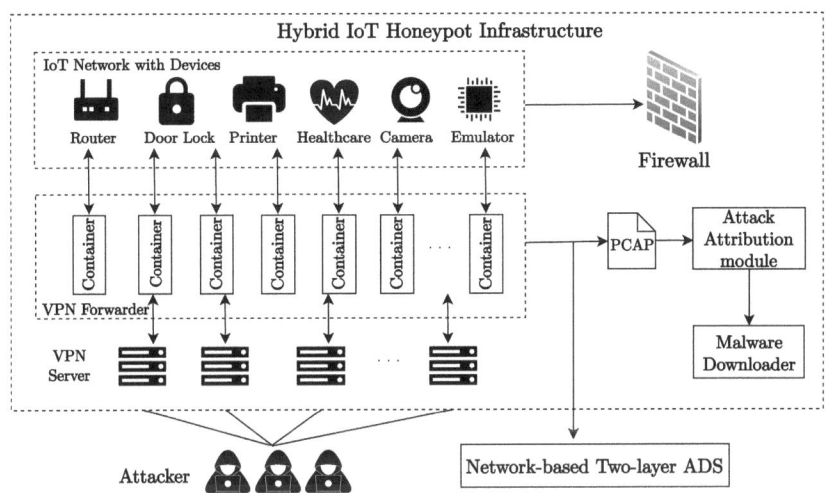

Fig. 1. Honeypot Infrastructure with Real IoT Devices

In order to scale the honeypot infrastructure as the number of devices increases, a lightweight approach is adopted to establish secure VPN tunnels to VPN servers and acquire public IP addresses. In each container of 'VPN Forwarder' in Fig. 1, the network traffic between attackers and IoT devices is captured and saved into PCAP files. The attack attribution module performs a further analysis of the PCAPs and detects outbound connections, which are potential malicious attempts executed by attackers, including the downloading of malware or establishing communication with Command & Control (C2) servers. Based on the connection attempts detected, the system inspects the captured PCAP files and attributes each outbound connection to its corresponding attack command. The malware downloader module parses the WGET[2] and Trivial File Transfer Protocol (TFTP) commands. The attack commands are then executed to download malware samples from the C2 server as attempted by the attackers.

---
[1] https://github.com/mushorg/conpot.
[2] https://www.gnu.org/software/wget/manual/wget.html.

To have a clear understanding of the insights between network traffic features and attack detection, we implement a network flow attribution module as described below. The attack attribution module makes use of *inotifywait* Linux utility[3] to detect new PCAP files written to the file system and check any outbound connection attempts from any of IoT devices. The module records the attribution relation between the malware samples downloaded and the network traffic captured in that specific attack. All network flows are attributed with the names of the malware files downloaded and timestamps. The information is stored in JavaScript Object Notation JSON format. Then it is analyzed and used as the labeling method for our anomaly detection system (explicitly described in Sect. 3.3).

3.2 Dataset Processing

Data Source. The construction of datasets and feature engineering provide an important foundation for the design, training, and evaluation of anomaly detection models. Hence, we introduce the methodologies to construct the network flow dataset. The malicious network traffic is captured from real-world IoT attacks as received by the honeypot and labeled by the network flow attribution module (see Sect. 3.1) and open source Network Intrusion Detection systems Snort[4] and Suricata[5]. The malicious traffic data is identified and filtered by the attack attribution module implemented by the honeypot for attacks performed via remote code execution behaviors or malware downloading attempts. Thus, network flows have a higher probability of being malicious traffic, and fewer false positive cases are generated under such labeling schemes. In terms of benign data, filtering benign networks from the honeypot-captured data does not have a clear behavioral pattern compared to malicious traffic. To avoid false negative samples in the labeling, we construct the benign component of the dataset by conducting simulation experiments on our honeypot devices and also introduce data from IoT-23 dataset [9], whose data is collected from real devices during their typical operations. Since both sources are IoT devices running in an isolated and attack-free setup, this dataset is taken as benign samples.

Dataset Construction and Class Labelling. At the high level, the dataset construction system consists of three main stages: i) capture, ii) filter, and iii) feature engineering. They are described as follows:

1. The first stage is performed by the VPN-forwarded IoT honeypots. The honeypots are manifested on 40 public IP addresses in the wild while forwarding the traffic to 17 real IoT devices. It detects network flows containing outbound attempts and saves the data in JSON format.

---

[3] https://linuxcommandlibrary.com/man/inotifywait.
[4] https://www.snort.org/.
[5] https://www.suricata-ids.org/.

2. The filter stage is performed using automated scripts to label malicious flows into attack families. The system detects the attack commands used by the attacker and labels the network flows accordingly. The filtered malicious network flows are then combined with the benign component of the simulation experiments and the public dataset, to form the original PCAP raw dataset.
3. The feature engineering stage converts the network PCAPs into statistical features and selects features based on feature correlation and variance. The PCAP files were converted into features using a feature extractor tool such as [6].

Dataset Description. The following elucidation is for our final dataset that consists of PCAP files and the proportion of different sources:

1. 86,231 (50.10%) malicious network flows obtained with VPN-forwarded honeypots implementation, and each network flow is related to malicious behaviors such as C2 server connections and malware downloading attempts.
2. 5,657 (3.30%) benign network flows obtained from isolated attack simulation experiments using the same honeypot devices.
3. 80,147 (46.60%) benign network flows taken from IoT-23 [9], which is a public dataset of network traffic from real IoT devices.

Table 1. Top 10 Features Selected

Level	Protocol	Feature Description
Flow	TCP	Number of packets sent by client with ACK flag
CW*	TCP	Number of duplicate ACKs
Flow	TCP	Number of bytes sent by the client
Session	HTTP	Standard deviation of interarrival time
Session	HTTP	Median of HTTP request bytes
Flow	HTTP	Number of unique HTTP user agents
CW*	TCP	Number of Keep-alive packets
CW*	TCP	Ratio between number of destination ports and flows
Session	TCP	Number of packets with RST flag
Flow	TCP	Standard deviation of client packets interarrival time

* Conversation Window.

Feature Engineering. We applied the correlation calculation and ranking algorithm for the feature selection process [6]. The top 25 features are selected from the 817 network features and used for training. Table 1 shows the top 10 selected network features. Most of them are statistical features that span across layers, protocols, and observation resolution, and reflect characteristics of network flows in different aspects. The raw features are normalized and stored as vector values for the later training process.

3.3 Model Structures

This section provides the detailed model structures of our two-layer ML-based anomaly detection method, named LAPIS, as shown in Fig. 2.

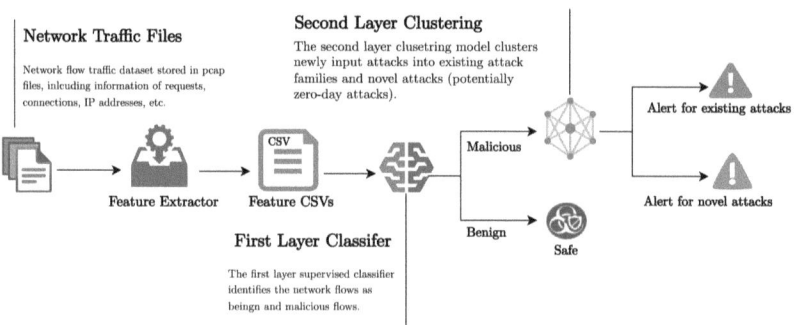

Fig. 2. LAPIS: Layered Anomaly Detection System

Malicious Traffic Classifier. In the first-layer traffic classifier, the model aims to identify malicious network traffic from benign ones. Real-time anomaly detection requires fast and efficient data processing, making traditional machine learning methods more suitable than deep learning models. Naïve Bayes and logistic regression are fast and lightweight algorithms that can handle large amounts of data in real-time without requiring a lot of computational resources. In contrast, deep learning models, such as convolutional neural networks (CNNs) and recurrent neural networks (RNNs), are compute intensive and require high-end hardware to operate in real-time. In addition, traditional machine learning methods are less prone to overfitting, making them more suitable for anomaly detection in real-time systems. Overfitting occurs when a model is trained too well on a particular dataset, making it less generalizable to new data. This is a common problem with deep learning models, which have many parameters and could easily overfit the training data. Naive Bayes and logistic regression have fewer parameters and are less prone to overfitting, making them more suitable for real-time anomaly detection.

Taking into account these factors, we have implemented and evaluated six machine learning algorithms in this layer, including both supervised and unsupervised machine learning algorithms. We include and test the following classification methods:

- *Decision Tree:* The Decision Tree algorithm is a tree-like model combined of decisions in the form of if-else branches.
- *XGBoost:* It is an ensemble learning method based on the Decision Tree. Based on its features of using gradient boost and tree pruning, it could achieve a fast training speed and high accuracy in some cases.

- *Random Forest:* It is an algorithm combining multiple Decision Trees. Compared with the Decision Tree, it only selects a subset of training input and features to prevent overfitting.
- *Logistic Regression:* A statistical model that uses a logistic function to model a binary dependent variable.
- *Naïve Bayes:* It is a probabilistic approach based on the Bayes theorem with the assumption of fully independent features.
- *K-Means:* It is a clustering approach that obtains k clusters out of the training input, where each input sample is placed in the cluster with the closest distance.

Algorithm 1. Second Layer Adaptive Clustering Algorithm

1: **procedure** ADAPTIVECLUSTERING(f)
2:     Get network flow features v extracted from network flow f
3:     Get a list of network flow features, V, of centroids of existing clusters
4:     $d = $ GETMINIMUMDISTANCE(V, f)
5:     **if** $d > n * \sigma$ **then**   ▷ New Cluster
6:         Create a new cluster with f
7:         Update the existing cluster list
8:     **else**
9:         Add f into the closest cluster c
10:        $\mu = $ GETNEWMEAN(c)
11:        $\sigma = \sqrt{\left|\frac{(n*(\sigma^2+\mu^2)+d^2)}{(n+1)} - \mu^2\right|}$ ▷ $n = $ # network flows in the closest cluster
12:     **end if**
13: **end procedure**

14: **procedure** GETMINIMUMDISTANCE(V, f)
15:     Initialize network flow feature distance list l
16:     **for** $i \leftarrow 1, n_c$ **do**   ▷ $n_c = $ # clusters
17:         $d_f = $ EUCLIDEAN_DISTANCE(V)
18:         Append d_f to l
19:     **end for**
20:     Get Minimum distance d from l
21:     **return** d
22: **end procedure**

23: **procedure** GETNEWMEAN(c)
24:     $m = $ FEATURE_EXTRACT(c)   ▷ Return 2d document-term matrix m
25:     $f = $ GET_FEATURE_NAMES   ▷ Column names for matrix m
26:     Sum every element in each feature from m ▷ Each row is a network flow feature set in cluster c.
27:     Compute average for each row
28:     **return** row r with minimum difference as new mean μ of this cluster c.
29: **end procedure**

Adaptive Clustering Model. Compared with the supervised learning method, unsupervised methods such as clustering do not include pre-defined classes and are more adaptive to detecting new categories. As a consequence, in the second layer of the system, we perform a clustering analysis on the malicious network flows and attempt to classify them into existing attack families and novel attacks.

The features used for training are also the top 25 features selected by the correlation and variance ranking method. For each network flow, all the feature values undergo a mean normalization and are converted into a range $[0, 10]$. We propose an adaptive clustering algorithm to process the normalized flow features. In general, the distance between network flow patterns is calculated by the Euclidean distance taking all the feature values. If the network flow pattern distance between the tested flow and other existing cluster centroids is larger than $n \times$ *cluster standard deviation*, a new cluster will be formed and the corresponding network flows will be identified as a novel attack. Otherwise, network flows will be added to existing network flow clusters and classified under existing attacks. That also means that in the evaluation process, only the occurrence of the first network flow under new attacks will be classified as novel. The formal clustering procedure is provided in Algorithm 1. In the second-layer clustering model, after each iteration of clustering new flows, the centroid feature value sets representing the corresponding clusters will be updated by calculating the new mean. The standard deviation value is also recomputed. The model saver and loader modules save real-time cluster information containing centroids, IDs of network flows under that cluster, and standard deviation values. Therefore, the calculation of the next clustering of network flows takes less time and the overall detection process is more effective.

3.4 Real-Time Detection Implementation

In the implementation of our anomaly detection system, another pivotal aspect is its real-time detection capabilities, achieved through the integration with the honeypot where the majority of malicious traffic is collected. This setup enables the anomaly detection system to continuously monitor network flows, identifying anomalies with a high degree of accuracy and low latency. The system processes incoming network data in 30-minute intervals and updates the two models accordingly, a design choice that balances between timely threat detection and computational efficiency.

The second layer clustering model saves the model states, including the adaptive clustering model parameters and existing cluster information, to a JSON file and train only on the newly collected data. This implementation enables the system to monitor potential zero-day IoT attacks captured by the honeypot, as well as update the detection models to detect up-to-date attacks. Remarkably, the model's update process is efficient, requiring on average 6 min to processing one-day data input as new training data and updating the model. This approach allows the second-layer model to focus on the most current data, avoiding the need to reprocess historical information, which in turn optimizes its performance and adaptability.

Moreover, the LAPIS is equipped with a comprehensive data-logging mechanism. During each process, the system will save the detection results of both layers to local log files. This functionality not only facilitates the detailed tracking of all detection activities, but also serves as a foundational element for subsequent in-depth analysis and visualization efforts. Through these logs, patterns and trends within the detected anomalies can be examined, enriching the understanding of potential threats and investigating further threat intelligence generated from attacks identified by the detection system.

4 Evaluation

To assess the efficacy of our system, we conducted a series of experiments designed to scrutinize various aspects of its performance. These evaluations aim to ascertain the system's proficiency in identifying both the presence of attack traffic and the specific families of attacks, utilizing a dataset procured by our honeypot network spanning over 12 months of operation from August 2020 through July 2021. Furthermore, we embarked on a detailed examination of the system's resilience when exposed to varying distributions of attack families, ensuring a robust defense mechanism against a diverse array of threats targeting IoT devices.

Additionally, we conducted chronological experiments to underscore our system's adeptness at detecting not only malicious network traffic but also the traffic flows indicative of potential emerging threats. This aspect was particularly emphasized in scenarios where network traffic is continuously monitored and the system undergoes periodic updates to enhance its detection capabilities. In such dynamic environments, our findings reveal a marked improvement in the system's capacity to identify and mitigate both known malicious activities and novel attack vectors. This continuous adaptation mechanism ensures that the system remains effective even as new threats emerge, highlighting its potential as a critical tool in the ongoing battle against diverse attacks.

4.1 Overall Intrusion Detection Performance

In the evaluation process, a ten-fold cross-validation process was conducted on the overall dataset. Figures 3 and 4 show how the accuracy results are converged after ten-fold cross-validation. For the first layer of supervised classification, the true positive rate, false positive rate, precision, recall, and F measures are used for evaluation. A cross-validation evaluation is implemented to keep the results stable and unbiased.

For the second layer unsupervised clustering, since the clustering results is generated automatically instead of defined in advance, we did a further enhancement on the clustering results. In the three-month chronological dataset, we split the timeline by a 6:4 ratio and classified the attack families into existing and

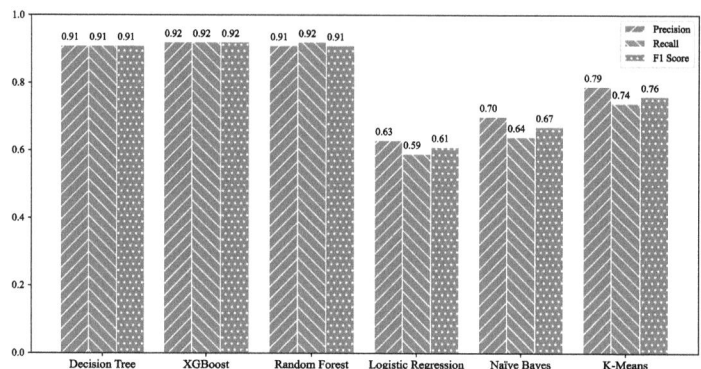

Fig. 3. First Layer Classification Results

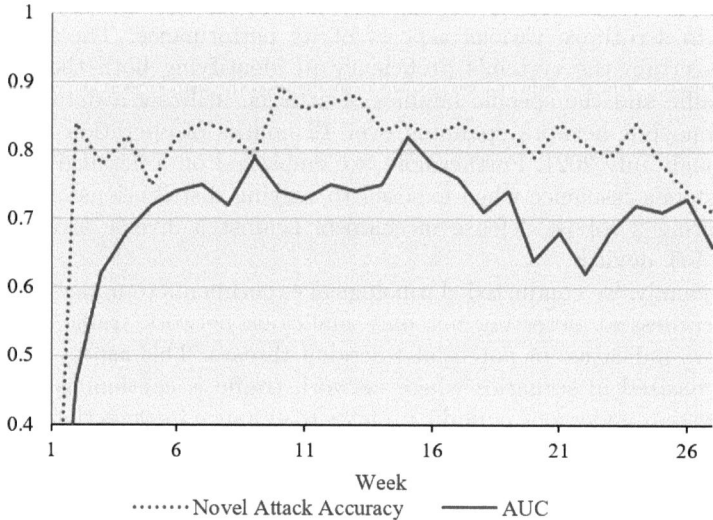

Fig. 4. Chronological Experiment Results for the Second Layer

novel types based on the first appearance timestamp. In the clustering results, for each cluster formed, we select the dominant attack families as the cluster's representative attack type and define the label of the clusters based on it.

In addition, the second-layer clustering aims to assist in discovering novel attack types. In the system clustering results, as long as one of the novel attack network flows is clustered as novel correctly, the attack family to which it belongs could be considered as identified.

4.2 Chronological Experiments

In this section, we would like to evaluate the ability and robustness of the system under a long period and network traffic distribution similar to realistic scenarios.

Based on the network traffic dataset used in the overall evaluation, we divided the dataset into unit of weeks. The models are trained and evaluated based on the simulated network traffic input. The results for the first and second layers are shown in respective Figs. 5 and Fig. 4.

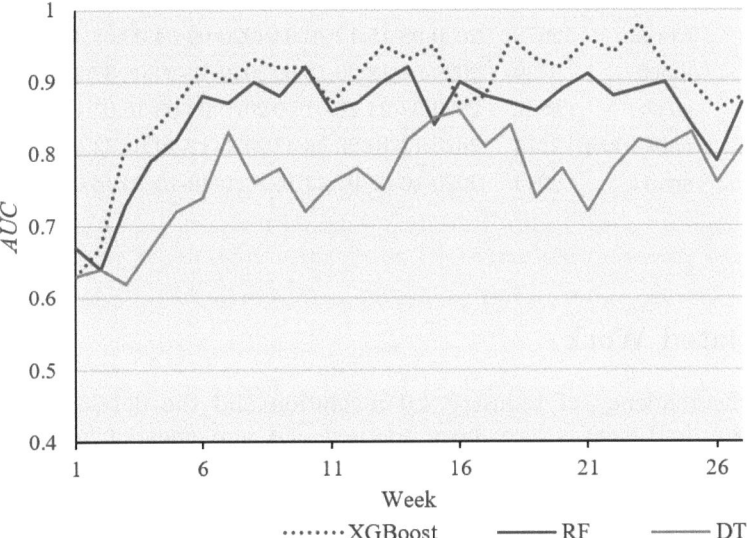

Fig. 5. Chronological Experiment Results for the First Layer

For the first layer, we used the Precision, Recall and the Area under the Curve (AUC) metrics to evaluate the performance of our detection results. For the second layer, we used AUC and the accuracy in detecting novel attacks to evaluate the performance of our detection results.

In general, the performance of the first and second layers showed a similar pattern. The AUC scores at the beginning four to five weeks were relatively low. This is as expected since the amount and types of network flow data used for training are limited. As more benign and attack traffic data was input into the system, the AUC performances continued to improve and tended to stabilize after around six weeks. The average AUC of the first layer and second layer in the last three months could reach 0.86 and 0.80 respectively. The average novel attack accuracy for potential zero-day attacks in the last three months could reach 0.81.

In addition to the AUC comparison, we also evaluated the second layer by comparing the discovery time in the simulation experiment with the earliest timestamp recorded in VirusTotal. In the 32,432 network flows related to novel attacks whose capture timestamp is earlier than the VirusTotal timestamp, 21,273 network flows are correctly identified as novel. The accuracy of the novel attack detection by second layer clustering compared to VirusTotal is 60.6%.

Detailed information on the top 5 novel attacks detected by layer 2 is provided in Table 2.

Table 2. Timestamps of the Captured Novel Attacks

Binary	# Flows	ADS Timestamp	VT Timestamp
Corona	12972	2020-08-15 12:16:04	2020-09-04 09:05:45
Skie6	9729	2020-08-12 20:18:00	2020-12-20 08:37:27
go.sh	5837	2020-08-24 18:01:00	2020-09-03 16:05:18
networkrip	2270	2020-12-10 20:08:47	2020-12-20 08:43:41
armvc	2043	2020-10-07 07:43:16	2020-10-10 20:46:04

5 Related Work

Under the tendency of Industry 4.0 revolution and the development of 5G technology, IoT devices have been adopted and implemented in more industrial domains and infrastructures. The attack surface and system vulnerabilities are also increasing. To address these challenges, researchers have proposed various detection systems. This section reviews the existing work on network-based anomaly detection systems.

D'Angelo et al. [7] represented a system named Uncertainty-managing Batch Relevance-based Artificial Intelligence (U-BRAIN). The U-BRAIN model is dynamic and operates on multiple machines. The dataset used in this work was binary NSL-KDD dataset as well as real traffic data from a university. The system in this work targets binary classification and does not include multiple attack families.

Work has also been done on specific IoT attack detection tasks. Kozik et al. [11] demonstrated a classification-based threat detection service utilizing cloud architecture. In this work, an Extreme Learning Machines (ELM), scaled in the Apache Spark cloud infrastructure is utilized to analyze simulated network flow structured data. The implementation is focused on three significant scenarios in IoT systems: scanning, command & control and infected host.

Liu et al. [16] designed a detector for the On and Off attack by a malicious network node in an industrial IoT scenario. The On and Off attack meant that the IoT network can be attacked by a malicious node when it is set to an active state. When the malicious node is in the inactive state, the IoT network behaves normally. This model uses a light probe routing mechanism that calculates the trust estimate of each neighbor node for the anomaly detection process. A series of experiments have been conducted to confirm the effectiveness of the system.

Diro et al. [8] presented an attack detection system using fog-to-things architecture. The main focus was to detect four predefined classes of attack and anomaly. The work also provided a comparison study of a deep and a shallow neural network using an open source dataset. For the four classes defined, the system achieved good performance for the shallow neural network model.

Meidan et al. [18] designed a network-based anomaly detection system to extract the behavioural characteristics of the network. The system is implemented by applying autoencoders to investigate malicious network traffic collected from compromised IoT devices. However, deep learning models need a large amount of data to train and validate. Despite that, models are usually computationally expensive, which is not suitable for the IoT live detection system due to resource constraints [19].

Anthi et al. [3] presented Pulse, an adaptive intrusion detection system for IoT devices. The network traffic dataset is collected for four subsequent days using Wireshark. Several ML classifiers have been used systematically to identify Denial of Service attacks and network scanning probing attempts. Weka was used to implement different ML classifiers together.

Similar works have been done on the implementation of ML approaches to detect network attacks. Pajouh et al. [20] proposed a detection system for intrusion detection based on a two-layer dimension reduction and two-tier classification module. The system mainly aimed at detecting malicious network behaviors such as User to Root (U2R) and Remote to Local (R2L) attacks. Linear discriminate analysis and component analysis have been used for dimensionality reduction. The NSL-KDD dataset is used for experiment training and validation. Of 41 features contained in the NSL-KDD dataset, 6 features were selected using the J-48 based algorithm. In the two-tier classification module, Naïve Bayes and Certainty Factor versions of K-Nearest Neighbor were implemented and tested.

Until recently, Li et al. [15] proposed an AI agent powered by large language models (LLM) for intrusion detection called IDS-Agent. Similar to LAPIS, the IDS-Agent predicts whether an input network traffic is benign or malicious and is able to identify previously unknown types of attacks. Using ACI-IoT and CIC-IoT benchmarks, IDS-Agent achieves 0.97 and 0.75 detection F1 scores for binary classification tasks and a recall of 0.61 to detect zero-day attacks. Although LAPIS uses a different dataset, the experimental results are comparable to the state-of-the-art work and even outperform IDS-Agent on unknown attack detection.

6 Conclusions

We proposed a machine learning-based IoT anomaly detection system combined with a honeypot infrastructure. The high-interaction hybrid honeypot infrastructure is capable of capturing network traffic data of the latest attacks targeting IoT devices and attributing network flows to attack families. We designed and implemented a two-layer network anomaly detection system that could detect both malicious intrusions and potential zero-day attacks. The system is trained and evaluated on the realistic dataset collected by the honeypot during 12 months of operation. The overall F1 score for anomaly detection and zero-day attack detection is 0.91 and 0.84, respectively, outperforming the closest state-of-the-work. In the chronological experiments that simulate live detection scenarios, the model also shows a stable and promising performance after a few weeks of data accumulation. For the detection of zero-day attack in the second layer, more than 61% of the novel attack network flows are identified to be true compared to VirusTotal records.

References

1. Netscout threat intelligence report 2h 2020. Comput. Fraud Sec. **2021**(7), 4–4 (2021)
2. Alalade, E.D.: Intrusion detection system in smart home network using artificial immune system and extreme learning machine hybrid approach. In: 2020 IEEE 6th World Forum on Internet of Things (WF-IoT), pp. 1–2 (2020). https://doi.org/10.1109/WF-IoT48130.2020.9221151
3. Anthi, E., Williams, L., Burnap, P.: Pulse: an adaptive intrusion detection for the Internet of Things. In: Living in the Internet of Things: Cybersecurity of the IoT - 2018, pp. 1–4 (2018). https://doi.org/10.1049/cp.2018.0035
4. Aung, Y.L., Ochoa, M., Zhou, J.: ATLAS: a practical attack detection and live malware analysis system for IoT threat intelligence. In: Susilo, W., Chen, X., Guo, F., Zhang, Y., Intan, R. (eds.) Information Security, pp. 319–338. Springer International Publishing, Cham (2022). https://doi.org/10.1007/978-3-031-22390-7_19
5. Aung, Y.L., Tiang, H.H., Wijaya, H., Ochoa, M., Zhou, J.: Scalable VPN-forwarded honeypots: dataset and threat intelligence insights, ICSS 2020, pp. 21–30. Association for Computing Machinery, New York (2020). https://doi.org/10.1145/3442144.3442146
6. Bekerman, D., Shapira, B., Rokach, L., Bar, A.: Unknown malware detection using network traffic classification. In: 2015 IEEE Conference on Communications and Network Security (CNS), pp. 134–142 (2015). https://doi.org/10.1109/CNS.2015.7346821
7. D'angelo, G., Palmieri, F., Ficco, M., Rampone, S.: An uncertainty-managing batch relevance-based approach to network anomaly detection. Appl. Soft Comput. **36**, 408–418 (2015). https://doi.org/10.1016/j.asoc.2015.07.029
8. Diro, A.A., Chilamkurti, N.: Distributed attack detection scheme using deep learning approach for Internet of Things. Futur. Gener. Comput. Syst. **82**, 761–768 (2018). https://doi.org/10.1016/j.future.2017.08.043
9. Garcia, S., Parmisano, A., Erquiaga, M.J.: IoT-23 dataset: a labeled dataset of malware and benign IoT traffic (2020). https://www.stratosphereips.org/datasets-iot23
10. Kolias, C., Kambourakis, G., Stavrou, A., Voas, J.: DDoS in the IoT: Mirai and other botnets. Computer **50**(7), 80–84 (2017). https://doi.org/10.1109/MC.2017.201
11. Kozik, R., Choraś, M., Ficco, M., Palmieri, F.: A scalable distributed machine learning approach for attack detection in edge computing environments. J. Parallel Distrib. Comput. **119**(C), 18–26 (2018). https://doi.org/10.1016/j.jpdc.2018.03.006
12. Kumar, A., Lim, T.J.: EDIMA: early detection of IoT malware network activity using machine learning techniques. In: 2019 IEEE 5th World Forum on Internet of Things (WF-IoT), pp. 289–294 (2019). https://doi.org/10.1109/WF-IoT.2019.8767194

13. Kumar, M., Singh, A.K.: Distributed intrusion detection system using blockchain and cloud computing infrastructure. In: 2020 4th International Conference on Trends in Electronics and Informatics (ICOEI)(48184), pp. 248–252 (2020). https://doi.org/10.1109/ICOEI48184.2020.9142954
14. Kumar, M., Mathur, R.: Unsupervised outlier detection technique for intrusion detection in cloud computing. In: International Conference for Convergence for Technology-2014, pp. 1–4 (2014). https://doi.org/10.1109/I2CT.2014.7092027
15. Li, Y., Xiang, Z., Bastian, N.D., Song, D., Li, B.: IDS-Agent: an LLM agent for explainable intrusion detection in IoT networks. In: NeurIPS 2024 Workshop on Open-World Agents (2024). https://openreview.net/forum?id=iiK0pRyLkw
16. Liu, X., Liu, Y., Liu, A., Yang, L.T.: Defending on–off attacks using light probing messages in smart sensors for industrial communication systems. IEEE Trans. Industr. Inf. **14**(9), 3801–3811 (2018). https://doi.org/10.1109/TII.2018.2836150
17. Malek, Z.S., Trivedi, B., Shah, A.: User behavior pattern -signature based intrusion detection. In: 2020 Fourth World Conference on Smart Trends in Systems, Security and Sustainability (WorldS4), pp. 549–552 (2020). https://doi.org/10.1109/WorldS450073.2020.9210368
18. Meidan, Y., et al.: N-BaIoT–network-based detection of IoT botnet attacks using deep autoencoders. IEEE Pervasive Comput. **17**(3), 12–22 (2018). https://doi.org/10.1109/MPRV.2018.03367731
19. Nawrocki, M., Wählisch, M., Schmidt, T.C., Keil, C., Schönfelder, J.: A survey on honeypot software and data analysis (2016)
20. Pajouh, H.H., Javidan, R., Khayami, R., Dehghantanha, A., Choo, K.K.R.: A two-layer dimension reduction and two-tier classification model for anomaly-based intrusion detection in IoT backbone networks. IEEE Trans. Emerg. Top. Comput. **7**(2), 314–323 (2019). https://doi.org/10.1109/TETC.2016.2633228
21. Palattella, M.R., et al.: Standardized protocol stack for the Internet of (important) Things. IEEE Commun. Surv. Tutorials **15**(3), 1389–1406 (2013). https://doi.org/10.1109/SURV.2012.111412.00158
22. Saxena, A.K., Sinha, S., Shukla, P.: General study of intrusion detection system and survey of agent based intrusion detection system. In: 2017 International Conference on Computing, Communication and Automation (ICCCA), pp. 421–471 (2017). https://doi.org/10.1109/CCAA.2017.8229866
23. Tambe, A., et al.: Detection of threats to IoT devices using scalable VPN-forwarded honeypots. In: Proceedings of the Ninth ACM Conference on Data and Application Security and Privacy, CODASPY 2019, pp. 85–96. Association for Computing Machinery, New York (2019). https://doi.org/10.1145/3292006.3300024
24. Vishwakarma, R., Jain, A.K.: A honeypot with machine learning based detection framework for defending IoT based botnet DDoS attacks. In: 2019 3rd International Conference on Trends in Electronics and Informatics (ICOEI), pp. 1019–1024. IEEE (2019)
25. Wang, Z., Fok, K.W., Thing, V.L.: Machine learning for encrypted malicious traffic detection: approaches, datasets and comparative study. Comput. Secur. **113**(C) (2022). https://doi.org/10.1016/j.cose.2021.102542

IoTCat: A Multidimensional Approach to Categorize IoT Devices in Order to Identify a Delegate for Cybersecurity Functions

Emiliia Geloczi[(✉)], Nico Mexis, Benedikt Holler, Henrich C. Pöhls, and Stefan Katzenbeisser

University of Passau, Innstr. 41, Passau, Germany
{emiliia.geloczi,nico.mexis,henrich.poehls,
stefan.katzenbeisser}@uni-passau.de, benedikt.holler@gmail.com

Abstract. Despite the extensive functionality and broad diversity of Internet of Things (IoT) devices, they remain vulnerable to cybersecurity attacks. Still, many of them are unable to protect themselves due to limited resources or missing security features. One solution is to delegate security functions to a "stronger" device "encapsulating" a "weaker" one in a secure environment. In order to identify a suitable IoT device within the system to take over security responsibilities, we propose a novel flexible multidimensional approach to IoT device categorization, named IoT-Cat, that considers not only the technical characteristics of devices (e.g., available memory) but also user experience (e.g., trust in the vendor). In this paper, we describe our approach, compare it with existing methods, and demonstrate its applicability by presenting a proof-of-concept software solution.

Keywords: Categorization · Security · IoT · Delegation · Identification

1 Introduction

The increasing number of Internet of Things (IoT) devices in everyday life [40] leads to more potential attack vectors, thereby increasing the risk to the personal data generated or exchanged in IoT networks [13]. At first glance, it may seem that IoT systems are powerful enough to ensure their own security, as they provide users with a wide range of functionality [29]. However, specific IoT devices are unable to ensure their own security, as most lack sufficient resources to perform complex cryptographic operations or store large amounts of data [25]. Nonetheless, these devices cannot be left unprotected, as they are also participants in the IoT system and generate, transmit, and receive potentially context-critical data [13].

It is reasonable to assume that if some devices are unable to protect themselves, they should be protected by another device. In other words, if security functions are not feasible for "weak" devices, they should be delegated to a "strong" device(s). In this case, the "strong" device is called a *delegate*, which "encapsulates" IoT devices in a secure environment (see Fig. 1). In order to use this delegation approach in an existing IoT network, the first task is to identify a device capable of acting as a delegate. Ideally, a suitable device can be identified among those already present in the network. Only if no appropriate device is found, should a "stronger" device be added to the system.

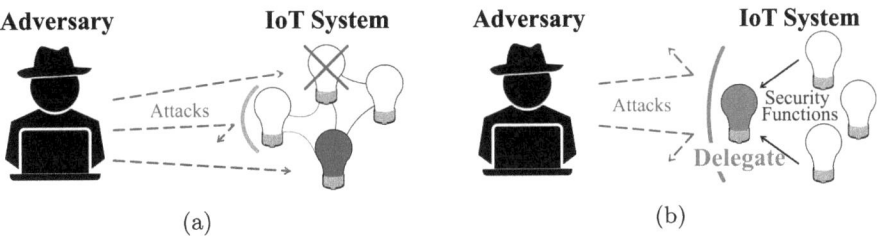

Fig. 1. IoT system (a) without and (b) with security delegation (based on [11]).

We assume that a device that outperforms others can become a delegate. Therefore, the devices connected to the network should be ranked based on a set of relevant characteristics. Depending on the purpose of selecting a delegate and its potential functions, the characteristics considered for ranking the existing devices may vary. To perform security functions (e.g., executing cryptographic protocols), the focus lies on technical characteristics organized into two groups: *Device-Related characteristics*, which we believe are most relevant to the ability to perform security tasks, and *Network-Related characteristics*, which we see as less relevant to security. Additionally, we consider *User-Related characteristics* to reflect user perception. However, since these characteristics are subjective, we assume they have the lowest weight among the groups.

Although a combination of technical and subjective characteristics reduces the likelihood of identifying multiple devices suitable for the delegate role, it does not eliminate this possibility. Having multiple devices that can act as delegates is not a disadvantage, but a benefit: it can enhance system reliability by balancing the load of delegation over several delegates or/and avoid a single point of failure by introducing redundancy. Additionally, splitting of functionality enables one to construct a defense-in-depth where devices on one level can jointly provide security functions to devices at higher levels.

1.1 Contribution

In this work, we introduce a novel flexible multidimensional approach, named *IoTCat*, which categorizes IoT devices based on their technical characteristics and the user's perspective, enabling the identification of a device(s) that can act as a delegate(s) and perform security functions on behalf of others.

1.2 Organization

Section 2 and Sect. 3 describe the methodology and implementation details of *IoTCat*. A review of existing related works is presented in Sect. 4, followed by a comparison of *IoTCat* with similar approaches and its discussion in Sect. 5. Finally, Sect. 6 concludes the paper and outlines potential directions for future research.

2 Methodology

We term our methodology *IoTCat*, as it categorizes IoT devices connected to a particular network according to nine characteristics in order to rank them for suitability in becoming a delegate for security functions. To achieve this, *IoTCat* collects device characteristics, calculates device scores, and performs ranking and classification of the devices (see Fig. 2).

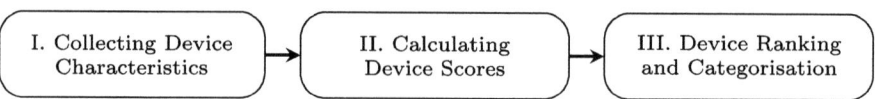

Fig. 2. Three-step workflow of *IoTCat*.

The pre-categorization task related to the identification of devices connected to a local network is not described in this section but is mentioned in Sect. 3, as it is performed using well-known technical tools. Since the primary novelty of our work lies in the categorization approach, we focus exclusively on the steps related to it.

Step I: Collecting Device Characteristics

Our categorization approach is based on nine device characteristics collected from devices within the network during this step. These characteristics are grouped into the following three categories:

Device-Related characteristics ($\mathcal{DR}$) include properties directly associated with a device:

1. *RAM* (Random Access Memory) is a limited resource in IoT devices. More RAM allows devices to use stronger security mechanisms, provide additional services, and better mitigate attacks.
2. *CPU* (Central Processing Unit) performance determines how fast a device can perform tasks.
3. *Availability (AV)* refers to a device's uptime. High AV indicates the absence of major faults, thereby ensuring more reliable service.

4. *Firmware Version (FV) Freshness* refers to the recency of a firmware version. Firmware updates improve functionality and should address recently disclosed vulnerabilities [5,9]. Therefore, it is generally assumed that newer firmware versions are more secure than older ones. We adhere to this assumption to simplify the demonstration of the general idea of *IoTCat*'s application. However, this assumption may not always apply, especially when comparing firmware versions across different devices. A newer firmware version of one device may provide a lower level of security than an older firmware version of another device. For more accurate categorization, a more detailed comparison of firmware is needed, for which a more complex algorithm could be implemented in the future. For example, Artificial Intelligence (AI) technologies could be employed to parse changelogs and identify which known vulnerabilities have been addressed by an update.

Network-Related characteristics ($\mathcal{NR}$) refer to properties associated with device communication:

5. *Wi-Fi* captures what kind of wireless communication technology is used. Newer standards improve the security, but also provide higher link rates, broader frequency support, and lower latency.
6. *Round-Trip Time (RTT)* is the time a signal takes to travel to a destination and back, also known as a delay.
7. *MPS* refers to the MQTT [36] protocol's Maximum Packet Size a device can process. A higher MPS reduces both transmission time and bandwidth usage.

User-Related characteristics ($\mathcal{UR}$) represent subjective aspects closely related to a user:

8. *Vendor Trust (VT)* is influenced by prior positive/negative experiences with the vendor or the user's perception of a vendor.
9. *Price (PR)* is not related to security, but it remains a key factor for many users when choosing an IoT device.

Each group of characteristics is weighted based on its relevance. In our context, $\mathcal{DR}$ is considered the most critical, as it directly reflects the device's ability to perform security tasks. While $\mathcal{NR}$ is also important, it is assigned a lower weight since it influences data transmission efficiency rather than the device's performance. $\mathcal{UR}$ has the lowest weight due to its subjectivity, though it remains relevant given the user-centric nature of IoT systems. These weights can be adjusted to fit specific application scenarios.

Step II: Calculation of Device Scores

Based on the data collected during Step I, the rank values for all devices are calculated using the formulas described below.

Definition 1. *Assume that there is an IoT system SM which consists of* $n \geqslant 2$ *IoT devices* d_i, $i = 1, \ldots, n$, *which can be denoted as*

$$SM := \{d_i \mid i = 1, \ldots, n\}.$$

Definition 2. *For every device* $d \in SM$, *the device can be characterized by a triple of characteristic groups as*

$$d := \{\mathcal{DR}, \mathcal{NR}, \mathcal{UR}\},$$

where $\mathcal{DR}$ *represents Device-Related,* $\mathcal{NR}$ *represents Network-Related, and* $\mathcal{UR}$ *represents User-Related characteristics.*

Definition 3. $\mathcal{DR}$, $\mathcal{NR}$, *and* $\mathcal{UR}$ *can be described as the following collections:*

$$\mathcal{DR} := \{RAM, CPU, AV, FV\},$$
$$\mathcal{NR} := \{WF, RTT, MPS\},$$
$$\mathcal{UR} := \{VT, PR\}.$$

Based on the definitions introduced, we can denote the device score S_d as follows:

$$S_d = 3 \times \mathcal{DR} + 2 \times \mathcal{NR} + 1 \times \mathcal{UR} =$$
$$= 3 \times (S_{RAM_d} + S_{CPU_d} + S_{AV_d} + S_{FV_d}) +$$
$$+ 2 \times (S_{WF_d} + S_{RTT_d} + S_{MPS_d}) + 1 \times (S_{VT_d} + S_{PR_d}),$$

where S_x is the characteristic score value of the device x. $\mathcal{DR}$, $\mathcal{NR}$, and $\mathcal{UR}$ are weighted according to their relevance, as discussed previously in Step I.

Table 1 illustrates how the individual scores for each characteristic of the device are calculated. Next, the values are normalized, with the best score being 1 and the worst score being 0. Once *IoTCat* collects and computes the scores for each device, it proceeds to the next and final step.

Step III: Ranking and Categorization of Devices

There are several methods for achieving device categorization, including linear ranking, $1/n$-dimensional k-means, or Kernel Density Estimation (KDE) [28,30]. We selected KDE because it is deterministic and provides clear categories of devices[1]. To apply KDE, we draw a graph for density estimation of device scores and identify one or more local minima. These minima serve as cut-off points for categories, as devices on opposite sides of these minima are likely significantly different from one another.

---

[1] In this paper, we present the most basic version of IoTCat, which means that other forms of ranking algorithms could be a possible extensions; as KDE provided good results for our prototype we did not investigate the choice further.

Table 1. Score calculation of each device characteristic.

Char.	Unit	Score S_x	Comment
RAM	kB	$\frac{RAM - RAM_{min}}{RAM_{max} - RAM_{min}}$	RAM is the available RAM value of the device.
CPU	ms	$\frac{CPU - CPU_{min}}{CPU_{max} - CPU_{min}}$	CPU denotes the time required for the device to complete a benchmark task.
AV	sec	$\frac{AV}{AV_{max}}$	AV is the uptime of d, AV_{max} is the uptime of the system.
FV	sec	$1 - \frac{FV - FV_{min}}{FV_{max} - FV_{min}}$	FV represents the time elapsed between the firmware build and the $IoTCat$ request.
WF	-	$\sum_{i=1}^{9} Sup_i \times S_{WFS_i}$	S_{WFS} is the score value of Wi-Fi standard (see Appendix A), Sup_i denotes whether a device supports (1) or does not support (0) the standard with index i.
RTT	ms	$\frac{RTT - RTT_{min}}{RTT_{max} - RTT_{min}}$	RTT represents the average ping time measured over multiple requests.
MPS	B	$\frac{MPS - MPS_{min}}{MPS_{max} - MPS_{min}}$	MPS denotes the maximum packet size supported by the device.
VT	-	$\frac{VT - VT_{min}}{VT_{max} - VT_{min}}$	VT of the device is equal to $VT_{IoTCat} + VT_{user}$, where VT_{IoTCat} and VT_{user} are trust values assigned by $IoTCat$ and user, respectively (see Appendix B).
PR	$	$1 - \frac{PR - PR_{min}}{PR_{max} - PR_{min}}$	PR is price of the device.

$X_{min/max}$ denotes the minimum/maximum value of the characteristic X among all devices.

3 Implementation Results

In order to demonstrate the application of $IoTCat$, we implemented a proof-of-concept software solution and tested it on 36 IoT devices. The test setup is illustrated in Fig. 3. All IoT devices are equipped with the custom open source Tasmota firmware [37] and communicate via the MQTT protocol with a Raspberry Pi (RPi) acting as a broker. The RPi performs all necessary operations and provides the user interface in the form of a web application.

Fig. 3. Test setup of $IoTCat$.

First, the pre-categorization step is performed, during which the RPi identifies the IoT devices connected via MQTT using the Python `paho.mqtt.client` library. Next, facilitating commands offered by the Tasmota firmware, the RPi requests data from each device regarding the characteristics specified in Section 3.I. For most characteristics, the RPi receives values in a ready-to-use format. However, the following of them still require pre-/post-processing:

- To evaluate *CPU* performance, the chip identifier can be retrieved and used to find the corresponding benchmark result in a pre-filled table. However, we decided to enhance the firmware to enable real-time performance testing. To achieve this, we extended the firmware to support the initiation of a benchmark calculation directly on the device, specifically, computing the dot product of two vectors, each containing 256 elements. This approach provides an indication of the device's performance not only on commonly used IoT chips (e.g., ESP8266EX) but also on a wide range of other platforms.
- To evaluate the RTT, the RPi sends n consecutive requests, records each individual RTT_i, and then calculates their average value. In our implementation, we set $n = 3$.
- VT cannot be directly obtained from the device and requires user input. Initially, the device's vendor is identified using the device's MAC address. The user should select the most trusted vendor. If any vendors are not automatically identified, the user is asked to enter them manually (see Appendix B).
- PR cannot be retrieved directly from a device. The user is required to either enter the device's price manually or provide the device's name, which is then used to identify the price using an AI engine. In *IoTCat*, `OpenAI` is used with the prompt: `Average price`+*Device_Name*+*Device_Vendor* in $.

From the obtained values, a `.csv` file is generated and passed to the web application, which calculates the scores, categorizes the devices, and provides the user interface.

Device scores are calculated as described in Table 1 (see Sect. 2.II), and categorization is performed using Gaussian KDE (see Sect. 2.III). By adjusting the bandwidth of KDE, we found that a value of 0.06 resulted in five device categories, while the "ideal" bandwidth of approximately 0.092 (calculated using Silverman's rule of thumb [35]) resulted in only two categories. We believe that the five categories provide a good balance between classification granularity and clarity (see Fig. 4a). The individual scores of the devices can be depicted using a radar chart, an example of which is shown in Fig. 4b.

The web application is implemented in C# using the `Microsoft .NET 8.0` platform, the `MathNet.Numerics` NuGet package and `Blazor` web framework with server-side rendering. Users can access *IoTCat* via a link and open it on any device. The interface is shown in Fig. 5.

4 Related Work

In our study, two interrelated topics are addressed: the *identification* of a suitable device for the delegate role and the *categorization* of devices based on their characteristics. Accordingly, in the literature review, we discuss works related to these topics with focus on studies most closely related to ours.

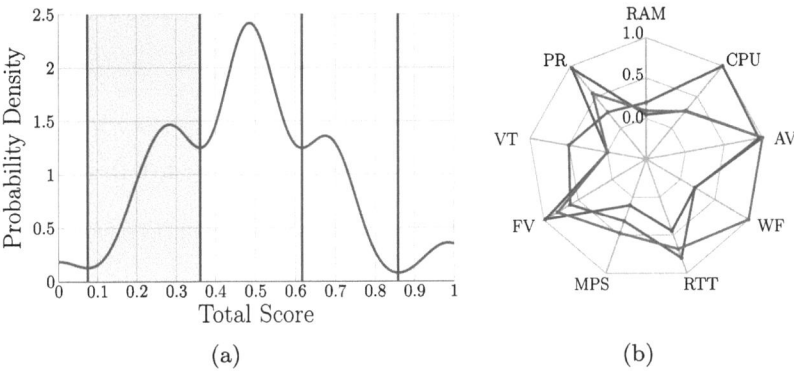

Fig. 4. (a) Gaussian probability density function. (b) Radar chart for: Arduino GIGA R1, Raspberry Pi Pico W RP2040, and nRF7002-DK Wi-Fi 6 DevKit.

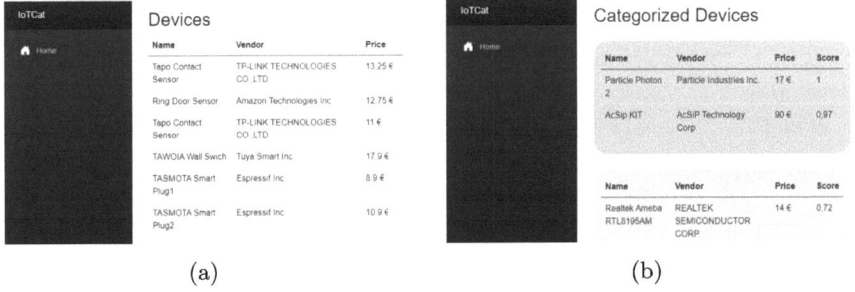

Fig. 5. *IoTCat* UI after (a) identification and (b) categorization of IoT devices.

4.1 Identification

During the study of literature on device identification, we observed that the works can be divided into two groups, based on the question each proposed approach aims to answer.

What Is/was It? The first group includes works that present approaches focused on identifying the device type, answering the question *"What is/was it?"* (see Table 2). For example, the authors analyze patterns of communication or device behavior and draw conclusions about the device type [7,22,38]. In general, all the approaches in this group rely on various AI technologies including Deep Learning, Machine Learning (ML). However, since our primary focus is not on device type identification, we do not review these approaches in detail.

What Is Good/bad? In the second group, we include papers that seek to answer the question *"What is good/bad?"* based on security implications. In general, the approaches are aimed at identifying trusted or suspicious devices. The

Table 2. Research works focus on IoT device type identification.

Author(s)	Title
Aksoy and Gunes [1]	Automated IoT Device Identification using Network Traffic
Ali et al. [2]	A Generic Machine Learning Approach for IoT Device Identification
Bao et al. [3]	IoT Device Type Identification Using Hybrid Deep Learning Approach...
Bezawada et al. [4]	Behavioral Fingerprinting of IoT Devices
Chen et al. [6]	IoT-ID: Robust IoT Device Identification...
Chowdhury et al. [7]	A Deep Learning Approach for Classifying ... IoT Devices...
Fan et al. [10]	An IoT Device Identification Method based on Semi-supervised Learning
Hamad et al. [15]	IoT Device Identification via Network-Flow ... Fingerprinting and Learning
Kotak and Elovici [18]	IoT device identification based on network communication analysis ...
Le et al. [19]	IoTFinder: Efficient Large-Scale Identification of IoT Devices ...
Liu et al. [21]	Class-Incremental Learning for Wireless Device Identification in IoT
Liu et al. [22]	Zero-Bias Deep Learning for Accurate Identification of ... (IoT) Devices
Meidan et al. [24]	ProfilIoT: A Machine Learning Approach for IoT Device Identification ...
Marchal et al. [23]	AuDI: Toward Autonomous IoT Device-Type Identification...
Salman et al. [31]	A machine learning based framework for IoT device identification ...
Scheidt and Adda [33]	Identification of IoT Devices for Forensic Investigation
Thom et al. [38]	FlexHash - Hybrid Locality Sensitive Hashing for IoT Device Identification
Wang et al. [42]	Efficient traffic-based IoT device identification ...
Yin et al. [43]	IoT ETEI: End-to-End IoT Device Identification Method

authors employ various techniques, such as blacklisting, whitelisting, and ML. We focus on this category in greater detail and discuss a few papers that we believe are most relevant to our approach.

Khalil et al. describe the trusted device identification approach based on several components: resource, trust, delegation repositories, and an ontology base [17]. In contrast to similar models, this approach uses a concept-weighting technique to organize the ontology, thereby addressing the shortcomings of previous studies. According to the authors' evaluation, this approach outperforms its competitors by accounting for additional features such as completeness, prioritization, and consistency.

Miettinen *et al.* present the automated system IoT Sentinel which identifies types of devices within IoT networks and restricts external communication with vulnerable devices to mitigate potential threats [26]. The system uses the pattern of packets sent during the device setup phase as unique fingerprints. The system uses packet patterns transmitted during the device setup phase as unique fingerprints. Based on these fingerprints, devices are identified and classified into different security levels: strict, restricted, or trusted. This approach enables effective device identification while maintaining high performance.

A method of selecting a trusted element in an IoT network based on a dynamic combination of white and blacklists is proposed by Wang *et al.* in [41]. The placement of items on either list is determined by the trust relationship between pairs of end users and between the users and the provider. Furthermore, both direct and indirect trust values are considered when assigning a to each end user. The proposed method is evaluated using the Lyapunov theory. The results demonstrate its robustness against attacks targeting a service provider and its suitability for scalable systems.

Tragos *et al.* present a trust model based on a combination of five metrics: communication-based trust (communication quality), security-based trust (device behavior), data-based trust (reliability of measurements produced by IoT devices), social relationship-based trust (owner/manufacturer characteristics), and reputation-based trust (reviews about the device). Based on the provided data analysis, the proposed model enables the detection of malfunctioning devices by verifying whether their output values are within a specified range [39].

4.2 Categorization

Next, we discuss papers that focus on the categorization of IoT devices based on various parameters.

An early concept for categorizing IoT devices was presented by Gigli and Koo [12]. The authors proposed that devices be classified into four categories according to the services they provide: identity-related (a device identifies an entity using a label), information aggregation (a device gathers data and sends it to a remote application for processing), collaborative-aware (a device uses the gathered information to make decisions and executes actions accordingly), and ubiquitous (a theoretical idea where collaborative-aware services are available, always connected and interoperable – "ultimate goal of IoT" [12]).

Liu *et al.* [20] propose a method for categorizing IoT devices within a multihop mesh network based on their reputation, and hence, the threat they pose to the rest of the system. This method includes two approaches: "Hard detection" [20], which groups devices into *benign* and *malicious* categories, and "soft detection" [20], which also includes an intermediate category for *suspicious* devices.

The model for categorizing IoT services based on their inherent security risks is presented in [8]. The service assessment is based on the DREAD model developed by Microsoft [34]. The authors define seven questions, the answers to which determine the rating of each service. Based on the resulting ratings, services can be allocated into four categories: critical, high, medium, and low risk.

A five-level IoT model consisting of cloud, fog, edge, mist, and dew computing layers is presented in [14]. Devices within the described IoT network are distributed across these layers based on their processing capabilities. Depending on the layer, the devices are assigned roles (such as cloud data manager, equipment provider, service provider, etc.), in order to ensure system security under the General Data Protection Regulation (GDPR).

Sawadogo *et al.* propose an approach to clustering IoT devices using unsupervised ML [32]. Network-level traffic characteristics serve as input, collected over multiple weeks, and are then categorized using both k-means and BIRCH (Balanced Iterative Reducing and Clustering using Hierarchies) clustering methods. The evaluation results show that this approach achieves an accuracy of 70%.

5 Discussion

This section examines *IoTCat*, focusing on its distinctions from existing approaches, potential security concerns, and application domains.

5.1 Comparison with Other Approaches

As described in Sect. 4, existing works can be grouped into two categories: approaches that focus on *identifying* a device's type or trustworthiness, and those that concentrate on *categorizing* devices. We believe that, in general, the second category is more relevant to our work. However, *IoTCat* is designed to identify device(s) with sufficient computational power to perform security functions as delegate(s), thereby addressing the question *"What is strong enough?"*. While this question may appear similar to one addressed by approaches from *identification* category, it is fundamentally different and highlights the distinct application goal of *IoTCat*.

Table 3 presents a comparison of *IoTCat* with the most closely related approaches from both categories.

The *Characteristics* column represents features of devices considered when determining their category.[2] From the table, we can see that most approaches evaluate the behavior-related characteristics, e.g., traffic patterns [20,26,32], or reputation [17,39,41]. Khalil *et al.* [17] consider also device resources, which we can interpret as analogous to our *Device-Related characteristics*. Furthermore, Tragos *et al.* [39] evaluate communication quality-related features that can be seen as similar to our *Network-Related characteristics*.

The *Evaluation Method* column describes the strategies used by the authors to evaluate devices. Some approaches adopt a concept-weighting method [17,39],

---

[2] For consistency, we assume that approaches focusing on *identification* classify devices into trusted/untrusted groups.

where characteristics are assigned s based on their significance, followed by the computation of rank values for the identification of a trusted device. *IoTCat* follows a similar method but also incorporates KDE for categorization. Other approaches classify devices based on their types [26], roles [12], capabilities [14], potential threats [20] and risks [8].

Regarding *Device Categories*, we can see that only *IoTCat* and the approach presented by Sawadogo et al. [32] offer the possibility of flexible categorization. Other approaches strictly define fixed categories. However, in contrast to our approach, Sawadogo et al. focuses on categorizing individual IoT devices but does not include any ranking mechanism.

Drawing conclusions from the comparison, we observe that *IoTCat* has a unique goal that is not commonly found in other approaches. Existing works primarily focus on either identifying the type or trustworthiness of devices or on categorizing them, typically without integrating these goals. In contrast, *IoTCat* combines both: it categorizes devices and identifies the "strongest" one(s) capable of acting as the delegate(s) and performing the required security functions. In addition, unlike other approaches, *IoTCat* provides users with a comprehensive overview of network device resources while taking user preferences into account.

Moreover, *IoTCat* offers flexible configuration to address specific needs. First, it provides customizable categorization, allowing devices to be distributed across a variable number of categories. This can be achieved by adjusting the bandwidth of the KDE or by using alternative methods (see Sect. 2.III). Second, using an evaluation method to calculate devices' scores allows for flexible customization of the ranking and categorization results, as the weights can be adjusted to emphasize the characteristics most relevant to the specific task. For our current research prototype presented here, we choose to give the subjective user-related characteristics a weight of 1, which is the lowest weight of the three groups; exploring the added flexibility by setting other weights to better match given real-life scenarios is subject to further research.

In this paper, we present the most basic version of *IoTCat*. However, we see significant potential for extending it by incorporating additional characteristics to enable more comprehensive device evaluation and more accurate categorization. We believe that *IoTCat* can seamlessly integrate any of the approaches presented in Table 3. For example, traffic pattern or behavior analysis could be implemented to identify devices that not only have sufficient resources for the required tasks but also exhibit trustworthy behavior. Such devices could then also be assigned tasks involving sensitive or critical data. Moreover, other aspects can be added to adapt the categorization to the real-world situation. For example, the following characteristics of the devices can be taken into account: the updateability [5], the availability of dedicated security hardware, or specific encryption abilities, or power limitations [27].

Also, it is important to note that a direct comparison of *IoTCat* with other approaches in terms of categorization results is not feasible. As discussed earlier, each approach is designed with a specific purpose, leading to inherently non-comparable outcomes.

Table 3. Comparison of *IoTCat* with the existing approaches.

Paper	Characteristics	Evaluation Method	Device Categories
Identification			
Khalil et al. [17]	resources, trust, ontology	concept-weighting	trusted, untrusted
Miettinen et al.[26]	traffic patterns	type-based	strict, restricted, trusted
Wang et al. [41]	relationships between nodes	black-and-white lists	trusted, untrusted
Tragos et al. [39]	communication quality, behavior, measurements reliability, social and reputational trust	concept-weighting	trusted, untrusted
Categorization			
Gigli and Koo [12]	services provided	role-based	identity, data aggregation, collaborative-aware, ubiquitous
Liu et al. [20]	traffic patterns	threat-based	benign, malicious, suspicious
Dominik et al. [8]	DREAD risks	numerical ranks	critical, high, medium, low
Hadzoovic et al.[14]	functions and capabilities	capability analysis following GDPR	cloud, fog, edge, mist, dew computing
Sawadogo et al. [32]	traffic patterns	k-means, BIRCH	flexible
IoTCat	RAM, CPU, AV, FV, WF, RTT, MPS, VT, PR	concept-weighting, KDE	flexible

5.2 Security Concerns

Applying the security delegation method to a system inevitably redirects an adversary's attack vector to a device acting as a delegate. On the one hand, delegation enhances the system's security, since weak devices are no longer the primary target and the delegate is able to perform more sophisticated protection mechanisms. However, on the other hand, the delegate becomes the main target of an adversary, resulting in a single point of failure vulnerability, which certainly introduces a new challenge to the security strategy. In order to address this vulnerability, *IoTCat* provides the device categorization functionality, enabling the selection of multiple devices for the delegate role. It ensures fault tolerance and distributes attack vectors across several devices, rather than concentrating them on a single target.

5.3 Possible Applications

Categorization and ranking of IoT devices can be applied not only within smart home systems but also across other domains. Regardless of the application goals, categorization solutions enhance the overall security of systems by enabling network load balancing, resource optimization, device monitoring, access control management, etc.

For example, in the healthcare and medical IoT device domain, the security and reliability of patient-critical devices must be strictly ensured. Conversely, non-medical devices such as smart beds and room thermostats can be designated as low priority. In the case of an emergency power outage, the load should be correctly distributed to prioritize critical devices. Furthermore, medical devices access data with varying levels of sensitivity. The more critical the data, the more security mechanisms must be applied; hence, more reliable and powerful devices should be employed.

Another example of the application of device categorization is in the Small or Medium-sized Enterprise (SME) domain. In SMEs that rely on IoT networks for their operations, such as manufacturing plants using smart sensors and microcontrollers to monitor production lines, categorization software similar to *IoTCat* can play a crucial role in optimizing network performance. For instance, in a manufacturing plant with multiple production lines, each line may have its own set of IoT devices monitoring various parameters. The software can identify which microcontroller consistently performs best under load and assign it the responsibility of managing inter-device communication and data aggregation. This delegated microcontroller can then handle more demanding tasks, such as coordinating real-time alerts when machines show signs of malfunction, thereby improving the overall efficiency and reliability of the production process. By using this software regularly, the company can adapt to changes in the IoT network. This ensures that the most capable microcontroller is always in charge, resulting in more reliable operations, reduced downtime, and better resource allocation, ultimately contributing to more streamlined and cost-effective production processes.

6 Conclusions and Future Works

In this paper, we introduce a novel multidimensional approach *IoTCat* designed to rank and categorize IoT devices. We use it to assess their suitability to act as a delegate for cybersecurity functions. By incorporating nine characteristics, covering both technical aspects of IoT devices and user preferences, our approach enables a comprehensive evaluation of devices within the system and identification of those "stronger" device(s) that are capable of performing critical security functions on behalf of "weaker" devices. Furthermore, we designed the *IoTCat* methodology to be highly flexible and customizable, allowing it to be adapted to a wide range of systems and use cases. Its full potential can be further explored through future research:

- Incorporation of continuous system monitoring and behavior/reputation-related metrics to determine whether the current delegate remains optimal.
- Exploration of *IoTCat*'s applicability beyond prototype settings, including its integration into real-world and large-scale IoT systems.
- Applying different clustering algorithms and ML techniques to offer even more flexible categorization.
- Design and implementation of a delegation protocol, to be applied following.
- Explore backup and fail-over strategies to avoid the delegate becoming a single-point of failure.

Acknowledgements. This work has been partially funded by the Bavarian State Ministry of Science and Arts (BayStMWK), under Project "ForDaySec: Security in Everyday Use of Digital Technologies (`fordaysec.de`)" of the Bavarian Research Association and by the Interreg VI-A Programme Germany/Bavaria–Austria 2021–2027, as part of Project BA0100016: "CySeReS-KMU: Cyber Security and Resilience in Supply Chains with focus on SMEs" of the European Union.

Disclosure of Interests. The authors have no competing interests to declare that are relevant to the content of this article.

A Appendix: Scoring of Wi-Fi Standards

Different Wi-Fi standards are maintained by the IEEE 802.11 working group. While each standard is assigned a unique letter code, major standard "generations" are also numbered chronologically [16]. Newer standards offer several advantages over older ones, e.g., higher maximum link rates, broader frequency band support, and reduced latency. In IoT environments, consistent and fast data transmission is essential for maintaining smooth interconnectivity. Furthermore, the ability to operate across a wider range of frequency bands enhances network flexibility.

The supported Wi-Fi standards of a device represent a qualitative rather than a quantitative characteristic. Therefore, to calculate a score for this characteristic, we first compute individual scores for each Wi-Fi standard in use (S_{WFS}) using the following formula (see Table 4):

$$S_{WFS} = CW_{WFS} + FREQ_{WFS} + DARA_{WFS},$$

where S_{WFS} is a score value of Wi-Fi standard WFS, CW_{WFS} and $FREQ_{WFS}$ are numbers of supported frequencies and channel widths by Wi-Fi standard WFS, respectively, and $DARA_{WFS}$ is a data rate of Wi-Fi standard WFS. All values are min-max normalized.

Table 4. Wi-Fi Standards scores.

№ Standard	Denotation*	Channel Width (MHz)	Frequency (GHz)	Data Rate (mbps)	Score
1 802.11	Wi-Fi 0	20	2.4	2	0.00
2 802.11b	Wi-Fi 1	20	2.4	11	0.00
3 802.11a	Wi-Fi 2	20	5	54	0.00
4 802.11g	Wi-Fi 3	20	2.4	6	0.00
5 802.11n	Wi-Fi 4	20/40	2.4/5	72	0.26
6 802.11ac	Wi-Fi 5	20/40/80	5	433	0.27
7 802.11ah	HaLow**	1/2/4/8/16	0.9	347	0.67
8 802.11ax	Wi-Fi 6	20/40/80/160	2.4/5/6	574	0.72
9 802.11be	Wi-Fi 7	20/40/80/160/320	2.4/5/6	1376	1.00

* Wi-Fi generations only received numerical nomenclature starting with Wi-Fi 4, others generations were numbered retroactively.

** During calculation, HaLow gets 1 additional score point to emphasize its low power consumption provided specifically for resource-constrained IoT devices.

B Appendix: Vendor Trust Calculation

Trust is a subjective characteristic of a device and can be influenced by various factors, such as prior positive or negative experiences. Therefore, we combine user preferences with a quantitative assessment of the vendors.

We calculate a vendor trust value for the device (VT) using the following formula:
$$VT = VT_{IoTCat} + VT_{user},$$

where VT_{IoTCat} is the weight value assigned to the vendor by *IoTCat*, and VT_{user} is the weight value that reflects the user's preference.

To determine VT_{IoTCat}, we analyzed multiple reports from the Statista.com portal on the most widely owned device brands across various countries (e.g., the USA, UK, India, China, Germany, and Italy). Based on this analysis, we identified 14 vendors with the highest overall popularity. These vendors were then clustered into three groups using the k-means algorithm, with each cluster assigned a specific weight value (see Table 5). Accordingly, if a device's vendor appears in this list, its VT_{IoTCat} is set to the corresponding weight value. Devices from vendors not included in the list receive $VT_{IoTCat} = 0$ by default.

It is important to note that for *IoTCat* we have compiled a generalized list of vendors and their corresponding weights. However, this list can be adjusted on demand to reflect specific market conditions and contextual factors such as country, application domain, or device type, as trust in vendors may vary in different environments.

In determining the value of VT_{user}, all vendors are initially assigned $VT_{user} = 0$. However, if the IoT system includes devices from multiple vendors, the user is required to indicate their preferred vendor, which is then assigned $VT_{user} = 1$.

Table 5. IoT device vendors and assigned weights.

№	Vendor Name	Weight
1	Samsung Electronics Co.	3
2	Philips	3
3	Google LLC	3
4	Robert Bosch GmbH	3
5	TP-LINK Technologies CO.	2
6	Amazon Technologies Inc.	2
7	Xiaomi Tech	2
8	Ring	2
9	Hive	2
10	LG Group	1
11	Siemens AG	1
12	Huawei Technologies Co.	1
13	D-Link	1
14	Espressif Inc.	1

References

1. Aksoy, A., Gunes, M.H.: Automated IoT device identification using network traffic. In: ICC 2019 - 2019 IEEE International Conference on Communications (ICC), pp. 1–7. IEEE, Shanghai, China (2019). https://doi.org/10.1109/ICC.2019.8761559
2. Ali, Z., Hussain, F., Ghazanfar, S., Husnain, M., Zahid, S., Shah, G.A.: A Generic Machine Learning Approach for IoT Device Identification. In: 2021 International Conference on Cyber Warfare and Security (ICCWS), pp. 118–123. IEEE, Islamabad, Pakistan (Nov 2021). https://doi.org/10.1109/ICCWS53234.2021.9702983
3. Bao, J., Hamdaoui, B., Wong, W.K.: iot device type identification using hybrid deep learning approach for increased IoT security. In: 2020 International Wireless Communications and Mobile Computing (IWCMC), pp. 565–570. IEEE, Limassol, Cyprus (2020). https://doi.org/10.1109/IWCMC48107.2020.9148110
4. Bezawada, B., Bachani, M., Peterson, J., Shirazi, H., Ray, I., Ray, I.: Behavioral Fingerprinting of IoT Devices. In: Proceedings of the 2018 Workshop on Attacks and Solutions in Hardware Security, pp. 41–50. ACM, Toronto Canada (Jan 2018). https://doi.org/10.1145/3266444.3266452
5. Brenner, R., Leithäuser, M., Jänich, S., Pöhls, H.C.: Updatefähigkeit als konstruktionsanforderung. Recht Digital (RDi), pp. 252 –264 (2024). https://beck-online.beck.de/Bcid/Y-300-Z-RDI-B-2024-S-252-N-1
6. Chen, Q., Song, Y., Jennings, B., Zhang, F., Xiao, B., Gao, S.: IoT-ID: robust IoT device identification based on feature drift adaptation. In: 2021 IEEE Global Communications Conference (GLOBECOM), pp. 1–6. IEEE, Madrid, Spain (2021). https://doi.org/10.1109/GLOBECOM46510.2021.9685693
7. Chowdhury, R.R., Idris, A.C., Abas, P.E.: A deep learning approach for classifying network connected iot devices using communication traffic characteristics. J. Netw. Syst. Manag. **31**(1), 26 (2023). https://doi.org/10.1007/s10922-022-09716-x

8. Dominik, O., Miljenko, M., Marin, V.: Categorizing IoT services according to security risks. In: Perakovic, D., Knapcikova, L. (eds.) FABULOUS 2021. LNICSSITE, vol. 382, pp. 154–166. Springer, Cham (2021). https://doi.org/10.1007/978-3-030-78459-1_11
9. European Commission: What constitutes the 'latest version of the firmware' under the regulation (eu) 2019/424? (2025). https://energy-efficient-products.ec.europa.eu/faqs-0/what-constitutes-latest-version-firmware-under-regulation-eu-2019424_en
10. Fan, L., et al.: An IoT Device Identification Method based on Semi-supervised Learning. In: 2020 16th International Conference on Network and Service Management (CNSM), pp. 1–7. IEEE, Izmir, Turkey (Nov 2020). https://doi.org/10.23919/CNSM50824.2020.9269044
11. Geloczi, E., Klement, F., Struck, P., Katzenbeisser, S.: SoK: delegated Security in the Internet of Things. Future Internet **17**(5), 202 (2025). https://doi.org/10.3390/fi17050202
12. Gigli, M., Koo, S.: Internet of Things: services and applications categorization. Adv. Internet of Things **1**(2), 27–31 (2011). https://doi.org/10.4236/ait.2011.12004
13. Gupta, B., Quamara, M.: An overview of internet of things (iot): architectural aspects, challenges, and protocols. Concurrency Comput. Pract. Exper. **32**(21), e4946 (2020). https://doi.org/10.1002/cpe.4946
14. Hadzovic, S., Mrdovic, S., Radonjic, M.: Identification of IoT Actors. Sensors **21**(6), 2093 (2021). https://doi.org/10.3390/s21062093
15. Hamad, S.A., Zhang, W.E., Sheng, Q.Z., Nepal, S.: IoT device identification via network-flow based fingerprinting and learning. In: 2019 18th IEEE International Conference On Trust, Security And Privacy In Computing and Communications/13th IEEE International Conference On Big Data Science And Engineering (TrustCom/BigDataSE), pp. 103–111. IEEE, Rotorua, New Zealand (2019). https://doi.org/10.1109/TrustCom/BigDataSE.2019.00023
16. Institute of Electrical and Electronics Engineers: IEEE 802.11, The Working Group Setting the Standards for Wireless LANs (2023). https://www.ieee802.org/11/
17. Khalil, U., Ahmad, A., Abdel-Aty, A.H., Elhoseny, M., El-Soud, M.W.A., Zeshan, F.: Identification of trusted IoT devices for secure delegation. Comput. Electr. Eng. **90**, 106988 (2021). https://doi.org/10.1016/j.compeleceng.2021.106988
18. Kotak, J., Elovici, Y.: IoT device identification based on network communication analysis using deep learning. J. Ambient. Intell. Humaniz. Comput. **14**(7), 9113–9129 (2023). https://doi.org/10.1007/s12652-022-04415-6
19. Le, F., Ortiz, J., Verma, D., Kandlur, D.: Policy-Based Identification of IoT Devices' Vendor and Type by DNS Traffic Analysis, pp. 180–201. Springer International Publishing, Cham (2019). https://doi.org/10.1007/978-3-030-17277-0_10
20. Liu, X., Abdelhakim, M., Krishnamurthy, P., Tipper, D.: Identifying malicious nodes in multihop IoT networks using diversity and unsupervised learning. In: 2018 IEEE International Conference on Communications (ICC), pp. 1–6. IEEE, Kansas City, MO (2018). https://doi.org/10.1109/ICC.2018.8422484
21. Liu, Y., Wang, J., Li, J., Niu, S., Song, H.: Class-incremental learning for wireless device identification in IoT. IEEE Internet Things J. **8**(23), 17227–17235 (2021). https://doi.org/10.1109/JIOT.2021.3078407
22. Liu, Y., et al.: Zero-bias deep learning for accurate identification of internet of things (IoT) devices. IEEE Internet Things J. **8**(4), 2627–2634 (2021). https://doi.org/10.1109/JIOT.2020.3018677

23. Marchal, S., Miettinen, M., Nguyen, T.D., Sadeghi, A.R., Asokan, N.: AuDI: toward autonomous IoT device-type identification using periodic communication. IEEE J. Sel. Areas Commun. **37**(6), 1402–1412 (2019). https://doi.org/10.1109/JSAC.2019.2904364
24. Meidan, Y., et al.: ProfilIoT: a machine learning approach for IoT device identification based on network traffic analysis. In: Proceedings of the Symposium on Applied Computing, SAC 2017, pp. 506–509. Association for Computing Machinery, New York, USA (Apr 2017). https://doi.org/10.1145/3019612.3019878
25. Mexis, N., Anagnostopoulos, N.A., Chen, S., Bambach, J., Arul, T., Katzenbeisser, S.: A lightweight architecture for hardware-based security in the emerging era of systems of systems. ACM JETC **17**(3), 1–25 (2021). https://doi.org/10.1145/3458824
26. Miettinen, M., Marchal, S., Hafeez, I., Asokan, N., Sadeghi, A.R., Tarkoma, S.: IoT sentinel: automated device-type identification for security enforcement in IoT. In: 2017 IEEE 37th International Conference on Distributed Computing Systems (ICDCS), pp. 2177–2184. IEEE (2017)
27. Mössinger, M., Petschkuhn, B., Bauer, J., Staudemeyer, R.C., Wójcik, M., Pöhls, H.C.: Towards quantifying the cost of a secure IoT: Overhead and energy consumption of ECC signatures on an ARM-based device. In: Proc. of The 5th workshop on IoT-SoS: Internet of Things Smart Objects and Services (WOWMOM SOS-IOT 2016). IEEE (July 2016). https://doi.org/10.1109/WoWMoM.2016.7523559, http://henrich.poehls.com/papers/2016_Moessinger_et_al-Towards_quantifying_the_cost_of_a_secure_IoT.pdf
28. Parzen, E.: On estimation of a probability density function and mode. Ann. Math. Stat. **33**(3), 1065–1076 (1962)
29. Pereira, F., Correia, R., Pinho, P., Lopes, S.I., Carvalho, N.B.: Challenges in resource-constrained iot devices: energy and communication as critical success factors for future iot deployment. Sensors **20**(22) (2020). https://doi.org/10.3390/s20226420
30. Rosenblatt, M.: Remarks on some nonparametric estimates of a density function. Ann. Math. Stat. **27**(3), 832–837 (1956). https://doi.org/10.1214/aoms/1177728190
31. Salman, O., Elhajj, I.H., Chehab, A., Kayssi, A.: A machine learning based framework for IoT device identification and abnormal traffic detection. Trans. Emerging Telecommun. Technol. **33**(3), e3743 (2022). https://doi.org/10.1002/ett.3743, e3743 ETT-19-0273.R1
32. Sawadogo, F., Violos, J., Hameed, A., Leivadeas, A.: An unsupervised machine learning approach for IoT device categorization. In: 2022 IEEE International Mediterranean Conference on Communications and Networking (MeditCom), pp. 25–30. IEEE, Athens, Greece (Sep 2022). https://doi.org/10.1109/MeditCom55741.2022.9928766
33. Scheidt, N., Adda, M.: Identification of IoT devices for forensic investigation. In: 2020 IEEE 10th International Conference on Intelligent Systems (IS), pp. 165–170. IEEE, Varna, Bulgaria (2020). https://doi.org/10.1109/IS48319.2020.9200150
34. Shostack, A.: Experiences Threat Modeling at Microsoft. In: MODSECMoDELS (2008). https://api.semanticscholar.org/CorpusID:2508643
35. Silverman, B.W.: Density Estimation for Statistics and Data Analysis. CRC Press, London (1986)
36. Spielvogel, K., Pöhls, H.C., Posegga, J.: TLS beyond the broker: enforcing fine-grained security and trust in publish/subscribe environments for IoT. In: Roman,

R., Zhou, J. (eds.) STM 2021. LNCS, vol. 13075, pp. 145–162. Springer, Cham (2021). https://doi.org/10.1007/978-3-030-91859-0_8
37. Tasmota Community: Tasmota Documentation (2025). https://tasmota.github.io/docs/, Accessed 3 April 2025
38. Thom, N., Thom, J., Charyyev, B., Hand, E., Sengupta, S.: FlexHash - hybrid locality sensitive hashing for IoT device identification. In: 2024 IEEE 21st Consumer Communications & Networking Conference (CCNC), pp. 368–371. IEEE, Las Vegas, NV, USA (Jan 2024). https://doi.org/10.1109/CCNC51664.2024.10454657
39. Tragos, E., et al.: Trusted IoT in the complex landscape of governance, security, privacy, availability and safety, p. 30. River Publishers (2016). https://doi.org/10.1201/9781003337966-6
40. Vailshery, L.S.: Number of IoT connected devices worldwide 2019-2023, with forecasts to 2030 (2023). https://www.statista.com/statistics/1183457/iot-connected-devices-worldwide/
41. Wang, B., Li, M., Jin, X., Guo, C.: A reliable IoT edge computing trust management mechanism for smart cities. IEEE Access **8**, 46373–46399 (2020). https://doi.org/10.1109/ACCESS.2020.2979022
42. Wang, B., Kang, H., Sun, G., Li, J.: Efficient traffic-based IoT device identification using a feature selection approach with Lévy flight-based sine chaotic sub-swarm binary honey badger algorithm. Appli. Soft Comput. **155**, 111455 (2024). https://doi.org/10.1016/j.asoc.2024.111455
43. Yin, F., Yang, L., Wang, Y., Dai, J.: IoT ETEI: end-to-End IoT Device Identification Method. In: 2021 IEEE Conference on Dependable and Secure Computing (DSC), pp. 1–8. IEEE, Aizuwakamatsu, Fukushima, Japan (Jan 2021). https://doi.org/10.1109/DSC49826.2021.9346251

QSHC – Quantum-Safe Hybrid Cryptography

Field-Tested Authentication for Quantum Key Distribution and DoS Attacks

Antoine Gansel[1](✉)[iD], Juliane Krämer[1][iD], Tim Schumacher[2],
Patrick Struck[3][iD], Maximilian Tippmann[2][iD], and Thomas Walther[2][iD]

[1] Universität Regensburg, Regensburg, Germany
{antoine.gansel,juliane.kraemer}@ur.de
[2] Technische Universität Darmstadt, Darmstad, Germany
tim.schumacher.64@stud.tu-darmstadt.de,
{maximilian.tippmann,thomas.walther}@physik.tu-darmstadt.de
[3] Universität Konstanz, Konstanz, Germany
patrick.struck@uni.kn

Abstract. Authentication is a crucial requirement for the security of Quantum Key Distribution (QKD). Yet, the integration of suitable methods in QKD systems tends to receive little attention from the research community. As a result, Wegman-Carter message authentication established itself as the go-to solution, leading to serious inefficiencies and additional trust assumptions, making it hard to recover from denial-of-service attacks. Another method is to use the lattice-based signature scheme Dilithium, as proposed by Wang et al. [36]. This method avoids the drawbacks of Wegman-Carter but, unfortunately, introduces new disadvantages. In this work, we implement and test several authentication methods on an actual QKD system. We compare and analyze three authentication variants, i.e., Wegman-Carter, Dilithium, and the established message-authentication code Chaskey, as a new method for authentication in QKD, which uses fewer quantum keys. We focus on the key consumptions, runtimes, and practicality in a field test of the QKD system. Lastly, we take a broader look at authentication for QKD in the context of Denial-of-Service attacks and propose a solution by combining several authentication methods to achieve their individual advantages while simultaneously avoiding several drawbacks.

Keywords: QKD · Authentication · Post-Quantum Security

1 Introduction

Cryptography is an indispensable tool to secure communication. A core concept of cryptography—and historically the first example—is the encryption of

---

This work was funded by the German Federal Ministry of Education and Research (BMBF) under the project Sequin (16KIS2123), by the German Research Foundation (DFG) – SFB 1119 CROSSING P1, P4 – 236615297, and by the Hector Foundation II.

messages between two parties Alice and Bob that share some key (symmetric encryption). In modern cryptography, keys for symmetric encryption are a sequence of random bits. A core challenge is how Alice and Bob can exchange such a key in a secure manner.

In their seminal work [10], Diffie and Hellman introduced the concept of asymmetric encryption where Alice and Bob do not need to share a key ahead of time. Due to efficiency reasons, however, asymmetric encryption is mainly used to securely exchange symmetric keys (the dedicated primitive is called key-encapsulation mechanism) which is then used to encrypt the actual messages. Constructions for asymmetric encryption based on number-theoretic problems like factoring and discrete logarithms that are used nowadays are known to be insecure once large-scale quantum computers exist, due to Shor's algorithm [33], which shows the devastating effects that quantum computers have on public-key cryptography. An alternative is post-quantum cryptography that relies on other hardness assumptions, e.g., the hardness of finding shortest vectors in lattices, which is assumed to be resistant to attacks with quantum computers. However, there is the possibility that an efficient quantum—or even classical—algorithm invalidating these assumptions will be found in the future. Luckily, quantum mechanics also offers methods to foster new promising candidates to securely exchange a secret between two parties: *Quantum Key Distribution* (QKD), introduced by Bennett and Brassard [5] forty years ago, indeed presents a method to harness the fundamental rules of quantum mechanics to exchange keys between two distant parties. Although QKD promises the exchange of information-theoretically secure keys thanks to quantum uncertainty (no-cloning theorem [38,39]) and verifiable entanglement, the practical application of this idea is faced with a couple of fundamental challenges. Among those—and the one of interest for this paper—is the problem of authenticating the classical communication needed between Alice and Bob, to ensure Eve cannot temper with the protocol's execution.

A typical method for authentication is to use the Wegman-Carter message authentication code (MAC) as mentioned in several works [8,20,34,37]. Here, messages are authenticated using one-time keys. A clear advantage of the Wegman-Carter authentication is that it achieves information-theoretic security. The disadvantage is that Alice and Bob need some pre-shared key to authenticate the first quantum key distribution session. A more recent approach [36] suggests to use Dilithium, a lattice-based signature scheme, for the authentication. While this avoids the problem of requiring a pre-shared key, the security now relies on computational hardness assumptions, more precisely, lattice assumptions.

An often neglected problem of QKD are Denial-of-Service (DoS) attacks. While Alice and Bob are able to determine whether an adversary was eavesdropping on the quantum channel, they cannot prevent the adversary from doing so—being able to identify such an eavesdropping adversary allows Alice and Bob to discard any potential key bits that the adversary might have learned. When using Wegman-Carter for authentication, every attempt to exchange a new quantum key—regardless of being successful or unsuccessful due to an eavesdropping adversary—consumes part of the Wegman-Carter key. By constantly eavesdropping on the quantum channel for a sufficiently long time, the adversary can "force" Alice and Bob to use all key material that they share.[1]

1.1 Contribution

In this work, we address the aforementioned issues. Besides the presented authentication methods, i.e., Wegman-Carter (mentioned in several works [8,20,34,37]) and Dilithium (considered in [36], and recently standardized by NIST as ML-DSA [30]), we additionally consider authentication via the message authentication code Chaskey [28] which has not been considered for QKD yet. In contrast to other MACs, Chaskey indeed comes with an explicit security proof against quantum adversaries [2], while it does not constantly consume one-time-pad keys, making it more interesting in the context of QKD.

We provide practical results for the three different authentication approaches recorded on the field-tested QKD network presented in [13]. Hereby, we demonstrate the operability of the authentication schemes in a real QKD system, investigating runtimes and key consumptions. While several QKD field tests mention the utilized authentication variant, the exact choice of parameters tends to get very little attention in most present works. Here, we take a detailed look into parameter choices, especially for the Wegman-Carter scheme, making impacts of the choice of security parameter and size of classical channel communication clear. Furthermore, we showcase that our implementations can handle the amount of data to be authenticated in the system without delaying the QKD operation.

Going further, we propose a combination of the three different authentication methods, Wegman-Carter, Dilithium, and Chaskey, to obtain their advantages while simultaneously avoiding many of their respective disadvantages. The initial QKD round (i.e., during the first key exchange) will be authenticated using Dilithium. From then on, authentication will be done by Wegman-Carter and Chaskey: The former is the default option, while the latter is used in case the key material for Wegman-Carter is depleted—for instance, due to a DoS attack—or in low QKD key rate scenarios where authentication would consume most of the newly generated key.

One advantage of our approach compared to [36] is that lattice assumptions are only required to hold for the very first round. Also, by ensuring that Alice and Bob always have a key for Chaskey as a backup, we limit the vulnerability to DoS attacks implied by a Wegman-Carter-only authentication approach, such as [17]. This, however, comes at the cost of assuming a random permutation used to instantiate Chaskey. Compared to lattice assumptions (or more generally post-quantum hardness assumptions), this is less critical as one can simply replace permutations if they turn out to be insufficient or their security becomes doubtful.

---

[1] Strictly speaking, Alice and Bob could refrain from using the system but they will not be able to determine a priori if an attempted QKD session will be successful or fail due to an eavesdropping adversary.

1.2 Related Work

The problem of authenticated QKD post-processing is far from being new. The first works that mention the need for an incorruptible public channel can be traced back as far as 1992, by Bennett et al. [4], where it was immediately suggested that Wegman-Carter [37] was a promising candidate to solve this issue.

Using Wegman-Carter or other Information-Theoretic secure (ITS) message authentication codes [1,18] indeed perfectly fits in with the goal of achieving unconditionally secure key exchange thanks to QKD. As such, Wegman-Carter remained the default go-to authentication method for QKD for numerous years. This method, however, uses a significant portion of the QKD key across its execution. In some high-loss, hence low-key-rate scenarios [22], this could cause no QKD key to be produced at all. Thus, many papers are working on optimising the key rate/key consumption ratio. While some of those works aimed to improve this ratio and retain the information theoretical security of the authentication (and thus of the QKD protocol) [17,25], we also saw the appearance of new protocols trading the ITS property for better performances [7,32].

Lately, more researchers voiced their concerns about ITS MACs' performances on key consumption and bootstrapping of QKD networks [19,41]. While many researchers still consider ITS to be the core property of interest of QKD [25], those concerns lead to significant works studying the incorporation of non-ITS MACs and post-quantum cryptography to QKD authentication [7,35,36]. A common argument to those works, to which we also stand by in this paper, is that the core property of interest of QKD is the unconditional forward-secrecy it provides (i.e., secrecy of the unused QKD key persists in time, independently of the evolution of Eve's computational power—also called everlasting security [7]), as long as we can provably authenticate the post-processing at a given time t.

While we, in this work, exclusively focus on classical authentication methods, it is important to note that some purely quantum-based authentication methods have been developed (quantum identity authentication [11]). Another authentication variant that maintains ITS properties are physically unclonable functions (PUFs) [31]. However, they require an addition to the physical setup and pre-sharing of a database (essentially containing the challenge-response pairs of the PUFs). While it may be interesting to compare their performances with classical techniques, this is out of scope for this paper.

1.3 Structure of This Work

The rest of this work is structured as follows. First, we introduce preliminaries in Sect. 2 on the QKD system used for testing and on the principles of Wegman-Carter, Dilithium and Chaskey authentication schemes. Section 3 contains the field test of the authentication schemes on the QKD system, including preparations and results. Section 4 concludes this work with the proposal of a combined protocol which is more resilient to DoS attacks on QKD systems.

2 Preliminaries

To implement a QKD system, a quantum channel and a classical channel are required [15,40]. The purpose of the quantum channel is to serve as a distribution platform for the quantum states between the two involved parties that want to exchange a symmetric key. For the quantum channel, photons are usually distributed via glass fiber or free-space optical links (e.g., satellite-to-ground QKD) [15,21,24] and are encoded in two non-orthogonal bases to leverage the no-cloning theorem of quantum mechanics. There are many different protocols to implement the quantum channel for QKD.

The QKD setup [13] we use across this paper implements an entanglement-based variant of the BBM92 protocol. Here, a central photon pair source distributes photon pairs to Alice and Bob, who both act as receivers. The source does not yield information on the secret key [6] and thus can be considered untrusted (i.e., controlled by the adversary). The exact implementation of the quantum channel and protocol is beyond the scope of this work. For a more detailed explanation, we refer the interested reader to [13].

The classical channel is an authenticated communication channel that serves as a data carrier for all information that Alice and Bob have to exchange during the protocol to extract a shared secret key from the quantum states [40]. Therefore, Alice and Bob perform the so-called post-processing phase of the protocol, which consists of several individual steps, including key sifting, error correction, error verification, and privacy amplification [40]. These post-processing steps are required to ensure that the resulting keys are indeed correct (identical) and secure (that means Eve's information on the shared key is minimized).

Notably, the authentication of this channel is necessary to prevent man-in-the-middle attacks on the QKD systems. However, the channel can be public, so no encryption is required.

In the QKD setup used for this work, Alice and Bob start with a calibration phase of the experimental setup to minimize errors on the quantum channel. Following that, they proceed with the actual key exchange by sending and measuring the quantum states via the quantum channel. For each QKD round, Alice and Bob record data for 90 s and afterwards immediately start evaluation (post-processing) of the recorded round, while at the same time, data acquisition for the next round is started. The post-processing via the classical channel employs the following steps:

The measured quantum states have bit values (0 and 1) assigned. Both parties now have individual bit arrays of 0's and 1's, which are referred to as raw keys. Upon completion of this process, key sifting takes place. Therefore, Alice and Bob bilaterally announce the bases they measured in but not the measurement outcome. They neglect all events where the bases did not match or only one party recorded an event. Consequently, they obtain a sifted key of the same length n.

However, Alice's and Bob's keys can still differ for a number of bits e, either due to imperfections of the measurement setup or the presence of an eavesdropper, Eve, attacking the quantum channel, for instance, intercepting and resending information on the quantum channel. The quantum bit error rate (QBER) q for a key is therefore defined as $q = \frac{e}{n}$. The errors on the remaining sifted key bits are corrected through classical error correction algorithms, i.e., low-density parity-check codes (LDPC) [12], or, for our demonstration, Cascade [27], which iteratively computes, sends, and compares block-wise parities of the key between Alice and Bob. Upon completion of the error correction, a key verification takes place to confirm whether Alice and Bob successfully generated an identical key.

As the final post-processing step, privacy amplification takes place. Hereby, both parties account for leaked information (e.g., through QBER, information published during post-processing) and shorten the error-corrected key by means of a two-universal hash function such that Eve's information on the key is minimized. As a result, Alice and Bob obtain a secure key whose length is shorter than the error-corrected key.

For communication during post-processing, a reliable authentication method must be implemented. Each of the listed steps requires the sending and receiving of messages of varying sizes, which can influence the parameters for authentication, as discussed in Sect. 3.1. Thus, it is especially important to customize authentication to the underlying QKD system.

Candidates to solve the authentication problem in QKD's post-processing can be found in both asymmetric (signature schemes) and symmetric (MAC) cryptography. Of the three primitives we consider in this paper, the first one, Dilithium [26] is a post-quantum signature scheme that thus requires a public-key infrastructure (PKI). While this means it does not achieve information-theoretic security, it does allow for starting a QKD session without any a priori shared secret. The two other schemes we consider, Wegman-Carter [17,37] and Chaskey [28], are MACs and thus use a fraction of the QKD key for authentication. The main difference between those two symmetric schemes lies in their security level (information-theoretic security vs. post-quantum security) and their key consumption. Indeed, as will be pointed out in Sect. 3.1, the one-time key approach of Wegman-Carter consumes significantly more key material than Chaskey.

In the following Sects. 2.1, 2.2, and 2.3, we revisit the basics of each of the three authentication variants.

2.1 Wegman-Carter

Wegman-Carter [37] is an information-theoretically secure MAC and is commonly suggested for the authentication of QKD systems [17]. In 1981, Wegman and Carter [37] indeed showed how to obtain information-theoretically secure MACs from strongly-universal$_2$ hash functions. That is, hash functions belonging to a set of functions H from M(essages) to T(ags) which have the following property: for any $m_1, m_2 \in M$ with $m_1 \neq m_2$ and any $t_1, t_2 \in T$, there are $\frac{|H|}{|T|^2}$ functions in H which map m_i to t_i (for $i \in \{1,2\}$). In particular, given sets M' and T' of messages and tags of respective sizes $s_{m'}$ and $s_{t'}$, the MAC will map block sizes of $2s$ to strings of size s, with $s = s_{t'} + \log_2 \log_2(s_{m'})$. To do so, a sequence $f_1, \ldots, f_n$ (for $n = \log_2 s_{m'} - \log_2 s_{t'}$) is selected from H such that all $f_x(m)$ are equal for a given $m \in M$. The tag t' for a given message m' is then computed as follows: m' is split in chunks of sizes s on which f_1 is applied before concatenating the results, which is processed similarly using f_2, etc. After applying f_n remains a final string of size s, of which the $s_{t'}$ lowest bits are used as final tag. The key size needed to create a MAC for a $2sn$ bits long message is then of $4s \log_2(m')$ bits, which they claim is close to optimal [17].

While we refer to it as Wegman-Carter, the exact Protocol studied in this paper is based on the work by Kiktenko et al. [17], where they proposed modifications to the trivial use of Wegman-Carter to limit key consumptions when authenticating QKD rounds (cf. performances in Sect. 3.1). Their new protocol involves two main changes. First, building on an idea already sketched in the original paper [37], they use a combination of XOR operations and hash functions in order to reuse part of the key without sacrificing the security of the scheme. Then, they update the message flow to a delayed authentication scheme, so that only one message needs to get authenticated per round per direction. Additionally, based on this delayed authentication scheme, they implement a "Ping Pong" scheme, such that only one direction is authenticated per round and each way is authenticated in alternating rounds. This method halves the key consumption. However, we did not implement this latter optimisation, due to the structure of the QKD test system, and only mention it here for the sake of completeness.

The fact that Wegman-Carter does not rely on hardness assumptions, thus achieving information-theoretic security, is the biggest incentive to use it for QKD round authentication. However, while it perfectly fits within the chase for unconditional security of QKD protocols, this property does come with serious drawbacks. In particular, it cannot be used if Alice and Bob do not already possess some shared secret. In QKD networks consisting of more than two nodes, this would lead to a dramatic increase in the number of key pairs needed when adding a new party. This can be solved by using trusted relays, such as to perform the key exchange in a party-to-relay manner [14]. A downside of this approach is that all communication going through a relay can potentially be decrypted by it, which introduces quite a serious single point of failure. While the first issue is typically solved by factory pre-shared keys, this still leaves the door open for serious consequences in the case of denial-of-service attacks that would consume the preshared key. Indeed, exclusively using Wegman-Carter (and more generally any symmetric cryptographic scheme) does not offer any solution to exchange a key from nothing. Thus, this would force us to exchange a new secret out-of-band, which is rather impractical.

2.2 Dilithium

Dilithium [26] is a lattice-based signature scheme that was recently standardized by NIST as ML-DSA [30]. The scheme follows the Fiat-Shamir with aborts framework and its security is based on the learning with errors problem; we depict it in Algorithm 1.

Algorithm 1. Template for the Dilithium signature scheme from [26, Figure 1]

Gen(1^λ)
1: $\mathbf{A} \leftarrow R_q^{k \times l}$
2: $(\mathbf{s}_1, \mathbf{s}_2) \leftarrow S_n^l \times S_n^k$
3: $\mathbf{t} := \mathbf{A}\mathbf{s}_1 + \mathbf{s}_2$
4: **return** $(pk = (\mathbf{A}, \mathbf{t}), sk = ((\mathbf{A}, \mathbf{t}), \mathbf{s}_1, \mathbf{s}_2))$

Sign(sk, M)
5: $\mathbf{z} := \bot$
6: **while** $\mathbf{z} = \bot$ **do**
7: $\quad \mathbf{y} \leftarrow S_{\gamma_1 - 1}^l$
8: $\quad \mathbf{w}_1 := \text{HighBits}(\mathbf{A}\mathbf{y}, 2\gamma_2)$
9: $\quad c \in B_\tau := H(M \| \mathbf{w}_1)$
10: $\quad \mathbf{z} := \mathbf{y} + c\mathbf{s}_1$
11: $\quad$ **if** $\|\mathbf{z}\|_\infty \geq \gamma_1 - \beta$ **or** $\|\text{LowBits}(\mathbf{A}\mathbf{y} - c\mathbf{s}_2, 2\gamma_2)\|_\infty \geq \gamma_2 - \beta$ **then**
12: $\quad\quad \mathbf{z} := \bot$
13: $\quad$ **end if**
14: **end while**
15: **return** $\sigma = (\mathbf{z}, c)$

Verify($pk, M, \sigma = (\mathbf{z}, c)$)
16: $\mathbf{w'}_1 := \text{HighBits}(\mathbf{A}\mathbf{z} - c\mathbf{t}, 2\gamma_2)$
17: **return** $[\![\|\mathbf{z}\|_\infty < \gamma_1 - \beta]\!]$ **and** $[\![c = H(M \| \mathbf{w'}_1)]\!]$

Wang et al. [36] considered Dilithium for the authentication of a QKD system, aiming at growing its short-term[2] post-quantum secure asymmetric keys in long-term (and arguably information-theoretically) secure QKD keys. In contrast with traditional QKD authentication methods, using a PKI eliminates the need for pre-shared symmetric keys. As a direct consequence, the previously mentioned scaling issue of Wegman-Carter is mitigated, as one only needs to store its own private key and a valid certificate in order to communicate with other nodes.

While solving the DoS issue mentioned earlier (cf. Sect. 2.1) and making it easier to work with QKD networks, using Dilithium presents a couple of drawbacks regarding performance and security. Traditionally, public-key cryptography indeed leads to higher signature sizes which, by its impact on the network, can be seen as a minor inconvenience. The security of Dilithium relies on lattice assumptions, which naturally poses two main issues. Most notably, the hardness assumption may end up being broken one day[3], which poses the issue of both finding a new suitable signature scheme and then updating the system to the new scheme, which is usually not trivial to do [16,23]. Moreover, reliance on a hardness assumption does not translate well in the context of a computation-

---

[2] We adopt this nomenclature from [36]. We stress that short-term secure keys are not to be confused with ephemeral keys.

[3] Chen [9] recently presented an efficient quantum algorithm for a lattice assumption; though it was later found to be flawed.

ally unbounded adversary, against which researchers usually try to prove QKD secure.

2.3 Chaskey

Chaskey [28] is an ISO-standardized MAC which is visualized in Fig. 1. Conceptually, Chaskey is very simple as it requires only a permutation and XOR operations.

To authenticate a message, Chaskey sets its key K as the initialisation vector for the first round of the computation's process. At round i, the message block m_i is first XORed with the input before applying Chaskey's permutation on the resulting string, and forwarding the output to the next round's input. For the last round, the last message block (padded if necessary) is XORed with the previous round's output, then XORed with a key K_j ($j \in \{1,2\}$), derived from the key K. The result is then passed through the permutation again, before being once again XORed with the same K_j, resulting in the final tag.

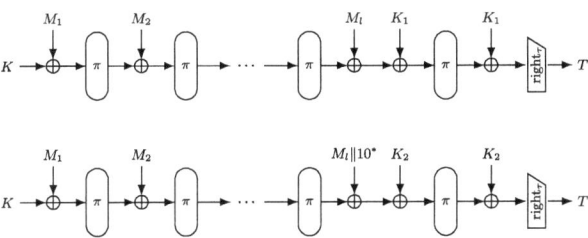

Fig. 1. Chaskey's mode of operation (taken from [28]) when $|M_l| = n$ (top), and when $0 \le |M_l| < n$ (bottom). The subkeys K_1 and K_2 are generated from the initial key K, and $M_l \| 10^*$ is shorthand for $M_l \| 10^{n-|M_l|-1}$.

Typically, Chaskey uses n-bit keys which also define the message blocks to be of length n. For $n = 128$, a key can be reused to authenticate up to 2^{48} n-bits message blocks (which, for $n = 128$, amounts to approximately 4 Petabytes of data). To prove security, Chaskey can be viewed as an instance of the (tweakable) Even-Mansour cipher, which recently resulted in an explicit security proof for Chaskey against quantum adversaries [2].

Chaskey provides an interesting middle ground between Wegman-Carter and Dilithium. Indeed, while it also belongs to symmetric cryptography and thus requires an a priori shared secret, its ability to authenticate many messages using the same key makes it practically invulnerable to DoS attacks[4]. However, Chaskey does rely on computational assumptions and therefore does not

---
[4] Strictly speaking, since there is an upper limit on how many messages can be authenticated with one key, an attacker against a QKD system could mount a DoS attack but due to the upper limit, it seems unrealistic that such an attack would succeed in practice.

achieve information-theoretic security. Its security indeed relies on the hardness assumption that its underlying permutation is indistinguishable from a truly random permutation. While an efficient algorithm for lattice problems would have a devastating effect by breaking all lattice-based cryptographic primitives, one can always replace a broken permutation of Chaskey (or one for which security seems doubtful). Another advantage of Chaskey over Dilithium follows from the inherent differences between symmetric and asymmetric cryptography. Indeed, because we can use Chaskey together with a QKD (thus long-term, information-theoretically secure) key, we do not have to worry about offline attacks as long as we never used the key beforehand. This implies a key can be stored for an indefinite amount of time until we need to use it without compromising the protocol's security. However, the key still needs to be stored securely.

3 Field-Test in a Live QKD-System

In the following, we elaborate on the implication of each scheme's properties in the context of a real-world QKD system, briefly discuss the difference in criticality between the hardness assumption used for Dilithium and Chaskey, and present their respective performances evaluated on the QKD network in Sects. 3.1 and 3.2.

3.1 Practical Implementation

Each of the schemes described in the previous section has been implemented and tested on the QKD infrastructure described in Sect. 2. In particular, we used Bouncy Castle's implementation of Dilithium (that was at the time following NIST's pre-standardisation recommendations), implemented Chaskey in Java according to a reference C implementation provided in [28] and implemented a new Wegman-Carter MAC in Java as well, following the variant by Kiktenko et al. [17], implementing a delayed authentication but without the ping-pong scheme.[5]

When testing, we used the parameter set for security level III for Dilithium as provided by the Bouncy Castle library, implemented 12 hashing rounds for Chaskey, as recommended by the ISO standard, and chose Wegman-Carter's parameters as per Kiktenko et al.'s work [17], that is $\epsilon = 10^{-12}$ which, together with $n = 100$ allowed reuses, yields $\epsilon_{\text{eff}} = n\epsilon = 10^{-10}$. While Dilithium does not consume QKD generated key material for later authentication rounds, and Chaskey does only require an initial key, the Wegman-Carter scheme has a regular key consumption from each newly generated QKD round. This consumption is impacted by the choice of ϵ, as the required One-Time-Pad (OTP) key length per authenticated QKD round and direction (i.e., Alice $\rightarrow$ Bob and Bob $\rightarrow$

---

[5] Note, that we did not manage to obtain Kiktenko et al.'s original implementation and thus could not thoroughly test ours with respect to the original.

Alice)[6] is given by [17]

$$\tau = \lfloor -\log_2 \epsilon \rfloor + 1 = 40 \text{ bits}. \tag{1}$$

Furthermore, the length of the recycled key L_{rec} depends on the maximum amount of data that has to be authenticated per QKD round per user μ. The recycled key is required to choose the applicable hash function. Hence, the key stays the same for several QKD rounds, before the hash function has to be refreshed to avoid disclosure and a new key is used (therefore the term recycled key). To choose an appropriate size for the recycled key, we have analyzed the data amount sent via the classical channel for a typical run of the QKD setup. The results of such a measurement are displayed in Fig. 2. Notably, most of the channel communication is caused by the exchange of measurement bases of the photon detections. We note a large difference in the total data amount sent by Alice and Bob. The reason for this is different fiber lengths (Source → Alice and Source → Bob) causing different photon losses and hence a difference in detection rates. The slowly varying drift of the total data amount sent per round per party is caused by a small change in photon production by the source and can be neglected for our analysis. The first few rounds (in the presented measurement it is six rounds) serve for calibration of the setup. These calibration rounds serve for timing synchronization[7] and to adjust the measurement devices such that in subsequent QKD rounds a low QBER can be achieved.[8] Therefore, data recorded during these rounds does not produce any secure key and hence, does not need to be authenticated. To extend on this argument, we discuss what happens, if Eve interferes with the system during the unauthenticated calibration rounds. Then, manipulation of the estimated QBER or timing offsets could occur, leading to an uncalibrated setup. However, if Alice and Bob proceed with the authenticated rounds to generate secure keys, while the setup is falsely calibrated, they will notice an increased QBER and therefore abort key generation and repeat the calibration. Hence, the worst-case scenario of Eve interfering during the unauthenticated calibration rounds would be a Denial-of-Service attack, which could be achieved by Eve anytime anyway, even during authenticated rounds. Therefore, not authenticating the calibration rounds saves QKD key consumption but does not reduce the security of the QKD protocol. For clarity, we do not display these calibration rounds in later figures. Note that the data amount sent each round can vary drastically in other QKD setups or when choosing different fiber lengths for the quantum channel. The results are also of importance for the use of Chaskey, as the expected data amount of one 90 s QKD round is much smaller

---

[6] Note, that both directions of communication have to be authenticated independently. Hence, two OTP keys are required per QKD round.

[7] Alice and Bob are required to estimate their timing offsets for detections such that they can compare corresponding events.

[8] In the setup used here, the temperature of an interferometer placed at each receiver's site has to be adjusted. The requirement of this process arises from a two-photon Franson interference and therefore is beyond the scope of this work. It is explained in more detail in [13].

than the maximum data size of ≈ 4 PiB. Hence, a very large number of QKD sessions will be possible with one key for Chaskey.

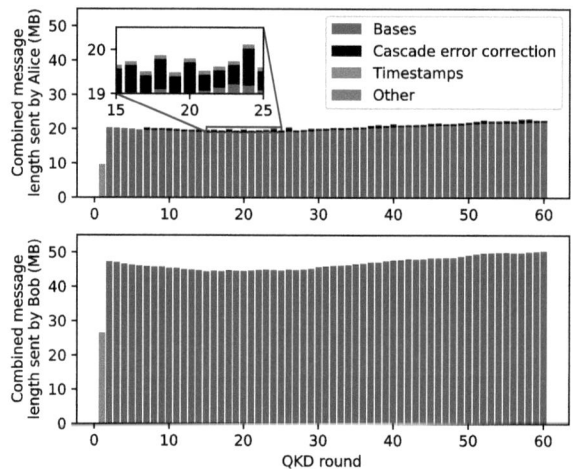

Fig. 2. Message sizes per QKD round via the classical channel between the two parties during key exchange. The first six rounds are for calibration of the setup (not authenticated). At round seven, the secure key generation starts. Most of the channel communication is caused by the basis exchange of the QKD measurements, a small amount by error-correction and a negligible amount by other communication. Alice and Bob sent different amounts of data as their respective photon detection rates differ.

Following [17] for a typical data amount of 50 MB in the setup, we have to choose the length of the recycled key by

$$L_{\text{rec}} = 2\lambda\omega + \lambda + \tau + 1 = 417 \text{ bits}, \qquad (2)$$

with $\omega = 31$ and λ being the smallest integer that fulfills

$$\left\lceil \frac{\mu}{\omega} \right\rceil^{\lambda} 2^{-\lambda\omega} \leq \epsilon - 2^{-\tau}. \qquad (3)$$

From the definition of the OTP and recycled key lengths, we can calculate an average total key consumption per QKD round. As the recycled key has to be renewed after $n = 100$ uses, and both directions of communication between the two parties have to be authenticated, we get an average key consumption per QKD round c of

$$c = 2L_{\text{OTP}} + 2\frac{L_{\text{rec}}}{n} \approx 88 \text{ bits per QKD round} \qquad (4)$$

for the used QKD setup when using the lightweight authentication scheme by Kiktenko et al. but without the ping-pong procedure. As one QKD round of the used setup takes 90 s, we obtain a key consumption of roughly 1 bit/s for $\epsilon = 10^{-12}$ and $\epsilon_{\text{eff}} = 10^{-10}$. The key consumption when using schemes based on the ideas of Wegman-Carter has to be considered for all QKD setups as it shrinks the effective rate a QKD system produces. This is especially important in high-loss and low-key-rate scenarios, as the authentication then consumes large chunks of the QKD keys. Hence, it is of particular interest to minimize the key consumption for a desired effective security parameter. Therefore, it might be desirable to change the length of the OTP key together with the recycled key and the number of rounds ($u = n/2$) it is reused. Therefore, we calculated $\epsilon = \epsilon_{\text{eff}}/n$ and subsequently the OTP and recycled key lengths following Eqs. (1) and (2). The results are depicted in Fig. 3a, with our current implementation marked. While a small number of QKD rounds before refreshing of the recycled key drastically increases the key consumption, there is only a small change in key consumption for more than 100 QKD rounds. We note that for our effective security parameter of 10^{-10}, a value of $u = 99$ would be optimal. However, we opted against changing the parameters of our authentication, as the improvement would be marginal and for practical reasons when testing the QKD system.

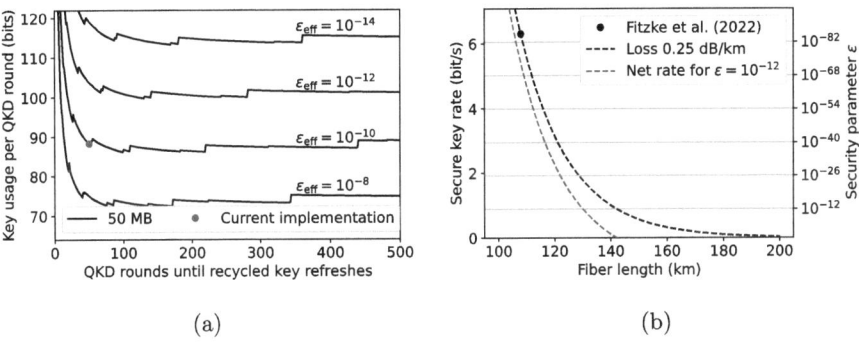

Fig. 3. (a) Total key consumption (recycled key + OTP key for both communication directions) for authentication with Wegman-Carter for various effective security parameters $\epsilon_{\text{eff}} = 2u\epsilon$, with u being the number of QKD rounds a recycled key remains valid. We assumed a maximum data amount of 50 MB per round to be authenticated per direction (Alice $\rightarrow$ Bob, Bob $\rightarrow$ Alice). (b) Secure key rate for various fiber lengths (black line), extrapolated from a previous QKD measurement via 108 km of fiber [13]. The right-hand side axis shows the maximum security parameter ϵ if the total generated key is used for authentication. In practice, one should choose the parameter such that a significant amount of QKD key is left for actual encryption. The red line shows the net key rate (=generated key minus authentication key) for an $\epsilon = 10^{-12}$.

In Fig. 3b we made an exemplary calculation based on a QKD test over 108 km fiber published in [13]. The plot extrapolates how the key rate varies when changing the fiber length by simply assuming a typical fiber loss of 0.25 dB/km[9]. On the right axis, we plotted the maximum security parameter ϵ that one could choose such that the complete secure key produced in a QKD round is consumed by the OTP keys for authentication. For a fixed $\epsilon = 10^{-12}$ we plotted the net key rate (difference between secure rate and OTP consumption for authentication). Clearly, in low key rate regimes, the key consumption for authentication drastically impacts the resulting key rate of the QKD system. Furthermore, this limits either the achievable quantum channel transmission distance or the choosable security parameter for authentication, thus impacting the practicality of such setups in real-world scenarios. Systems like the long-distance QKD experiment over 1000 km fiber [22] achieved a key rate for this distance of just 0.0034 bits per second, leaving basically no key for authentication via information-theoretically secure MACs. Hence, it is of interest to consider other options for authentication, such as Chaskey.

Table 1. Comparison of runtimes for generation of the authentication tag (Auth. time) and its verification (Verif. time) of the various algorithms. The test was run on an Intel i5-12400 with 64 GB RAM, Windows 10 Pro 22H2.

Algorithm	Data size (10^6 Bytes)	Auth. time (ms)	Verif. time (ms)
Dilithium-3 [26]	10	30	28
	25	69	69
	50	139	136
	100	280	274
	150	434	422
Chaskey-12 [28]	10	16	16
	25	40	40
	50	80	80
	100	160	160
	150	242	242
Wegman-Carter [17]	10	59	60
	25	149	152
	50	301	299
	100	598	601
	150	899	899

The runtime of an authentication scheme should be short to not delay the protocol execution and key generation. However, to this extent, it is not necessary

---

[9] For the sake of simplicity, we waived the impact of detector dark count rates on the key rate. Also note that in other regimes like short distances or high-detection rates, detector saturation effects have to be taken into account when calculating the key length.

to optimize for a few milliseconds of additional speed. For all three schemes (Dilithium, Wegman-Carter, Chaskey) we measured the times to compute the authentication tag and verify this tag for various amounts of arbitrary data. All show fairly similar capabilities and a linear time complexity with respect to the input data (cf. Table 1), with a slight edge to Chaskey in terms of overall speed.

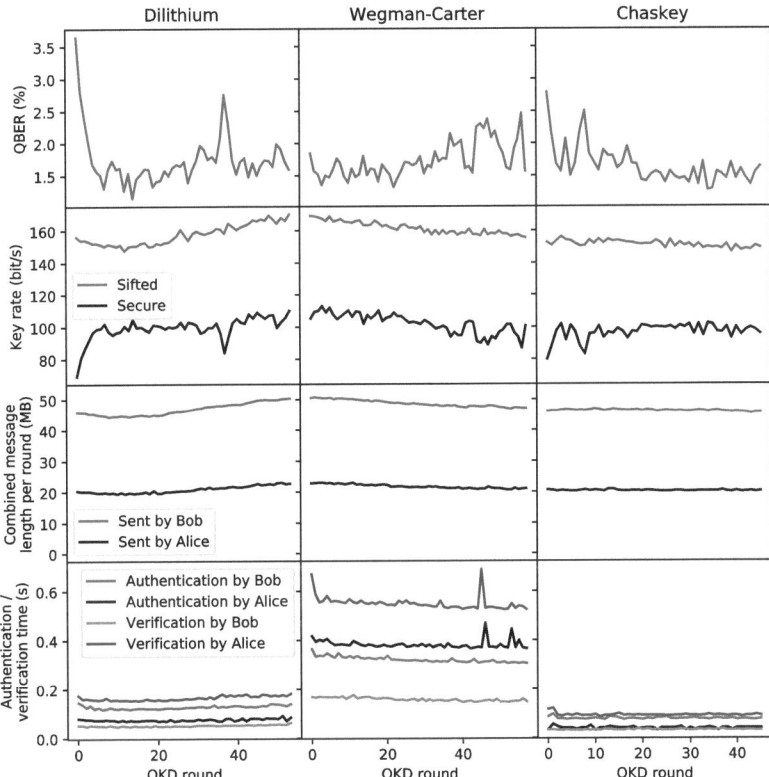

Fig. 4. Demonstration runs of the authentication algorithms on the live QKD-system. The calibration phases of the system before each measurement are not displayed here. QBER (quantum bit error rate) and key rates vary due to experimental reasons unrelated to the authentication. All QKD rounds were completed successfully without failing the authentication regardless of the used algorithms. The runtime advantage of Chaskey is clearly visible.

3.2 Results

All three authentication methods have been tested in the QKD setup [13] with approximately 26 km of glass fiber for the quantum channel between Alice and Bob. If the algorithm requires a symmetric key at the beginning of the protocol

(Chaskey and Wegman-Carter) it is taken from the key database of the system from an earlier QKD run. For Wegman-Carter, subsequent rounds repeatedly pull keys from earlier QKD rounds for the OTP key and renew the recycled key if necessary. For Dilithium no symmetric key from the key storage is required, however, we exchange the public keys of the involved parties before the actual QKD takes place. In particular, the results plotted in Fig. 4 have been obtained by executing the QKD system for 60 rounds. The results do not display the rounds required for calibration as they are not authenticated and thus are of no interest for this work. All three implementations have been tested successfully, i.e., every QKD round that generated secure keys has been authenticated successfully. The variation of sifted key rates and QBERs, and consequently also secure key rates during the measurements, are caused by variations of the physical measurement setup (i.e., temperature fluctuations, drifting photon pair production rates at the source) and is thus independent of the software and authentication schemes in place. In fact, every measurement produced sifted key rates, averaging at roughly 150 bits/s and secure key rates of approximately 100 bits/s. For Wegman-Carter we have to deduct approximately 1 bit/s from the secure key rate as cost for authentication. The key consumption of Chaskey is negligible when conducting QKD over several rounds and maintaining the initial key, while Dilithium does not require a QKD key at all for authentication. The data size to be authenticated per QKD round was similar for all three runs. While Bob sent data of close to 50 MB per round, Alice sent approximately 20 MB. This is reflected in the authentication time of Bob being longer than authentication for Alice, and verification for Alice being longer than verification for Bob. However, in the used QKD system a delay much smaller than 1 s is still sufficiently short to not stop the QKD key generation with its blocks of 90 s. Nevertheless, as predicted by the runtime benchmark, we observe Chaskey to be the fastest algorithm. This property can make Chaskey an interesting option for QKD systems that have higher demands in terms of authentication speed such as high-key-rate systems.

In summary, we successfully tested three different means of authentication in a real QKD setup. While all variants proved to be sufficiently fast in the system, and are thus all suitable solutions for authentication, they all present different advantages. The biggest advantage of Wegman-Carter is its information-theoretic security, which comes with a few disadvantages, however. A minor downside is a small amount of secure key consumption ($\approx 1\%$), while the bigger downsides are the necessity of initial shared keys and its vulnerability to DoS attacks. Dilithium offers post-quantum secure authentication via public-key infrastructures, thus not requiring the QKD keys for authentication. The obvious downside is the potential vulnerability due to advances in cryptanalysis against lattices. Chaskey as a new solution for QKD's authentication has been successfully tested, offering negligible key consumption, easy-to-use implementation and fast computation times, making it a serious candidate for tailored QKD scenarios such as high-rate systems or high-loss links. It essentially avoids the downside of DoS attacks that Wegman-Carter has at the cost of giving up information-theoretic security, nevertheless maintaining the long-term security of the QKD key.

4 Combined Authentication Methods

While the performance of each scheme presented herein makes them all suitable for authenticating QKD rounds, they all come with their share of drawbacks. Their respective strengths and weaknesses, however, do seem to be complementary, drawing a picture for an efficient authentication protocol that would leverage all three schemes studied in this work. In the following sections, we sketch a new authentication protocol that uses Dilithium, Wegman-Carter, and Chaskey to compensate for each other's weaknesses and attain a satisfactory practicality-security trade-off. We then briefly study the proposed solution's security in the classical authenticated key-exchange framework, showing it retains unconditional forward secrecy.

4.1 Protocol Idea

The first step when creating a QKD network from scratch (or adding new nodes to the network) is the initial bootstrapping, meaning the establishment of an initial shared secret between the new node(s) and the already existing members of the network. As mentioned in Sect. 2.1, this is typically done through a combination of factory keys and trusted relays, which introduces a rather unsatisfactory single point of failure in the system. Instead of fully replacing Wegman-Carter by Dilithium, as done in [36], a natural idea would be to use Dilithium exclusively for the initial bootstrapping, such as to compensate for Wegman-Carter's need for pre-shared keys. This shifts the trust to the underlying public-key infrastructure. While this does threaten the effective information-theoretic security of the scheme, we can play on the validity duration of emitted certificates to obtain a satisfyingly low adversarial success rate, such as not compromising the QKD key's practical security.

When two parties communicate for the first time across the network, they would thus use the signature scheme (i.e., Dilithium) to authenticate the first QKD round, so they can extract a first symmetric key. From this point on, we rejoin the traditional QKD authentication method [17], i.e., every subsequent authentication is performed exclusively using this symmetric key (and those derived from it through a QKD execution), such as using the PKI as little as possible. Ideally, those symmetric keys should be used together with Wegman-Carter (cf. Sect. 2.1), eliminating all concerns related to a potential break of some underlying computationally hard problem as is the case with PKI.

A persisting problem of only using Dilithum and Wegman-Carter, however, are DoS attacks. By performing such an attack, an adversary can make Alice and Bob use up the entire shared key from their storage—effectively taking them back to round one, where they would need to, again, rely on Dilithium to establish a shared key. To mitigate this issue, we introduce the additional use of Chaskey in the protocol. We impose the first QKD session to exchange not only a key for Wegman-Carter but also one for Chaskey. This additional secret is safely stored as long as the protocol succeeds using Wegman-Carter. In case the Wegman-Carter key gets fully used up, rather than using Dilithium, one would use the stored Chaskey key instead. As stated in Sect. 2.3, Chaskey's key consumption is negligible, and any DoS attack aiming at using up its key would thus most likely fail, thus mitigating the chances that we would ever need to fall back to public-key cryptography. Switching back to Wegman-Carter authentication, once the QKD key storage is sufficiently filled up again, avoids relying on Chaskey's security for the remaining time.

4.2 Security

Considering a computationally bounded adversary, we write ϵ_{QKD}, as the advantage of the adversary in guessing the key information exchanged in a QKD round, and ϵ_{WC}, ϵ_{C}, and ϵ_{D}, its advantage in breaking Wegman-Carter with key recycling [17, Definition 2], Chaskey [2, Thererom 7] and Dilithium [3], respectively. The final security parameter of any QKD protocol authenticated according to the proposed scheme can be upper bounded as per Eq. (5) [29].

$$\epsilon_{\text{full}} \leq \epsilon_{\text{env}} + N_{\text{WC}}(\epsilon_{\text{QKD}} + 2\epsilon_{\text{WC}}) + \delta_{\text{C}}(N_{\text{C}}\epsilon_{\text{QKD}} + \epsilon_{\text{C}}) \qquad (5)$$

where $N = N_{\text{C}} + N_{\text{WC}}$ the total number of QKD rounds, with N_{C} (N_{WC}) the number of QKD rounds authenticated through Chaskey (Wegman-Carter); $\delta_{\text{C}} = 1$, if $N_{\text{C}} \neq 0$, and 0 otherwise. $\epsilon_{\text{env}} = \epsilon_{\text{D}} + \epsilon_{\text{Store}}$ encompasses the security of the key used in the first round, where ϵ_{Store} is the security parameter of its storage as meant in [17, Appendix B].

In particular, ϵ_{C} and ϵ_{D} only appear once (independently of how many rounds Chaskey and Dilithium authenticate) because their respective security bounds are computed on the whole lifespan of their key. In Chaskey's case, given a 128-bit key, it means the bound holds for the authentication of up to 2^{48} bits (cf. Sect. 2.3), which is well above the communication required for thousands of QKD rounds (cf. Sect. 3.1). If the limit of 2^{48} bits is reached, another instance of Chaskey would be required. In Wegman-Carter's case, the advantage is refreshed with each new tag. That is, it is refreshed each time we authenticate a message with it [17]. Because we have two authentications per round, it thus amounts to $2N_{\text{WC}} \cdot \epsilon_{\text{WC}}$ in the final bound.

Notice that, because we consider a computationally bounded adversary, we cannot claim information theoretic security anymore. However, as QKD authentication only needs to be secure at the time of the protocol's execution, forward secrecy is ensured with respect to any adversary.

A Data Availability

Our results build upon an existing QKD setup. The code to run the QKD setup is not part of this work and we can therefore not provide it. We can and will provide the data and code related to the authentication variants we present in this paper and the data extracted from the presented QKD measurements. Since this data is very large (many gigabytes per measurement), it is available upon request.

References

1. Abidin, A., Larsson, J.Å.: New universal hash functions. In: Armknecht, F., Lucks, S. (eds.) WEWoRC 2011. LNCS, vol. 7242, pp. 99–108. Springer, Heidelberg (2012). https://doi.org/10.1007/978-3-642-34159-5_7
2. Alagic, G., Bai, C., Katz, J., Majenz, C., Struck, P.: Post-quantum security of tweakable even-mansour, and applications. In: Joye, M., Leander, G. (eds.) Advances in Cryptology – EUROCRYPT 2024, pp. 310–338. Springer, Cham (2024)
3. Barbosa, M., et al.: Fixing and mechanizing the security proof of Fiat-Shamir with aborts and dilithium. Cryptology ePrint Archive, Paper 2023/246 (2023)
4. Bennett, C.H., Bessette, F., Brassard, G., Salvail, L., Smolin, J.: Experimental quantum cryptography. J. Cryptol. **5**(1), 3–28 (1992)
5. Bennett, C.H., Brassard, G.: Quantum cryptography: public key distribution and coin tossing. Theoret. Comput. Sci. **560**, 7–11 (2014). Theoretical Aspects of Quantum Cryptography – celebrating 30 years of BB84
6. Bennett, C.H., Brassard, G., Mermin, N.D.: Quantum cryptography without Bell's theorem. Phys. Rev. Lett. **68**(5), 557 (1992)
7. Bibak, K., Ritchie, R.: Quantum key distribution with PRF(hash, nonce) achieves everlasting security. Quantum Inf. Process. **20**(7), 228 (2021)
8. Chapuran, T.E., et al.: Optical networking for quantum key distribution and quantum communications. New J. Phys. **11**(10), 105001 (2009)
9. Chen, Y.: Quantum algorithms for lattice problems. Cryptology ePrint Archive, Paper 2024/555 (2024). https://eprint.iacr.org/2024/555
10. Diffie, W., Hellman, M.E.: New directions in cryptography. IEEE Trans. Inf. Theory **22**(6), 644–654 (1976)
11. Dutta, A., Pathak, A.: A short review on quantum identity authentication protocols: how would bob know that he is talking with Alice? (2021)
12. Elkouss, D., Leverrier, A., Alléaume, R., Boutros, J.J.: Efficient reconciliation protocol for discrete-variable quantum key distribution. In: 2009 IEEE International Symposium on Information Theory, pp. 1879–1883. IEEE (2009)
13. Fitzke, E., et al.: Scalable network for simultaneous pairwise quantum key distribution via entanglement-based time-bin coding. PRX Quant. **3**(2), 020341 (2022)
14. Fröhlich, B., Dynes, J.F., Lucamarini, M., Sharpe, A.W., Yuan, Z., Shields, A.J.: A quantum access network. Nature **501**(7465), 69–72 (2013)
15. Gisin, N., Ribordy, G., Tittel, W., Zbinden, H.: Quantum cryptography. Rev. Modern Phys. **74**(1), 145 (2002)
16. Holz, R., et al.: Tracking the deployment of TLS 1.3 on the web: a story of experimentation and centralization. SIGCOMM Comput. Commun. Rev. **50**(3), 3–15 (2020)
17. Kiktenko, E.O., et al.: Lightweight authentication for quantum key distribution. IEEE Trans. Inf. Theory **66**(10), 6354–6368 (2020)
18. Krawczyk, H.: LFSR-based hashing and authentication. In: Desmedt, Y.G. (ed.) CRYPTO 1994. LNCS, vol. 839, pp. 129–139. Springer, Heidelberg (1994). https://doi.org/10.1007/3-540-48658-5_15

19. Kunz-Jacques, S., Jouguet, P.: Using hash-based signatures to bootstrap quantum key distribution. *CoRR*, abs/1109.2844 (2011)
20. Li, Q., Zhao, Q., Le, D., Niu, X.: Study on the security of the authentication scheme with key recycling in QKD. Quantum Inf. Process. **15**, 3815–3831 (2016)
21. Liao, S.-K., et al.: Satellite-to-ground quantum key distribution. Nature **549**(7670), 43–47 (2017)
22. Liu, Y., et al.: Experimental twin-field quantum key distribution over 1000 km fiber distance. Phys. Rev. Lett. **130**(21), 210801 (2023)
23. Loebenberger, D., Gazdag, S.-L., Herzinger, D., Hirsch, E., Näther, C.: Formalizing the cryptographic migration problem. *CoRR*, abs/2408.05997 (2024)
24. Lucamarini, M., Yuan, Z.L., Dynes, J.F., Shields, A.J.: Overcoming the rate-distance limit of quantum key distribution without quantum repeaters. Nature **557**(7705), 400–403 (2018)
25. Luo, Y., Mao, H.-K., Li, Q., Chen, N.: An information-theoretic secure group authentication scheme for quantum key distribution networks. IEEE Trans. Commun. **71**(9), 5420–5431 (2023)
26. Lyubashevsky, V., et al.: CRYSTALS-DILITHIUM. Technical report, National Institute of Standards and Technology (2020). https://csrc.nist.gov/projects/post-quantum-cryptography/post-quantum-cryptography-standardization/round-3-submissions
27. Martinez-Mateo, J., Pacher, C., Peev, M., Ciurana, A., Martin, V.: Demystifying the information reconciliation protocol cascade. Quant. Inf. Comput., 453–477 (2015)
28. Mouha, N., Mennink, B., Van Herrewege, A., Watanabe, D., Preneel, B., Verbauwhede, I.: Chaskey: an efficient MAC algorithm for 32-bit microcontrollers. In: Joux, A., Youssef, A. (eds.) SAC 2014. LNCS, vol. 8781, pp. 306–323. Springer, Cham (2014). https://doi.org/10.1007/978-3-319-13051-4_19
29. Mueller-Quade, J., Renner, R.: Composability in quantum cryptography. New J. Phys. **11**(8), 085006 (2009). arXiv:1006.2215 [quant-ph]
30. National Institute of Standards and Technology: Module-lattice-based digital signature standard. Federal Information Processing Standards Publication NIST FIPS 204, Department of Commerce, Washington, D.C. (2024)
31. Nikolopoulos, G.M., Fischlin, M.: Quantum key distribution with post-processing driven by physical unclonable functions. Appl. Sci. **14**(1), 464 (2024)
32. Peev, M., et al.: A novel protocol-authentication algorithm ruling out a man-in-the-middle attack in quantum cryptography (2004)
33. Shor, P.W.: Algorithms for quantum computation: discrete logarithms and factoring. In: Proceedings 35th Annual Symposium on Foundations of Computer Science, pp. 124–134. IEEE (1994)
34. Tajima, A., et al.: Quantum key distribution network for multiple applications. Quant. Sci. Technol. **2**(3), 034003 (2017)
35. Termos, H.: Quantum authentication evolution: novel approaches for securing quantum key distribution. Entropy **26**(6) (2024)
36. Wang, L.-J., et al.: Experimental authentication of quantum key distribution with post-quantum cryptography. npj Quant. Inf. **7**(1), 67 (2021)
37. Wegman, M.N., Carter, J.L.: New hash functions and their use in authentication and set equality. J. Comput. Syst. Sci. **22**(3), 265–279 (1981)
38. Wootters, W.K., Zurek, W.H.: A single quantum cannot be cloned. Nature **299**(5886), 802–803 (1982)
39. Wootters, W.K., Zurek, W.H.: The no-cloning theorem. Phys. Today **62**(2), 76–77 (2009)

40. Feihu, X., Ma, X., Zhang, Q., Lo, H.-K., Pan, J.-W.: Secure quantum key distribution with realistic devices. Rev. Mod. Phys. **92**(2), 025002 (2020)
41. Yang, Y.-H., et al.: All optical metropolitan quantum key distribution network with post-quantum cryptography authentication. Opt. Express **29**(16), 25859–25867 (2021)

Integration of PQC and QKD: Applications, Challenges and Implementation Frameworks

Elina Kalnina(✉), Rihards Balodis, Edgars Celms, Sergejs Kozlovics, Inara Opmane, Krisjanis Petrucena, Edgars Rencis, and Juris Viksna

Institute of Mathematics and Computer Science, University of Latvia,
Raiņa bulv. 29, Riga 1459, Latvia
{elina.kalnina,rihards.balodis,edgars.celms,sergejs.kozlovics,
inara.opmane,krisjanis.petrucena,edgars.rencis,juris.viksna}@lumii.lv

Abstract. The advent of quantum computing poses a significant threat to classical cryptographic systems, necessitating the development of quantum-resistant solutions. Post-Quantum Cryptography (PQC) and Quantum Key Distribution (QKD) have emerged as complementary approaches to achieving quantum-safe communications. This paper explores the integration of PQC and QKD technologies, emphasising their potential applications, practical implementation frameworks, and the challenges associated with their deployment. We have also analysed key use cases that are compatible with our existing network equipment, such as the Centauris encryptors, Juniper devices, and Cisco routers. Through an examination of the use cases and experimental findings, this work provides valuable insights into building scalable, robust, and quantum-resistant infrastructures for long-term data security.

Keywords: PQC · QKD · quantum resistant cryptography · post-quantum cryptography · quantum cryptography

1 Introduction

The rapid advancement of quantum computing poses a significant threat to current cryptographic systems, which are heavily reliant on classical algorithms that are vulnerable to quantum attacks. To address this, two primary technologies have emerged: Post-Quantum Cryptography (PQC) and Quantum Key Distribution (QKD). While PQC aims to replace traditional cryptographic algorithms with quantum-resistant alternatives, QKD enables secure key exchange through quantum mechanics, offering theoretically unbreakable encryption when combined with one-time-pad encryption. However, both methods have distinct limitations. The resilience of PQC against future quantum computing developments remains uncertain, as there are currently no definitive security proofs confirming its complete resistance to all quantum attacks [1]. Conversely, QKD, although promising, faces practical limitations due to hardware requirements and infrastructure dependencies, which increase the costs and complexities of deployment.

"It is important to clarify that the choice between QKD and PQC is not binary. The integration of QKD with PQC can offer a hybrid solution that is based on the strengths of both technologies" [1]. It has sparked interest in a hybrid approach that combines PQC and QKD. Notably, PQC can provide essential authentication for QKD processes, safeguarding against potential man-in-the-middle attacks, which is crucial in maintaining the integrity of QKD's key exchange mechanism. By combining QKD with PQC-based authentication, it becomes possible to achieve a balance between short-term and long-term security: PQC can secure immediate authentication, while QKD enables the generation of long-term secure keys [2]. This integration ensures that even if PQC were compromised in the future, previous authentication and QKD-generated keys would remain unaffected, adding a layer of resilience to cryptographic infrastructure.

Ultimately, the integration of PQC and QKD can adapt to diverse security needs, creating a robust and flexible framework for quantum-safe communications. Although this approach requires investment in both advanced algorithms and QKD-compatible hardware, the combined security benefits make it a promising solution for environments where information integrity and confidentiality are of paramount importance.

We start with an overview of post-quantum cryptography in Sect. 2. Section 3 discusses the math problems that PQC algorithms rely on. Section 4 discusses QKD algorithms. The literature review of PQC and QKD integration examples and approaches is given in Sect. 5. We analyse PQC and QKD support by the network equipment in Sect. 6. We complete with the analyses of potential use case scenarios in Sect. 7 and the testbed description in Sect. 8.

2 Overview of PQC Algorithms

PQC develops cryptographic algorithms that are considered secure against potential quantum computer threats while remaining compatible with existing digital communication protocols and infrastructure. Unlike QKD, which also resists quantum attacks but requires specialised and costly equipment, PQC relies on mathematically hard problems for classical and quantum computers. PQC enables a gradual transition to quantum-resistant algorithms without disrupting current systems.

2.1 Why We Need PQC

RSA, one of the earliest and widely used public-key cryptosystems, relies on the prime factorisation problem. Its difficulty lies in finding the product of two large prime numbers. Elliptic-curve cryptography (ECC), another approach, uses the algebraic structure of elliptic curves over finite fields and achieves equivalent security to RSA with smaller key sizes, making it suitable for key exchange, digital signatures, and pseudorandom generation.

In 1994, Peter Shor introduced a quantum algorithm for factoring integers and solving discrete logarithm problems [3]. The algorithm can break RSA and ECC in polynomial time on a sufficiently large quantum computer. While such computers are not yet available, advancements in quantum technology suggest they might be implemented in 5–10 years. This has enabled "harvest now, decrypt later" attacks, where encrypted network traffic is stored and decrypted once quantum computers are available. Long-term sensitive data, such as government documents or financial records, is already at risk.

2.2 NIST Standardisation

To address quantum threats, NIST initiated a standardisation process in 2016 to identify quantum-resistant cryptographic algorithms. Out of 69 initial submissions, the process, involving four evaluation rounds, categorised algorithms into "Public-Key Encryption and Key-Establishment Algorithms" and "Digital Signature Algorithms." Some algorithms were broken, and others merged, leading to the selection of four algorithms in 2022: CRYSTALS-KYBER (encryption) [4] and three digital signature schemes: CRYSTALS-DILITHIUM [5], FALCON [6], and SPHINCS+ [7].

In August 2024, NIST published three PQC standards:

- **FIPS 203:** Based on CRYSTALS-KYBER for key encapsulation, relying on the Module Learning with Errors problem [8].
- **FIPS 204:** Based on CRYSTALS-DILITHIUM, a digital signature scheme also leveraging Module Learning with Errors [9].
- **FIPS 205:** Based on SPHINCS+, a hash-based signature scheme that combines few-time (FORS) and multi-time (XMSS) signature schemes [10].

FALCON, another digital signature scheme, has been selected but not standardised. Its reliance on floating-point arithmetic raises concerns regarding processor compatibility and resistance to side-channel attacks, such as timing and energy consumption. Additionally, the larger signature sizes of PQC schemes compared to the classical ones may hinder crypto agility, particularly in use cases requiring long signature chains that could exceed protocol limits. Code-based KEM - HQC [11] was selected for standardisation by NIST in March 2025.

3 Math Problems Used in PQC Algorithms

This section discusses key mathematical problems that serve as the foundation for post-quantum cryptographic algorithms, highlighting their principles and applications.

3.1 Hash-Based Cryptography

Hash-based cryptography relies on the collision resistance of cryptographic hash functions to provide secure digital signatures. A prominent example is the Merkle signature scheme [12], which employs binary hash trees to sign messages securely. In this scheme, a root hash serves as the public key, and each message signature reveals a specific path within the tree, proving authenticity without relying on vulnerable mathematical assumptions. The core building block of all hash-based schemes is the concept of one-time signatures introduced by [13]. The NIST standard SLH-DSA [10] integrates other hash-based signature schemes: Forest of random subsets (FORS) [14], the eXtended Merkle Signature Scheme (XMSS) [15] and Winternitz One-Time Signature Plus (WOTS+) [16]. SLH-DSA attacks include side channel and fault attacks [17–21].

Despite its quantum resistance, hash-based cryptography faces limitations such as large signature sizes and the need for careful tracking of used keys in stateful schemes. However, it remains a highly secure and practical alternative, exemplified by its adoption in the NIST SLH-DSA digital signature standard [10].

3.2 Code-Based Cryptography

Code-based cryptography derives its security from the computational hardness of decoding random linear codes, as demonstrated by the McEliece cryptosystem [22]. The public key is a scrambled error-correcting code, while the private key enables efficient decoding. Encryption involves introducing random errors that make decryption without the private key infeasible. Classic McEliece advanced to the final rounds but was not standardized due to key size [23]. However, a severe attack has recently occurred on the McElice cryptosystem [24]. Despite challenges, the simplicity and robustness of code-based cryptography make it a valuable post-quantum candidate. Code-based KEM - HQC [11] was selected for standardization by NIST in March 2025. It is based on Hamming Quasi-Cyclic codes [25].

3.3 Lattice-Based Cryptography

Lattice-based cryptography leverages the structure of n-dimensional lattices, utilizing problems such as the Shortest Vector Problem (SVP) and the Closest Vector Problem (CVP). These problems, especially in their approximate forms, are computationally hard to solve even with quantum computers. The Learning With Errors (LWE) problem [26,27], a variant involving noisy linear algebra, forms the foundation for many lattice-based schemes.

The inherent hardness of these problems makes lattice-based cryptography highly secure and versatile. For example, the NIST standards ML-KEM [8] and ML-DSA [9] are based on the Modulus Learning with Errors problem. Lattice-based cryptography is also favoured for its efficiency and scalability, with applications in encryption, digital signatures, and key exchanges.

The best-known attacks on LWE and its variants include lattice sieving [28, 29], enumeration [30,31], basis reduction algorithms like LLL [32] and BKZ [33] and machine learning-based techniques like SALSA [34].

3.4 Multivariate Quadratic Cryptography

Multivariate Quadratic (MQ) cryptography is based on the difficulty of solving systems of multivariate quadratic equations over finite fields, a problem known to be NP-hard. MQ cryptography is particularly robust against quantum and classical attacks due to the lack of efficient algorithms to solve these equations.

MQ cryptography is widely used for digital signatures. In these schemes, the private key allows efficient signature generation, while the public key enables verification by checking specific quadratic equations. However, the Rainbow [35] signature scheme, once a prominent MQ system, was compromised in 2022 [36] due to vulnerabilities that exposed its private keys. Despite this, MQ cryptography remains an active research area, with ongoing efforts to enhance its robustness and utility.

3.5 Isogeny-Based Cryptography

Isogeny-based cryptography leverages the complexity of finding isogenies between elliptic curves. The Supersingular Isogeny Key Encapsulation (SIKE) scheme was a notable candidate in this field but was broken in 2022 [37] when researchers discovered an efficient attack on SIDH.

Despite this setback, isogeny-based cryptography continues to attract interest due to its compact key sizes and bandwidth efficiency. Alternative approaches and modified schemes are being explored to address vulnerabilities, ensuring the field remains a promising avenue for quantum-resistant cryptographic protocols.

4 Overview of QKD Algorithms

Quantum Key Distribution is a secure key agreement protocol that enables two parties, commonly referred to as Alice and Bob, to generate a shared secret key using the principles of quantum mechanics and classical communication. Unlike traditional cryptographic methods, QKD leverages the fundamental laws of physics to ensure that any attempt by a third party (commonly called Eve) to intercept or tamper with the key can be detected. The security of QKD originates from the no-cloning theorem and the probabilistic nature of quantum measurements, which make eavesdropping inherently detectable. This unique property provides perfect forward secrecy, making QKD resistant to future quantum-based threats, including so-called "harvest now, decrypt later" attacks. As a result, QKD offers a robust foundation for long-term secure communication in the era of quantum computing.

The foundational QKD protocol, BB84 [38], was proposed as early as 1984, although a formal security proof was not published until 2000 [39]. Since then, several other notable protocols have been introduced, including B92 [40], SARG04 [41], and the Ekert protocol [42]. These protocols fall into different categories - some are based on the prepare-and-measure paradigm, others leverage quantum entanglement, and some exist in both forms. A crucial requirement for all QKD implementations is an authenticated classical communication channel, without which the system remains vulnerable to man-in-the-middle attacks. Typically, authentication is achieved using a pre-shared key (PSK) between the two communicating parties (Alice and Bob). In this context, QKD functions as a mechanism to amplify or extend the initial PSK, generating a long (potentially unbounded) sequence of secure, shared key bits that are guaranteed to be free from tampering or interception.

Several commercial QKD devices are available on the market. The most mature manufacturers in the market are Toshiba[1] and IDQ[2]. The Toshiba devices use efficient BB84 protocol with decoy states and phase encoding. The newest ID Quantique devices (e.g. Clavis XG QKD System) also use BB84 protocol with decoy states. Some models (e.g. Cerberis XGR QKD System) use the COW (Coherent One-Way) protocol [43].

5 Overview of PQC and QKD Integration

In this chapter, we review and summarise information from the scientific literature and documented case studies on the integration of PQC and QKD. This overview includes theoretical insights and practical experiences, highlighting current challenges, solutions, and advancements in merging these two technologies.

In [44], the potential for integrating PQC and QKD in mobile networks is discussed. To protect communication between user equipment and the base station, PQC is employed. QKD is integrated within the backbone of the communication network to enhance overall security. QKD is utilised to secure communication between base stations and the 6G core. PQC is also used for authenticating devices with a software-defined network controller. On the other hand, authors admit that QKD equipment is expensive and requires dedicated optical lines; therefore, for large networks, creating QKD links between all base stations and 6G core nodes would be very expensive. The work is theoretical and only provides suggestions where QKD and PQC could be used but doesn't discuss implementation and adoption details. It focuses more on different PQC algorithm types and where each of them could be useful in the mobile network. However, some of the claims, at the time of writing, are already outdated, as some of the suggested algorithms are broken and others have been standardised.

In [45], a hybrid protocol Muckle is presented. It integrates various potential key sources: QKD, PQC KEM and Classical KEM. The Muckle relies on the existence of a pre-shared key. A HAKE framework for the security evaluation of

---

[1] https://www.toshiba.eu/quantum/.
[2] https://www.idquantique.com/quantum-safe-security/products/#quantum_key_distribution.

such hybrid protocols is also proposed. The work doesn't cover real QKD implementations. It abstracts QKD as an array of independent, uniformly random bits available to both parties.

Muckle++ protocol is proposed in [46]. The protocol integrates PQC and QKD if a QKD link is available. If QKD is not available, it combines PQC with classical cryptography. The authors claim that protocol is provably ITS (information-theoretically secure) if QKD is used and provable quantum secure otherwise. The paper does not contain the proofs. Muckle++ augments an earlier presented Muckle protocol [45], by excluding the need to pre-share keys and instead rely on quantum-resistant digital signature schemes for authentication [46]. The authors were able to run the protocol for 20 h using a physical QKD link (with Toshiba QKD equipment) and FPGA (Field-Programmable Gate Array). However, there were technical problems running it longer due to error correction overload. The authors also used PUF (Physically Unclonable Function) to identify devices. For PQC, the CRYSTALS-Kyber [4] was used as KEM and Falcon [6] as digital signature schema.

Muckle+ [47] for joining PQC and QKD uses KDF (key derivation functions) with security proofs and provides signature authentication. Muckle# is inspired by KEM TLS. It is a modification of TLS where KEMS are used for authentication instead of digital signatures. The reason is that, currently, PQC KEMs are shorter than PQC digital signatures.

In [2], the significance of QKD device authentication is explained. It is proposed to replace pre-shared keys for authentication with PQC algorithms. The Aigis.Sig algorithm is used here. However, the idea is still valid by replacing the PQC algorithm. The stability of PQC authentication was tested with a pair of QKD devices. The fibre length is 40 km, and it was running continuously for 30 h. The PQC program keeps running normally, and the QKD systems continuously generate keys.

In [48], PQC algorithm Aigis-Sig [49] is used for authentication in the Jinan metropolitan QKD network (14 QKD nodes, 5 optical switching nodes). The PQC algorithm replaced pre-shared symmetric keys used previously. The PQC algorithm was integrated into the ARM chip of the QKD device to realise the authentication process. The average key rate and QBER of each connection during 36 days of network operation were analysed. There were no significant performance issues.

According to [50], their encryptors are stated to support PQC and can be integrated with their QKD equipment. Meanwhile, [51] reports that the backbone of the Paris QCI network was implemented using QKD, while relays were secured with PQC.

6 PQC and QKD Support in the Equipment

This section analyses the capabilities of the equipment to support Quantum Key Distribution and Post-Quantum Cryptography in secure communication systems, referencing specific examples.

6.1 PQC and QKD Support in Centauris

Centauris encryptors secure data links between remote sites using symmetric key cryptography with AES-256, which is currently considered quantum-safe when appropriate key lengths are used. For enhanced long-term security, AES-512 may be preferred, but Centauris encryptors do not yet support it.

The encryptors integrate with QKD systems, such as Clavis XG, to regularly update symmetric keys (e.g., every minute). Clavis XG can generate four new keys per second, ensuring frequent updates and quantum-safe keys. If the QKD system becomes unavailable, the last obtained key is reused, and a warning is issued via a light on the device. To extend the secure usage of symmetric keys, AES key modification techniques are employed [52].

Device authentication and management of Centauris encryptors are handled via the CM7 software tool. CM7 authenticates devices using digital signatures, allowing the selection of predefined certificates from a list that includes NIST PQC standards, such as CRYSTALS-DILITHIUM and SPHINCS+. However, compatibility between certificate types, CM7 versions, and encryptor releases varies.

Alternative encryptors, such as the Thales High-Speed Encryptor, offer similar functionality, integrating with QKD devices that conform to the ETSI eQKD v14.01 standard. Thales also includes a PQC Starter Kit that supports built-in PQC algorithms [52].

6.2 PQC and QKD Support in Juniper

Juniper devices do not directly support QKD and/or PQC but can integrate pre-shared keys, namely post-quantum pre-shared keys, into IPSec IKEv2 encryption. These keys may then be periodically replaced via calls to the key management system (KMS). The KMS, on the other hand, may use a QKD network or external PQC systems to acquire and distribute symmetric keys.

An experiment conducted by Juniper Networks, ID Quantique, and Deutsche Telekom tested ETSI's REST API in a multivendor environment. Two Juniper SRX380 firewalls connected via a classical 10GbE link were secured using MACsec (AES-256). The QKD devices used were ID Quantique's Cerberis XG systems, connected via standard single-mode fibre optic links and an IDQ eavesdropping simulator. The experiment confirmed that the API is ready for productized environments, though further enhancements to standards are required [53].

Juniper devices running JUNOS 22.4R1 support quantum-safe IPsec using IETF RFC 8784 and the ETSI QKD014 [54] REST API. This implementation merges classical and quantum-safe key material (e.g., from QKD or PQC) to create quantum-resistant IPsec tunnels. Despite these developments, Juniper is cautious about PQC's long-term security and instead focuses on Distributed Symmetric Key Establishment (DSKE) to achieve quantum-safe communications [53, 55].

6.3 PQC and QKD Support in Cisco

Cisco devices support secure connections through IPsec protocols such as SKIP (1995), IKEv1, and IKEv2. SKIP (1995) is an early protocol designed for stateless key distribution but is now largely obsolete. However, the SKIP (2024) draft integrates QKD systems to generate symmetric encryption keys dynamically. In this workflow, QKD devices generate Key IDs and keys, share these with routers, and enable secure key distribution for IPsec communications. SKIP (2024) aligns with ETSI GS QKD 014 but includes additional features such as an optional entropy source endpoint [56,57].

IKEv2 is widely adopted for its efficiency and improved security. However, IKEv2 systems relying on Elliptic Curve Diffie-Hellman (ECDH) are vulnerable to quantum attacks if sufficiently powerful quantum computers become available. These vulnerabilities can be mitigated by integrating post-quantum preshared keys (PPKs) obtained through QKD or PQC mechanisms. For example, IKEv2 Key Derivation with PPK, described in [58], requires at least 256 bits of entropy for PPKs to ensure 128 bits of post-quantum security and protection against dictionary attacks. Though the current approach supports only static PPKs, extensions to dynamic PPKs are possible [59].

Cisco devices also support MACsec (IEEE 802.1AE), a Layer 2 protocol that secures traffic on a frame-by-frame basis defending against attacks such as replay and MAC address spoofing. However, MACsec relies on symmetric pre-shared keys (PSKs), which are not quantum-resistant. Using QKD-generated keys or PQC mechanisms for PSKs could significantly enhance MACsec's quantum safety. Additionally, EAP-TLS can establish mutual authentication using certificates, though it does not provide quantum resistance [60,61].

In summary, Cisco's IPsec and MACsec implementations are being enhanced to integrate QKD and PQC capabilities, aligning with emerging quantum-safe standards [56,57,62].

7 Use Cases Integrating PQC and QKD

We discuss use cases that integrate QKD and PQC technologies to enhance security.

7.1 Connecting Two LANs Using Bump-in-the-Wire Encryptors

This use case connects two local area networks (A and B) using a QKD link and an encrypted classical communication channel. While traffic within the local area networks remains unencrypted, encryptors secure the communication between the networks using symmetric cryptography keys derived from the QKD system. Centauris encryptors (discussed in Sect. 6.1) are employed for this purpose, with authentication currently performed using ECC, but it is planned to transition to SPHINCS+. The communication scheme is shown in Fig. 1.

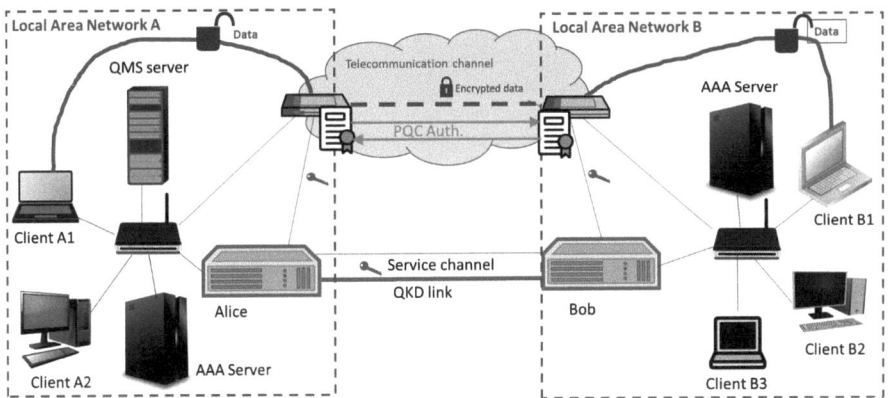

Fig. 1. Schema of the use case QKD as a Service without local area network encryption.

Cisco routers could also replace Centauris encryptors in this use case by employing MACsec for traffic encryption and SKIP to inject QKD keys. Authentication between QKD devices is performed using pre-shared keys and digital certificates. Combining PQC (e.g., SPHINCS+) with a classical algorithm (e.g., ECDH) in certificates provides multi-layer security, ensuring protection even if one algorithm is compromised.

7.2 Integration of QKD Into TLS-Based Communication

This modification extends the previous use case by encrypting traffic within the local area networks. In addition to QKD-generated keys used by encryptors and post-quantum cryptography mechanisms for authentication, network users must also ensure mutual identity verification and secure their communications through encryption.

To facilitate this, a Key Management Server (KMS) with shared entropy is introduced. The server acts as a Relying Party (RP), authenticating users via client-server authentication in a TLS v1.3 flow. Certificates signed with PQC algorithms (e.g., SPHINCS+) are negotiated alongside post-quantum KEMs, as explained in [63]. Implementation can utilize repositories like Bouncy Castle [64–66].

The KMS also serves as a key provider, managing QKD-derived and QRNG-generated keys. Symmetric keys are distributed to users who wish to communicate. The scheme is shown in Fig. 2, with PQC-based authentication indicated in orange and KMS-provided keys in green.

7.3 QKD as a Service for External Partners

This use case involves QKD links connecting two local area networks, with external users accessing the networks via VPN servers at the perimeter. The schema within the networks mirrors the one described in Sect. 7.2, as shown in Fig. 3.

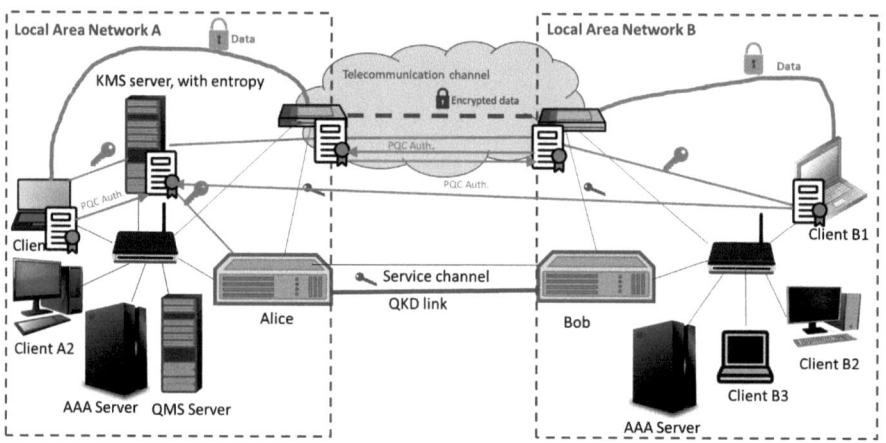

Fig. 2. Schema of the use case QKD as a Service with local area network encryption. (Color figure online)

A critical vulnerability in this scenario is the VPN link between a client and the VPN server. Post-quantum VPNs can mitigate this risk. Microsoft's post-quantum OpenVPN fork [67,68] integrates PQC and is part of the Open Quantum Safe project's OpenVPN subproject [69]. Other VPNs, such as Mullvad (using Kyber and Classic McEliece) and ExpressVPN (evaluated by Cure53), also offer PQC support [70,71].

PAN-OS 11.2 Quasar enables quantum-safe hybrid keys for IKEv2 VPNs, implementing RFC 8784 and RFC 9370 [72,73]. Despite being experimental, the Open Quantum Safe OpenVPN subproject appears to be the most promising candidate for the implementation.

7.4 QKD-Protected Messenger

In this use case, two clients with direct access to a QKD link securely exchange text messages. Keys from the QKD link encrypt messages using OTP as the encryption algorithm. Authentication is essential in the use case. A hybrid signature scheme that combines classical signatures (e.g., ECC) with PQC signatures (ML-DSA or SLH-DSA) is preferred.

This use case leverages the QKD link's direct access for secure communication while ensuring robust authentication through hybrid cryptographic methods.

8 Site-to-Site Quantum-Safe Interconnect Testbed

Our experimental two LAN quantum-safe interconnect testbed integrated QKD devices with post-quantum cryptography. It utilized ID Quantique's QKD hardware specifically the Clavis and Cerberis models which implement the BB84 protocol and the COW protocol respectively. The testbed was tested with Cisco

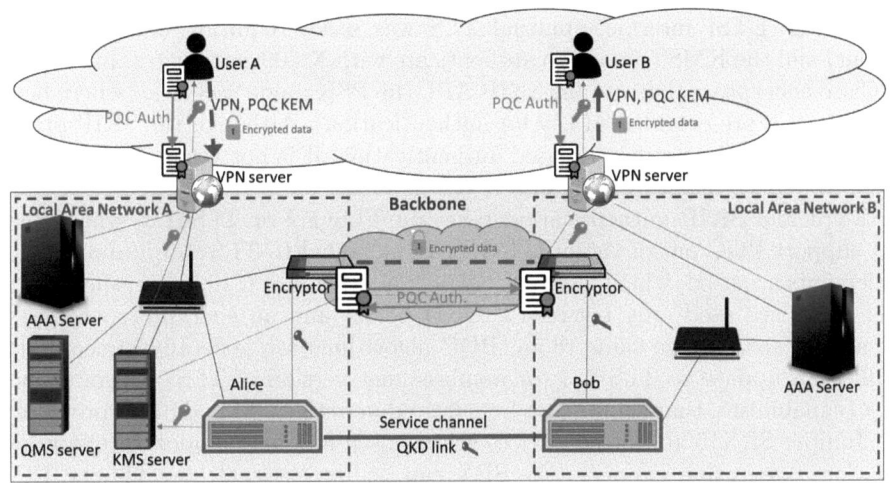

Fig. 3. Schema of the use case QKD as a Service for external partners.

NCS 540 routers, Juniper SRX1500 firewalls, and IDQ Centauris bump-in-the-wire encryptors. For brevity, we later briefly detail the deployment with Juniper devices as encryptors.

Both QKD devices rely on a small pre-shared secret for initial mutual authentication; this PSK is used to authenticate their classical communications (e.g. error-correction data) and thus securely bootstrap the quantum key exchange.

The two QKD nodes were interconnected by a dedicated quantum channel (a dark fibre carrying single-photon signals) and a parallel classical service channel. The service channel operated as a 2.5 Gbps bidirectional optical link on standard telecom wavelengths in the C-band (compliant with ITU-T G.694.1 DWDM grid), and was used for synchronization, basis reconciliation, error correction and other auxiliary communications.

To utilize the keys generated by these QKD links, a Key Management System (KMS) layer is necessary, abstracting away vendor-specific details and enabling integration with standard network encryptors. Essentially, the KMS ingests raw keys from the QKD devices (via the devices' proprietary interfaces) and presents them to the network layer through well-defined, interoperable APIs. In our testbed, KMS service is integrated into QKD devices. It provides support for the following two APIs that allow encryptors (referred to as Secure Application Entities, SAE-s) to request QKD keys from Alice and Bob endpoints:

- the ETSI GS QKD 014 API [54], used by the majority of QKD-capable devices; it is a REST-based API, which has a standard since 2019;
- the Cisco SKIP v00 [74], used only by Cisco routers with recent firmware update. The SKIP protocol is currently in draft status. Our IDQ and Cisco devices support the draft version 00 (as of August 2024); however, the draft version 01 was proposed in March 2025.

For the ETSI interface, mutual TLS was used, requiring each encryptor (client) and the KMS (server) to authenticate with X.509 certificates. In the case of Cisco encryptors that use the SKIP API, the PSK mode was used (where both sides share a pre-established key for authentication). Although the SKIP protocol draft supports certificate-based authentication, it is not yet implemented by the latest Cisco firmware available at the moment.

ETSI and SKIP authentication relies on TLSv1.2 or TLSv1.3, which does not support PQC out-of-the-box. PQC can be added to TLSv1.3 if appropriate codepoints are used, which have not been standardized yet. However, since ETSI and SKIP are used only between a QKD device and an encryptor, which are usually located in the same room, PQC algorithms are generally unnecessary. Still, if an update to TLSv1.3 (or a subsequent version of TLS) will introduce PQC capabilities, that should also be reflected in both ETSI and SKIP protocols.

Juniper SRX1500 firewall devices were chosen for their support of quantum-safe key integration support (the SRX can utilize external keys via the RFC 8784 mechanism). The IPsec tunnels were set with short-lived keys so that new keys would be frequently requested from the KMS. Instead of a continuously running QKD link during testing, a simulated QKD key server nicknamed "SNEK" (Single-node ETSI KMS) was also deployed for observability. SNEK emulated the behaviour of real QKDs to test the encryptors' compliance with the ETSI GS QKD 014 protocol and to observe request/response patterns over time. The experiments showed that the encryptors successfully retrieved keys in sync, applied them to the IPsec SAs (Security Associations), and maintained encrypted traffic flow without packet loss or downtime.

Cisco devices, in their turn, rely on the proprietary MACSec protocol, while Centauris devices use a proprietary TLS-like protocol. Interestingly, Centauris devices can use PQC algorithms for mutual authentication. However, they have to rely on algorithm identifiers and key encodings that are subject to change since not all PQC algorithms have these standards yet.

9 Conclusions

We analysed the state-of-the-art advancements in Post-Quantum Cryptography. Currently, three algorithms have been standardised by NIST: one key encapsulation mechanism (KEM) and two digital signature schemes. The KEM and one of the signature schemes are based on lattice-based cryptography using the Learning With Errors problem, while the second signature scheme relies on hash-based cryptography. Despite the standardisation of these two signature schemes, an ongoing competition seeks to identify additional signature schemes, primarily due to concerns regarding the large signature sizes of the currently standardised schemes. Additionally, some vendors remain hesitant to integrate post-quantum standards into their network solutions, citing insufficient real-world testing and the lack of long-term validation.

In this context, we also investigated the extent to which PQC and QKD are supported by the network equipment we use. Our findings indicate that not all devices natively support PQC or QKD keys. Nevertheless, in most cases, workarounds can be implemented to enable the integration of QKD keys and PQC algorithms with the equipment.

We reviewed scientific literature addressing the integration of PQC and QKD. While several papers discuss experimental implementations of PQC and QKD integration, no widely accepted or standardised approach currently exists for achieving such integration. This highlights the need for further research and development in this domain.

Based on our experience and the literature review, we discussed four use cases. The use cases explicitly define the utilisation of QKD links. Consequently, we focused on identifying where PQC could provide additional value within these scenarios. Three primary areas for the application of PQC were identified:

1. **Device Authentication**: QKD does not inherently provide authentication. Pre-shared keys are typically used for QKD authentication, but this approach can become problematic in larger networks due to scalability issues. PQC offers a robust solution for device authentication in such scenarios.
2. **Quantum-Safe Communication for Remote Users**: PQC can enable secure communication for users who do not have direct access to the local area network. This is typically achieved through PQC-based VPNs, which replace classical VPNs to ensure quantum-safe communication. While several PQC-based VPN solutions are currently available, many remain experimental.
3. **Quantum-Safe IPSec Communication**: Integrating PQC libraries into IPSec implementations enables quantum-safe communication between users. We identified libraries that provide both PQC support and compatibility with IPSec, making them well-suited for adaptation in the targeted use cases.

We have developed a testbed currently supporting some of the proposed use cases. We plan to extend the testbed to support all discussed use cases. Given that many of these solutions incorporate experimental components, modifications or adaptations are likely necessary to implement the planned approaches effectively.

Acknowledgment. The research is supported by the European Union, project No. 101091559 "Development of experimental quantum communication infrastructure in Latvia (LATQN)".

References

1. Regulatory Horizons Council, Regulating Quantum Technology Applications (2024)
2. Wang, L.J., Zhang, K.Y., Wang, J.Y., et al.: Experimental authentication of quantum key distribution with post-quantum cryptography. npj Quant. Inf. **7**, 67 (2021). https://doi.org/10.1038/s41534-021-00400-7

3. Shor, P.W.: Algorithms for quantum computation: discrete logarithms and factoring. In: Goldwasser, S. (ed.) Proceedings of the 35th Annual Symposium on Foundations of Computer Science (FOCS), pp. 124–134. IEEE Computer Society Press, Los Alamitos (1994). https://doi.org/10.1109/SFCS.1994.365700
4. Avanzi, R., et al.: CRYSTALS-Kyber algorithm specifications and supporting documentation, Third-round submission to the NIST's post-quantum cryptography standardization process (2020). https://csrc.nist.gov/Projects/post-quantum-cryptography/post-quantum-cryptography-standardization/round-3-submissions
5. Bai, S., et al.: CRYSTALS-Dilithium: algorithm specifications and supporting documentation, Version 3.1. (2021). https://pq-crystals.org/dilithium/data/dilithium-specification-round3-20210208.pdf
6. Prest, T., et al.: Falcon: Fast-Fourier Lattice-based Compact Signatures over NTRU. Submission to the NIST's post-quantum cryptography standardization process, Version 1.2. (2020). https://falcon-sign.info/falcon.pdf
7. Aumasson, J.P., et al.: SPHINCS+ – Submission to the NIST post-quantum project, Version 3.1. (2022). https://sphincs.org/data/sphincs+-r3.1-specification.pdf
8. NIST: FIPS 203 Module-Lattice-Based Key-Encapsulation Mechanism Standard. Information Technology Laboratory National Institute of Standards and Technology Gaithersburg, MD 20899-8900 (2024). https://doi.org/10.6028/NIST.FIPS.203
9. NIST: FIPS 204 Module-Lattice-Based Digital Signature Standard. Information Technology Laboratory National Institute of Standards and Technology Gaithersburg, MD 20899-8900 (2024). https://doi.org/10.6028/NIST.FIPS.204
10. NIST: FIPS 205 Stateless Hash-Based Digital Signature Standard. Information Technology Laboratory National Institute of Standards and Technology Gaithersburg, MD 20899-8900 (2024). https://doi.org/10.6028/NIST.FIPS.205
11. Aguilar-Melchor, C., et al.: Hamming Quasi-Cyclic (HQC) – Submission to the NIST post-quantum project, Fourth round version, Updated version 19/02/2025 (2025). https://pqc-hqc.org/doc/hqc-specification_2025-02-19.pdf
12. Merkle R.C.: Secrecy, authentication, and public key systems. Ph.D. thesis, Stanford university (1979). http://www.ralphmerkle.com/papers/Thesis1979.pdf
13. Lamport, L.: Constructing digital signatures from a one way function. Technical Report SRI-CSL-98, SRI International Computer Science Laboratory (1979)
14. Bernstein, D.J., Hülsing, A., Kölbl, S., Niederhagen, R., Rijneveld, J., Schwabe, P.: The SPHINCS+ signature framework. In: Proceedings of the 2019 ACM SIGSAC Conference on Computer and Communications Security (CCS 2019), pp. 2129–2146. Association for Computing Machinery, New York (2019). https://doi.org/10.1145/3319535.3363229
15. Buchmann, J., Dahmen, E., Hülsing, A.: XMSS - a practical forward secure signature scheme based on minimal security assumptions. In: Yang, B.-Y. (ed.) PQCrypto 2011. LNCS, vol. 7071, pp. 117–129. Springer, Heidelberg (2011). https://doi.org/10.1007/978-3-642-25405-5_8
16. Hülsing, A.: W-OTS+ – shorter signatures for hash-based signature schemes. In: Youssef, A., Nitaj, A., Hassanien, A.E. (eds.) AFRICACRYPT 2013. LNCS, vol. 7918, pp. 173–188. Springer, Heidelberg (2013). https://doi.org/10.1007/978-3-642-38553-7_10
17. Kannwischer, M.J., Genêt, A., Butin, D., Krämer, J., Buchmann, J.: Differential power analysis of XMSS and SPHINCS. In: Fan, J., Gierlichs, B. (eds.) COSADE 2018. LNCS, vol. 10815, pp. 168–188. Springer, Cham (2018). https://doi.org/10.1007/978-3-319-89641-0_10

18. Castelnovi, L., Martinelli, A., Prest, T.: Grafting trees: a fault attack against the SPHINCS framework. In: Lange, T., Steinwandt, R. (eds.) PQCrypto 2018. LNCS, vol. 10786, pp. 165–184. Springer, Cham (2018). https://doi.org/10.1007/978-3-319-79063-3_8
19. Genêt, A., Kannwischer, M.J., Pelletier, H., McLauchlan, A.: Practical fault injection attacks on SPHINCS, Cryptology ePrint Archive, Paper 2018/674 (2018). https://ia.cr/2018/674
20. Amiet, D., Leuenberger, L., Curiger, A., Zbinden, P.: FPGA-based SPHINCS+ implementations: mind the glitch. In: 2020 23rd Euromicro Conference on Digital System Design (DSD), Kranj, Slovenia, pp. 229–237. IEEE (2020). https://doi.org/10.1109/DSD51259.2020.00046
21. Genêt, A.: On protecting SPHINCS+ against fault attacks. IACR Trans. Cryptogr. Hardw. Embed. Syst., **2023**(2), 80–114 (2023). https://doi.org/10.46586/tches.v2023.i2.80-114
22. McEliece, R.J.: A public-key cryptosystem based on algebraic coding theory. DSN Progr. Rep., 42–44 (1978)
23. Niebuhr, R., Meziani, M., Bulygin, S., Buchmann, J.: Selecting parameters for secure McEliece-based cryptosystems. Int. J. Inf. Secur. **11**, 137–147 (2012). https://doi.org/10.1007/s10207-011-0153-2
24. Randriambololona, H.: The syzygy distinguisher. In: Fehr, S., Fouque, P.A. (eds.) EUROCRYPT 2025. LNCS, vol. 15606, pp. 324–354, Springer, Cham (2025). https://doi.org/10.1007/978-3-031-91095-1_12
25. Aguilar-Melchor, C., Blazy, O., Deneuville, J.C., Gaborit, P., Zémor, G.: Efficient encryption from random Quasi-cyclic codes. IEEE Trans. Inf. Theory **64**(5), 3927–3943 (2018). https://doi.org/10.1109/TIT.2018.2804444
26. Regev, O.: On lattices, learning with errors, random linear codes, and cryptography. J. ACM **56**(6), 1–40 (2009). https://doi.org/10.1145/1568318.1568324. Article 34
27. Lyubashevsky, V., Peikert, C., Regev, O.: On ideal lattices and learning with errors over rings. J. ACM **60**(6), 1–35 (2013). https://doi.org/10.1145/2535925. Article 43
28. Ajtai, M., Kumar, R., Sivakumar, D.: A sieve algorithm for the shortest lattice vector problem. In: Proceedings of the 33th Annual ACM Symposium on Theory of Computing, STOC 2001, pp. 601–610. ACM (2001). https://doi.org/10.1145/380752.380857
29. Nguyen, P.Q., Vidick, T.: Sieve algorithms for the shortest vector problem are practical. J. Math. Cryptol. **2**, 181–207 (2008). https://doi.org/10.1515/JMC.2008.009
30. Schnorr, C.P.: lattice basis reduction: improved practical algorithms and solving subset sum problems. J. Math. Program. **66**, 181–191 (1994). https://doi.org/10.1007/BF01581144
31. Gama, N., Nguyen, P.Q., Regev, O.: Lattice enumeration using extreme pruning. In: Gilbert, H. (ed.) EUROCRYPT 2010. LNCS, vol. 6110, pp. 257–278. Springer, Heidelberg (2010). https://doi.org/10.1007/978-3-642-13190-5_13
32. Lenstra, A., Lenstra, H., Lovasz, L.: Factoring polynomials with rational coefficients. J. Mathematische Annalen **261**(4), 515–534 (1982). https://doi.org/10.1007/BF01457454
33. Schnorr, C.P.: A hierarchy of polynomial time lattice basis reduction algorithms. J. Theoret. Comput. Sci. **53**(2-3), 201–224 (1987). https://doi.org/10.1016/0304-3975(87)90064-8. ISSN 0304-3975

34. Wenger, E., Chen, M., Charton, F., Lauter, K.: SALSA: attacking lattice cryptography with transformers. In: Proceedings of the 36th International Conference on Neural Information Processing Systems (NIPS 2022), pp. 34981–34994. Curran Associates Inc., Red Hook (2022). Article 2535
35. Ding, J., Schmidt, D.: Rainbow, a new multivariable polynomial signature scheme. In: Ioannidis, J., Keromytis, A., Yung, M. (eds.) ACNS 2005. LNCS, vol. 3531, pp. 164–175. Springer, Heidelberg (2005). https://doi.org/10.1007/11496137_12
36. Beullens, W.: Breaking rainbow takes a weekend on a laptop. In: Dodis, Y., Shrimpton, T. (eds) CRYPTO 2022. LNCS, vol. 13508, pp. 464–479, Springer, Cham (2022). https://doi.org/10.1007/978-3-031-15979-4_16
37. Maino, L., Martindale, C., Panny, L., Pope, G., Wesolowski, B.: A direct key recovery attack on SIDH. In: Hazay, C., Stam, M. (eds.) EUROCRYPT 2023. LNCS, vol. 14008, pp. 448–471. Springer, Cham (2023). https://doi.org/978-3-031-30589-4_16
38. Bennett, C.H., Brassard, G.: Quantum cryptography: public key distribution and coin tossing. In: Proceedings of IEEE International Conference on Computers, Systems and Signal Processing, Bangalore, India, pp. 175–179 (1984)
39. Shor, P.W., Preskill, J.: Simple proof of security of the BB84 quantum key distribution protocol. Phys. Rev. Lett. **85**(2), 441–444 (2000). https://doi.org/10.1103/PhysRevLett.85.441
40. Bennett, C.H.: Quantum cryptography using any two nonorthogonal states. Phys. Rev. Lett. **68**(21), 3121–3124 (1992). https://doi.org/10.1103/PhysRevLett.68.3121
41. Scarani, V., Acín, A., Ribordy, G., Gisin, N.: Quantum cryptography protocols robust against photon number splitting attacks for weak laser pulse implementations. Phys. Rev. Lett. **92**(5), 057901 (2004). https://doi.org/10.1103/PhysRevLett.92.057901
42. Ekert, A.K.: Quantum cryptography based on Bell's theorem. Phys. Rev. Lett. **67**(6), 661–663 (1991). https://doi.org/10.1103/PhysRevLett.67.661
43. Stucki, D., Brunner, N., Gisin, N., Scarani, V., Zbinden, H.: Fast and simple one-way quantum key distribution. Appl. Phys. Lett. **87**(19), 194108 (2005). https://doi.org/10.1063/1.2126792
44. Hoque, S., Aydeger, A., Zeydan, E.: Exploring post quantum cryptography with quantum key distribution for sustainable mobile network architecture design. In: Proceedings of the 4th Workshop on Performance and Energy Efficiency in Concurrent and Distributed Systems (PECS 2024), pp. 9–16. Association for Computing Machinery (2024). https://doi.org/10.1145/3659997.3660033
45. Dowling, B., Hansen, T.B., Paterson, K.G.: Many a mickle makes a muckle: a framework for provably quantum-secure hybrid key exchange. In: Ding, J., Tillich, J.-P. (eds.) PQCrypto 2020. LNCS, vol. 12100, pp. 483–502. Springer, Cham (2020). https://doi.org/10.1007/978-3-030-44223-1_26
46. Garms, L., et al.: Experimental integration of quantum key distribution and post-quantum cryptography in a hybrid quantum-safe cryptosystem. Adv. Quantum Technol. **7**(4), 2300304 (2024). https://doi.org/10.1002/qute.202300304
47. Bruckner, S., Ramacher, S., Striecks, C.: Muckle+: end-to-end hybrid authenticated key exchanges. In: Johansson, T., Smith-Tone, D. (eds.) Post-Quantum Cryptography (PQCrypto 2023). LNCS, vol. 14154, pp. 601–633. Springer, Cham (2023). https://doi.org/10.1007/978-3-031-40003-2_22
48. Yang, Y.H., et al.: All optical metropolitan quantum key distribution network with post-quantum cryptography authentication. Opt. Express **29**(16), 25859–25867 (2021). https://doi.org/10.1364/OE.432944

49. Zhang, J., Yu, Yu., Fan, S., Zhang, Z., Yang, K.: Tweaking the asymmetry of asymmetric-key cryptography on lattices: KEMs and signatures of smaller sizes. In: Kiayias, A., Kohlweiss, M., Wallden, P., Zikas, V. (eds.) PKC 2020. LNCS, vol. 12111, pp. 37–65. Springer, Cham (2020). https://doi.org/10.1007/978-3-030-45388-6_2
50. Telsy SpA: Quantum Key Distribution (QKD) and Post-Quantum Cryptography (PQC). https://www.telsy.com/en/quantum-key-distribution-qkd-and-post-quantum-cryptography-pqc/
51. ID Quantique SA: PQC-QKD Hybridization in Orange's Fiber Network (2024). https://www.idquantique.com/pqc-qkd-hybridization-in-orange-fiber-network/
52. Ginga, S.: Shielding Your Network: Preparing for a Quantum-Safe Future Now. In: THALES BLOG (2024). https://cpl.thalesgroup.com/blog/encryption/preparing-for-a-quantum-safe-future-now
53. Juniper Networks, Inc.: Validation of Quantum Safe MACsec Implementation (2022). https://www.juniper.net/content/dam/www/assets/white-papers/us/en/2022/validation-of-quantum-safe-macsec-white-paper.pdf
54. European Telecommunications Standards Institute (ETSI): Quantum Key Distribution (QKD); Protocol and data format of REST-based key delivery API. ETSI GS QKD 014 V1.1.1 (2019)
55. Aelmans, M.: NIST Finalizes Post-Quantum Encryption Standards. Blog post in Juniper Networks, Inc. (2024). https://blogs.juniper.net/en-us/industry-solutions-and-trends/nist-finalizes-post-quantum-encryption-standards
56. Singh, R., Hill, C., Kawaguchi, S., Lupo, J.: Secure Key Integration Protocol (SKIP). In: draft-cisco-skip-00 (2024). https://datatracker.ietf.org/doc/draft-cisco-skip/00/
57. ETSI: Quantum Key Distribution (QKD); Protocol and Data Format of REST-based Key Delivery API. In: ETSI GS QKD 014 V1.1.1 (2019-02) (2019). https://www.etsi.org/deliver/etsi_gs/QKD/001_099/014/01.01.01_60/gs%5Ctextbf_QKD014v010101p.pdf
58. Fluhrer, S., Kampanakis, P., McGrew, D., Smyslov, V.: mixing preshared keys in the internet key exchange protocol version 2 (IKEv2) for post-quantum security. In: RFC 8784, Internet Engineering Task Force (IETF) (2020). https://datatracker.ietf.org/doc/html/rfc8784
59. Cisco Systems, Inc.: Chapter: configuring quantum-safe encryption using postquantum preshared keys. In: Security and VPN Configuration Guide, Cisco IOS XE 17.x (2021). https://www.cisco.com/c/en/us/td/docs/routers/ios/config/17-x/sec-vpn/b-security-vpn/m-sec-cfg-quantum-encryption-ppk.html
60. Kaufman, C., Hoffman, P., Nir, Y., Eronen, P., Kivinen, T.: Internet key exchange protocol version 2 (IKEv2). In: STD 79, RFC 7296 (2014). https://doi.org/10.17487/RFC7296
61. Hoffman, P.: The transition from classical to post-quantum cryptography. In: Network Working Group (2020). https://datatracker.ietf.org/doc/html/draft-hoffman-c2pq-07
62. Aziz, A., Markson, T., Prafullchandra, H.: Simple Key-Management For Internet Protocols (SKIP) (1996). https://datatracker.ietf.org/doc/draft-ietf-ipsec-skip/06/
63. Kozlovičs, S., Petručeņa, K., Lāriņš, D., Vīksna, J.: Quantum key distribution as a service and its injection into TLS. In: Meng, W., Yan, Z., Piuri, V. (eds.) Information Security Practice and Experience (ISPEC 2023). LNCS, vol. 14341, pp. 527–545. Springer, Singapore (2023). https://doi.org/10.1007/978-981-99-7032-2_31

64. IMCS SysLab: Bouncy Castle Fork at IMCS SysLab for Implementing the TLS Injection Mechanism (for Adding PQC/QKD-Related Code to TLS). https://github.com/LUMII-Syslab/tls-injection-mechanism
65. IMCS SysLab: Integration of PQC Algorithms into the BouncyCastle TLS Injection Mechanism. https://github.com/LUMII-Syslab/tls-injection-pqc
66. IMCS SysLab: TLS Client Example with Injected PQC Algorithm. https://github.com/LUMII-Syslab/tls-injection-pqc
67. Microsoft: Post-Quantum Crypto and VPNs. https://www.microsoft.com/en-us/research/project/post-quantum-crypto-vpn
68. Microsoft: Post-Quantum Cryptography VPN. https://github.com/microsoft/PQCrypto-VPN
69. Open Quantum Safe: OQS-Demos / OpenVPN. https://github.com/open-quantum-safe/oqs-demos/tree/main/openvpn
70. Powell, O.: Why Every VPN Should Use Post-Quantum Encryption. Tom's Guide (2024). https://www.tomsguide.com/computing/vpns/why-every-vpn-should-use-post-quantum-encryption
71. Tamašiūnas, L.: NordVPN Launches First App with Post-Quantum Encryption Support. NordVPN Blog (2024). https://nordvpn.com/blog/nordvpn-linux-post-quantum-encryption-support/
72. Meshi, Y.: PAN-OS 11.2 Quasar Helps Customers Secure Networks Everywhere, Faster. Palo Alto Networks Blog (2024). https://www.paloaltonetworks.com/blog/network-security/quasarlaunch/
73. Palo Alto Networks, Inc.: Network Security, Quantum Security Concepts (2023). https://docs.paloaltonetworks.com/network-security/quantum-security/administration/quantum-security-concepts
74. Internet Engineering Task Force (IETF): Secure Key Integration Protocol (SKIP). Version: draft-cisco-skip-00. https://datatracker.ietf.org/doc/draft-cisco-skip/00/

Author Index

A

Aggarwal, Akshit   III-207, III-213
Aghili, Farhad   III-141
Arya, Kislay   I-3
Aung, Yan Lin   I-204
Azzabi, Radhouene   III-162

B

Balachandran, Vivek   III-179, III-197
Balodis, Rihards   I-266
Barbu, Guillaume   II-3
Basurto-Becerra, Abraham   I-77
Battagliola, Michele   II-251
Bhattacharya, Sarani   I-3

C

Cao, Yunfei   II-41, II-118
Celms, Edgars   I-266
Che, Anda   II-229
Chen, Luoqi   II-81
Chetry, Reejit   I-113
Chiku, Sohto   II-274
Chithambara Moorthii, J.   I-113
Chowdhury, Siddhartha   I-3

D

D'Alconzo, Giuseppe   II-251
Damie, Marc   III-109
Dehghantanha, Ali   III-70
Del Bino, Leonardo   III-191
Ding, Yaoling   II-23
Dong, Ye   I-204

E

Edu, Jide   I-185
Eisenbarth, Thomas   III-43

F

Felde, Hendrik Meyer Zum   III-162
Fu, Haoyue   II-118

Fujino, Takeshi   I-94
Fukuda, Yuta   I-94

G

Gangemi, Andrea   II-251
Gansel, Antoine   I-245
Gao, Jing   II-23
Gay, Maël   I-58
Geloczi, Emiliia   I-222
Gil, Amaia   III-162
Goldmann, Mirko   III-191
Gong, Weiping   II-23
Gong, Zheng   II-81, II-211
Gonzalez, Ruben   II-173
Goswami, Bhanprakash   I-113
Gouy-Pailler, Cédric   III-162
Grémy, Laurent   II-3

H

Hahn, Florian   III-109
Haiqi, He   III-179
Hao, Xinpeng   II-152
Hara, Keisuke   II-274
Hara, Yuko   I-144, III-223
He, Junlin   II-132
He, Yituo   II-152
Hirata, Haruka   I-144
Hoffmann, Clément   II-101
Holler, Benedikt   I-222
Hristoskova, Anna   III-141
Hu, Xi   II-41

I

Ise, Kenshiro   III-223

J

Janetschek, Matthias   I-163
Jia Jing, Caleb Lee   III-179
Jing, Jiwu   II-132, II-229

K

Kalnina, Elina I-266
Kalvin, Lee Ling Yi III-121
Karatsiolis, Evangelos II-337
Karayalçin, Sengim I-40
Katzenbeisser, Stefan I-222
Khairallah, Mustafa I-22
Kharitonov, Alexander I-58
Kiefer, Franziskus II-337
Kiggins, Andrew I-185
Kissner, Michael III-191
Kou, Chunjing II-132
Kozlovics, Sergejs I-266
Kozlovičs, Sergejs III-185
Krämer, Juliane I-245, II-337
Kristen, Meret III-218

L

Le Jeune, Laurens III-141
Lehmann, Gilles III-162
Lescuyer, Roch II-3
Li, Juanru II-152
Li, Meixuan III-121
Li, Yang I-144, III-207, III-213
Li, Zhen II-193
Limbasiya, Trupil I-204
Lin, Zihe II-23
Liu, Anjiang II-193
Liu, Zhenyuan I-124
Loiero, Mirjam II-337
Long, Chongyu II-229

M

Malmqvist, Lars III-52
Malnicof, Andrew I-124
Mandal, Upasana I-3
Maurer, Felix III-43
Merkle, Florian I-163
Mexis, Nico I-222
Mishra, Rina III-89
Miyahara, Daiki I-144
Momin, Charles II-101
Mottok, Jürgen III-218
Mouiche, Inoussa III-3
Mukhopadhyay, Debdeep I-3

N

Nambiar, Sanjana III-23
Nocker, Martin I-163

O

Odoh, Kenneth III-202
Opmane, Inara I-266

P

Padhye, Sahadeo II-318
Peng, Jin II-211
Peters, Thomas II-101
Petručeça, Krišjānis III-185
Petrucena, Krisjanis I-266
Picek, Stjepan I-40, I-77
Pöhls, Henrich C. I-222
Polian, Ilia I-58
Pöpper, Christina III-23

Q

Qian, Yuhan II-23

R

Rabieinejad, Elnaz III-70
Raj, Amal III-197
Rencis, Edgars I-266
Rezaeezade, Azade I-77
Rieder, Vincent II-296

S

Saad, Sherif III-3
Sahu, Rajeev Anand II-318
Sakiyama, Kazuo I-144
Sander, Jonas III-43
Saraswat, Vishal II-318
Sarkar, Tishya Sarma I-3
Schaumont, Patrick I-124
Schoenauen, Thibaud II-101
Schöttle, Pascal I-163
Schumacher, Tim I-245
Schwartzentruber, Jeff III-70
Shanmugam, Dillibabu I-124
Shikata, Junji II-274
Shukla, Shubhi I-3
Spadafora, Chiara II-251
Standaert, François-Xavier II-101

Struck, Patrick I-245
Suri, Manan I-113
Swain, Srinibas III-207, III-213

T
Tang, Yufeng II-81
Tippmann, Maximilian I-245
Tobias, Christian II-337

U
Upadhyay, Rohitkumar R. II-318

V
van Dartel, Bram III-109
Varshney, Gaurav III-89
Viksna, Juris I-266
Vīksna, Juris III-185

W
Walther, Thomas I-245
Wang, An II-23, II-193
Wang, Cheng I-204
Wang, Dachao II-211
Wang, HengSheng II-61
Wang, Wei II-61

Wang, WeiJia II-193
Weishäupl, Maximiliane II-337
Welling, Tarick I-58
Wen, ShuShang II-61
Wu, Jingjie II-23

X
Xiang, Hong II-41, II-118
Xing, Haoyang II-229

Y
Yamasaki, Hirokatsu I-94
Yap, Trevor I-22
Yoshida, Kota I-40, I-94
Yousaf, Awais III-121
Yu, Yu II-152

Z
Zarrinkalam, Fattane III-70
Zhang, Congyi II-118
Zhao, Liangju II-81
Zhao, Yiyan II-132
Zheng, Fangyu II-132, II-229
Zhong, Yuchen II-23
Zhou, Jianying I-204, III-121

MIX
Papier aus verantwortungsvollen Quellen
Paper from responsible sources
FSC® C105338

If you have any concerns about our products,
you can contact us on
ProductSafety@springernature.com

In case Publisher is established outside the EU,
the EU authorized representative is:
**Springer Nature Customer Service Center GmbH
Europaplatz 3, 69115 Heidelberg, Germany**

Printed by Libri Plureos GmbH
in Hamburg, Germany